Illustrations

Colonialism in Question

Colonialism in Question

Theory, Knowledge, History

FREDERICK COOPER

University of California Press

BERKELEY   LOS ANGELES   LONDON

University of California Press
Berkeley and Los Angeles, California

University of California Press, Ltd.
London, England

Library of Congress Cataloging-in-Publication Data

Cooper, Frederick, 1947–
  Colonialism in question : theory, knowledge, history / Frederick
Cooper.
    p.   cm.
  Includes bibliographic references and index.
  ISBN-13 978-0-520-24414-6 (pbk. : alk. paper)
  ISBN-10 0-520-24414-1 (pbk. : alk. paper)
    1. Africa—Colonization—Historiography.   2. Decolonization—
Africa—Historiography.   3. Imperialism—Historiography.   4. Decolo-
nization—Historiography.   I. Title.

DT30.C5953   2005
325.6—dc22   2004021043

Manufactured in the United States of America

13   12   11   10   09   08   07
10   9   8   7   6   5   4   3

Printed on Ecobook 50 containing a minimum 50% post-consumer
waste, processed chlorine free. The balance contains virgin pulp, including 25% Forest Stewardship Council Certified for no old growth tree
cutting, processed either TCF or ECF. The sheet is acid-free and meets the
minimum requirements of ANSI/NISO Z39.48–1992 (R 1997) (Permanence of Paper).

Contents

Acknowledgments

The biggest debt I owe is to the people who appear in its notes: writers who have devoted much thought and much effort to pondering the question of colonialism in world history. The strongest compliment a scholar can pay to another is to engage her or his ideas critically, and this book has been written in such a spirit. These pages address subjects that have been given considerable attention in the past two decades, and I have had the privilege not only of following and participating in exchanges that have occurred in print, but in attending some of the conferences where colonial issues have been debated and in hearing presentations by visitors to the University of Michigan and New York University, the two institutions at which I have taught in these decades. I can no longer trace what I learned where, but the programs at the University of Michigan in Anthropology and History, Comparative Studies of Social Transformations, and Postemancipation Societies have contributed greatly to bringing new perspectives to my attention, and, however critical I may be of certain arguments and concepts, the ideas expressed there have provoked a great deal of thought. The notes to this book refer to many people who at one time were colleagues at the University of Michigan, reflecting a particularly engaged academic culture in which it was my good fortune to participate for over eighteen years. Keeping to people whose work is actually cited in what follows (and risking forgetting a few), I would like to acknowledge the writing and influence of Rebecca Scott, Tom Holt, Nancy Hunt, Mamadou Diouf, Bill Sewell, David Hollinger, Geoff Eley, Ron Suny, Julia Adams, Müge Göçek, Ann Stoler, Simon Gikandi, Fernando Coronil, Nick Dirks, Jane Burbank, Matthew Connelly, Juan Cole, Sue Alcock, and George Steinmetz. The stream of visitors coming to Michigan whom I had a chance to hear and meet—including Partha Chatterjee, Gyan Pandey, Gyan Prakash, and

Dipesh Chakrabarty—opened up what was to me, and many others, a new field of inquiry and new perspectives. A special word of thanks to Partha Chatterjee and Gyan Pandey for their hospitality when I visited Calcutta and Delhi in 1996, and to Mamadou Diouf for his generosity when we first met in Dakar in 1986 and for the many exchanges we have had since then. The parts of this book (and previous publications) focused on francophone Africa benefited also from the tutelage of Mohamed Mbodj, Boubacar Barry, and Babacar Fall. The African side of the work also benefited from conversations with my Michigan colleagues, especially David Cohen.

The Michigan empire—on which the sun never seems to set—can also be traced in what follows to many former graduate students on whose committees I served and who have taught me a great deal as they became influential contributors to a field of history in its key stage of development: Susan Thorne, Lora Wildenthal, Christopher Schmidt-Nowara, Ada Ferrer, Lisa Lindsay, Pamela Scully, Lynn Thomas, Tim Scarnecchia, Steven Pierce, Dorothy Hodgson, Aims McGuiness, Andy Ivaska, Sarah Womack, Moses Ochonu, Vukile Khumalo, and Kerry Ward among them. Since moving to NYU in 2002, I have found new intellectual homes in the History Department, the Institute of French Studies, and the Center for Middle Eastern Studies; they all have welcomed and encouraged thinking and research on colonial questions. I encountered here another set of scholars whose research and writing on a wide range of empires has informed and influenced the writing of this book, including Lauren Benton, Mike Gomez, Manu Goswami, Emmanuelle Saada, Harry Harootunian, Rebecca Karl, Khaled Fahmy, Antonio Feros, Tim Mitchell, Louise Young, and, as ever, Jane Burbank. I have particularly profited from extensive conversations on colonial questions with Manu, Emmanuelle, Antonio, and Jane. My graduate classes on empires and on decolonization at NYU have sent me back to rethink or rewrite sections of the book; I am particularly grateful for the critical reading that my decolonization class in the fall of 2003 gave to an earlier version of the introduction. And thanks to Marc Goulding for meticulously checking notes.

Ann Stoler realized that I was studying colonial questions before I did, and our collaboration in organizing an international conference, sponsored by the Wenner-Gren Foundation in 1988, and later in editing *Tensions of Empire: Colonial Cultures in a Bourgeois World,* has been instrumental in shaping the research trajectory that has gone into this book. During this time, Jane Burbank was telling me that my perspective on colonial questions was limited by its focus on nineteenth- and twentieth-century empires coming out of Western Europe. The message finally got through and led to our working together on a graduate seminar that we have taught at both Michigan and NYU on Empires, States, and Political Imagination as well as to conferences at Michigan and Istanbul in which we participated together. The formative influence of these classes, meetings, and numerous conversations is reflected in the title of a chapter in this book and arguments developed there and in the introduction.

I have been lucky enough to be working on French colonialism at a time when—after historians of France long persisted in taking a "national" view of their subject—a group of younger scholars have begun to open up the field. Emmanuelle Saada, Emmanuelle Sibeud, Benoît de l'Estoile, Isabelle Merle, Alice Conklin, Jim LeSueur, and Todd Shepherd have kindly brought me into ongoing discussions. Thanks too to Didier Fassin and Jean-Pierre Dozon for inviting me to present seminars at the Ecole des Hautes Etudes en Sciences Sociales as this work was being completed, and to José Kagabo and Jean-Claude Penrad for many congenial and stimulating conversations. And finally thanks to Catherine Coquery-Vidrovitch for her welcome to the French Africanist community.

Particularly valuable for critical readings of my work and exposure to the thinking of others during the writing of parts of this book were conferences on colonial studies and related topics in New Delhi in 1996 (organized by SEPHIS and hosted by Gyan Pandey and some of his colleagues), at New York University (brought together by Emmanuelle Saada), the University of Illinois at Urbana-Champagne (organized by Ania Loomba and Suvir Kaul), and the School of American Research at Santa Fe (led by Ann Stoler and Carol McGranahan). Two visits to the University of the Bosphorus, as well as a conference on the Ottoman, Russian, and Habsburg empires at the University of Michigan—permitting repeated discussions with Selim Deringil and Faruk Birtek as well as my Michigan colleague Müge Göçek—have influenced my thinking on these empires, and a conference entitled "Empires in Modern Times," at the Institut des Hautes Etudes Internationales in Geneva, organized by Jürgen Osterhammel and Philippe Burrin, widened my perspective still further. A conference on settler colonialism at Harvard University, organized by Susan Pedersen and Caroline Elkins, brought African and East Asian perspectives into useful confrontation. Miniconferences on "globalization" at the Centre d'Etudes et de Recherche International in Paris and the University of California at Irvine got me going on a paper that has become a chapter in this book.

I am grateful to the editors of *Theory and Society* for permission to republish as chapter 3 the essay originally entitled "Beyond Identity" (vol. 29, 2000, pp. 1–47), and I wish to thank my co-author, Rogers Brubaker, for letting me reprint it in this volume. I can only reciprocate by calling attention to Rogers' new book of essays, *Ethnicity without Groups,* forthcoming with Harvard University Press. Thanks to *African Affairs* and Oxford University Press for allowing me to reprint as chapter 4 an article originally entitled "What Is the Concept of Globalization Good For? An African Historian's Perspective" (vol. 100, 2001, pp. 189–213). Finally, my thanks to *French Politics, Culture, and Society* for permission to reprint as chapter 2 an article originally published as "Decolonizing Situations: The Rise, Fall and Rise of Colonial Studies, 1951–2001" (vol. 20, 2002, pp. 47–76). I have made some cuts and fixed up some notes in these articles but, except for rectifying a few serious omissions, have avoided the temptation to reflect on new material appearing in the few years since their publication, for the simple reason that writing on such subjects is pouring forth at such a rate that the new will be overshadowed by the still newer while this book is in press.

Most of the previously unpublished material here was written in 2002–2003, when I was a fellow at the Center for Advanced Study in the Behavioral Sciences, which provides the most supportive atmosphere imaginable for scholarly writing. Special thanks to the Mellon Foundation, which contributed to my support, to Doug McAdam, director of the center, and to Kathleen Much, who provided astute editorial comments on chapter 5.

The new chapters or the manuscript as a whole have also benefited from the critiques of Bin Wong, Lynn Thomas, Mamadou Diouf, Steven Pierce, Jane Burbank, Emmanuelle Saada, Jane Guyer, Michael Watts, and James Clifford. Monica McCormick of the University of California Press is largely responsible for my deciding to write this book, for providing excellent advice on how to go about it, and for shepherding it through the editorial process. Working with Monica has made me understand why writers like to use the possessive pronoun in the phrase "my editor." Monica has since defied the pronoun in order to pursue endeavors outside of publishing, so her authors can only wish her well and hope that their writing will prove worthy of the confidence she has placed in us over the years. Jane Burbank has read more of this manuscript more times than anyone else and has provided sound advice on everything from its title to the footnotes, besides sharing with me the richness of her own thinking about empires and a great deal else besides.

New York City
April 2004

PART I

Colonial Studies and Interdisciplinary Scholarship

1 Introduction

Colonial Questions, Historical Trajectories

The burst of scholarship on colonial studies in the last two decades—crossing the disciplinary boundaries of literature, anthropology, and history—has begun to fill one of the most notable blind spots in the Western world's examination of its history. Yet there is something strange about the timing: scholarly interest in colonialism arose when colonial empires had already lost their international legitimacy and ceased to be viable forms of political organization. Earlier, when colonialism was an object of mobilization, scholars and intellectuals were most captivated by the drama of liberation movements and the possibilities of "modernization" and "development" for people whom colonialism and racism had excluded from the march of progress.

Part of the impetus behind the recent research and writing on colonial situations has been to ensure that this past is not forgotten. But the colonial past is also invoked to teach a lesson about the present, serving to reveal the hypocrisy of Europe's claims to provide models of democratic politics, efficient economic systems, and a rational approach to understanding and changing the world, by connecting these very ideas to the history of imperialism. Such concerns have led some scholars to examine thoughtfully the complex ways in which Europe was made from its colonies and how the very categories by which we understand the colonies' past and the ex-colonies' future were shaped by the process of colonization.

Yet a significant part of this body of work has taken colonial studies out of the history whose importance has just been asserted, treating colonialism abstractly, generically, as something to be juxtaposed with an equally flat vision of European "modernity." This side of the field has focused more on *stance*—on critical examination of the subject position of the scholar and political advocate—than on process, on how the trajectories of a colonizing Europe and a colonized Africa and Asia shaped each other over time. Not only does such an approach obscure the details of colonial history and the experience of people in colonies, but the aspirations and challenges posed by political movements in the colonies over the course of history disappear beneath the ironic gaze that critics have directed toward claims for progress and democracy.

The refusal to leave the "colonial" as a neatly bounded, excisable dimension of European history marks an important challenge to historical analysis. Yet unbounding colonialism risks leaving us with a colonial project vaguely situated between 1492 and the 1970s, of varying contents and significance, alongside an equally atemporal "post-Enlightenment" Europe, missing the struggles that reconfigured possibilities and constraints across this period. This is why a reconsideration of colonialism's place in history should both engage deeply with the critical scholarship of the last two decades and insist on moving beyond the limitations that have emerged within it.

Europe's ambivalent conquests—oscillating between attempts to project outward its own ways of understanding the world and efforts to demarcate colonizer from colonized, civilized from primitive, core from periphery—made the space of empire into a terrain where concepts were not only imposed but also engaged and contested. From the very moment of the French Revolution, rebels in the plantation colony of Saint Domingue raised the question of whether the Declaration of the Rights of Man and of the Citizen applied to the French empire as well as the French nation, and in so doing, they, as Laurent Dubois puts it, " 'universalized' the idea of rights."[1] Ever since, political activism in and about empire has posed not only possibilities of accepting or rejecting the application to colonial worlds of ideas and structures asserted by Europe, but also the possibility, however difficult, of changing the meaning of the basic concepts themselves.

Conceptual issues are the focus of this book. How can one study colonial societies, keeping in mind—but not being paralyzed by—the fact that the tools of analysis we use emerged from the history we are trying to examine?

INTERDISCIPLINARITY AND THE CONFORMISM OF THE AVANT-GARDE

Historians' quite recent interest in colonial situations owes much to the influence of literary studies and anthropology; scholarly work on colonial issues gave rise to a cutting-edge interdisciplinary field of scholarship. Yet the basic problem with interdisciplinary scholarship is the same as that within the disciplines: conformism, gatekeeping, conventions that one should publish in the "right" journals—whether the *American Political Science Review* or *Social Text*—and cite the right people, be they Gary Becker or Homi Bhabha. The economist—to take the most theoretically monolithic of the disciplines within the American academy—generally has to write within the confines of neoclassical theory and to devise and test abstract models; he or she gets little credit for fieldwork into the complexities of actually experienced economic relations. In cultural studies, the assistant professor is required to decenter, destabilize, and disrupt socially constructed categories and to empower subaltern discourse. To transgress the norm of transgressivity is to be unaware of one's own positionality. The cultural critic may relish her disciplinary hybridity yet have a great deal in common with the economist who thinks that more work within neoclassic models has a higher marginal utility than an excursion into anthropology. Interdisciplinary studies can be impoverished by once provocative constructs that have become clichés, just as a discipline can be narrowed by professional hierarchies, required methodologies, or theoretical conservatism.

The urge to conform is evident in some favorite phrases of scholars charting trends: the "cultural turn," the "linguistic turn," and the "historical turn." These expressions imply that scholars in history, cultural studies, or the social sciences take their intellectual curves together, and anyone who does not is off on a tangent or has entered a dead end. The cultural turn of the 1980s and 1990s corrected to a significant extent the excesses of a previous turn, toward social history and political economy in the 1970s, but after a time scholars were told that we were "beyond the cultural turn," which meant—as some of the more thoughtful participants in these discussions frankly put it—bringing back questions of social and economic history. Excellent research and valuable reflection came out of the cultural turn, as from previous and subsequent turns.[2] Meanwhile, however, a generation of graduate students experienced pressure from their mentors and peers to focus their work in one direction, just as a previous generation had been influenced to conform to a different trend. In African history, my generation avoided colonial history for fear of being thought to do "white history"—and contributed thereby to the doldrums of imperial history of which many later complained—whereas now the history of Africa before the European conquests is neglected. Scholars' openness to new ideas and directions is one thing, taking "turns" together another.[3]

Interdisciplinary studies have their own pitfalls, in particular credulity toward other fields that do not apply to one's own, such as the historian's belief that a quotation from Geertz means doing anthropology or that a reference to Bakhtin means mastery of literary criticism. One is likely to fall for conventional wisdom in another discipline, miss internal debates, and pick up tidbits without exploring their relationship. The remedy for these difficulties of interdisciplinary work, however, is not disciplinarity but discipline: a more thorough and critical engagement with other fields, a more rigorous and wider reading of social theory that both reconfigures and deepens methodological understandings.

Writing on colonialism in the last two decades has had a double—and positive—impact in regard to established verities: calling into question a narrative of progress radiating from Europe that ignored how deeply this history was entwined with overseas conquest, and rejecting the consignment of "non-Europe" to static backwardness regardless of how those regions' fates were shaped by interaction with Europe, including the sidetracking of other modes of change and interaction. The bandwagon effect within colonial studies or postcolonial theory is probably no more severe than in other areas of academic inquiry, but rather is illustrative of a wider problem in intellectual life. Like other new fields, colonial studies has been the object of a dismissive backlash that ignores the insights and the healthy debate within the field—indeed, the considerable heterogeneity that characterizes writing on colonial subjects.[4] I hope in these pages to steer between the conformism of the avant-garde and the dismissiveness of the old regime in the study of colonization, colonial history, and decolonization by focusing on specific conceptual and methodological issues.

Bashing the Enlightenment and criticizing modernity have become favorite activities within colonial and postcolonial studies. Such positioning has been answered by a defense of modernity and Enlightenment against the barbarians at the gates who threaten the universal principles on which democratic societies are based.[5] Debate at such levels of abstraction is unedifying, not least because both sides are content to treat Enlightenment rationality as an icon separated from its historical significance. There is a delicious irony here, for Europeans become the "people without history," a notion once reserved for the colonized. Both sides are content to let unchanging and unmediated images of reason, liberalism, and universality stand in for a much more convoluted trajectory, in which the status and the meaning of such concepts were very much in question.[6] The not-so-delicious irony is that the critique of modernity aimed at destabilizing a smug, Europe-centered narrative of progress has ended up preserving this category as a defining characteristic of European history to which all others must respond. Only a more precise historical practice will get us out of the involuted framing of such a debate.

In chapter 2, I take up the paradox noted at the beginning of this essay, that scholarly interest in analyzing colonialism peaked at a time when it was no longer a political issue. Its starting point is Georges Balandier's article of 1951, "The Colonial Situation," which was a call for analysis of colonial rule using tools perfected in studying indigenous groups but now directed at the "totality" of coercive, structural, and ideological mechanisms of colonial power. This call—timely as it was—went largely unanswered, because scholars, including Balandier himself, were more fascinated by the possibilities of modernizing societies that had been held back and by the liberation movements themselves. My essay surveys the changing focus of scholarship on colonial societies in the half-century since Balandier's intervention, not as a succession of turns, but as overlapping and often conflicting perspectives, all in relation to the shifting politics of decolonization.

Part 2 of this book turns to key concepts that epitomize the current direction of scholarship—in colonial studies and other interdisciplinary endeavors. The use of these concepts has provoked new thinking and important research, but they deserve a scrutiny that the bandwagon effect of scholarly trends has to a large extent repressed. I will examine in detail three concepts—identity, globalization, and modernity—and later in this introduction raise questions about concepts like coloniality, postcoloniality, and post-Enlightenment rationality. In questioning the analytic value of such concepts, my intent is not to step away from the objects of inquiry envisaged by those who use these concepts, but rather to ask if they are adequate to the work at hand.

Identity, globalization, and modernity occupy a large and growing place in scholarly fashions. Figure 1 shows how often these terms have appeared as keywords in a leading web-based index of scholarly articles over the past decade, while references to the buzzwords of a prior era, like *industrialization, urbanization,* and *modernization,* have stagnated at lower levels.[7] *Identity* wins the prize, and if *modernity* isn't as "in" as *identity,* it passed *modernization*—a related concept with a different valence—in 1995.

The use of such concepts addresses important subjects: subjectivity and particularity in people's collective vision of themselves, the apparently increasing importance of cross-border interaction in today's world, and the apparent power—for good or for evil—of a view of historical change as moving in a forward direction. In all three cases, I argue, the concepts are important as indigenous categories, as terms used in today's politics and culture. They need to be understood in the often conflicting ways in which they are deployed. The problem comes with scholars' widespread use of these terms as analytic categories, as tools for description and analysis. This

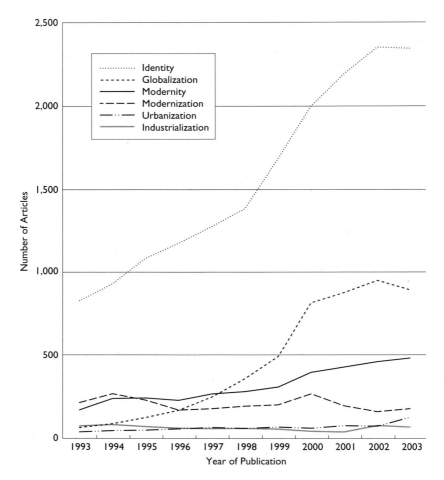

FIGURE 1. "In" words and "out" words in published articles.

usage does more to obscure than to illuminate the problems of social connection, cross-border interaction, and long-term change that they are thought to address. There is nothing inherently wrong in using the same term as both an analytic category and an indigenous one, but there are two problems that need to be confronted if one does so. First, the usefulness of an analytic category doesn't follow from its salience as an indigenous one: such concepts must perform analytic work, distinguishing phenomena and calling attention to important questions. Second, the academic's endeavor to refine and sharpen analytic categories may obscure the ways in which historical actors deployed similar terms, thereby complicating the task of understanding forms of discourse in their own contexts.

These chapters address not just the words as such—although in all three cases academic language adds confusion to ordinary English definitions—but the conceptual questions to which writing about them gives rise. To question the analytic usefulness of the category *identity* is not to presume that people's particularistic and subjective concerns—about gender, ethnicity, or any other form of affinity—should be downplayed in favor of the great universalisms, be they the liberal idea of a citizenry of equivalent individuals or the Marxist idea of class. But understanding how people conceive of commonality, belonging, and affinity does require a precise and differentiated set of concepts.

Much recent scholarship on identity uses the same word for something that is claimed to be general but soft—that is, everybody seeks an identity, but identity is fluid, constructed, and contested—and for something that is specific and hard, that is, the assertion that being "Serbian," "Jewish," or "lesbian" implies that other differences within the category should be overlooked in order to facilitate group coherence. This contradictory usage leaves us powerless to examine what scholars most need to understand and explain: why some affinities in some contexts give rise to groups with a hard sense of uniqueness and antagonism to other groups, while in other instances people operate via degrees of affinity and connection, live with shades of grey rather than white and black, and form flexible networks rather than bounded groups. In chapter 3, written by Rogers Brubaker and myself, we do not argue for a more refined or precise word to replace *identity*, but rather for the use of a range of conceptual tools adequate to understand a range of practices and processes.

With globalization and modernity, we again encounter two words and two bodies of scholarships that confuse normative and analytic categories and reinforce the metanarratives that they pretend to take apart. It is hard for anyone who lived through the modernization debates of the 1970s to read the globalization and modernity debates without a sense of déjà vu. The idea that people were being liberated from the stultifying edifice of colonialism or the backwardness of tradition—producing a convergence toward the social practices and living standards of the West—was the hallmark of modernization theory in the 1950s and 1960s. More recently, some pundits and scholars insist that globalization is inevitable as well as desirable. Critics again decry as malignant what advocates insist is beneficial, while some scholars accept the narrative of ever-increasing interaction but deny that it is producing convergence. My argument is neither for nor against globalization; rather, I attempt to reframe the issue, pointing out that the globalization story claims as new what is not new at all, confuses "long-distance" with "global," fails to complement discussion of connections across space with analysis of their limitations, and distorts the history of empires and colonization in order to fit it into a story with a predetermined end.[8] The alternative to the concept of globalization is not to reify the state or any other container of interaction, but to detach mechanisms of connection from the artificial notion of globality and to study the marking of territory and the crossing of territorial boundaries in more specific ways than those implied by the linear concept of globalization.

The critique of modernization theory that emerged in the 1970s brought out the teleological and Eurocentric nature of the theory. But if the teleology is gone, the telos remains in the form of a burgeoning literature on modernity, colonial modernity, and alternative modernities, the former two with a negative valence instead of a positive one, the latter as the positive, non-Eurocentric reflection of the others. In chapter 5, I argue that the modernity now in question is hopelessly confused by the divergent meanings given to it and that any effort to refine the analytic concept would result in loss of the ability to understand the meanings of *modern* as an indigenous category—where it was in fact used. The appeal of the modernization concept in the 1970s was above all that it constituted a package, pulling together such changes as urbanization, the growth of market economies, and achievement-oriented status systems. Modernity in the 1990s was still a package, sometimes decried instead of celebrated, sometimes repackaged as "alternative modernities," but still assuming that the alternatives must be modernities. When Partha Chatterjee talks about the "bitter truth" that no one in Europe believes that Indians "could be producers of modernity," he concedes that modernity is what Europe produced.[9] The package is still on its pedestal, and debate about a wide range of issues— from the equality of women in society to the desirability of free markets— will be conducted in relation to a presumed distinction between modern and backward rather than in more specific and less teleological terms.

As scholars, we need to understand what people mean when they engage in identity politics, when they argue for the inevitability and desirability of the global marketplace, or when they articulate aspirations for clean water and better education. We also need to develop a precise and incisive vocabulary for analyzing affinity, connections, and change. We should try to explain why such concepts evoked passions at some moments but not at others. Colonial elites—sometimes—claimed legitimacy on the grounds that they were remaking Asian or African societies in the image of Europe's self-proclaimed modernity, and at other times they insisted that colonies could never be modern, that they would only go astray if their status hierarchies were undermined, and that European rule was necessary to preserve this conservative order. Such arguments are best analyzed as debates *within* the history of colonization rather than as a "colonial modernity" located vaguely between the Enlightenment and the present. Understanding indigenous categories—be they those of a French colonial minister, an African trade unionist, or an Islamic religious leader—requires asking how people put their thoughts together; in other words, scholars must make an effort to get out of their own categories.

Part 3 develops alternatives to the flattening of time, space, and interaction in the concepts considered above, first via a general argument and then through a case study. Chapter 6 argues that instead of telling a story of the inevitable rise over the last two centuries of the nation-state and the national imagination, one can tell a more revealing story by looking over a longer period of time at a more varied set of political forms. For imperial rulers from the Roman Empire through the Ottoman and Austro-Hungarian Empires to the French Community and the British Commonwealth, governing an imperial polity produced a different set of structures and a different way of imagining political space than did a nation-state. Empires should not be reduced to national polities projecting their power beyond their borders. They always had to balance the incorporation of people and territory and differentiation that maintained the power and sense of coherence of the ruling elite. The chapter puts in a single framework continental and overseas, "modern" and "premodern," European and non-European empires, for all participated in the calculus of balancing incorporation and differentiation, and interacted and competed with each other for resources—but did so in different ways.

Similarly, there is much to learn by looking at political mobilization within and against empire not just in terms of a community or nation rallying against an intrusive, distant power. Political movements developed more varied repertoires, including deterritorialized forms of affinity—pan-Africanism, pan-Slavism, pan-Arabism, Islamism, Christian humanitarianism, proletarian internationalism—as well as attempts to reform and restructure the imperial unit itself, often by turning imperial ideology into a claim on the rulers of empire. It was only with the collapse of the last empires in the 1960s that the nation-state became the generalized form of sovereignty. Up to the very end of those empires, some people within them were trying to turn the empires' incorporative needs into demands for imperial resources and for political voice. Empire is, unregrettably, no longer in the political repertoire, but appreciating the recent roots of the nation-state might help to foster more precise discussion of different forms of political organization and their consequences, without falling into the teleology of nation-building, sweeping denunciations of all forms of state power, the use of empire as an epithet for any form of power, or the sentimental reimagining of past empires as models of stern and responsible governance of the fit over the unfit.

Chapter 7, based on my research in Senegal and France, provides an example of how both the makers of empire and the leaders of social movements operated within an imperial framework and by using that framework changed it. Labor and political movements in French West Africa in the 1940s and 1950s seized the language of postwar French imperialism—in a moment when France needed more than ever for colonies to be orderly, productive, and legitimate—and turned it into demands for equality of wages, benefits, and ultimately standard of living among all people whom the government asserted to be French. This impeccable logic of equivalence—backed by well-organized protest movements and in the context of worldwide debates over self-determination and anticolonial revolutions in Vietnam and North Africa—presented the French government with the dilemma of either giving up the idea of Greater France or facing its metropolitan citizens with never-ending demands and an unpayable bill. The national conception of France was consolidated in the same process that give rise to nation-states in North and sub-Saharan Africa.

CRITICAL HISTORY AND AHISTORICAL HISTORY

The arguments presented here are historical. They do not, however, imply a polarization between a domain that might be called colonial studies—or more generally, interdisciplinarity—and another called history. Such a division would mask the extensive differences and debate within all such designations, as well as the cross-fertilization across whatever lines scholars use to mark their territory. My goal is not to criticize any scholarly field as a whole, or even to pin down exactly what such field labels signify, but instead to focus on key concepts themselves, to assess the work they do, the blind spots as well as insights they entail, and the difficulties of using them to examine change over time.[10]

The historical profession has without doubt been reinvigorated by challenges to it, coming from new entrants into the academy—not least of all, scholars from Africa and Asia—by ferment in other disciplines, and by the tense but frequently crossed frontier between academic history and diverse people's interest in the past. In my experience and that of many of my generation of professional historians, the study of colonial empires had by the 1970s become one of the deadest of dead fields within history. Students interested in pushing the frontiers of historical research looked to Africa, Asia, or Latin America, or they sought to look at Europe and North America "from the bottom up." The revival of interest in the colonial world a generation later reflects the influence of literature and anthropology and, most importantly, wider intellectual currents that threw into question the most basic narratives and the most basic ways in which knowledge is configured. Historians were having to face the fact that the new challenges were not simply to add an African or Asian component to a previously Europe-centered curriculum, but to think about what we mean by Europe, Africa, Asia, and how they shaped each other over time (see chapter 2).

But it is now the interdisciplinary domains of colonial and postcolonial studies that could use a new sense of direction, particularly a more rigorous historical practice. These fields of inquiry have introduced to a large and transcontinental public the place of colonialism in world history. Yet in much of the field, a generic colonialism—located somewhere between 1492 and the 1970s—has been given the decisive role in shaping a postcolonial moment, in which invidious distinctions and exploitation can be condemned and the proliferation of cultural hybridities and the fracturing of cultural boundaries celebrated.

Meanwhile, historians can at times be faulted for treating own engagement with sources from the place and time in question as unproblematic, as if sources spoke on their own. The outsider's characterization of academic history as one damn thing after another has a grain of truth. Historians' narratives are built on conventions of narrativity that are not always examined. Nevertheless, the historian's displacement in time itself generates a bias against the homogenization of categories; while some historians narrate the past as if it inevitably led to the present, they still distinguish past from present, and another historian in the same present might interpret that past differently. Historical practice suggests that however varied the impetus and context for the actions of men and women, interactions unfold over time; contexts are reconfigured and shape future possibilities and closures.

At least some of the criticism has had a positive effect. The June 2004 congress of the once staid and nationally-focused Society for French Historical Studies included seventeen panels on topics related to colonial history, with nearly four dozen presentations, mostly by young historians with fresh material from archives and other sources that enlarged from colonial vantage points the meanings of citizenship, law, social welfare, and "France" itself. In the following pages, I will point both to the importance of the critique of the historical profession and to its limitations, especially when ahistorical methodologies are deployed to answer questions that are unavoidably historical.

Ashis Nandy argues that history is inseparable from its imperialist origins, that it necessarily imposes the imperialist's understanding of people's past over their own. To some scholars, history confines the zigzags of time into linear pathways, privileges state-building over other forms of human connection, and tells a story of progress that inevitably leaves Africans or Asians on the side, lacking some crucial characteristic necessary to attain what is otherwise universal.[11] Such arguments are valid criticisms of many histories, but do they amount to an indictment of the study of history itself? In fact, the indictment of history is itself historical. To trace history to imperialism is to give power to a phenomenon that is historically located. The question such an observation leaves is whether it is enough to *name* imperialism as the dark side of modernity, or if understanding it requires a more searching examination, which in some form is historical. Meanwhile, the practices of many historians may well suggest an "irrevocable link between History and the Nation-State," but the evidence that the nation-state is not so universal is another sort of history, which documents more varied sorts of political imagination.[12] Academic history, like all others, has its particularities, and the argument that other visions of the past are more diverse and lively is valid only if one aggregates them—itself a quintessentially academic exercise.

Historians' complacency about the European boundaries of their field was shaken up by Edward Said's *Orientalism* (1978). Said showed how certain visions of Asiatic societies are deeply woven into canonical European literature. Colonization was no longer out there, in exotic places, but in the heart of European culture. Said was soon criticized for presenting such a closed view of the colonized "other" that there was no room for alternative constructions, including those by Arabs, Africans, or South Asians. In his subsequent book, *Culture and Imperialism*, Said tried to restore balance by emphasizing not the stark separation of European and indigenous discourses but the efforts of colonized intellectuals to work between them and to develop crosscutting languages of liberation.[13] Such an argument, too, is a historical one.

The Saidian view of Europe constructing itself and its others in relation to each other has had wide influence in many disciplines and has fostered an examination of those disciplines. The categories used by social scientists from the nineteenth through the twenty-first century to examine colonized societies have been shown to be less a neutral means of analysis of bounded societies located elsewhere than part of a process of intellectual pacification and ordering of the world. Vocabularies and methods of elite control for handling distinctions of gender, class, and race—of the respectable and the civilized in contrast to the unruly and the dangerous—were developed in both metropoles and colonies. Esthetics and science helped order an imperial world. The scholarship on such subjects in the last quarter century adds up to a impressive reconsideration of intellectual and cultural history. The question it leaves is that which Said faced after *Orientalism*: whether such work will be read as a solid edifice of colonial modernity or colonial governmentality imposed from Europe, or whether it will be seen as a framework for contestation and debate over the nature of social distinctions and social knowledge across the colony-metropole divide.[14]

To some postcolonial theorists, the goal has been no less than to overthrow the place of reason and progress as the beacons of humanity, insisting that the claims to universality that emerged from the Enlightenment obscure the way colonialism imposed not just its exploitative power but its ability to determine the terms—democracy, liberalism, rationality—by which political life the world over would be conducted from then on. By contrasting this universalizing modernity with the ugly particularity of colonialism, postcolonial theorists attack head-on a historical metanarrative that shows Europe repudiating step by step the oppressiveness of its own past and making itself into a model for the rest of the world. Some hope to persuade us to "give up the seemingly powerful corollary *presumption* that liberalism and indeed democracy (even a purportedly radical one) have any *particular* privilege among ways of organizing the political forms of our collective lives."[15]

Before we give such ideas up, we would do well to examine carefully not only what they are, but how they have been used—and perhaps, in being used by people in colonies, given a new meaning. We should be careful about what else we might be giving up: perhaps the tools with which to analyze and critique various forms of oppression, from local patriarchies to global capitalism?[16]

My focus is on the double occlusion that results from turning the centuries of European colonization overseas into a critique of the Enlightenment, democracy, or modernity. First is the obscuring of European history, for the counterpart of reducing non-Western history to a lack of what the

West had is to assume that the West actually had it. All the debate and conflict within post-1789 European history is reduced within the critique of the post-Enlightenment to an essence of modernity, producing a label attached to an entire epoch, and this abstraction is assigned causal weight in shaping what happened in colonies in the nineteenth and twentieth centuries. Second is the occlusion of the history of the people who lived in colonies. Positing a colonial modernity (see chapter 5) reduces the conflicting strategies of colonization to a modernity perhaps never experienced by those being colonized, and gives insufficient weight to the ways in which colonized people sought—not entirely without success—to build lives in the crevices of colonial power, deflecting, appropriating, or reinterpreting the teachings and preachings thrust upon them. Within this line of argument, resistance might be celebrated or subaltern agency applauded, but the idea that struggle actually had effects on the course of colonization is lost in the timelessness of colonial modernity. The Haitian Revolution—and especially the possibility that the Haitian Revolution actually affected the meanings of citizenship or freedom in Europe and the Americas—is as strikingly absent in prominent postcolonial texts as in conventional narratives of European progress.[17] The result is that ownership of notions like human rights and citizenship is conceded to Europe—only to be subjected to ironic dismissal for their association with European imperialism.

The "colonial" of postcolonial studies is often the generic one, what Stuart Hall sweeps together in a single phrase—"European and then Western capitalist modernity after 1492." It is spatially diffuse and temporally spread out over five centuries; its power in determining the present can be asserted even without examining its contours.[18] But might not this generic colonial history produce an equally generic postcolonial present?[19]

I agree with the postcolonial critic's insistence that the evils of nineteenth- and twentieth-century colonialism lie firmly within the political structures, values, and understandings of its era; colonialism was not an atavistic holdover from the past. Less convincing is the juxtaposition of post-Enlightenment universality and colonial particularity isolated from the dynamics ensuing from the tensions within any ideological formation and from the tensions produced by efforts of empires to install real administrations over real people. Such an approach privileges the stance of the critic, who decodes this transhistorical phenomenon; hence the label Gyan Prakash and others have attached to their project: "colonial critique."[20]

Such a critique has had its value, above all in forcing historians—like anthropologists or other social scientists—to question their own epistemological positions. The question is how one understands and gets beyond the limits inherent in the stance of the critic. Let me turn now to a brief analysis of modes of writing that can be called ahistorical history, which purport to address the relationship of past to present but do so without interrogating the way processes unfold over time. I will mention four modes of looking at history ahistorically: story plucking, leapfrogging legacies, doing history backward, and the epochal fallacy. My purpose is not to defend one discipline or condemn another, for some of the most searching historical questions have been asked by literary critics or anthropologists. Historians are familiar with many ways of doing history ahistorically, not only from criticizing the shortcomings of other disciplines but from engaging in such practices themselves. Nonetheless, theoretical perspectives that operate in vaguely specified temporalities and that give explanatory weight to agentless abstractions—like coloniality and modernity—both depend on and reinforce the methodological shortcomings described below.

Story Plucking

The "colonial" has itself become an object of study, literary and otherwise—a phenomenon appearing in many places and times. The weighty *-ity* in such widely used words as *coloniality* or *postcoloniality* implies that there is an essence of being colonized independent of what anybody did in a colony.[21] One can pluck a text from Spanish America in the sixteenth century, a narrative of the slave colonies of the West Indies in the eighteenth, or a description of moderately prosperous African cocoa planters in the twentieth-century Gold Coast, and compare it to other texts. This gives rise to the question of how far we can go in discussing coloniality when the fact of having been colonized is stressed over context, struggle, and the experience of life in colonies. Colonial power, like any other, was an object of struggle and depended on the material, social, and cultural resources of those involved. Colonizer and colonized are themselves far from immutable constructs, and such categories had to be reproduced by specific actions.

Leapfrogging Legacies

Here I refer to claiming that something at time A caused something in time C without considering time B, which lies in between. African political scientist Mahmood Mamdani, in his *Citizen and Subject: Contemporary Africa and the Legacy of Late Colonialism*,[22] draws a direct causal connection between a colonial policy—important in the 1920s and 1930s—of ruling through African chiefdoms given authority under colonial auspices and the brittle politics of authoritarianism and ethnicity in Africa in the 1980s and 1990s. Mamdani has a point at either end of his leapfrog, but he misses what lies in between. His book says almost nothing about the 1950s and 1960s, and thus does not consider another dimension of Africa's malaise: that there was indeed effective mobilization in those years that cut across ethnic divisions and urban/rural distinctions. Through such mobilizations, Africans made strong claims to citizenship. African politicians built a powerful challenge to colonial regimes—either to make good on the implied promises of imperial citizenship or to give way to governments that could truly represent their citizens (see chapter 7). But once in power, such leaders understood all too well how dangerous such claims were. The explosion of citizenship in the final years of colonial rule appears nowhere in Mamdani's book. He thus misses not only the sequence of processes in the decolonization era, but the tragedy of recent African history, people's heightened sense of possibility and the thwarting of their hopes.[23]

Doing History Backward

Trying to illuminate present issues is a fine motivation for exploring the past, but as one looks backward, one risks anachronism: confusing the analytic categories of the present with the native categories of the past, as if people acted in search of identity or to build a nation when such ways of thinking might not have been available to them. Even more important is what one does not see: the paths not taken, the dead ends of historical processes, the alternatives that appeared to people in their time. Two common, and in many ways meritorious, approaches to historical analysis can easily fall into backward-looking history. One is the idea of *social construction,* a useful antidote to claims that race, ethnicity, or nationality are primordial characteristics of given groups, and which is also helpful in recognizing that race or any other category may be no less important for having been constructed historically. The trouble with constructivism, as it is most often practiced, is that it doesn't go far enough: we talk of the social construction of racial categories, but it is rare that we even ask about categories that are not now important, and we thus lose sight of the quest of people in the past to develop connections or ways of thinking that mattered to them but not to us.[24] The study of nationalism in colonial societies is a case in point: because we know that the politics of the 1940s and 1950s did indeed end up producing nation-states, we tend to weave all forms of opposition to what colonialism did into a narrative of growing nationalist sentiment and nationalist organization. That the motivations and even the effects of political action at several junctures could have been something else can easily be lost.[25]

At a more abstract level, seeking the *genealogy* of concepts or ideas also easily turns into a backward-gazing approach to history. Just as an ordinary genealogy starts with "ego" (the person looking backward) and produces a tree of connection, genealogical approaches to ideas look backward to find their roots, sometimes finding them in a discredited colonial past. What gets lost here is the historical context in which concepts emerged, the debates out of which they came, the ways in which they were deflected and appropriated. Genealogical and constructivist approaches when done in a historically grounded way—that is, by working forward— become other words for doing . . . history. To the extent that such approaches both call attention to the non-neutral position of the present-day observer and see the conceptual vision of that observer in historical terms, they are valuable, albeit hardly new.[26] Good historical practice should be sensitive to the disjunctures between the frameworks of past actors and present interpreters.

The Epochal Fallacy

Historical analysis can point to moments of uncertainty—when stabilizing institutions were weakened and expectations of change heightened—and to moments of stability, and it can point to change. But to see history as a succession of epochs is to assume a coherence that complex interactions rarely produce. Whatever makes an era distinct should not only be present but be its defining feature; otherwise, the identification of an epoch says little. It is ironic that postmodernists, who distinguish themselves by a refusal of high theory and grand narrative, have to jimmy modernity into an epochal straightjacket in order to claim to have moved beyond it.[27] A more nuanced approach involves assessing change in whatever dimensions it occurs and analyzing the significance and limitations of conjunctures when multidimensional change became possible.

The term *postwar* has a clear meaning if the war in question has ended, and *postcolonial* is meaningful if one accepts—as I do—that the decolonizations of the postwar era extinguished the category of colonial empire from the repertoire of polities that were legitimate and viable in international politics.[28] The *post-* can usefully underscore the importance of the colonial past to shaping the possibilities and constraints of the present, but such a process cannot be reduced to a colonial effect, nor can either a colonial or a postcolonial period be seen as a coherent whole, as if the varied efforts and struggles in which people engaged in different situations always ended up in the same place. One is not faced with a stark choice between a light-switch view of decolonization—once independence was declared, the polity became "African"—and a continuity approach (i.e., colonialism never really ended), but one can look at what in the course of struggle be-

fore and after that moment could or could not be reimagined or reconfigured, what structural constraints persisted, what new forms of political and
economic power impinged on ex-colonial states, and how people in the
middle of colonial authority systems restructured their ties within and outside of a national political space.[29]

Skepticism is especially in order in regard to the modern epoch. Modernization theory was justly criticized for claiming that a certain societal
form came to define a modern era.[30] Era labeling has been given a new interdisciplinary lease on life, in part through the work of Michel Foucault,
which locates modern governmentality in a space that is amorphous in
time and amorphous in agency and causality, and provides a blueprint for
a wide range of scholars to attribute practices and discourses to the fact of
modernity, often elided with post-Enlightenment rationalism, bourgeois
equality, and liberalism.[31]

Dipesh Chakrabarty, for example, justly criticizes versions of Indian history, colonialist, nationalist, or Marxist, which measure the colonized by
how well they succeeded in class formation and state-building—where Europe supposedly led the way—and attribute their failures to certain lacks
on their part (of a proper working class, of a proper bourgeoisie). He instead
calls for the "provincialization" of Europe, its history seen as particular
rather than as a universal model.[32]

Then he proceeds to do the opposite. Post-Enlightenment rationality,
bourgeois equality, modernity, or liberalism become not provincial ideologies but a grid of knowledge and power, forcing people to give up diverse
understandings of community in favor of a one-to-one relationship of the
unmarked individual and the nation-state, at best seeking "alternatives" to
a modernity that is decidedly singular and decidedly European. European
history is flattened into a single post-Enlightenment era. A reference to
Hegel stands in for a European history reduced to the claim of progress.[33]

Yet nineteenth-century Europe was immersed in struggles within and
among many parochialisms and many universalities. Secularism was more
often beleaguered than triumphant; ancien régimes and aristocracies didn't
die out on the guillotine.[34] The balancing of the universalized rights-
bearing individual against questions of "difference" was a vital debate
within and after the Enlightenment. Intellectuals who called themselves
modernists between 1890 and 1930 were in "revolt against positivism, rationalism, realism, and liberalism," something lost in the stark opposition
between Enlightenment reason and the "posts" in vogue today.[35]

Sankar Muthu has brought out the debate over empire among Enlightenment thinkers. For Diderot, most notably, coming to grips with the hu-

manity of non-European people also meant confronting their subjection. Rather than seeing universal values as effacing difference, Diderot insisted on the fundamentally cultural nature of humanity. Others, like the Abbé Grégoire, were deeply sympathetic to slaves and the other victims of imperial oppression, but assumed that people, once liberated, would abandon their particularity. Still others—those most emphasized by critics of Enlightenment reason—advanced taxonomic structures, which in some (but not all) hands implied distinctions that put some outside the realm of the rights-bearing individual and made them a potential subject for colonization. "The" Enlightenment implied no one view of race or difference. It provided no clear basis either for legitimizing the subordination of certain non-European societies on the basis of universalistic criteria or for claiming that cultural difference precluded criticizing different political practices, in Europe or elsewhere.[36] What Enlightenment implied in its time—and since—was the necessity of having the debate. The historians' contribution is not to decide which Enlightenment was the authentic one, but to point to the responsibility of those who advanced particular arguments and the consequences of their interventions.

Too ready identification of an actual Europe with post-Enlightenment rationality not only leaves out the conflict and uncertainty within that continent's history, but also the extent to which even such constructs as bourgeois equality were not some essence of the West but products of struggle. The ascension of a liberal idea of a rights-bearing individual over the equally liberal idea of rights as earned by the civilized behavior of a collectivity reflected the labors not only of a Toussaint L'Ouverture or a Frederick Douglass, but of unnamed ex-slaves, dependent laborers, and colonized peasants who revealed the limits of colonial power and defined alternative modes of living and working in the crevices of authority.[37]

Doing history historically does more to challenge the supposedly dominant narrative of Western-led progress, of nation-building, or of development than an approach to the past based on story plucking, leapfrogging legacies, doing history backward, or the epochal fallacy. Criticisms of historians for writing everything into a linear history of human progress are often accurate and appropriate, but understanding different forms of temporality is not assisted by positing a flattened modern era against the linearity of a history of continual Western-centered progress. Historical temporality, as William Sewell puts it, is "lumpy": the tendency for innovations and breaks to be reabsorbed into ongoing discursive and organizational structures is sometimes broken by a cascade of events that reconfigures the imaginable and the conceivable.[38] Historical time is lumpy in

another sense—across different conceptions of temporality held by different people at the same moment. But if time is plural, it is not divided into
self-contained compartments. One circles back to the problem that in order
to understand how ideas of history were shaped by colonialism, one has to
understand colonization and challenges to it over time. The critical insistence that historians examine their own concepts of time is valuable, but so
too is the historian's insistence on attention to process, on how what happens at one moment in time configures possibilities and constraints on
what can happen the next.[39]

IMPERIAL SPACE

Can one really provincialize Europe? One way to do so is to dig more
deeply into European history itself, and there is no more central myth to
be dissected than that of narrating European history around the triumph of
the nation-state. Much recent scholarship has exaggerated the centrality of
the nation-state in the "modern" era, only to exaggerate its demise in the
present.[40] Post-Revolutionary France, as I will explain in chapter 6, cannot
be understood as a nation-state pushing into colonies external to it. The
Haitian Revolution of 1791 revealed how much questions of slavery and
citizenship, of cultural difference and universal rights, were part of debate
and struggle across imperial space.[41] This complex, differentiated empire,
expanded into continental Europe by Napoleon, did not produce a clear and
stable duality of metropole/colony, self/other, citizen/subject. Political activists in the colonies, until well into the 1950s, were not all intent upon asserting the right to national independence; many sought political voice
within the institutions of the French Empire while claiming the same
wages, social services, and standard of living as other French people. If one
wants to rethink France from its colonies, one might argue that France only
became a nation-state in 1962, when it gave up its attempt to keep Algeria
French and tried for a time to define itself as a singular citizenry in a single
territory.

A fuller version of the story of European colonial empires in the nineteenth and twentieth centuries can also come from telling it alongside the
histories of the continental empires with which they shared time and space,
the Habsburg, the Russian, and the Ottoman, and those empires that lay
outside Europe, notably the Japanese and the Chinese, not to mention two
powers with wide reach and an ambivalent sense of themselves as imperial
powers: the United States and, after 1917, the Soviet Union. At times colonialism was layered: late-nineteenth-century Sudan, for instance, was col-

onized by Egypt, which was part of the Ottoman Empire but itself experienced heavy British intervention.[42] The sharp separation of a certain kind of empire—which produces colonial and postcolonial effects—not only precludes the posing of important questions about critical historical moments and interrelated processes, but reproduces a form of Eurocentrism. Central Asian Muslims conquered by the tsars and subjected to the violent and modernizing project of the Soviets do not receive the attention devoted to North African Muslims colonized by the French; 1989 is not marked in postcolonial circles as a milestone of decolonization.[43]

The narrowing of the range of inquiry is based on certain assumptions: that these empires were not truly colonial, and above all that they were, except for the Soviet case, not "modern." The latter argument reads backward the collapse of the Ottoman, Habsburg, and Russian Empires in 1917–23 into a thesis of the inevitable transition from empire to nation-state. But excellent historical research has shown that far from being beleaguered holdouts against claims to the nation, these empires produced a strong empire-centered imagination that captured the minds of many self-conscious minority activists within their territories until World War I, a theme developed in chapter 6.

At the heart of colonialism, Partha Chatterjee has argued, is the rule of difference.[44] It might be more useful to emphasize the *politics* of difference, for the meanings of difference were always contested and rarely stable. As broad comparative study suggests, all empires, in one way or another, had to articulate difference with incorporation. Difference had to be grounded in institutions and discourses, and that took work. "Modern" empires were in some ways more explicit about codifying difference—and particularly codifying race—than aristocratic empires, for the giving way of status hierarchies to participation in a rights-bearing polity raised the stakes of inclusion and exclusion. Just where lines of exclusion would be drawn—in terms of territory, race, language, gender, or the respectability of personal or collective behavior—was not a given of the "modern state," but rather the focus of enormous and shifting debate in nineteenth- and twentieth-century Europe. The openings and closures of such debates deserve careful examination.[45]

New imperial endeavors confronted the dilemmas of older ones: geographic dispersion, extended chains of command, the need to make use of regional economic circuits and local systems of authority and patronage. The most technologically sophisticated, bureaucratized, self-consciously rational empires were compelled to give elites of conquered and subordinated people a stake in the imperial system and to produce subordinates and intermediaries who also had a stake in the system, a problem also faced by the Romans and the Ottomans. The most powerful empires were often in danger of being hijacked by their agents, by settlers, or by indigenous collectivities in search of alternatives to cooperation with an imperial center. Within empires, Enlightenment thought, liberalism, and republicanism were neither intrinsically colonial nor anticolonial, neither racist nor antiracist, but they provided languages of claim-making and counter claim-making, whose effects were shaped less by grand abstractions than by complex struggles in specific contexts, played out over time.

Ideologies of imperial inclusion and differentiation were challenged by people acting within the ideological and political structures of empire, as well as by people who tried to defend or create a political space wholly outside. At certain moments, empires needed to soften differentiation and enhance incorporation, when the need for colonial soldiers rose—in the French Caribbean of the 1790s or European campaigns of 1914—or at many other moments when people in the middle of relations of authority proved too important to making colonies work, too reflective of the actual ambiguities of colonial societies. At other moments, sometimes in reaction to activism in the colonies, rulers became more intent on articulating a colonizer/colonized dualism, a more national conception of the polity. But such conceptions were as hard to sustain in practice as the fiction of belonging to a unified polity. And colonial elites did not always agree on which direction they should lean. Among colonizing elites—even if they shared a conviction of superiority—tensions often erupted between those who wanted to save souls or civilize natives and those who saw the colonized as objects to be used and discarded at will. Among metropolitan populations, colonized people sometimes provoked sympathy or pity, sometimes fear—as well as the more complex sentiments that emerged during the actual encounters and political struggles in the colonies themselves.

IMPERIAL SPACE AND THE VARIETIES OF POLITICAL IMAGINATION

The backward projection of the post-1960s world of nation-states into a two-century-long path of inevitability affects our understanding not only of the relationship of national and imperial regimes but of the diversity of opposition to them. Pan-Arab, pan-Slavic, and pan-African movements put political affinity into a nonterritorial framework. Territory-crossing politics today, far from being a new response to a new "globalization," have a long pedigree—and, beginning with antislavery movements, a record of some effectiveness.

As I will argue in the final essay in this volume, there is a danger that ahistorical history encourages an apolitical politics. To write as if "post-Enlightenment rationality" or "the cunning of reason" or the "insertion of modernity" were what shaped the political possibilities of colonial situations is to give excessive weight to the determining power of agentless abstractions and offer little insight into how people acted when facing the possibilities and constraints of particular colonial situations. We lose the power of their example to remind us that our own moral and political choices, made in the face of the ambivalences and complications of our present situation, will have consequences in the future.

The view of an atemporal modern colonialism goes along with a notion of resistance as heroic but vain. Only at the end, in some views at least, could it have much effect—in an anticolonial moment in which iconic figures like Nkrumah and Fanon stand in for an epoch. But the heroic moment proved ephemeral, and much of the impetus behind postcolonial theory has been the failure of decolonized states to fulfill an emancipatory project—a disillusionment that then turns its critique toward the emancipatory project itself, now seen as fatally linked to its imperial genealogy.[46] The view expounded in these pages acknowledges the impetus behind this version of postcolonial theory but takes a different view of the history. I argue that colonial regimes and oppositions to them reshaped the conceptual frameworks in which both operated. Struggle was never on level ground, but power was not monolithic either. The intersection of locally or regionally rooted mobilizations with movements deploying a liberal-democratic ideology, with attempts at articulating a Christian universalism, with the mobilization of Islamic networks, with the linkages of anti-imperialist movements in different continents, or with trade union internationalism helped to shape and reshape the terrain of contestation. Collaborators and allies of colonial regimes—or people simply trying to make their way within empire—also pushed rulers of empire to change the way they acted. Subtle and dramatic changes at critical conjunctures are both part of the story.

The conjuncture of the post–World War II era indeed produced a situation in which longer-term political processes, with diverse goals, focused on fundamentally transforming the colonial state. Revolutionary mobilization, especially in Indonesia and Vietnam, as well as the climax of India's nationalist movement, had effects well beyond the immediate territories involved. But attempts at change within empires had a profound effect too (see chapter 7), for the danger that social movements operating within imperial frameworks could effectively make demands upon colonial states for resources equivalent to those of the other—metropolitan—members of the polity raised the question of whether a postwar empire could aspire to legitimacy without taking on an impossible burden of social and economic expenditures, with the threat of violence lying behind the demands. That such demands were phrased in a language of citizenship, progress, democracy, and rights both reflected social movements' serious engagement with the categories of colonizers and profoundly changed the meaning of those categories because of who was speaking. At the same time, movements outside of such frameworks—sometimes denounced by colonial rulers as atavistic, demagogic, or antimodern—raised the stakes for colonial regimes to contain tensions within familiar institutions and allowed African political movements room to maneuver between different visions of the future. One needs to appreciate the sense of possibility of these years and to understand what ensued not as an imminent logic of colonial history but as a dynamic process with a tragic end.

EMPIRES, COLONIES, AND THE POLITICS OF NAMING

For many postcolonial theorists, the naming of the colonial makes a point with relevance beyond the specificities of bygone regimes. Doing so links the history of the West and its identification with civilization and progress to its colonial genealogy. The colonial evokes above all the marking of certain people as distinct, in need of special forms of surveillance and supervision, and unable to participate fully in the projects of a modernizing society. The colonial phenomenon is thus located broadly—it may appear within "national" territory as well as in institutions of empire.[47] The use of such a general conception has its costs: a diminished ability to make distinctions among the various forms of discrimination and exclusion and a tendency to look away from the actual histories of colonization toward a homogenized coloniality. Politically as well as analytically, a more precise use of categories may be enabling.

Hence the potential value of leaning away from a dilute use of the concept of the colonial and toward a focus on the institutionalization of a set of practices that both defined and reproduced over time the distinctiveness and subordination of particular people in a differentiated space.[48] Hence the importance of concepts that bring together a range of polities across time and space all sharing basic characteristics, all the while emphasizing distinctions among them and change over time. We can set out a family description of *empire*, if not a precise definition: a political unit that is large, expansionist (or with memories of an expansionist past), and which reproduces differentiation and inequality among people it incorporates. The extent to which difference across space is institutionalized is important to constituting empire. Empire could be a phase in a polity, for if incorporation ceased to entail differentiation, it could result in a relatively homogeneous polity that becomes more nation-like and less empire-like—sometimes as the result of extremely brutal tactics of coerced assimilation or extermination, possibly a more gradual (if still asymmetrical and at times violent) process of mixing.[49] Nation-states and empire-states are, first of all, states, and power is unevenly distributed in all kinds of states.[50] In empires, power does not necessarily cohere in a core collectivity or a "people," for all members of the polity might be subordinated to greater or lesser degrees to a monarch, dictator, oligarchy, or lineage. An empire-state is a structure that reproduces distinctions among collectivities while subordinating them to a greater or lesser degree to the ruling authority.[51]

How starkly should *colonial* empires be separated from other types of empire? At stake in such a question is how one thinks about an institutionalizion of distinction that it is collective, invidious, and spatial, the marking of particular people as subject to distinct regimes of discipline and exploitation. But let us back up a moment. The spatial referent of colonization goes back to Greek and Roman meanings of the word—the bringing of new territory into use by an expanding society, including settlements for trade and agriculture. Such a referent remained part of the word's significance into the twentieth century, so that French officials, for example, could write about—without deploying an oxymoron—indigenous colonization in Africa, that is, the movement of African peasants onto new land.[52] But the principal meaning of colonization has come to involve people rather than land: coercive incorporation into an expansionist state and invidious distinction. The political salience of the colonial has been sharpened by the addition of an "ism": either an accusation—set against the alternative of a more inclusive, more consensual polity—or a defense of the legitimacy of a polity in which some people ruled over others. The power of both accusation and defense lay in bounding the colonial phenomenon to make it appear to be an exceptional form of political organization. Here definitional exercises need to enter the historical realm. Maintaining the colonial required coercive and administrative work and cultural work—to define hierarchies and police social boundaries. Such work was always subject to contestation, by those who sought to exit from the colonial polity or to make the polity less colonial.[53]

Was empire in the nineteenth and twentieth centuries more colonial than its predecessors? Brutality, enslavement, land grabbing, the denigration of indigenous cultures, and coerced religious conversion are not unique to any era or place. The more profound argument lies both in a supposedly post-Enlightenment penchant for classification—and hence invidious distinction based not on the give and take of relations between unequals but on systemic rankings of peoples (see above)—and, more persuasively, in the contention that as European publics claimed rights and citizenship for themselves, they defined a sharper division between a metropolitan polity for which such claims were relevant and an external sphere for which they were not. Subordination was no longer a fate to which anyone might be subject, but a status assigned to specific people, whose marking therefore became an issue. Overcoming such marking required evidence of acquiring the prerequisites of inclusion, hence the importance both of civilizing missions and of tightly controlling the passage from one status to another. There is something in this long-term view of a shift toward sharper distinction between a potentially democratic imperial core, located in Europe, and a colonial periphery, where access to rights, if attainable at all, required evidence of personal transformation. Even some of the old empires—the Russian and the Ottoman, for instance—began to act more colonial in the late nineteenth century, trying to impose an imperial civilization along the edges of empires, although constrained by the practical necessity of working with local elites.[54]

But if empires could become more colonial, could they get away from the dilemmas of still being empires? I will argue that they could not, because of both the *old* problem—administrative and political constraints intrinsic to the vastness and diversity of imperial spaces—and the ambiguities of the spatial referents of *new* ideologies of rights and citizenship. The old problem would not go away: colonial rulers needed to co-opt old elites and generate new collaborators, but such ties might soften the colonizer-colonized distinction and strengthen the indigenous social and cultural practices colonial ideology was trying to denigrate; rulers hoped at times to profit from indigenous trade networks and productive systems without fostering the autonomy of indigenous economic elites; they needed to raise levels of exploitation without fostering rebellion or undermining local authorities vital to the maintenance of order. The new problem was a question not simply of the ambiguity of rights discourse, but of struggle. Could concepts of rights, human dignity, and participation be confined to national units and be kept from contaminating imperial ones?[55] The Haitian Revolution in the French Empire, the combination of slave revolts and antislavery mobilization in the British Empire, and the tensions between creole elites and peasants and slaves in the era of revolution in Spanish America all point to the possibility that politics in metropoles could not be neatly segregated from colonies. Somebody might take imperial space seriously. When British or French rulers wanted Africans or Asians to be soldiers as well as workers and cash crop producers, they appealed to a notion that subjects had membership and a stake in an imperial polity. I argue in chapter 7 that the French government after 1946, faced with challenges to the legitimacy and security of its colonies, explicitly effaced the colonial nature of the regime in favor of an imperial vision of Greater France as a differentiated unit of belonging, in which all people were now considered rights-bearing citizens, but with a range of political relationships to the state. Such initiatives from above provided openings to more demands for equivalence—economic and social as well as political—from below.

The empire perspective allows us to appreciate not only the significance of the racialization of difference within nineteenth-century imperial polities, but the instability of that racialization. It gives us more options with which to understand the variety of political forms in the past and present than those of colony, nation-state, and amorphous globality.[56]

The naming of empire has acquired in the first years of the twenty-first century a political salience it seemed to have lost in the last half of the twentieth, and once again the politics of naming need to be understood. One contemporary use of *empire* is as a metaphor for the extremes of state power. The Bush administration in the United States has been denounced from the Left for behaving like an empire, and encouraged from the Right to act like an empire in order to bring more order to the world.[57] Whether either argument makes effective polemical use of the word is not for a historian to pronounce upon. But one can point to the risks either usage entails for understanding political processes: if every form of asymmetrical power is termed empire, we are left without ways of distinguishing among the actual options we might have. Liberals may be sliding into a denunciation of power that fails to distinguish different motivations and mechanisms for deploying it. Conservatives who evoke the empire analogy seem little interested in an essential dimension of historic empires: the long-term incorporation of territory and people *into* a polity. Iraqis and Afghanis are not about to become American subjects. Even proponents of the empire analogy doubt that the United States has the gumption to undertake imperial responsibilities—but such responsibilities are not actually at stake.[58] The empire word is being used to delegitimize the sovereignty of particular regimes, to mark "rogue" states, to separate the world into the fit and the unfit, the modern and the backward. Conservative empire talk is about domination, not incorporation, and most fundamentally of all, its political purpose is to mark the excluded.[59]

Empires have a large place in history, but the exercise of power across territorial lines also took other forms and can be described in other words: hegemony as used by international relations theorists, the gunboat diplomacy that was part of American foreign policy, or the "imperialism of free trade" of nineteenth-century Britain.[60] We need to consider both the entire range of forms of power and the consequences each one entails. Some scholars argue that the adjective *imperial,* applied to power, should be separated from the noun *empire* to underscore the diverse methods by which power is sometimes exercised on a vast scale: by Great Britain in the early nineteenth century or the United States in the twenty-first. One can accept this argument without losing sight of the specificity of actual empires. If we don't pay attention to what empires did—the marking and policing of boundaries, the design of systems of punishment and discipline, the attempt to instill awe as well as a sense of belonging in diverse populations—we will not understand any better the other ways in which powerful states act, and their limitations. Nor, if we wish to study power from "below" (or from in between), can we afford to miss the importance of making claims for resources, rights, or access on an empire on the basis of *belonging*—a claim that rulers of empire in certain circumstances needed to take seriously. In short, the need to understand the range of forms of imperial power entails appreciating both the general condition and its specific forms, including empire and colonies. Such analysis should be a dynamic one: states could be dragged into colonization when other means of exercising imperial power failed, and they could decolonize without giving up indirect means of authority.[61] Thinking carefully about such distinctions in historical terms underscores the misleading nature of discussions about "empire" today.

One should neither avoid the specific trajectories of Western European expansion nor fetishize them. To enlarge *empire* to include non-Western or ancient empires is not to dilute responsibility for what European empire entailed, but on the contrary to enable a more specific discussion of choice, responsibility, and consequences. To take the story of European colonization out of the metanarratives of globalization, the triumph of the nation-state, colonial modernity, or post-Enlightenment reason is, in fact, to provincialize Europe.

Chakrabarty and others are quite right to point out that historical asymmetry is reproduced in the practice of historians: scholars who examine

Asia or Africa refer continuously to European models and European styles of history writing, whereas those who study Europe are free to ignore or compartmentalize the experience of Asians and Africans and need not refer to modes of apprehending the past outside their own imaginations.[62] On an imperial scale, Zulus or Bengalis, whatever their political strategies were to be, had a much greater need to learn the English language and frame their projects in relation to European models than Europeans had to learn Zulu or Bengali or envisage the modes of understanding that Zulu or Bengali brought to their histories.[63] But scholars have enormous difficulty in separating the asymmetry of power from a totality. They can show that such successful challenges to power as antislavery, anticolonial, and anti-apartheid movements did not fully overthrow the inequalities they challenged or escape the frameworks of social order that imperial expansion produced. Scholars are less willing to acknowledge to what extent asymmetrical power is assailable power, or that the terrain labeled "Europe" might in fact change even as other people seem to be conducting their battles for recognition on "European" terms. Chakrabarty, in the end, contributes to the asymmetry he rightly deplores by focusing his attention on what he calls a "hyperreal" Europe instead of taking on a more historical, more provincial Europe.[64]

There is no ready formula for analyzing power structures that are neither symmetrical nor dichotomous. The work that has gone under the name of colonial studies and postcolonial theory is both vital and insufficient to such a task, vital because of the fundamental role of imperialism and colonialism in shaping the geography of power, insufficient because discussion at the general level of the colonial does not tell us enough about the ways in which conflict and interaction have reconfigured imaginative and political possibilities. As we address ways in which people of different origins within states or in international fora can interact, our task becomes much more difficult as we recognize that the issue is not difference per se, but rather a history that has placed differences in fundamentally unequal relationship.[65] But such relationships are not static either. We are not faced with a dichotomous choice between a *universality* that is really European and an *alternative* that can be located within an irreducible "community," and rather than resolve the tensions in favor of one such pole, we are best off using those tensions to think through issues and conflicts in their painful concreteness.

Scholarship in the 1980s and afterward has rewritten French, British, Spanish, and American histories to show that Europe was reshaped in the colonies even as people in Asia, Africa, the Pacific, and the Americas were confronting the categories of colonizers. This work has invested these histories with a moral fervor as well as an expanded horizon of inquiry. We should not lose that fervor, even while taking inspiration from it to explore the historical trajectories of colonial situations. We can examine the constraints imposed by the insinuation of Western social categories into daily life and political ideology in conquered spaces without assuming that the logic imminent in those categories determined future politics. We can recognize the instability and contested nature of colonizing ideologies and ask how political leaders in the colonies sought to reinterpret, appropriate, deflect, and resist the political ideas they gleaned from colonial rulers, their own experiences, and their connections across colonial boundaries.

We do not need to romanticize anticolonial movements in their moment of triumph or treat colonial history as if the actions of the colonized never changed its course up to the final crisis; colonialism was as much threatened by fissures within its modes of action and representation as by the threat that the last might become first.[66] We can probe the continued traces today of colonial histories while still acknowledging that these histories are not reducible to a colonial effect. Far from having to choose between examining the complexities of a colonial past and broadening our sense of the opportunities and constraints of the future, a critical and sensitive historical practice can help us retain our focus on the possibilities of political imagination and the importance of accountability for the consequences of our actions.

2 The Rise, Fall, and Rise of Colonial Studies, 1951–2001

When Georges Balandier published "La situation coloniale" (The Colonial Situation) in 1951, colonial empires were at the heart of profound debates and struggles. By the 1970s, colonialism had been banished from the realm of legitimate forms of political organization. What remained "colonial" in world politics passed itself off as something else. The burst of scholarship on colonial societies in the 1980s and 1990s thus appears paradoxical, and so too does the lack of response and follow-up to Balandier's brilliantly incisive article in the two decades after its appearance.

Colonialism, about which European publics—including left publics—had been ambivalent for decades, was an object of attack in the 1950s and 1960s, but not an object for careful examination. French Algeria, above all, attracted the attention of French scholar-intellectuals. They argued intensely about the *wrongs* being done by France, as colonizer and as brutal agent of repression. Some opened up a multisided debate about the possibilities and dangers of reform within the French system and the possibilities and dangers of independence.[1] But analytically, Balandier may have won too easy a victory: once the colonial situation had been identified, it became something recognizable, compartmentalized, and—in not too many years—transcended.

Sub-Saharan Africa in the 1950s had particular salience for that side of French progressive opinion which believed that a humanist, socialist, or revolutionary tradition originating in Europe could foster progress in the colonial world. Parts of the Left fought valiantly to give meaningful contents to ideas of French citizenship, education, and development, and anticolonial forces within Africa sometimes sought to use such ideas for their own purposes rather than assuming that national sovereignty was the only alternative to empire. African and European intellectuals took up the challenge implied in Senghor's famous phrase—that Africans should assimilate what Europe had to offer but without being assimilated—and debated the extent to which the universal values of freedom and social progress and the particularities of African culture were compatible.

In the 1950s and 1960s, the great subjects for scholarly attention, in anthropology and sociology above all, were the "-izations": modernization, urbanization, industrialization. Balandier himself turned his focus in that direction, not to applaud such processes but to engage them critically. What was lost to scholarly eyes was colonialism in the sense that Balandier's article delineated it: as a relationship of power, deriving from a particular history and with profound but complex social, economic, political, and cultural meanings.[2] At the height of decolonization struggles, notably during the Algerian war, intellectuals were most likely to see colonialism as a solid obstacle that should and could be removed. It was the process and consequences of the removal that were exciting, not the object blocking the path. Many students thought that all they needed to know about colonialism was its horrors, and a text from Fanon was sufficient to convey that. Historians, by the 1960s, also started to look away from colonial history, for to study it too much, even critically, was to reinforce the old canard that real history meant the history of white people in Africa; the new history that new nations needed was a history of either the precolonial past or the anticolonial past; colonial history could be taken as a too-familiar given.

The burst of interest in colonial studies in the 1980s needs explanation. It clearly reflects the failures of modernization projects in their liberal and radical guises. To some, the trend that has come to call itself postcolonial theory reflects growing awareness that colonial societies could not be seen as "out there," a consequence of European expansionism that could be clearly marked and eventually excised. Rather, the incorporation into a European-centered system of physical, political, and cultural power of a large portion of the world's population via colonization profoundly shaped European as well as Afro-Asian history. To a growing extent in recent decades, the presence of intellectuals of ex-colonial origin in visible academic and literary institutions in Europe, the United States, and Australia facilitated a discussion of the centrality of the colonial experience to world history. And the increasing visibility of colonial immigrants in Europe—although this is in fact a much longer history than is commonly recognized—made plausible the argument that colonial situations cannot be bounded in either time or place, that they are fundamental to any history of the present, in London as much as Calcutta.

More cynically, one might argue that the increased prominence of colonial studies comes at a time when intellectuals are profoundly disillusioned with their own possibilities for influencing social change. To locate racial and cultural hierarchy and exclusion in the heart of "post-Enlightenment rationality" is to make such a sweeping point that one is justified in doing nothing about it. Such a move privileges one side of the intellectual's place in society, that of the critic.

My goal in this chapter is not to resolve the issues it raises. A serious intellectual history of writing on colonialism could be done, but not here and not by me; to link such a history to political trends in the post-1945 era in a nonreductionist way is even more difficult. What makes intellectuals think what they think is always elusive—the intellectual in question may be the last to know—and figuring out what resonates with a larger public is more elusive still. This article is intended to provoke discussion and reflection on the way that the "colonial situation" has moved in and out of intellectual focus. I am particularly interested in issues of framing: how unposable questions come to be asked, how angles of vision change.

THE END OF EMPIRE AND THE MARGINALIZATION OF COLONIAL STUDIES

Balandier's 1951 article is notable for taking the sociological tradition in a new direction. His emphasis was on the colonial problem in the postwar era as a "totality." What was new was primarily the unit of analysis: not the ethnic group favored by anthropologists of his era[3] but a unit in which power was actually exercised, which nonetheless needed to be analyzed in the comprehensive way that anthropology had emphasized. Here, the emphasis would be not on kinship and witchcraft, but on military conquest, economic extraction, and racist ideology. Equally important was his historical sensibility: colonization was a historically specific process, and the crisis of the postwar moment exposed "the totality of relationships between colonial peoples and colonial powers and between the cultures of each of them . . . when the antagonism and the gulf between a colonial people and a colonial power are at their maximum."[4] As Balandier later pointed out, his new departure came out of prewar discussions over Marcel Mauss's concern with analyzing society not in terms of fixed forms but as a "total social phenomenon" that was living and in motion, and it was profoundly inflected by the experience of war, with the immediacy of a historical "situation."[5]

The most important predecessor and a companion piece to Balandier's article was Max Gluckman's "Analysis of a Social Situation in Modern Zululand," originally published in 1940 and cited by Balandier.[6] Gluckman broke with the notion of the bounded ethnic group and wrote about whites and blacks, officials and subjects within the same framework. His was an essay on the micropolitics of *a* colonial situation, just as Balandier's was on the macropolitics of *the* colonial situation. Rereading these two essays a half century later, I am struck by the possibilities that they opened up for an analysis of power relations within colonial societies and for allowing the units of analysis to vary with the relationships and networks as they were established over space and through interaction. They significantly prefigure some of the best work in anthropology and history of the last twenty years, and they run counter to the debunking of anthropology as a field that could not avoid its preoccupation with the "savage slot."[7] In comparison to recent anthropological writing that posits a vaguely defined mutual constitution of "the local" and "the global," concepts like the situation, the social field, and the network in 1950s anthropology offered opportunities for analyzing actual territory-crossing patterns of movement and connection (see chapter 5). Balandier's article resolutely insisted that such processes could not be usefully designated as "culture contact"—Malinowski's formulation—but should be understood above all in terms of a system for the exercise of power.

Situational anthropology had its fullest development in the work of the Copperbelt anthropologists of the 1950s, notably A. L. Epstein, J. Clyde Mitchell, and Gluckman himself. It was the situation analyzed by Gluckman rather than that of Balandier that was their focus: analysis of the ways in which urban migrants constituted distinct sets of social relations in the mine town—notably based on class relations—as compared to their villages of origin.[8] They were opening up new fields to anthropological analysis, but they were also eliding the central issue of Balandier's article. Analysis of the colonial situation was being trumped by the process of socio-economic change that seemed to be overwhelming it.

Modernizing the Colonial Situation

By 1955, Balandier himself was putting urbanization at the center of his vision of social change. In a series of studies, culminating in his *Sociologie des Brazzavilles noires* (1955),[9] he presented a picture of precarious living conditions, rapid mobility, breakdown of previous kinship structures, and individualization but continued connections with regions of origin. What Balandier found in the towns was not the colonial planner's dream, but "makeshifts" and "unrest," Africans struggling to build new communities in their own ways. Balandier used developmentalist rhetoric: social classes were "embryonic," "what might be called a middle class spirit is gaining ground" among certain groups. But counter-evolutionary tendencies were clear as well, and the deepening roots of a working class in some neighborhoods did not, after all, diminish rural connections or the flux and reflux between other neighborhoods and village life or the harsh conditions born of insecurity and instability.[10] The modernization project of late colonialism was not just incompletely realized, but badly realized.

One cannot appreciate the fascination of social scientists in the early 1950s with the dynamics of social change without recognizing the heightened sense of possibility in this era. Fundamental conceptions of how the world was ordered were in question: a neat division of labor between dynamic social sciences focused on Europe—sociology, economics, political science, history—and an anthropology focused on static, primitive Africa, divided into discrete tribal units.[11] For economists and sociologists, a new domain of intellectual conquest was opening up; for anthropologists, units of analysis as well as subjects for investigation were no longer self-evident.

The sense of new possibility did not line up on a "pro-" versus "anti-" colonial front. With the British Colonial Development and Welfare Act of 1940 and its French equivalent, the Fond d'Investissement pour le Développement Economique et Social (FIDES) of 1946, and with the reorganization of scientific research within colonial establishments, the leading colonial powers signaled their reorientation toward a modernized imperialism and their need for new sorts of expertise.[12] Both the French Socialists and the British Labour Party were divided over the question of whether or not colonial regimes could be converted into forces for economic and social progress, without which "traditional" societies might be condemned to a backward and uncompetitive existence.[13]

Colonial regimes in the 1950s were moving targets for criticism, for they sought to reposition themselves in a progress-oriented world. The colonial civil servant who "knew his natives"—so important to French and British administrations and to both country's ethnographic establishments in the interwar years—lost status to new sorts of experts, not just in relation to technical issues of health, engineering, and medicine but to a sense that social problems, labor most notably, could be managed in a rational way as well. Socialist and Communist approaches to the colonial world were determinedly modernizing too. Nationalist parties often claimed that only they could offer a true modernization in the interests of Africans. Social movements in Africa—the labor movement most prominently—were using the rhetoric of modernization to advance their claims for the resources needed to for them to advance.[14]

Balandier's position—and that of his colleagues—reflects an ambivalent engagement with the shifting project of social engineering in the 1950s.

His opportunities for research support were shaped by the needs of the administration for different kinds of knowledge, and Balandier saw his contribution as simultaneously practical and theoretical. The possibility of influencing social change in Africa stemmed from his ability to make a case for particular policy approaches based on his stature as a social scientist. It was not a position of innocence—of self-conscious distancing from any colonial taint. Nor was it uncritical. From 1949, Balandier conducted research projects that in his view helped solve administrative problems, advanced the sociology of Africa, and confronted decision-makers with the social consequences of their actions.

On the whole, social scientists working in sub-Saharan Africa in the 1950s were more eager to see what Africans could do with the opportunities of a decolonizing world than to dwell on the specificity of the colonial situation. It is worth noting the discrepancy between the mid-1950s politics of social change south of the Sahara and that in Algeria. By 1954, when the Algerian war began, African social and political movements had won a major victory in the struggle for a nonracial labor code, and they were continuing to claim one form of equivalence after another.[15] By 1956, French officials were so frustrated with the escalating claims on French resources that they now favored devolving substantial budgetary authority to elected territorial legislatures, who would be constrained by the willingness of their own electorates to vote the necessary taxes. African cities were privileged loci for colonial planning efforts, for African associations to make claims to "modern" resources, and for a wide variety of ways in which city-dwellers tried to make their lives. Balandier, Paul Mercier, and others were revealing the complexity of this urban situation: they deflated social engineers' project to remake the world in their own image, but still provided planners with useful information.[16] Their findings helped African leaders document the precariousness and insalubrity of the living conditions faced by most Africans. They both underscored the importance and revealed the failings of theories of transition from tradition to modernity.

The politics of decolonization in sub-Saharan Africa in the 1950s seemed to offer what the Algerian war denied: the opportunity of centering political debate and social science research on the possibilities of social and economic transformation rather than on the fact of rule itself. In the end, the French government would decide that the costs of an empire of claim-making citizens were more than it was willing to pay, while African political leaders would find that desires for cultural and political autonomy needed to be conjugated with the quest for material improvement.[17] The Algerian war, meanwhile, was opening a colonial sore that would, for years thereafter, prove too painful to examine in such a complex and nuanced manner.[18]

Social science research would soon prove of interest not just to colonial regimes contemplating the costs and possible benefits of modernizing imperialism, but to African leaders playing an increasing role in the self-government of African territories and eventually in their sovereign autonomy.[19] The most widely shared theme of 1950s social science research in sub-Saharan Africa, notably in sociology and anthropology, was "adaptation," particularly adaptation to the city. Research pointed to new forms of association that cut across ethnic lines—from occupational groupings to mutual aid societies—but also to "tribal" associations that developed among migrants from a particular place and which gave new significance to urban ethnicity.[20] When UNESCO, in cooperation with the French government, sponsored a conference in 1954 in Abidjan entitled "Social Impact of Industrialization and Urban Conditions in Africa," urban studies had matured sufficiently to allow for an extensive exchange of information and the publication two years later of a 743-page book on the subject. Most contributors to the UNESCO volume wrote in a progressive mold: labor forces and urban populations were growing; women were coming to the cities; families were being raised in urban environments. No one seemed to want to resurrect the fantasy of primitive Africa. Although classes were often called "embryonic," at least the metaphor implied they would one day be born. At the same time, most of the papers revealed relentless poverty and insecurity in African cities; they presented evidence of joblessness, which colonial officials were slow to see; they reported on low skill levels among workers and the continued presence of "large floating populations" in cities. Not only a sense of common language and a common past but the insecurities of urban life encouraged the maintenance of rural ties. The quest to fit African urbanization and industrialization into a universal model was strong among the urban specialists, but so too was the willingness to bring out the countertendencies and complexities in the urbanization process, as well as the pain it entailed.[21]

Among social scientists, the most influential competitor for this empirically focused, engaged form of scholarship was a more teleological, theoretically-driven vision of modernization. This eventually acquired the name of modernization theory. Modernization theory had two tenets that went beyond other progress-oriented theories of social change: first, "tradition" and "modernity" were dichotomous, modernization being understood "in terms of the goals toward which its is moving"; second, modernity, like tradition, was a package, and modernization signified a series of co-varying changes, from subsistence to market economies, from subject to participant political culture, from ascriptive status systems to achievement status systems, from extended to nuclear kinship, from religious to secular ideology.[22] To some leading American exponents of modernization theory, this conception of change was an explicit alternative to a communist vision of progress.[23]

The differences in politics and perspective among social scientists focused in the 1950s and 1960s on modernization were considerable. Some—W. W. Rostow, for instance—believed that people all over the world must tread the same path pioneered by Europe, and if they deviated it was to their detriment. Others argued that capitalism, as it then was structured, prevented the poor from following such a path, and they looked to another path—also based on European models—which would lead to socialism. There were pessimistic variants that stressed the obstacles and dangers along whichever path was chosen, and there were scholars—notably anthropologists like Balandier—who saw the complexities and problems of social change and questioned the existence of an a priori end point and the duality between tradition and modernity, but still were moved by the opportunity for new ways of life and higher standards of living that were opening to people of all origins in the era of decolonization.

Intellectuals and scholars, as well as political leaders, from former colonies were attracted to the idea of modernization. Notable among them was W. Arthur Lewis, born in the British Caribbean, who early in his career wrote pamphlets denouncing colonial rule and the planter class in the West Indies and went on to become a founding father of development economics. He never lost his disdain for colonial regimes that retarded the advance of the modern sector, but his efforts were redirected toward analysis of the bases and implications of that sector's growth. He looked to liberation in a dual sense: from the backwardness of colonial capitalism toward a more dynamic variant and from the backwardness of tradition into a modern world now open to all.[24]

The failures of modernization theory, disillusionment with the development process, and heightened sensitivity to the imperiousness of Western social science should not lead the present-day observer to miss the poignancy of the era of development, when a young and talented scholar from the British West Indies was writing the textbook on how an academic discipline should restructure itself and how the relations of rich and poor should be remade.

Colonial economies and colonial societies were discussed within such approaches, but in a particular way: as the baseline against which progress could be measured or as marks of the rigidity that dynamic nationalists, committed revolutionaries, or forward-looking experts were overcoming. Forms and strategies of modernization were hotly debated precisely because the decline of colonial empires seemed to be opening up such possibilities for liberation, as well as the dangers following from the reordering of world power.

Psychologizing the Colonial Situation

Balandier, in the first pages of his article, criticized O. Mannoni's *Psychologie de la colonisation* (1950) for treating colonization from a "purely psychological or psychoanalytical point of view"; he accused Mannoni of focusing on an ill-defined aspect of the colonial situation rather than the situation as a totality. The elision of the psychological and the sociological must have caused alarm bells to go off in a social scientist steeped in the Durkheimian tradition.

Balandier's dislike of Mannoni's psychologizing was shared by Aimé Césaire, as was his critique of the notions of primitive Africa and of culture contact. Césaire's *Discourse on Colonialism* (1955) was as ardent as Balandier's article was measured. Most commentators emphasize Césaire's searing denunciation of colonialism's power to "decivilize" and "brutalize" the colonizer as much as the colonized. Less noted is that anticolonialism, for Césaire, did not take the sole form of a movement for national independence. His book ends with a call for the "salvation of Europe" both by a "new policy founded on respect for peoples and cultures" and by "Revolution" (with a capital *R*) that would establish within Europe a classless society. Césaire, since 1945, served as a deputy from Martinique in the French legislature (and he became mayor of Fort-de-France as well); he had been a prime mover in the drive to gain for Martinique the status of a French department.[25]

Césaire balanced his concern for African cultural specificity—shorn, in his writings, of association with a racial mystique—with a direct address to issues of social and political power. Like Balandier, he didn't quite fit the trends of the late 1950s, and particularly the way the eventual movement for territorial independence put social questions on the back burner.[26] But if Balandier by 1955 was recentering his argument on social change, Césaire remained focused on colonialism—as a relationship of power among people and between classes rather than as a relation between nations.

However, the psychologizing version of the colonial situation continued to resonate among influential writers, albeit in an increasingly critical form. Albert Memmi's *The Colonizer and the Colonized* (1957) stressed the psychological effects on both parties of living in a colonial situation. It is an often insightful and even poignant book—especially in its treatment of the leftist intellectual's dilemma in the face of struggles over colonialism—but the two figures of its title remain stripped of history, social relations, or aspirations other than the fact of colonization. Colonization to Memmi was a "disease of the European," and those among the colonized who worked with Europeans could only be seen in pathological terms. Decolonization could then be understood in terms of the model of disease and cure. "If he [the colonized] ceases to be a colonized—he will become something else . . . a man like any other."[27]

The most durable of the psychologizing accounts is of course Frantz Fanon's The Wretched of the Earth (1961).[28] Even more striking than the text itself has been the extent of its influence. Many scholars today are still content to use this text as the best description of what French colonialism was really like. Yet Fanon's insistence on the Manichean nature of colonial society was more an attempt to define a politics that excluded a middle ground than to describe an observable reality. Above all, he was attacking the contention of other French-speaking intellectuals that a "colonialisme du progrès" was still a possibility; hence his insistence on the total reversal of colonialism: "The last shall be first and the first last."[29] Fanon was trying to eliminate the options that modernizing imperial governments, modernizing social scientists, and modernizing nationalists were seeking to develop. The language of mental pathology served as an indictment not only of colonial brutality, but of rival positions among its critics.

Fanon saw nationalism as a petit bourgeois ideology espoused by those intent on stepping into the colonial structure rather than turning it upside down. He had little interest in the history of Algeria or Africa and no sympathy for négritude or any other assertion of racial or cultural specificity, except insofar as it created symbols of anticolonial determination. The only history he saw was a history of oppression. His sociology of struggle was deterministic: the Algerian petite bourgeoisie was pathological, able only to imitate the colonizer; the working class had become an aristocracy intent on capturing the privileges of white workers. The peasantry and the lumpen proletariat, by contrast, were the true anticolonialists.

The Algerian revolution, pace Fanon, was a highly differentiated movement—moving between overlapping mobilizations and internecine struggles—growing out of a differentiated colonial situation. The struggle against the exploitation and humiliation of French colonialism in Algeria was a long one, and the importance of frustrated claims to a meaningful version of French citizenship, of the Communist connections of the hundreds of thousands of Algerians who had worked in France as well as in Algeria, of the Islamist politics within the Algerian population, of regional tensions within Algeria, and of alliances with Nasser's Egypt and other external forces are not easily reduced to a distinction between true anticolonialist and pathologized social categories. What is notable is how Fanon's attempt to redirect the struggle in Algeria served as a substitute for a social analysis of colonialism and of the Algerian revolution.[30]

Historicizing the Colonial Situation

It might be more accurate to entitle this section, which focuses on the 1950s and 1960s, "Historicizing Africa, Except for the Colonial Situation." African history, particularly in anglophone scholarship, took shape by differentiating itself from colonial history. K. Onwuka Dike's *Trade and Politics in the Niger Delta* (1956)[31] was a foundational text, written by a Nigerian trained by British imperial historians, staking out new territory by writing about the interaction of European and Africa traders, focusing on the structure and actions of the African trading houses. Dike's preface was more militant than his text: he argued for an African perspective using African sources to write African history. What followed was a matter-of-fact study of interaction, using a range of sources. But the distancing from imperial history was clear.

His followers went further: the most important objective for an African historian in the 1960s was to show that Africa really did have a history, above all a history of African initiative. J. F. Ade Ajayi argued that colonialism should be considered an "episode in African history." It was no more important than any other episode. Above all, Ajayi and his colleagues posited a direct link between precolonial and postcolonial history, both instances of African self-rule, the former legitimating the latter. The other acceptable topic was African resistance, and Terence Ranger linked this topic directly with the nationalist movements that had led African states to independence: resistance to conquest created traditions and forged linkages across ethnic divides, which would provide a mobilizing base later on.[32]

The domination of precolonial history and resistance was never complete; the very fact that African history was becoming a legitimate subject in the 1960s created room for students to spread out beyond the norm. The older school of history framed by the actions of European states and white colonists did not die out, although it was stripped of the racial assumptions of a bygone era and strengthened by more sophisticated historical methodologies.[33] But the Africanizing of African history was still the central item on the agenda of the 1960s.

Anthropology in these years seemed uncertain where it was going, its hegemonic position within African studies now challenged by historians, political scientists, and sociologists. What remained strong was its field-work tradition, an insistence that detailed empirical research be the basis of whatever was done: urban anthropology continued to be the most important subfield that focused explicitly on a dynamic present, while much work on religion, spirit possession, dispute resolution, and other classic topics continued, with perhaps a more explicit sense that research had to be located in time, but less often a specific effort to undertake examination of the colonial past.[34]

Economizing the Colonial Situation

What spurred a reexamination of the colonial situation was above all the discovery that it was not so easily banished. This became evident first of all in economics—building a "national economy" proved difficult and the constraints of international capitalism severe. The sense that the break with the past was more elusive and complex than anticipated took on an increasingly political aspect, in particular after the coup that overthrew Nkrumah and the Biafran war.

The word *neocolonial* expressed this disillusionment, to some extent an indictment of African regimes that had remained too cozy with former colonial powers or with the United States, and more profoundly a critique of a world economy that imposed tight constraints on African economic policy or of Western powers that punished independent states which deviated too far from certain expectations. The trouble with the neocolonial concept was that it provided a framework too simple for analyzing with precision just what had changed and what had not.

The most influential theoretical work of the 1970s, however, did not focus on the colonial situation in particular. Rather, the emphasis was on the longer term and on capitalism. Walter Rodney in *How Europe Underdeveloped Africa* (1972) took his theoretical lead from Latin American theorists of underdevelopment and dependency and fashioned this theory into a comprehensive and penetrating analysis of the history of Africa's economic relations to European capitalism. Although Rodney dealt specifically with the colonial era, the lynchpin of his analysis appeared earlier, with the slave trade and the incorporation of Africa into an unequal and exploitative world economy. Immanuel Wallerstein's writings on the world-system of capitalism also placed the focus on an earlier era. Much more satisfying was detailed work done on particular colonial institutions, situations, and time periods.[35]

A more theoretically sophisticated approach came from the French school of Marxist anthropology. The focus was still not on colonialism per se, but on the "articulation of modes of production." But by putting so much emphasis on the articulation and not simply on the production, such theories justified close examination of how the intersection played out. By drawing attention to Marx's notion of primitive accumulation—the separation of producers from the means of production—in defining capitalism, Marxist anthropology opened the question of how to analyze the specific forms in which access to resources was mediated, hence to the role of states in regulating and enforcing access and in regulating the different forms of labor.

At one level of abstraction, this school tended toward a functionalist answer to the complex question of why colonial capitalism preserved noncapitalist modes of production: so that they could pay some of the social costs of reproduction and thereby lower capital's wage bill. But if that answer was too simple, the theoretical debate gave rise to good questions that were both empirical and theoretical: just what was the relationship of different modes of resource control? What were the different possibilities and shortcomings in varying labor regimes, in different organizations of agriculture? How could one analyze the strengths and weaknesses of colonial states in regulating, stimulating, or suppressing such processes? How did the efforts of Africans to use family and kinship ties to balance different economic strategies within the constraints of colonial rule operate over time?[36]

The theoretical ferment of the 1970s and early 1980s reinforced a tradition of empirical research that had all along been strong in African studies. This served economic history quite well, and the complexities uncovered raised serious questions about the more rigid theoretical claims of world-system theory and the articulation of modes of production.[37] That economic patterns didn't quite conform to theoretical predictions put a bigger focus on agency and on the social and cultural dimensions of economic behavior: on what mining capitalists or import-export firms could think about organizing and what they could accomplish, how African traders could build diasporic networks, how workers could navigate between village production, temporary jobs, and longer-term urban activities, and what state officials could imagine and what they could do.[38]

A renewed interest in colonial states and societies reflected growing discomfort with theoretically driven agendas that focused on economic and social process. Modernization theory had provided a model of a supposedly ongoing process, but research—when conducted with integrity—revealed that change was a much more convoluted process. Economic models claimed that certain relationships were persistent because they were functional to capitalism, but it wasn't clear that capital was getting its way. And most important, the ferment that had caused the opening of new perspectives in the social sciences, the collapse of a world order based on the relationship of imperial center to colonies, was not resolving itself in the production of new principles of international order. Transitional societies weren't transitioning, and the baseline for change, the end point, and everything in between were very much in question three decades after Balandier had called for an integrated analysis of the colonial situation.

THE COLONIAL SITUATION—AGAIN

By the late 1970s, the colonial question was no longer a political issue. The remnants of white rule in Africa struggled to maintain their place in world politics by asserting themselves as nation-states. Meanwhile, scholars' renewed interest in the colonial situation had much to do with confronting intellectual dead-ends and disappointments in the previous decades. The colonial was not proving to be a temporally bounded and readily excisable element of world history.

Anthropology Puts Itself in the Picture

Talal Asad's collection *Anthropology and the Colonial Encounter* (1973) was an important breakthrough not because it was a disciplinary mea culpa, confessing anthropology's multifaceted complicity in colonial projects, but because it focused attention on the ambiguity of the relationship.[39] Anthropolgists had both served and criticized colonial regimes; they had frequently been in a position to bear witness to activities that regimes would have preferred to go unseen and unreported.[40] In the interwar years, anthropologists had had to work within the structures of "indirect rule" or "association," and their work reinforced the historically problematic notion that "tribe" was the fundamental unit of African society. Yet the information that anthropologists collected often complicated this very picture. In the 1960s, historians seeking to replace a view of age-old cultural solidarity with one of regional interaction, adaptation, and change could reinterpret older ethnographic data, turning the regional distribution of cultural traits into evidence for boundary crossing instead of for the integrity of bounded units. And they could draw on earlier challenges, such as Gluckman's or Godfrey Wilson's, to the tribal school of Africanist anthropology.[41]

The effort to see social and natural sciences as part of history and not simply as neutral observers has been one of the most stimulating trends in historical and anthropological analysis in the last decades: botany, geography, medicine, and ecology, as well as history, anthropology, and development studies, have been subject to such scrutiny.[42] Such analysis has its simplistic versions too, particularly a tendency to read all analytic schemes into an imposed "modernity." It is easy to miss the possibility that social and natural science can be reinterpreted and selectively used as well as imposed.[43]

Locating the Colonial Situation within European Civilization

Edward Said's *Orientalism*, published in 1978, showed how deeply certain visions of Asiatic societies were woven into canonical European literature. Colonization was no longer in exotic places, but in the heart of European culture.[44] Said's influence has been profound, and not limited to literary studies: his approach opened up analysis of a wide range of cultural productions and their representations of difference, power, and progress (see chapter 1). Examining the mutual constitution of an "occident" and an "orient" has helped to explain how different kinds of political processes became imaginable or inconceivable. Some scholars have insisted that the very meaning of a term like *Africa* needs to be taken apart.[45]

The bandwagon effect in colonial studies has brought with it considerable repetitiveness and distortion. The trope of otherness or alterity has become a cliché in literary studies, problematic not just because of its increasing banality but because it discourages attention to nondualistic forms of cross-cultural linkage. Looking for a "textual colonization" or a "metaphoric colonization" distinct from the institutions through which colonial power is exercised risks making colonialism appear everywhere— and hence nowhere (chapter 1). Even the most engaging of such texts, such as Homi Bhabha's elegant short essay on mimicry, leaves the two stick figures of colonizer and colonized interacting with each other independent of anything except their mutual relationship.[46] Bhabha's emphasis on hybridity problematizes the dualistic nature of previous arguments about culture in colonial contexts, but the very abstracting of his figures makes it hard to give content to this hybridity or to see how modes of interaction and engagement might differ from each other.

Rehistoricizing the Colonial Situation

In anthropology from the 1980s, one can see at last a return to the agenda that Balandier left on the table thirty years previously. The anthropological

perspective on this resurrected object of study is important in a double
sense: an application of anthropological analysis to a different sort of society, that defined by a mission community or a colonial regime, and an extension of the fieldwork method to archival sources, which would be examined with the same kind of quest for the relationship of different parts of the
story to each other. Thomas Beidelman's *Colonial Evangelism* (1982) was a
pioneering text in this regard, among other things for the author's noting
that this was a rereading of field notes from earlier research, reflecting his
new awareness that the missionaries were as interesting a community to
study as the indigenous population.[47]

An influential program for an anthropology of colonialism came from
John and Jean Comaroff, whose study of the missionary project among the
Tswana situates missionaries in relation to the tensions in English society
from which they emerged and the tensions within South Africa—between
government, settlers, and missionaries—in which they operated. Their
concern is not simply with the mission as a social entity, but with the long-
term impact of the experience, particularly the insinuation of new discourses and practices into daily life, in such a way that notions of age and
kinship among Tswana become less useful as guides to daily interactions,
and new relations between individuals and the mission institutions, between people and commodities, between people and the labor market become ordinary parts of life. They face greater difficulties in using historical
sources to demonstrate the ways in which Tswana forms of self-representation actually changed than in documenting the missionaries' intentions
and perceptions; it is not clear how far "the colonization of the mind" went
beyond the minds of missionaries.[48] But the rootedness of this project in
multiple contexts and interactions—all laden with power relationships,
with conflicts over racial and cultural distinctions—points to key themes in
the resurgence of an anthropology of colonialism.[49]

The field has been greatly influenced by Michel Foucault, and much discussion has revolved around the question of how and to what extent the
modes of "governmentality" that he saw as characteristic of modern Europe were worked out in a field of power that included both metropoles and
colonies. The grid of understanding through which colonizing regimes
enumerated and described their subjects drew on and perfected such institutions as the census, but developed specifically colonial modes of classification—tribe, caste. The Foucauldians have contributed to a far-reaching
discussion of what power means, but how far one wants to go with such an
approach is open to question. If Foucault saw power as "capillary," it was arguably arterial in most colonial contexts—strong near the nodal points of

colonial authority, less able to impose its discursive grid elsewhere, often little interested in obtaining or dispensing much knowledge about its subjects. Colonial rule in many contexts depended *not* on making the individual subject understandable within the categories of the state, but on a collectivized and reified notion of traditional authority. When, after World War II, French and British officials, reversing past policies, decided to shape an African working class using the mechanisms developed in Europe of industrial relations and the welfare state, they faced a large obstacle in the absence of civil registers and other mechanisms of tracking the individual body or understanding the social body. Efforts to delineate a realm within which the "modern subject" could actually be found widened cleavages within colonial societies—between wage workers and non–wage workers, between urban and rural. To the extent that Foucauldian approaches open up a debate over such issues, they have proved useful, but if the overall experience of nineteenth- and twentieth-century colonizers is slotted into a notion of "colonial governmentality" or "colonial modernity," the effort obscures more than it reveals. Equally important to consider is whether the Foucauldian approach gives adequate tools to understand the deflections, reinterpretations, and reconfigurations to which indigenous peoples subjected colonial power systems.[50]

If to an earlier generation of scholars what was colonial about colonial societies appeared obvious, to a new generation this has become a central issue. Ann Stoler has pointed to social reproduction both as a key marker of the fundamental problem of colonial societies and a key index of the variability of colonial regimes. The distinction between colonizer and colonized, rather than being self-evident, had to be continually reproduced, which led colonial regimes to pay inordinate attention to relatively small categories of people on crucial fault lines: racially mixed children, colonizers who "went native." In some circumstances, a male settler, trader, military man, or official could see in colonial society a domain where he could exercise masculine privilege, ignoring the consequences. But movements in late-nineteenth-century European colonies toward a more regulated colonialism consistent with bourgeois virtues subjected the sexual and reproductive dimensions of colonization to control and sanction. There was a danger of reproducing the wrong kind of colonization.[51]

Later in the twentieth century, as I have argued elsewhere, French and British indifference to how wage labor was reproduced—a task that could be foisted off on rural villages steeped in their peculiar and ill-understood cultural matrixes—turned into an obsession with reproducing the right kind of working class. To this end, the families of male wage workers needed to be brought out of their primitive contexts into locations near places of work, where the workers and their children could be properly acculturated and subject to surveillance. Such a move would open up questions of why a specifically colonial system of control made sense when African men, women, and children were being subjected to the same kind of regulatory regime as those in France or Britain—a question that cut to the heart of the colonial question in the decade after World War II.[52]

If for a time the study of resistance eclipsed the study of what was being resisted, influential currents now focus on the complexity and mutual constitution of both phenomena. The most influential scholarship has come from the Subaltern Studies collective of Indian historians. Influenced by Foucault and Gramsci and rebelling against both the nationalist and Marxist traditions in Indian history, they have examined the ways in which the imposition of a kind of colonial governmentality in India shaped the very conditions in which knowledge could be obtained and organized. They have also tried to reveal that there existed a much richer range of oppositional movements and ways of thinking than colonial or nationalist elites were capable of seeing or acknowledging. In Ranajit Guha's formulation, the particular form of power in colonial situations—domination without hegemony, he terms it—has given rise to particular forms of subaltern politics, in which the very nonhegemonic nature of the state allowed subaltern groups a considerable measure of autonomy. Such an argument is suggestive but not convincing: nineteenth- and twentieth-century colonial regimes had neither the capacity for coercive domination that Guha attributes to them nor a disinterest in articulating hegemonic strategies, however inconsistent. The history of anticolonial politics does not easily split into autonomous subalterns and colonized elites channeled into patterns of opposition bounded by the categories of imperial rulers; the politics of engagement are more complex than that. The idea of a post-Enlightenment rationality defining the terms in which both colonial power and opposition could be articulated represents a confining reading of both European and Afro-Asian histories, and above all of the ways they shaped each other. Nonetheless, the debates provoked by Subaltern Studies scholars—as intense among Indian historians as they are influential outside—have given to the study of colonial societies a vitality that it lacked fifteen years ago.[53]

To a significant extent, the former focus on the political structure of the colonial state and the economics of empires has more recently taken a backseat to an emphasis on cultural conceptions of politics. But the colonial state, as a construct and an object for empirical investigation, has not gone away. It remains the object of considerable attention, but still of puzzlement. A breakthrough text was a 1979 article by John Lonsdale and Bruce Berman, "Coping with the Contradictions."[54] They took off from the then influential contention in Marxist state theory that the state was not a mere instrument of capital but "semiautonomous." Only a state capable of distancing itself from the immediate imperatives of capital could, paradoxically, provide the conditions for the orderly reproduction of capitalism. It had to referee disputes among factions of capitalist classes and be sure that excessive exploitative zeal did not bring on conflict that might threaten the system. Extended to colonial situations, the semiautonomy argument drew attention to the disjunction between the imperial state, centered in a metropolitan location, and the colonial states that were its offshoots. Neither the state nor capital was unified; imperial/colonial interests could diverge, and tensions could be considerable. Most important, the colonial state existed in relation to different modes of production, each animated by people distinct from each other, distinctions that were crucial if a clear order were to be preserved and if capital were to exploit the labor power it found in the colonies. Such labor power was not simply there for the taking; rather the state had to hitch itself to the interests of indigenous elites in order to gain access to the labor power that imperial capital needed. Each colonial state had to manage a particularly complex set of contradictions, if that state was to promote the interests of "its" economic actors in a competitive world economy. It would be simplistic to assume that colonial states actually managed these contradictions very well or that empires effectively integrated their diverse parts. Such an approach opens the door to exploring a range of structures, strategies, and capabilities of such states, as well as a range of outcomes.

Lonsdale and Berman have helped take political economy out of a reductive approach to the state. Their approach is compatible with more Weberian or Foucauldian approaches, open to thinking about the cultural idioms in which power is expressed and contested. But the study of colonial states still produces curiously wooden results. Two of the more important overviews by political scientists are cases in point. Crawford Young's *The African State in Comparative Perspective* (1994) takes the Congolese term for the brutal state, *bula matari*, as an exemplar of colonial states across time and space, missing the basic ways in which colonial states reconstituted their forms of governance and their reigning ideologies in interaction with their subjects. Mahmood Mamdani's *Citizen and Subject* (1996) argues that colonial regimes, above all in the 1920s and 1930s, ruled through "decentralized despotisms," and that these structures constituted the framework within which opposition had to act, so that decolonization entailed deracialization but not detribalization. His case for interwar colonial policy is a strong one, but he misses the extent to which Africans developed networks that cut across these divisions, and most importantly the strength of the claims to citizenship that exploded in the late 1940s and 1950s. Instead of a colonial legacy determining postcolonial political structures, it is more telling—and more tragic—to emphasize the openings of those years and the closures that followed them.[55]

But the problem within colonial studies is more fundamental than this particular analysis. The explosion of colonial studies in the 1980s and 1990s, and particularly their popularity in literary studies, has been misleading as well as eye-opening, for the field has become unmoored from analysis of processes unfolding over time. An even greater abstraction—to turn the exercise from the historical and institutional specificity of Balandier's analysis of the colonial situation into a "critique of modernity" or an "ethnography of modernity"—is a notable departure, which makes the identification of structures, agency, and causality fade from view (see chapters 1 and 5).

Colonial Situations: Widening Perspectives on Empire

The reading of colonialism against modernity, post-Enlightenment rationality, or liberalism is in part a consequence of the bias within colonial/postcolonial studies in the past two decades toward the empires of Western Europe in the nineteenth and twentieth centuries. British India and French and British Africa occupy privileged places in this literature. There is a very rich scholarship on the Iberian empires of the sixteenth century onward, but how it is to be integrated with scholarship on the more recent period is less evident. Empires necessarily reproduced difference, but they did not necessarily reproduce a self-other distinction. Imperial rule always entailed command, but patrimonial forms of authority, systems of rule that recognized corporate structures within empires, rule via ethnic networks and group structures, and recruitment of high-level administrative personnel from conquered provinces complicate the relationship of ruler and ruled, of insider and outsider. Even the history of the nineteenth and twentieth centuries can be reconfigured if the range is expanded beyond the usual notion of imperialism as a projection of a European state. It is not terribly demanding to ask historians of Europe to acknowledge that colonies mattered. It is another thing to ask them to rethink the narrative of the growth of the nation-state. That the Haitian Revolution should stand alongside the French one because it immediately threw into question the universe to which universal rights was applied—in metropolitan France as well as overseas—is to suggest a more radical revisioning of historiography (chapter 6).

Imperialisms existed in relation to one another. Interaction was not only a matter of high diplomacy but also a question of how different ways of articulating ideologies and social norms traveled. The possibilities for organizing colonial societies could shift sharply in particular conjunctures. To take the end of the nineteenth century as an example, one can examine how different imperial trajectories intersected in the scramble for Africa, the American recolonization of the Philippines and Puerto Rico, the uncompleted reform efforts in the Ottoman, Romanov, and Habsburg Empires, the clash of a growing Japanese imperialism and a stalled Russian one, and the crises of a Chinese empire beset from without and challenged from within. Likewise, the rapidity of decolonization in the fifteen years after World War II can only be understood as a conjunctural, interactive phenomenon of wide scale.

Finally, empires established circuits along which personnel, commodities, and ideas moved, but were also vulnerable to redirection by traders and subordinate officials. Empires were crosscut by circuits that they could not necessarily control—the ethnic diaspora of Chinese traders in Southeast Asia, for example, or the diasporas created by imperialism and enslavement, such as the linkages established by African Americans across the Atlantic world. Benedict Anderson has used the idea of a circuit to explain the origins of creole nationalisms, but that was only one form of political imagination that grew up within and across colonial systems.[56] The metanarrative of a long-term shift from empire to nation risks masking these diverse forms of political imagination in a singular teleology.

To add a plural to the colonial situation is not to diminish the importance of the specific forms of colonization that spread out from Europe in the nineteenth and twentieth centuries. Rather, it enables an analysis of the importance of such a process, and its limitations as well.

CONCLUSION

Colonial history in the era of decolonization has suffered a double form of occlusion. From the 1950s into the 1970s, the idea of modernization occluded the colonial. In the 1980s and 1990s, the idea of modernity occluded history. It was into the hopes for making a new future that the specificity of Balandier's 1951 project disappeared for a time. The bitterness of the dénouement of French colonialism in Algeria, as much as the transition of modernizing imperialism into dependent sovereignty in sub-Saharan

Africa, fostered the nonreckoning that accompanied and followed the end of empires. More recently, the treatment of colonization as an ugly reflection of modernity placed the unevenness of colonizing processes and the small and profound effects of the evasions, deflections, and struggles within colonized territories in a vaguely defined metahistory rather than in the situations in which people actually acted.

The most thought-provoking dimension of the "new" scholarship on colonial situations, in relation to the "old," is the way it calls into question the position of the observer, not simply in terms of social biases but in terms of the ways in which forms of knowledge and conceptions of change are themselves shaped by a history of which imperialism is a central element. But looking back at the scholarship of the early 1950s, one cannot escape its political engagement, the sense among intellectuals that what they said mattered. They could try to reshape discourses, criticize certain kinds of interventions, identify oppression or indifference where they saw it, reform political and economic structures where possible, point out the unintended consequences of interventions, and above all affirm that the organization of power across the world needed to be rethought and remade. Such scholarship—be it modernization theory or Balandier's notion of a colonial situation—was a call to action, and it was subject to examination and opposition based on its real-world influences and effects. Now, it is not so clear what anyone should do next, once one has located colonialism as post-Enlightenment rationality's evil twin.

To look back on Balandier's 1951 article is to reenter an era when the definition of the possible in world politics changed fundamentally. Colonial empires were a fact of political life in 1940. In 1951, their normality and their future were more in doubt, and struggles to retain, reform, and eliminate colonial systems were all ongoing. By the 1960s, a normative transformation had taken place on a worldwide level; the colonial empire was no longer a legitimate or viable form of political organization. This transformative process took in not only political structures but the very way in which people and roles could be talked about and understood. Extreme forms of defining certain people as irredeemably "other" still resurface, and they lie beneath the surface in much of the media, as well as in academic discussions. They are also fiercely contested within Europe and the United States, just as in the former colonies. Africans, meanwhile, face the opposite danger: of submergence in notions of generalized economic or political behavior, namely that the individual person or the individual territory is supposed to function within an open world market and a generalized system of sovereignty, whose basic contours are taken as a given in which people and governments must either sink or swim.[57] Aimé Césaire had this figured out by 1956: "There are two ways to lose oneself: by a walled segregation in the particular or by a dilution in the 'universal.' "[58]

Balandier's 1951 article was an effort to address the uncertainty and complexity of a dynamic period. Africans, he insisted, were not living within tribal cages from which their emergence was always temporary and risky. They lived within a system of power exercised on a large territorial scale and drawing on even broader symbolic resources, but they maneuvered within and challenged that system. Fifty years later, Balandier's contribution retains the vitality of writing that is both engaged and rigorous.

PART II

Concepts in Question

3 Identity

WITH ROGERS BRUBAKER

"The worst thing one can do with words," wrote George Orwell half a century ago, "is to surrender to them." If language is to be "an instrument for expressing and not for concealing or preventing thought," he continued, one must "let the meaning choose the word, and not the other way about."[1] The argument of this paper is that the social sciences and humanities have surrendered to the word *identity*; that this has both intellectual and political costs; and that we can do better. *Identity*, we will argue, tends to mean too much (when understood in a strong sense), too little (when understood in a weak sense), or nothing at all (because of its sheer ambiguity). We take stock of the conceptual and theoretical work *identity* is supposed to do, and suggest that this work might be done by terms that are less ambiguous and unencumbered by the reifying connotations of *identity*.

We argue that the prevailing constructivist stance on identity—the attempt to soften the term, to acquit it of the charge of essentialism by stipulating that identities are constructed, fluid, and multiple—leaves us without a rationale for talking about identities at all and ill-equipped to examine the "hard" dynamics and essentialist claims of contemporary identity politics. "Soft" constructivism allows putative identities to proliferate. But as they proliferate, the term loses its analytical purchase. If identity is everywhere, it is nowhere. If it is fluid, how can we understand the ways in which self-understandings may harden, congeal, and crystallize? If it is constructed, how can we understand the sometimes coercive force of external identifications? If it is multiple, how do we understand the terrible singularity that is often striven for—and sometimes realized—by politicians seeking to transform mere categories into unitary and exclusive groups? How can we understand the power and pathos of identity politics?

Identity is a key term in the vernacular idiom of contemporary politics, and social analysis must take account of this fact. But this does not require us to use "identity" as a category of analysis or to conceptualize identities as something that all people have, seek, construct, and negotiate. Conceptualizing all affinities and affiliations, all forms of belonging, all experiences of commonality, connectedness, and cohesion, all self-understandings and self-identifications in the idiom of identity saddles us with a blunt, flat, undifferentiated vocabulary.

We do not aim here to contribute to the ongoing debate on identity politics.[2] We focus instead on identity as an analytical category. This is not a merely semantic or terminological issue. The use and abuse of *identity*, we suggest, affects not only the language of social analysis but also—inseparably—its substance. Social analysis—including the analysis of identity politics—requires relatively unambiguous analytical categories. Whatever its suggestiveness, whatever its indispensability in certain practical contexts, *identity* is too ambiguous, too torn between "hard" and "soft" meanings, essentialist connotations, and constructivist qualifiers, to serve well the demands of social analysis.

THE "IDENTITY" CRISIS IN THE SOCIAL SCIENCES

Identity and cognate terms in other languages have a long history as technical terms in Western philosophy, from the ancient Greeks through contemporary analytical philosophy. They have been used to address the perennial philosophical problems of permanence amidst manifest change, and of unity amidst manifest diversity.[3] Widespread vernacular and social-analytical use of *identity* and its cognates, however, is of much more recent vintage and more localized provenance.

The introduction of *identity* into social analysis and its initial diffusion in the social sciences and public discourse occurred in the United States in the 1960s (with some anticipations in the second half of the 1950s).[4] The most important and best-known trajectory involved the appropriation and popularization of the work of Erik Erikson (who was responsible, among other things, for coining the term *identity crisis*).[5] But as Philip Gleason has shown,[6] there were other paths of diffusion as well. The notion of identification was pried from its original, specifically psychoanalytic context (where the term had been initially introduced by Freud) and linked to ethnicity on the one hand (through Gordon Allport's influential 1954 book *The Nature of Prejudice*) and to sociological role theory and reference group theory on the other (through figures such as Nelson Foote and Robert Merton). Symbolic interactionist sociology, concerned from the outset with "the self," came increasingly to speak of "identity," in part through the influence of Anselm Strauss.[7] More influential in popularizing the notion of identity, however, were Erving Goffman, working on the periphery of the symbolic interactionist tradition, and Peter Berger, working in social constructionist and phenomenological traditions.[8]

For a variety of reasons, the term *identity* proved highly resonant in the 1960s,[9] diffusing quickly across disciplinary and national boundaries, establishing itself in the journalistic as well as the academic lexicon, and permeating the language of social and political practice as well as that of social and political analysis. In the American context, the prevalent individualist ethos and idiom gave a particular salience and resonance to identity concerns, particularly in the contexts of the 1950s thematization of the "mass society" problem and the 1960s generational rebellions. And from the late 1960s on, with the rise of the Black Power movement, and subsequently other ethnic movements for which it served as a template, concerns with and assertions of individual identity, already linked by Erikson to "communal culture,"[10] were readily, if facilely, transposed to the group level. The proliferation of identitarian claim-making was facilitated by the comparative institutional weakness of leftist politics in the United States and by the concomitant weakness of class-based idioms of social and political analysis. As numerous analysts have observed, class can itself be understood as an identity.[11] Our point here is simply that the weakness of class politics in the United States (vis-à-vis Western Europe) left the field particularly wide open for the profusion of identity claims.

Already in the mid 1970s, W. J. M. Mackenzie could characterize identity as a word "driven out of its wits by over-use," and Robert Coles could remark that the notions of identity and identity crisis had become "the purest of cliches."[12] But that was only the beginning. In the 1980s, with the rise of race, class, and gender as the "holy trinity" of literary criticism and cultural studies,[13] the humanities joined the fray in full force. And "identity talk"—inside and outside academia—continues to proliferate today.[14] The "identity" crisis—a crisis of overproduction and consequent devaluation of meaning—shows no sign of abating.[15]

Qualitative as well as quantitative indicators signal the centrality—indeed the inescapability—of identity as a topos. In recent years, two new interdisciplinary journals devoted to the subject, complete with star-studded editorial boards, have been launched.[16] And quite apart from the pervasive concern with identity in work on gender, sexuality, race, religion, ethnicity, nationalism, immigration, new social movements, culture, and "identity politics," even those whose work has *not* been concerned primarily with these topics have felt obliged to address the question of identity. A selective listing of major social theorists and social scientists whose main work lies *outside* the traditional homelands of identity theorizing yet who have nonetheless written explicitly on identity in recent years includes Zygmunt Bauman, Pierre Bourdieu, Fernand Braudel, Craig Calhoun, S. N. Eisenstadt, Anthony Giddens, Bernhard Giesen, Jürgen Habermas, Claude Lévi-Strauss, Paul Ricoeur, Amartya Sen, Margaret Somers, Charles Taylor, Charles Tilly, and Harrison White.[17]

CATEGORIES OF PRACTICE AND CATEGORIES OF ANALYSIS

Many key terms in the interpretative social sciences and history—*race, nation, ethnicity, citizenship, democracy, class, community,* and *tradition,* for example—are at once categories of social and political *practice* and categories of social and political *analysis.* By *categories of practice,* we mean, following Bourdieu, something akin to what others have called *native* or *folk* or *lay* categories. These are categories of everyday social experience, developed and deployed by ordinary social actors, as distinguished from the experience-distant categories used by social analysts. We prefer the expression *category of practice* to the alternatives, for while the latter imply a relatively sharp distinction between native or folk or lay categories on the one hand and scientific categories on the other, such concepts as race, ethnicity, or nation are marked by close reciprocal connection and mutual influence between their practical and analytical uses.[18]

Identity, too, is both a category of practice and a category of analysis. As a category of practice, it is used by "lay" actors in some (not all!) everyday settings to make sense of themselves, of their activities, of what they share with, and how they differ from, others. It is also used by political entrepreneurs to persuade people to understand themselves, their interests, and their predicaments in a certain way, to persuade certain people that they are (for certain purposes) "identical" with one another and at the same time different from others, and to organize and justify collective action along certain lines.[19] In these ways the term *identity* is implicated both in everyday life and in identity politics in its various forms.

Everyday identity talk and identity politics are real and important phenomena. But the contemporary salience of identity as a category of practice does not require its use as a category of analysis. Consider an analogy. *Nation* is a widely used category of social and political practice. Appeals and claims made in the name of putative nations—for example, claims to self-determination—have been central to politics for a hundred and fifty years. But one does not have to use *nation* as an analytical category in order to understand and analyze such appeals and claims. One does not have to take a category inherent in the *practice* of nationalism—the realist, reifying conception of nations as real communities—and make this category central to the *theory* of nationalism.[20] Nor does one have to use *race* as a category of analysis—which risks taking for granted that race exists—in order to understand and analyze social and political practices oriented to the presumed existence of putative races.[21] Just as one can analyze "nation-talk" and nationalist politics without positing the existence of nations, or "race-talk" and race-oriented politics without positing the existence of races, so one can analyze "identity-talk" and identity politics without, as analysts, positing the existence of identities.

Reification is a social process, not only an intellectual practice. As such, it is central to the politics of ethnicity, race, nation, and other putative identities. Analysts of this kind of politics should seek to *account* for this process of reification. We should seek to explain the processes and mechanisms through which what has been called the "political fiction" of the nation—or of the ethnic group, race, or other putative identity—can crystallize, at certain moments, as a powerful, compelling reality.[22] But we should avoid unintentionally *reproducing* or *reinforcing* such reification by uncritically adopting categories of practice as categories of analysis.

The mere use of a term as a category of practice, to be sure, does not disqualify it as a category of analysis.[23] If it did, the vocabulary of social analysis would be a great deal poorer, and more artificial, than it is. What is problematic is not *that* a particular term is used, but *how* it is used. The problem, as Loïc Wacquant has argued with respect to *race*, lies in the "uncontrolled conflation of social and sociological . . . [or] folk and analytic understandings."[24] The problem is that *nation, race,* and *identity* are used analytically a good deal of the time more or less as they are used in practice, in an implicitly or explicitly reifying manner, in a manner that implies or asserts that nations, races, and identities exist and that people "have" a nationality, a race, an identity.

It may be objected that this overlooks recent efforts to avoid reifying identity by theorizing identities as multiple, fragmented, and fluid.[25] Essentialism has indeed been vigorously criticized, and constructivist gestures now accompany most discussions of identity.[26] Yet we often find an

uneasy amalgam of constructivist language and essentialist argumentation.[27] This is not a matter of intellectual sloppiness. Rather, it reflects the
dual orientation of many academic identitarians as both *analysts* and *pro-
tagonists* of identity politics. It reflects the tension between the constructivist language that is required by academic correctness and the founda-
tionalist or essentialist message that is required if appeals to identity are to
be effective in practice.[28] Nor is the solution to be found in a more consistent constructivism, for it is not clear why that which is routinely characterized as "multiple, fragmented, and fluid" should be conceptualized as
identity at all.

THE USES OF *IDENTITY*

What do scholars mean when they talk about identity? What conceptual
and explanatory work is the term supposed to do? This depends on the context of its use and the theoretical tradition from which the use in question
derives. The term is richly—indeed, for an analytical concept, hopelessly—
ambiguous. But one can identify a few key uses:

1. Understood as a ground or basis of social or political action, *identity* is
   often opposed to *interest* in an effort to highlight and conceptualize *noninstrumental* modes of social and political action.[29] With a slightly different analytical emphasis, it is used to underscore the manner in which
   action—individual or collective—may be governed by *particularistic
   self-understandings* rather than *by putatively universal self-interest*.[30]
   This is probably the most general use of the term; it is frequently found
   in combination with other uses. It involves three related but distinct
   contrasts in how action is conceptualized and explained. The first is between self-understanding and (narrowly understood) self-interest.[31]
   The second is between particularity and (putative) universality. The
   third is between two ways of construing social location. Many (though
   not all) strands of identitarian theorizing see social and political action as
   powerfully shaped by position in social space. In this they agree with
   many (though not all) strands of universalist, instrumentalist theorizing. But *social location* means something quite different in the two
   cases. For identitarian theorizing, it means position in a multidimensional space defined by *particularistic categorical attributes* (race, ethnicity, gender, sexual orientation). For instrumentalist theorizing, it
   means position in a *universalistically conceived social structure* (for example, position in the market, the occupational structure, or the mode of
   production).

2. Understood as a specifically *collective* phenomenon, *identity* denotes a fundamental and consequential *sameness* among members of a group or category. This may be understood objectively (as a sameness "in itself") or subjectively (as an experienced, felt, or perceived sameness). This sameness is expected to manifest itself in solidarity, in shared dispositions or consciousness, or in collective action. This usage is found especially in the literature on social movements;[32] on gender;[33] and on race, ethnicity, and nationalism.[34] In this usage, the line between identity as a category of analysis and identity as a category of practice is often blurred.

3. Understood as a core aspect of (individual or collective) selfhood or as a fundamental condition of social being, identity is invoked to point to something allegedly *deep, basic, abiding, or foundational.* This is distinguished from more superficial, accidental, fleeting, or contingent aspects or attributes of the self, and is understood as something to be valued, cultivated, supported, recognized, and preserved.[35] This usage is characteristic of certain strands of the psychological (or psychologizing) literature, especially as influenced by Erikson,[36] though it also appears in the literature on race, ethnicity, and nationalism. Here too the practical and analytical uses of identity are frequently conflated.

4. Understood as a product of social or political action, identity is invoked to highlight the *processual, interactive* development of the kind of collective self-understanding, solidarity, or groupness that can make collective action possible. In this usage, found in certain strands of the new social movement literature, identity is understood both as a *contingent product* of social or political action and as a ground or basis of further action.[37]

5. Understood as the evanescent product of multiple and competing discourses, identity is invoked to highlight the *unstable, multiple, fluctuating, and fragmented* nature of the contemporary "self." This usage is found especially in the literature influenced by Foucault, poststructuralism, and postmodernism.[38] In somewhat different form, without the poststructuralist trappings, it is also found in certain strands of the literature on ethnicity—notably in situationalist or contextualist accounts of ethnicity.[39]

Clearly, the term *identity* is made to do a great deal of work. It is used to highlight noninstrumental modes of action; to focus on self-understanding rather than self-interest; to designate sameness across persons or sameness over time; to capture allegedly core, foundational aspects of selfhood; to deny that such core, foundational aspects exist; to highlight the processual, interactive development of solidarity and collective self-understanding; and to stress the fragmented quality of the contemporary experience of self, a self unstably patched together through shards of discourse and contingently activated in differing contexts.

These usages are not simply heterogeneous; they point in sharply differing directions. To be sure, there are affinities between certain of them, notably between the second and third, and between the fourth and fifth. And the first usage is general enough to be compatible with all of the others. But there are strong tensions as well. The second and third uses both highlight *fundamental sameness*—sameness across persons and sameness over time—while the fourth and fifth uses both *reject* notions of fundamental or abiding sameness.

Do we really need this heavily burdened, deeply ambiguous term? The overwhelming weight of scholarly opinion suggests that we do.[40] Even the most sophisticated theorists, while readily acknowledging the elusive and problematic nature of identity, have argued that it remains indispensable. Critical discussion of identity has thus sought not to jettison but to save the term by reformulating it so as to make it immune from certain objections, especially from the dreaded charge of essentialism. Thus Stuart Hall characterizes identity as "an idea which cannot be thought in the old way, but without which certain key questions cannot be thought at all." What these key questions are, and why they cannot be addressed without identity, remain obscure in Hall's sophisticated but opaque discussion.[41] Hall's comment echoes an earlier formulation of Claude Lévi-Strauss's, characterizing identity is "a sort of virtual center *[foyer virtuel]* to which we must refer to explain certain things, but without it ever having a real existence."[42] Lawrence Grossberg, concerned by the narrowing preoccupation of cultural studies with the "theory and politics of identity," nonetheless repeatedly assures the reader that he does "not mean to reject the concept of identity or its political importance in certain struggles" and that his "project is not to escape the discourse of identity but to relocate it, to rearticulate it."[43] Alberto Melucci, a leading exponent of identity-oriented analyses of social movements, acknowledges that "the word *identity* . . . is semantically inseparable from the idea of permanence and is perhaps, for this very reason, ill-suited to the processual analysis for which I am arguing."[44] Ill-suited or not, *identity* continues to find a central place in Melucci's writing.

We are not persuaded that identity is indispensable. We will sketch below some alternative analytical idioms that can do the necessary work without the attendant confusion. Suffice it to say for the moment that if one wants to argue that particularistic self-understandings shape social and political action in a noninstrumental manner, one can simply say so. If one wants to trace the process through which persons sharing some categorical attribute come to share definitions of their predicament, understandings of their interest, and a readiness to undertake collective action, it is best to do so in a manner that highlights the contingent and variable relationship between mere categories and bounded, solidary groups. If one wants to examine the meanings and significance people give to constructs such as race, ethnicity, and nationality, one already has to thread one's way through conceptual thickets, and it is not clear what one gains by aggregating them under the flattening rubric of identity. And if one wants to convey the sense of a self being constructed and continuously reconstructed out of a variety of competing discourses—and remaining fragile, fluctuating, and fragmented—it is not obvious how the word *identity* captures the meaning being conveyed.

STRONG AND WEAK UNDERSTANDINGS OF IDENTITY

Our inventory of the uses of *identity* has revealed not only great heterogeneity but a strong antithesis between positions that highlight fundamental or abiding sameness and stances that expressly reject notions of basic sameness. The former can be called strong or hard conceptions of identity, the latter, weak or soft conceptions.

Strong conceptions of identity preserve the common-sense meaning of the term—the emphasis on sameness over time or across persons. And they accord well with the way the term is used in most forms of identity politics. But precisely because they adopt for analytical purposes a category of everyday experience and political practice, they entail a series of deeply problematic assumptions:

1. Identity is something all people have, or ought to have, or are searching for.

2. Identity is something all groups (at least groups of a certain kind—e.g., ethnic, racial, or national) have, or ought to have.

3. Identity is something people (and groups) can have without being aware of it. In this perspective, identity is something to be *discovered*, and something about which one can be *mistaken*. The strong conception of identity thus replicates the Marxian epistemology of class.

4. Strong notions of collective identity imply strong notions of group boundedness and homogeneity. They imply high degrees of groupness, an identity or sameness between group members, a sharp distinctiveness from nonmembers, a clear boundary between inside and outside.[45]

Given the powerful challenges from many quarters to substantialist understandings of groups and essentialist understandings of identity, one might think we have sketched a straw man here. Yet in fact strong conceptions of identity continue to inform important strands of the literature on gender, race, ethnicity, and nationalism.[46]

Weak understandings of identity, by contrast, break consciously with the everyday meaning of the term. It is such weak or soft conceptions that have been heavily favored in theoretical discussions of identity in recent years, as theorists have become increasingly aware of and uncomfortable with the strong or hard implications of everyday meanings of identity. Yet this new theoretical common sense has problems of its own. We sketch three of these.

The first is what we call "clichéd constructivism." Weak or soft conceptions of identity are routinely packaged with standard qualifiers indicating that identity is multiple, unstable, in flux, contingent, fragmented, constructed, negotiated, and so on. These qualifiers have become so familiar—indeed obligatory—in recent years that one reads (and writes) them virtually automatically. They risk becoming mere placeholders, gestures signaling a stance rather than words conveying a meaning.

Second, it is not clear why weak conceptions of identity are conceptions *of identity*. The everyday sense of *identity* strongly suggests at least some self-sameness over time, some persistence, something that remains identical, the same, while other things are changing. What is the point in using the term *identity* if this core meaning is expressly repudiated?

Third, and most important, weak conceptions of identity may be *too* weak to do useful theoretical work. In their concern to cleanse the term of its theoretically disreputable hard connotations, in their insistence that identities are multiple, malleable, fluid, and so on, soft identitarians leave us with a term so infinitely elastic as to be incapable of performing serious analytical work.

We are not claiming that the strong and weak versions sketched here jointly exhaust the possible meanings and uses of *identity*. Nor are we claiming that sophisticated constructivist theorists have not done interesting and important work using soft understandings of identity. We will argue, however, that what is interesting and important in this work often does not depend on the use of identity as an analytical category. Consider three examples.

Margaret Somers, criticizing scholarly discussions of identity for focusing on categorical commonality rather than on historically variable relational embeddedness, proposes to "reconfigur[e] the study of identity formation through the concept of narrative," to "incorporate into the core conception of identity the categorically destabilizing dimensions of time, space, and relationality." Somers makes a compelling case for the importance of narrative to social life and social analysis, and argues persuasively for situating social narratives in historically specific relational settings. She focuses on the ontological dimension of narratives, on the way in which narratives not only represent but, in an important sense, constitute social actors and the social world in which they act. What remains unclear from her account is why—and in what sense—it is *identities* that are constituted through narratives and formed in particular relational settings. Social life is indeed pervasively "storied"; but it is not clear why this storiedness should be axiomatically linked to identity. People everywhere and always tell stories about themselves and others, and locate themselves within culturally available repertoires of stories. But in what sense does it follow that such "narrative location endows social actors with identities—however multiple, ambiguous, ephemeral, or conflicting they may be"? The major analytical work in Somers's article is done by the concept of narrativity, supplemented by that of relational setting; the work done by the concept of identity is much less clear.[47]

Introducing a collection on *Citizenship, Identity, and Social History*, Charles Tilly characterizes identity as a "blurred but indispensable" concept and defines it as "an actor's experience of a category, tie, role, network, group or organization, coupled with a public representation of that experience; the public representation often takes the form of a shared story, a narrative." But what is the relationship between this encompassing, open-ended definition and the work Tilly wants the concept to do? What is gained, analytically, by labeling *any* experience and public representation of *any* tie, role, or network as an *identity?* When it comes to examples, Tilly rounds up the usual suspects: race, gender, class, job, religious affiliation, national origin. But it is not clear what analytical leverage on these phenomena can be provided by the exceptionally capacious, flexible concept of identity he proposes. Justly well known for fashioning sharply focused, hardworking concepts, Tilly here faces the difficulty that confronts most social scientists writing about identity today: that of devising a concept soft and flexible enough to satisfy the requirements of relational, constructivist social theory, yet robust enough to have purchase on the phenomena that cry out for explanation, some of which are quite hard.[48]

Craig Calhoun uses the Chinese student movement of 1989 as a vehicle for a subtle and illuminating discussion of the concepts of identity, interest, and collective action. Calhoun explains students' readiness to "knowingly risk death" in Tiananmen Square on the night of June 3, 1989, in terms of an honor-bound identity or sense of self, forged in the course of the movement itself, to which students became increasingly and, in the end, irrevocably committed. His account of the shifts in the students' lived sense of self during the weeks of their protest—as they were drawn, in and through the dynamics of their struggle, from an originally "positional," class-based self-understanding as students and intellectuals to a broader, emotionally charged identification with national and even universal ideals—is a compelling one. Here too, however, the crucial analytical work appears to be done by a concept other than identity—in this case, that of honor. Honor, Calhoun observes, is "imperative in a way interests are not." But it is also imperative in a way *identity*, in the weak sense, is not. Calhoun subsumes honor under the rubric of identity, and presents his argument as a general one about the "constitution and transformation of identity." Yet his fundamental argument in this paper, it would seem, is not about identity in general, but about the way in which a compelling sense of honor can, in extraordinary circumstances, lead people to undertake extraordinary actions, lest their core sense of self be radically undermined.[49]

In his edited volume on *Social Theory and the Politics of Identity*, Calhoun works with this more general understanding of identity. "Concerns with individual and collective identity," he observes, "are ubiquitous." It is certainly true that we "know of no people without names, no languages or cultures in which some manner of distinctions between self and other, we and they are not made."[50] But it is not clear why this implies the ubiquity of identity, unless we dilute identity to the point of designating *all* practices involving naming and self-other distinctions. Calhoun—like Somers and Tilly—goes on to make illuminating arguments on a range of issues concerning claims of commonality and difference in contemporary social movements. Yet while such claims are indeed often framed today in an idiom of identity, it is not clear that adopting that idiom for *analytical* purposes is necessary or even helpful.

IN OTHER WORDS

What alternative terms might stand in for *identity*, doing the theoretical work *identity* is supposed to do without its confusing, contradictory connotations? Given the great range and heterogeneity of the work done by *identity*, it would be fruitless to look for a *single* substitute, for such a term would be as overburdened as *identity* itself. Our strategy has been rather to unbundle the thick tangle of meanings that have accumulated around the term *identity*, and to parcel out the work to a number of less congested terms. We sketch three clusters of terms here.

Identification and Categorization

As a processual, active term derived from a verb, *identification* lacks the reifying connotations of *identity*.[51] It invites us to specify the agents that do the identifying. And it does not presuppose that such identifying (even by powerful agents, such as the state) will necessarily result in the internal sameness, the distinctiveness, the bounded groupness that political entrepreneurs may seek to achieve. Identification—of oneself and of others—is intrinsic to social life; identity in the strong sense is not.

One may be called upon to identify oneself—to characterize oneself, to locate oneself vis-à-vis known others, to situate oneself in a narrative, to place oneself in a category—in any number of different contexts. In modern settings, which multiply interactions with others not personally known, such occasions for identification are particularly abundant. They include innumerable situations of everyday life, as well as more formal and official contexts. How one identifies oneself—and how one is identified by others—may vary greatly from context to context; self- and other-identification is fundamentally situational and contextual.

One key distinction is between *relational* and *categorical* modes of identification. One may identify oneself (or another person) by position in a relational web (a web of kinship, for example, or of friendship, patron-client ties, or teacher-student relations). On the other hand, one may identify oneself (or another person) by membership in a class of persons sharing some categorical attribute (such as race, ethnicity, language, nationality, citizenship, gender, sexual orientation, and so on). Craig Calhoun has argued that, while relational modes of identification remain important in many contexts even today, categorical identification has assumed ever greater importance in modern settings.[52]

Another basic distinction is between self-identification and the identification and categorization of oneself by others.[53] Self-identification takes place in dialectical interplay with external identification, and the two need not converge.[54] External identification is itself a varied process. In the ordinary ebb and flow of social life, people identify and categorize others, just as they identify and categorize themselves. But there is another key type of external identification that has no counterpart in the domain of self-identification: the formalized, codified, objectified systems of categorization developed by powerful, authoritative institutions.

The modern state has been one of the most important agents of identification and categorization in this latter sense. In culturalist extensions of the Weberian sociology of the state, notably those influenced by Bourdieu and Foucault, the state monopolizes, or seeks to monopolize, not only legitimate physical force but also legitimate symbolic force, as Bourdieu puts it. This includes the power to name, to identify, to categorize, to state what is what and who is who. There is a burgeoning sociological and historical literature on such subjects. Some scholars have looked at identification quite literally: as the attachment of definitive markers to an individual via passport, fingerprint, photograph, and signature, and the amassing of such identifying documents in state repositories. When, why, and with what limitations such systems have been developed turns out to be no simple problem.[55] Other scholars emphasize the modern state's efforts to inscribe its subjects onto a classificatory grid: to identify and categorize people in relation to gender, religion, property ownership, ethnicity, literacy, criminality, or sanity. Censuses apportion people across these categories, and institutions—from schools to prisons—sort out individuals in relation to them. To Foucauldians in particular, these individualizing and aggregating modes of identification and classification are at the core of what defines governmentality in a modern state.[56]

The state is thus a powerful identifier, not because it can create identities in the strong sense—in general, it cannot—but because it has the material and symbolic resources to impose the categories, classificatory schemes, and modes of social counting and accounting with which bureaucrats, judges, teachers, and doctors must work and to which nonstate actors must refer.[57] But the state is not the only identifier that matters. As Charles Tilly has shown, categorization does crucial organizational work in all kinds of social settings, including families, firms, schools, social movements, and bureaucracies of all kinds.[58] Even the most powerful state does not monopolize the production and diffusion of identifications and categories; and those that it does produce may be contested. The literature on social movements—"old" as well as "new"—is rich in evidence on how movement leaders challenge official identifications and propose alternative ones.[59] It highlights leaders' efforts to get members of putative constituencies to identify themselves in a certain way, to see themselves—for a certain range of purposes—as identical with one another, to identify emotionally as well as cognitively with one another.[60]

The social movement literature has valuably emphasized the interactive, discursively mediated processes through which collective solidarities and self-understandings develop. Our reservations concern the move from discussing the work of identification—the efforts to build a collective self-understanding—to positing identity as their necessary result. By considering authoritative, institutionalized modes of identification together with alternative modes involved in the practices of everyday life and the projects of social movements, one can emphasize the hard work and long struggles over identification, as well as the uncertain outcomes of such struggles. However, if the outcome is always presumed to be an identity—however provisional, fragmented, multiple, contested, and fluid—one loses the capacity to make key distinctions.

Identification, we noted above, invites specification of the agents that do the identifying. Yet identification does not *require* a specifiable identifier; it can be pervasive and influential without being accomplished by discrete, specified persons or institutions. Identification can be carried more or less anonymously by discourses or public narratives.[61]

There is one further meaning of *identification*, briefly alluded to above, that is largely independent of the cognitive, characterizing, classificatory meanings discussed so far. This is the psychodynamic meaning, derived originally from Freud.[62] While the classificatory meanings involve identifying oneself (or someone else) *as* someone who fits a certain description or belongs to a certain category, the psychodynamic meaning involves identifying oneself emotionally *with* another person, category, or collectivity. Here again, *identification* calls attention to complex (and often ambivalent) *processes*, while the term *identity*, designating a *condition* rather than a *process*, implies too easy a fit between the individual and the social.

Self-Understanding and Social Location

Identification and *categorization* are active, processual terms, derived from verbs and calling to mind particular acts of identification and categorization performed by particular identifiers and categorizers. But we need other kinds of terms as well to do the varied work done by *identity*. Recall that one key use of *identity* is to conceptualize and explain action in a noninstrumental, nonmechanical manner. In this sense, the term suggests ways in which individual and collective action can be governed by particularistic understandings of self and social location rather than by putatively universal, structurally determined interests. *Self-understanding* is therefore the second term we would propose as an alternative to *identity*. It is a dispositional term that designates what might be called situated subjectivity: one's sense of who one is, of one's social location, and of how (given the first two) one is prepared to act. As a dispositional term, it belongs to the realm of what Pierre Bourdieu has called *sens pratique*, the practical sense—at once cognitive and emotional—that persons have of themselves and their social world.[63]

The term *self-understanding*, it is important to emphasize, does not imply a distinctively modern or Western understanding of the self as a homogeneous, bounded, unitary entity. A sense of who one is can take many forms. The social processes through which persons understand and locate themselves may in some instances involve the psychoanalyst's couch and in others participation in spirit possession cults.[64] In some settings, people may understand and experience themselves in terms of a grid of intersecting categories; in others, in terms of a web of connections of differential proximity and intensity. Hence the importance of seeing self-understanding and social locatedness in relation to each other, and of emphasizing that both the bounded self and the bounded group are culturally specific rather than universal forms.

Like the term *identification*, *self-understanding* lacks the reifying connotations of *identity*. Yet it is not restricted to situations of flux and instability. Self-understandings may be variable across time and across persons, but they may be stable. Semantically, *identity* implies sameness across time or persons; hence the awkwardness of continuing to speak of identity while repudiating the implication of sameness. *Self-understanding*, by contrast, has no privileged semantic connection with sameness or difference.

Two closely related terms are *self-representation* and *self-identification*. Having discussed identification above, we simply observe here that, while the distinction is not sharp, self-understandings may be tacit; even when they are formed, as they ordinarily are, in and through prevailing discourses, they may exist, and inform action, without themselves being discursively articulated. Self-representation and self-identification, on the other hand, suggest at least some degree of explicit discursive articulation.

Self-understanding cannot, of course, do *all* the work done by *identity*. We note here three limitations of the term. First, it is a subjective, autoreferential term. As such, it designates *one's own* understanding of who one is. It cannot capture *others'* understandings, even though external categorizations, identifications, and representations may be decisive in determining how one is regarded and treated by others, indeed in shaping one's own understanding of oneself. At the limit, self-understandings may be overridden by overwhelmingly coercive external categorizations.[65]

Second, *self-understanding* would seem to privilege cognitive awareness. As a result, it would seem not to capture—or at least not to highlight—the affective or cathectic processes suggested by some uses of *identity*. Yet self-understanding is never purely cognitive; it is always affectively tinged or charged, and the term can certainly accommodate this affective dimension. However, it is true that the emotional *dynamics* are better captured by the term *identification* (in its psychodynamic meaning).

Finally, as a term that emphasizes situated subjectivity, *self-understanding* does not capture the objectivity claimed by strong understandings of identity. Strong, objectivist conceptions of identity permit one to distinguish "true" identity (characterized as deep, abiding, and objective) from "mere" self-understanding (superficial, fluctuating, and subjective). If identity is something to be discovered, and something about which one can be mistaken, then one's momentary self-understanding may not correspond to one's abiding, underlying identity. However analytically problematic these notions of depth, constancy, and objectivity may be, they do at least provide a reason for using the language of identity rather than that of self-understanding.

Weak conceptions of identity provide no such reason. It is clear from the constructivist literature why weak understandings of identity are *weak*, but it is not clear why they are conceptions *of identity*. In this literature, it is the various *soft predicates* of identity—constructedness, contestedness, contingency, instability, multiplicity, fluidity—that are emphasized and elaborated, while that which they are predicated *of*—identity itself—is taken for granted and seldom explained. When identity itself is elucidated, it is often represented as something—a sense of who one is,[66] a self-conception[67]—that can be captured in a straightforward way by "self-understanding." This term lacks the allure, the buzz, the theoretical pretensions of *identity*, but this should count as an asset, not a liability.

Commonality, Connectedness, Groupness

One particular form of affectively charged self-understanding that is often designated by *identity*—especially in discussions of race, religion, ethnicity, nationalism, gender, sexuality, social movements, and other phenomena conceptualized as involving *collective* identities—deserves separate mention here. This is the emotionally laden sense of belonging to a distinctive, bounded group, involving both a felt solidarity or oneness with fellow group members and a felt difference from or even antipathy to specified outsiders.

The problem is that *identity* is used to designate *both* such strongly groupist, exclusive, affectively charged self-understandings *and* much looser, more open self-understandings, involving some sense of affinity or affiliation, commonality or connectedness to particular others, but lacking a sense of overriding oneness vis-à-vis some constitutive "other."[68]

Both the tightly groupist and the more loosely affiliative forms of self-understanding—as well as the transitional forms between these polar types—are important, but they shape personal experience and condition social and political action in sharply differing ways.

Rather than stirring all self-understandings based on race, religion, ethnicity, and so on into the great conceptual melting pot of identity, we would do better to use a more differentiated analytical language. Terms such as *commonality, connectedness,* and *groupness* could be usefully employed here in place of the all-purpose *identity*. This is the third cluster of terms we propose. *Commonality* denotes the sharing of some common attribute, *connectedness* the relational ties that link people. Neither commonality nor connectedness alone engenders groupness—the sense of belonging to a distinctive, bounded, solidary group. But commonality and connectedness together may indeed do so. This was the argument Charles Tilly put forward some time ago, building on Harrison White's idea of the catnet, a set of persons comprising both a *category,* sharing some common attribute, and a *network.*[69] Tilly's suggestion that groupness is a joint product of "catness" and "netness"—categorical commonality and relational connectedness—is suggestive. But we would propose two emendations.

First, categorical commonality and relational connectedness need to be supplemented by a third element, what Max Weber called a *Zusammenge-hörigkeitsgefühl,* a feeling of belonging together. Such a feeling may indeed depend in part on the degrees and forms of commonality and connectedness, but it will also depend on other factors, such as particular events, their encoding in compelling public narratives, prevailing discursive frames, and so on. Second, relational connectedness, or what Tilly calls "netness," while crucial in facilitating the sort of collective action Tilly was interested in, is not always necessary for groupness. A strongly bounded sense of groupness may rest on categorical commonality and an associated feeling of belonging together with minimal or no relational connectedness. This is typically the case for large-scale collectivities such as "nations": when a diffuse self-understanding as a member of a particular nation crystallizes into a strongly bounded sense of groupness, this is likely to depend not on relational connectedness, but rather on a powerfully imagined and strongly felt commonality.[70]

The point is not, as some partisans of network theory have suggested, to turn from commonality to connectedness, from categories to networks, from shared attributes to social relations.[71] Nor is it to celebrate fluidity and hybridity over belonging and solidarity. The point in suggesting this last set of terms is rather to develop an analytical idiom sensitive to the multiple forms and degrees of commonality and connectedness, and to the widely varying ways in which actors (and the cultural idioms, public narratives, and prevailing discourses on which they draw) attribute meaning and significance to them. This will enable us to distinguish instances of strongly binding, vehemently felt groupness from more loosely structured, weakly constraining forms of affinity and affiliation.

THREE CASES: *IDENTITY* AND ITS ALTERNATIVES IN CONTEXT

Having surveyed the work done by *identity*, indicated some limitations and liabilities of the term, and suggested a range of alternatives, we seek now to illustrate our argument—both the critical claims about *identity* and the constructive suggestions regarding alternative idioms—through a consideration of three cases. In each case, we suggest, the identitarian focus on bounded groupness limits the sociological—and the political—imagination, while alternative analytical idioms can help open up both.

A Case from Africanist Anthropology: "The" Nuer

African studies has suffered from its version of identitarian thinking, most extremely in journalistic accounts that see Africans' "tribal identity" as the main cause of violence and of the failure of the nation-state. Academic Africanists were troubled by this reductive vision of Africa since at least the 1970s and attracted to a version of constructivism, well before such an approach had a name.[72] The argument that ethnic groups are not primordial but the products of history—including the reifying of cultural difference through imposed colonial identifications—became a staple of African studies. Even so, scholars tended to emphasize boundary formation rather than boundary crossing, the constitution of groups rather than the development of networks.[73] In this context, it is worth going back to a classic of African ethnology: E. E. Evans-Pritchard's *The Nuer*.[74]

Based on research in northeast Africa in the 1930s, *The Nuer* describes a distinctively relational mode of identification, self-understanding, and social location, one that construes the social world in terms of the degree and quality of connection among people rather than in terms of categories, groups, or boundaries. Social location is defined in the first instance in terms of lineage, consisting of the descendants of one ancestor reckoned through a socially conventional line: patrilineal, via males in the case of Nuer, via females or more rarely via double descent systems in other parts of Africa. Children belong to the lineage of their fathers, and while relationships with

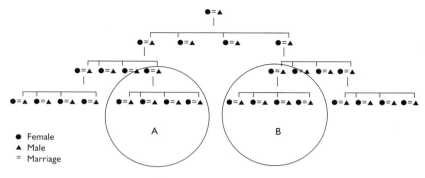

FIGURE 2. A segmentary patrilineage. Lines represent descent; marriage partners come from another lineage; children of daughters belong to the lineage of the husband and are not shown; children of sons belong to this lineage and are represented here.

the mother's kin are not ignored, they are not part of the descent system. A segmentary lineage can be diagrammed as shown in figure 2.

Everybody in this diagram is related to everybody else, but in different ways and to different degrees. One might be tempted to say that the people marked in circle A constitute a group, with an identity of A, as distinct from those in circle B, with an identity of B. The trouble with such an interpretation is that the very move which distinguishes A and B also shows their relatedness, as one moves back one generation and finds a common ancestor, who may or may not be living but whose social location links people in A and B. If someone in set A gets into a conflict with someone in set B, such a person may well try to invoke the commonality of "A-ness" to mobilize people against B. But someone genealogically older than these parties can invoke the linking ancestors to cool things off. The act of going deeper in a genealogical charter in the course of social interaction keeps reemphasizing relational visions of social location at the expense of categorical ones.

One could argue that this patrilineage as a whole constitutes an identity, distinct from other lineages. But Evans-Pritchard's point is that segmentation represents an entire social order, and that lineages themselves are related to one another as male and female lineage members are to each other. Let us then consider marriage. Virtually all segmentary societies insist on exogamy; and, in evolutionary perspective, the prevalence of exogamy may reflect the advantages of cross-lineage connectedness. So the male-centered lineage diagram presumes another set of relationships, through women who are born into the lineage of their fathers but whose sons and daughters belong to the lineage they married into.

One could then argue that all the lineages which intermarried constitute the "Nuer" as an identity distinct from "Dinka" or any of the other groups in the region. But here recent work in African history offers a more nuanced approach. The genealogical construction of relationality offers possibilities for extension more supple than the twentieth-century scholar's tendency to look for a neat boundary between inside and outside. Marriage relations could be extended beyond the Nuer (both via reciprocal arrangements and coercively by forcing captive women into marriage). Strangers—encountered via trade, migration, or other form of movement—could be incorporated as fictive kin or more loosely linked to a patrilineage via blood brotherhood. The people of northeastern Africa migrated extensively, as they tried to find better ecological niches or as lineage segments moved in and out of relations with each other. Traders stretched their kinship relations over space, formed a variety of relationships at the interfaces with agricultural communities, and sometimes developed lingua franca to foster communication across large spatial networks.[75] In many parts of Africa, one finds certain organizations—religious shrines, initiation societies—that cross linguistic and cultural distinctions, offering what Paul Richards calls a "common 'grammar'" of social experience within regions, for all the cultural variation and political differentiation that they contain.[76]

The problem with subsuming these forms of relational connectedness under the "social construction of identity" is that linking and separating get called by the same name, making it harder to grasp the processes, causes, and consequences of differing patterns of crystallizing difference and forging connections. Africa was far from a paradise of sociability, but war and peace both involved flexible patterns of affiliation as well as differentiation.

One should not assume that the principles of a sliding scale of connection are unique to small-scale "tribal" society. We know from the study of larger-scale political organizations—with authoritative rulers and elaborate hierarchies of command—that kinship networks remained an important principle of social life. African kings asserted their authority by developing patrimonial relations with people from different lineages, creating a core of support that crosscut lineage affiliations, but they also used lineage principles to consolidate their own power, cementing marriage alliances and expanding the size of the royal lineage.[77] In almost all societies, kinship concepts are symbolic and ideological resources, yet while they shape norms, self-understandings, and perceptions of affinity, they do not necessarily produce kinship *groups*.[78]

To a greater extent than the forms of domination that preceded it, colonial rule attempted a one-to-one mapping of people with some putatively common characteristic onto territory. These imposed identifications could be powerful, but their effects depended on the actual relationships and symbolic systems that colonial officials—and indigenous cultural entrepreneurs as well—had to work with, and on countervailing efforts of others to maintain, develop, and articulate different sorts of affinities and self-understandings. The colonial era did indeed witness complex struggles over identification, but it flattens our understanding of these struggles to see them as producing identities. People could live with shadings—and continued to do so day by day, even when political lines were drawn.

Sharon Hutchinson's remarkable reanalysis of Evans-Pritchard's "tribe" takes such an argument into a contemporary, conflict-ridden situation. Her aim is "to call into question the very idea of 'the Nuer' as a unified ethnic identity."[79] She points to the fuzziness of the boundaries of people now called Nuer: culture and history do not follow such lines. And she suggests that Evans-Pritchard's segmentary schema gives excessive attention to the dominant male elders of the 1930s, and not enough to women, men in less powerful lineages, or younger men and women. In this analysis, it not only becomes difficult to see Nuerness as an identity, but imperative to examine with precision how people tried both to extend and to consolidate connections. Bringing the story up to the era of civil war in the southern Sudan in the 1990s, Hutchinson refuses to reduce the conflict to one of cultural or religious difference between the warring parties and insists instead on a deep analysis of political relationships, struggles for economic resources, and spatial connections.

In much of modern Africa, indeed, some of the most bitter conflicts have taken place within collectivities that are relatively uniform culturally and linguistically (Rwanda, Somalia) and between loose economic and social networks based more on patron-client relations than ethnic affiliation (Angola, Sierra Leone), as well as in situations where cultural distinction has been made into a political weapon (Kwa Zulu in South Africa).[80] To explain present or past conflict in terms of how people construct and fight for their identities risks providing a prefabricated, presentist, teleological explanation that diverts attention from questions such as those addressed by Hutchinson.

East European Nationalism

We have argued that the language of identity, with its connotations of boundedness, groupness, and sameness, is conspicuously ill suited to the analysis of segmentary lineage societies—or to present-day conflicts in Africa. One might accept this point yet argue that identitarian language is well suited to the analysis of other social settings, including our own, where public and private identity talk is widely current. But we are not arguing only that the concept of identity does not travel well, that it cannot be universally applied to all social settings. We want to make a stronger argument: that identity is neither necessary nor helpful as a category of analysis, even where it *is* widely used as a category of practice. To this end, we briefly consider East European nationalism and identity politics in the United States.

Historical and social scientific writing on nationalism in Eastern Europe—to a much greater extent than writing on social movements or ethnicity in North America—has been characterized by relatively strong or hard understandings of group identity. Many commentators have seen see the post-Communist resurgence of ethnic nationalism in the region as springing from robust and deeply rooted national identities—from identities strong and resilient enough to have survived decades of repression by ruthlessly antinational Communist regimes. But this "return-of-the-repressed" view is problematic.[81]

Consider the former Soviet Union. To see national conflicts as struggles to validate and express identities that had somehow survived the regime's attempts to crush them is unwarranted. Although anti-*nationalist,* and of course brutally repressive in all kinds of ways, the Soviet regime was anything but anti-*national.*[82] Far from ruthlessly suppressing nationhood, the regime went to unprecedented lengths in institutionalizing and codifying it. It carved up Soviet territory into more than fifty putatively autonomous national homelands, each belonging to a particular ethnonational group; and it assigned each citizen an ethnic nationality, which was ascribed at birth on the basis of descent, registered in personal identity documents, recorded in bureaucratic encounters, and used to control access to higher education and employment. In doing so, the regime was not simply *recognizing* or *ratifying* a pre-existing state of affairs; it was *newly constituting* both persons and places *as national.*[83] In this context, strong understandings of national identity as deeply rooted in the pre-Communist history of the region, frozen or repressed by a ruthlessly antinational regime, and returning with the collapse of Communism are at best anachronistic, at worst simply scholarly rationalizations of nationalist rhetoric.

What about weak, constructivist understandings of identity? Constructivists might concede the importance of the Soviet system of institutionalized multinationality, and interpret this as the institutional means through which national identities were constructed. But why should we assume it is identity that is constructed in this fashion? To assume that it is risks conflating a system of *identification* or *categorization* with its presumed result, *identity*. Categorical group denominations—however authoritative, however pervasively institutionalized—cannot serve as indicators of real groups or robust identities.

The formal institutionalization and codification of ethnic and national categories implies nothing about the *depth, resonance,* or *power* of such categories in the lived experience of the persons so categorized. A strongly institutionalized ethno-national classificatory system makes certain categories readily and legitimately available for the representation of social reality, the framing of political claims, and the organization of political action. This is itself a fact of great significance, and the breakup of the Soviet Union cannot be understood without reference to it. But it does not mean that these categories will have a significant role in framing perception, orienting action, or shaping self-understanding in everyday life—a role that is implied by even constructivist accounts of identity.

The extent to which official categorizations shape self-understandings, the extent to which the population categories constituted by states or political entrepreneurs approximate real groups—these are open questions that can only be addressed empirically. The language of identity is more likely to hinder than to help the posing of such questions, for it blurs what needs to be kept distinct: external categorization and self-understanding, objective commonality and subjective groupness.

Consider one final, non-Soviet example. The boundary between Hungarians and Romanians in Transylvania is certainly sharper than that between Russians and Ukrainians in Ukraine. Here too, however, group boundaries are considerably more porous and ambiguous than is widely assumed. The language of both politics and everyday life, to be sure, is rigorously categorical, dividing the population into mutually exclusive ethno-national categories, and making no allowance for mixed or ambiguous forms. But this categorical code, important though it is as a *constituent element* of social relations, should not be taken for a *faithful description* of them. Reinforced by identitarian entrepreneurs on both sides, the categorical code obscures as much as it reveals about self-understandings, masking the fluidity and ambiguity that arise from mixed marriages, from bilingualism, from migration, from Hungarian children attending Romanian-language schools, from intergenerational assimilation (in both directions), and—perhaps most importantly—from sheer indifference to the claims of ethno-cultural nationality.

Even in its constructivist guise, the language of identity disposes us to think in terms of bounded groupness. It does so because even constructivist thinking on identity takes the *existence* of identity as axiomatic. Identity is always already "there," as something that individuals and groups "have," even if the content of particular identities, and the boundaries that mark groups off from one another, are conceptualized as always in flux

This tendency to objectify identity deprives us of analytical leverage. It makes it more difficult for us to treat groupness and boundedness as *emergent properties* of particular structural or conjunctural settings rather than as always already there in some form. The point needs to be emphasized today more than ever, for the unreflectively groupist language that prevails in everyday life, journalism, politics, and much social research as well—the habit of speaking without qualification of Albanians and Serbs, for example, as if they were sharply bounded, internally homogeneous groups—not only weakens social analysis but constricts political possibilities in the region.

Identity Claims and the Enduring Dilemmas of "Race" in the United States

The language of identity has been particularly powerful in the United States in recent decades. It has been prominent both as an idiom of analysis in the social sciences and humanities and as an idiom in which to articulate experience, mobilize loyalty, and formulate symbolic and material claims in everyday social and political practice.

The pathos and resonance of identity claims in the contemporary United States have many sources, but one of the most profound is that central problem of American history—the importation of enslaved Africans, the persistence of racial oppression, and the range of African American responses to it. The African American experience of "race" as both imposed categorization and self-identification has been important not only in its own terms, but from the late 1960s on as a template for identity claims of all sorts, including those based on gender and sexual orientation, as well as those based on ethnicity or race.[84]

In response to the cascading identitarian claims of the last three decades, public discourse, political argument, and scholarship in nearly every field of the social sciences and humanities have been transformed. There is much that is valuable in this process. History textbooks and prevailing public narratives tell a much richer and more inclusive story than those of a generation ago. Specious forms of universalism—the Marxist category of worker, who always appears in the guise of a male, the liberal category of citizen, who turns out to be white—have been powerfully exposed. First-generation identitarian claims themselves—and scholarly literatures informed by them—have been criticized for their blindness to crosscutting particularities: African American movements for acting as if African American women did not have gender-specific concerns, feminists for assuming that all women were white and middle-class.

Constructivist arguments have had a particular influence in Americanist circles, allowing scholars to stress the contemporary importance of imposed identifications and the self-understandings that have evolved in dialectical interplay with them, while emphasizing that such self- and other-identified groups are not primordial but historically produced. The treatment of race in the historiography of the United States is an excellent example.[85] Even before *social construction* became a buzz-word, scholars were showing that far from being a given dimension of America's past, race as a political category originated in the same moment as America's republican and populist impulses. Edmund Morgan argued that in early-eighteenth-century Virginia, white indentured servants and black slaves shared a subordination that was not sharply differentiated; they sometimes acted together. It was when Virginian planter elites started to mobilize against the British that they needed to draw a sharp boundary between the politically included and the excluded, and the fact that black slaves were more numerous and necessary as laborers and less plausible as political supporters led to a marking of distinction, which poor whites could in turn use to make claims.[86] From such an opening, historians have charted several key moments of redefinition of racial boundaries in the United States—and several points at which other sorts of ties showed the possibility of giving rise to other kinds of political affiliation. Whiteness and blackness were both historically created and historically variable categories. Comparative historians, meanwhile, have shown that the construction of race can take still more varied forms, showing that many people who were black under North American classificatory systems would have been something else in other parts of the Americas.[87]

American history thus reveals the power of imposed identification, but it also reveals the complexity of the self-understandings of people defined by circumstances they did not control. Pre–Civil War collective self-definitions situated black Americans in particular ways in regard to Africa—often seeing an African (or an "Ethiopian") origin as placing them close to the heartlands of Christian civilization. Yet early back-to-Africa movements often treated Africa as a cultural tabula rasa or as a fallen civilization to be redeemed by African American Christians.[88] Asserting one-

self as a diasporic people did not necessarily imply claiming cultural commonality—the two concepts have been in tension with each other ever
since. One can write the history of African American self-understanding as
the rise over time of a black nationality, or one can explore the interplay of
such a sense of collectivity with the efforts of African American activists to
articulate different kinds of political ideologies and to develop connections
with other radicals. The most important point is to consider the range of
possibilities and the seriousness with which they were debated.

It is not the historical analysis of social construction as such that is problematic, but the presumptions about what is constructed. Whiteness or race
is taken as the typical object of construction, not other, looser forms of
affinity and commonality. Setting out to write about *identifications* as they
emerge, crystallize, and fade away in particular social and political circumstances may well inspire a rather different history than setting out to write
of an *identity*, which links past, present, and future in a single word.

Cosmopolitan interpretations of American history have been criticized
for taking the pain out of the distinct ways in which that history has been
experienced: above all, the pain of enslavement and discrimination, and of
struggle against enslavement and discrimination, a history that marks
African Americans in ways that white Americans do not share.[89] Here is
where calls for the understanding of the particularity of experience resonate powerfully, but it is also here that the dangers of flattening those histories into a static and singular identity are serious. There may be gains as
well as losses in such a flattening, as thoughtful participants in debates over
the politics of race have made clear.[90] But to subsume further under the
generic category of identity the historical experiences and allegedly common cultures of other groups as disparate as women and the elderly, Native
Americans and gay men, poor people and the disabled is not in any obvious
way more respectful of the pain of particular histories than are the universalist rhetorics of justice or human rights. And the assignment of individuals to such identities leaves many people—who have experienced the uneven trajectories of ancestry and the variety of innovations and adaptations
that constitute culture—caught between a hard identity that doesn't quite
fit and a soft rhetoric of hybridity, multiplicity, and fluidity that offers neither understanding nor solace.[91]

The question remains whether we can address the complexity of history—including the changing ways in which external categorizations have
both stigmatized and humiliated people and given them an enabling and
empowering sense of collective selfhood—in more supple and differentiated language. If the real contribution of constructivist social analysis—

that affinities, categories, and subjectivities develop and change over time—is to be taken seriously and not reduced to a presentist, teleological account of the construction of currently existing groups, then bounded groupness must be understood as a contingent, emergent property, not an axiomatic given.

Representing contemporary American society poses a similar problem—avoiding flat, reductive accounts of the social world as a multichrome mosaic of monochrome identity groups. This conceptually impoverished identitarian sociology, in which the intersection of race, class, gender, sexual orientation, and perhaps one or two other categories generates a set of all-purpose conceptual boxes, has become powerful in American academia in the 1990s—not only in the social sciences, cultural studies, and ethnic studies, but also in literature and political philosophy. In the remainder of this section, we shift our angle of vision and consider the implications of the use of this identitarian sociology in the latter domain.

"A moral philosophy," wrote Alisdair MacIntyre, "presupposes a sociology";[92] the same holds a fortiori of political theory. The problem with much contemporary political theory is that it is built on questionable sociology—indeed precisely on the group-centered representation of the social world just mentioned. We are not taking the side of universality against particularity here. Rather, we are suggesting that the identitarian language and groupist social ontology that informs much contemporary political theory occludes the problematic nature of groupness itself and forecloses other ways of conceptualizing particular affiliations and affinities.

There is a considerable literature now that is critical of the idea of universal citizenship. Iris Marion Young, one of the most influential of such critics, proposes instead an ideal of group-differentiated citizenship, built on group representation and group rights. The notion of an "impartial general perspective," she argues, "is a myth," since "different social groups have different needs, cultures, histories, experiences, and perceptions of social relations." Citizenship should not seek to transcend such differences, but should recognize and acknowledge them as "irreducible."[93]

What sort of differences should be ratified with special representation and rights? The differences in question are those associated with "social groups," defined as "comprehensive identities and ways of life," and distinguished from mere aggregates on the one hand—arbitrary classifications of persons according to some attribute—and from voluntary associations on the other. Special rights and representation would be accorded not to all social groups, but to those who suffer from at least one of five forms of oppression. In practice, this means "women, blacks, Native Americans, Chicanos, Puerto Ricans and other Spanish-speaking Americans, Asian Americans, gay men, lesbians, working-class people, old people, and mentally and physically disabled people."[94]

What constitutes the groupness of these "groups"? What makes them groups rather than categories around which self- and other-identifications may but certainly do not necessarily or always crystallize? This is not addressed by Young. She assumes that distinctive histories, experiences, and social location endow these groups with different "capacities, needs, culture, and cognitive styles" and with "distinctive understandings of all aspects of the society and unique perspectives on social issues."[95] Social and cultural heterogeneity is construed here as a juxtaposition of internally homogeneous, externally bounded blocs. The "principles of unity" that Young repudiates at the level of the polity as a whole—because they "hide difference"—are reintroduced, and continue to hide difference, at the level of the constituent groups.

At stake in arguments about group-differentiated or multicultural citizenship are important issues that have been long debated outside as well as inside the academy, all having to do in one way or another with the relative weight and merits of universalist and particularist claims.[96] Sociological analysis cannot and should not seek to resolve this robust debate, but it can seek to shore up its often shaky sociological foundations. It can offer a richer vocabulary for conceptualizing social and cultural heterogeneity and particularity. Moving beyond identitarian language opens up possibilities for specifying other kinds of connectedness, other idioms of identification, other styles of self-understanding, other ways of reckoning social location. To paraphrase what Adam Przeworski said long ago about class, cultural struggle is a struggle about culture, not a struggle between cultures.[97] Activists of identity politics deploy the language of bounded groupness not because it reflects social reality, but precisely because groupness is ambiguous and contested. Their groupist rhetoric has a performative, constitutive dimension, contributing, when it is successful, to the making of the groups it invokes.[98]

Here we have a gap between, on the one hand, normative arguments and activist idioms that take bounded groupness as axiomatic and, on the other hand, historical and sociological analyses that emphasize contingency, fluidity, and variability. At one level, there is a real-life dilemma: preserving cultural distinctiveness depends at least in part on maintaining bounded groupness, and hence on policing the "exit option," and accusations of "passing" and of betraying one's roots serve as modes of discipline.[99] Critics of such policing, however, would argue that a liberal polity should protect individuals from the oppressiveness of social groups as well as that of the state. At the level of social analysis, though, the dilemma is not a necessary one. We are not faced with a stark choice between a universalist, individualist analytical idiom and an identitarian, groupist idiom. Framing the options in this way misses the variety of forms that affinity, commonality, and connectedness can take—hence our emphasis on the need for a more supple vocabulary. We are not arguing for any specific stance on the politics of cultural distinction and individual choice, but rather for a vocabulary of social analysis that may help open up and illuminate the range of options. The politics of group "coalition" that is celebrated by Young and others, for example, certainly has its place, but the groupist sociology that underlies this particular form of coalition politics—with its assumption that bounded groups are the basic building blocks of political alliances—constricts the political imagination.[100]

We need not in fact choose between an American history flattened into the experiences and cultures of bounded groups and one equally flattened into a single national story. Reducing the heterogeneity of American society and history to a multichrome mosaic of monochrome identity groups hinders rather than helps the work of understanding the past and pursuing social justice in the present.

CONCLUSION: PARTICULARITY AND THE POLITICS OF IDENTITY

We have not made an argument about identity politics. Nonetheless, the argument does have political as well as intellectual implications. To persuade people that they are one; that they comprise a bounded, distinctive, solidary group; that their internal differences do not matter, at least for the purpose at hand—this is a normal and necessary part of politics, and not only of what is ordinarily characterized as identity politics. It is not all of politics, and we do indeed have reservations about the way in which the routine recourse to identitarian framing may foreclose other equally important ways of framing political claims. But we do not seek to deprive anyone of identity as a political tool, or to undermine the legitimacy of making political appeals in identitarian terms.

Our argument has focused, rather, on the use of identity as an *analytical* concept. Throughout the article, we have asked what work the concept is supposed to do, and how well it does it. We have argued that the concept is deployed to do a great deal of analytical work—much of it legitimate and important. The term *identity*, however, is ill suited to perform this work, for it is riddled with ambiguity, riven with contradictory meanings, and encumbered by reifying connotations. Qualifying the noun with strings of adjectives—specifying that identity is multiple, fluid, constantly renegotiated, and so on—does not solve the Orwellian problem of entrapment in a word. It yields little more than a suggestive oxymoron—a multiple singularity, a fluid crystallization—but still begs the question of why one should use the same term to designate all this and more. Alternative analytical idioms, we have argued, can do the necessary work without the attendant confusion.

At issue here is not the legitimacy or importance of particularistic claims, but how best to conceptualize them. People everywhere and always have particular ties, self-understandings, stories, trajectories, histories, predicaments. And these inform the sorts of claims they make. To subsume such pervasive particularity under the flat, undifferentiated rubric of *identity*, however, does nearly as much violence to its unruly and multifarious forms as would an attempt to subsume it under "universalist" categories such as *interest*.

Construing particularity in identitarian terms, moreover, constricts the political as well as the analytical imagination. It points away from a range of possibilities for political action other than those rooted in putatively shared identity—and not only those that are praised or damned as universalist. Identitarian political advocates, for example, construe political cooperation in terms of the building of coalitions between bounded identity groups. This is one mode of political cooperation, but not the only one.

Kathryn Sikkink and Margaret Keck, for example, have drawn attention to the importance of "transnational issue networks," from the antislavery movement of the early nineteenth century to international campaigns about human rights, ecology, and women's rights in recent years. Such networks necessarily cross cultural as well as state boundaries and link particular places and particularistic claims to wider concerns. To take one instance, the anti-apartheid movement brought together South African political organizations that were themselves far from united—some sharing universalist ideologies, some calling themselves Africanist, some asserting a quite local, culturally defined identity—with international church groups, labor unions, pan-African movements for racial solidarity, human rights groups, and so on. Particular groups moved in and out of cooperative arrangements within an overall network; conflict among opponents of the apartheid state was sometimes bitter, even deadly. As the actors in the network shifted, the issues at stake were reframed. At certain moments, for example, issues amenable to international mobilization were highlighted, while others—of great concern to some would-be participants—were marginalized.[101]

Our point is not to celebrate such networks over more exclusively iden- titarian social movements or group-based claims. Networks are no more. intrinsically virtuous than identitarian movements, and groups are intrin- sically suspect. Politics—in southern Africa or elsewhere—is hardly a con- frontation of good universalists or good networks versus bad tribalists. Much havoc has been done by flexible networks built on clientage and fo- cused on pillage and smuggling; such networks have sometimes been linked to "principled" political organizations; and they have often been connected to arms and illegal merchandise brokers in Europe, Asia, and North Amer- ica. Multifarious particularities are in play, and one needs to distinguish be- tween situations where they cohere around particular cultural symbols and situations where they are flexible, pragmatic, readily extendable. It does not contribute to precision of analysis to use the same words for the extremes of reification and fluidity, and everything in between.

To criticize the use of *identity* in social analysis is not to blind ourselves to particularity. It is rather to conceive of the claims and possibilities that arise from particular affinities and affiliations, from particular commonali- ties and connections, from particular stories and self-understandings, from particular problems and predicaments in a more differentiated manner. So- cial analysis has become massively, and durably, sensitized to particularity in recent decades; and the literature on identity has contributed valuably to this enterprise. It is time now to go beyond identity—not in the name of an imagined universalism, but in the name of the conceptual clarity required for social analysis and political understanding alike.

ACKNOWLEDGMENTS

The authors wish to thank Zsuzsa Berend, John Bowen, Jane Burbank, Margit Feischmidt, Jon Fox, Mara Loveman, Jitka Malečková, Peter Stam- atov, Loïc Wacquant, Roger Waldinger, and two anonymous *Theory and Society* reviewers for valuable comments and suggestions on earlier drafts. Thanks as well to the Center for Advanced Study in the Behavioral Sci- ences, where this article was conceived during a lunchtime conversation, and to participants in the Sociology Department Colloquium at UCLA and in the faculty seminar of the program on the Comparative Study of Social Transformation at the University of Michigan, where earlier versions of the chapter were presented. And a final word of thanks to our graduate stu- dents, who have put up in good spirit—but not necessarily in agreement— with our querying their use of a seemingly indispensable concept.

4 Globalization

There are two problems with the concept of globalization, first the "global," and second the "-ization." The implication of the first is that a single system of connection—notably through capital and commodities markets, information flows, and imagined landscapes—has penetrated the entire globe, and the implication of the second is that it is doing so now, that this is the global age. There are certainly those, not least of them the advocates of unrestricted capital markets, who claim that the world should be open to them, but that does not mean that they have gotten their way. But many critics of market tyranny, social democrats who lament the alleged decline of the nation-state, and people who see the eruption of particularism as a counterreaction to market homogenization give the boasts of the globalizers too much credibility. Crucial questions don't get asked: about the limits of interconnection, about the areas where capital cannot go, and about the specificity of the structures necessary to make connections work.

Behind the globalization fad is an important quest for understanding the interconnectedness of different parts of the world, for explaining new mechanisms shaping the movement of capital, people, and culture, and for exploring institutions capable of regulating such transnational movement. What is missing in discussions of globalization today is the historical depth of interconnections and a focus on just what the structures and limits of the connecting mechanisms are. It is salutary to get away from whatever tendencies there may have been to analyze social, economic, political, and cultural processes as if they took place in national or continental containers; but to adopt a language that implies that there is no container at all, except the planetary one, risks defining problems in misleading ways. The world has long has been—and still is—a space where economic and political relations are very uneven; it is filled with lumps, places where power coalesces

surrounded by those where it does not, places where social relations become dense amid others that are diffuse. Structures and networks penetrate
certain places and do certain things with great intensity, but their effects
tail off elsewhere.

Specialists on Africa, among others, have been drawn into the globalization paradigm, positing "globalization" as a challenge that Africa must
meet or else as a construct through which to understand Africa's place in a
world whose boundaries are apparently becoming more problematic. My
concern here is with seeking alternative perspectives to a concept that emphasizes change over time but remains ahistorical, and which seems to be
about space, but which ends up glossing over the mechanisms and limitations of spatial relationships. Africanists, I argue, should be particularly
sensitive to the time depth of cross-territorial processes, for the very notion of *Africa* has itself been shaped for centuries by linkages within the
continent and across oceans and deserts—by the Atlantic slave trade, by the
movement of pilgrims, religious networks, and ideas associated with Islam,
by cultural and economic connections across the Indian Ocean. The concept
cannot, I will also argue, be salvaged by pushing it backward in time, for the
histories of the slave trade, colonization, and decolonization, as well as the
travails of the era of structural adjustment fit poorly in any narrative of
globalization—unless one so dilutes the term that it becomes meaningless.
To study Africa is to appreciate the long-term importance of the exercise of
power across space, but also the limitations of such power. The relevance of
this history today lies not in assimilation of old (colonial) and new (global)
forms of linkages but in the lessons it provides about both the importance
and the boundedness of long-distance connections. Historical analysis does
not present a contrast between a past of territorial boundedness and a present of interconnection and fragmentation, but rather a back-and-forth, varied combination of territorializing and deterritorializing tendencies.

Today, friends and foes of globalization debate "its" effects. Both assume
the reality of such a process, which can either be praised or lamented, encouraged or combated.[1] Are we asking the best questions about issues of
contemporary importance when we debate globalization? Instead of assuming the centrality of a powerful juggernaut, might we do better to define more precisely what it is we are debating, to assess the resources pos-
sessed by institutions in different locations within patterns of interaction,
to look toward traditions of transcontinental mobilization with considerable time depth?

Globalization is clearly a significant native's category for anyone studying contemporary politics. Anyone wishing to know why particular ideo-

logical and discursive patterns appear in today's conjuncture needs to examine how it is used. But is it also a useful analytic category? My argument here is that it is not. Scholars who use it analytically risk being trapped in the very discursive structures they wish to analyze. Most important in the term's current popularity in academic circles is how much it reveals about the poverty of contemporary social science faced with processes that are large-scale, but not universal, and with the fact of crucial linkages that cut across state borders and lines of cultural difference but which nonetheless are based on specific mechanisms within certain boundaries. That global should be contrasted to local, even if the point is to analyze their mutual constitution, only underscores the inadequacy of current analytical tools to analyze anything in between.

Can we do better? I would answer with a qualified yes, but mainly if we seek concepts that are less sweeping, more precise, which emphasize both the nature of spatial linkages and their limits, which seek to analyze change with historical specificity rather than in terms of a vaguely defined and unattainable endpoint.

VIEWS OF GLOBALIZATION

The first style of talking about globalization can be termed the Banker's Boast. With the collapse of the Soviet Union and the market orientation of Communist China, investments supposedly can go anywhere. Pressure from the United States, the IMF, and transnational corporations brings down national barriers to the movement of capital. This is in part an argument for a new regulatory regime, one which lowers barriers to capital flow as well as trade, and which operates on a global level. It is also an argument about discipline: the world market, conceived of as a web of transactions, now forces governments to conform to its dictates. Globalization is invoked time and time again to tell rich countries to roll back the welfare state and poor ones to reduce social expenditures—all in the name of the necessity of competition in a globalized economy.[2]

Next comes the Social Democrat's Lament. It accepts the reality of globalization as the bankers see it, but instead of claiming that it is beneficial for humankind, it argues the reverse. The social democratic left has devoted much of its energy to using citizenship to blunt the brutality of capitalism. Social movements thus aim for the nation-state—the institutional basis for enforcing social and civic rights. Whereas the enhanced role of the nation-state reflected organized labor's growing place within the polity, globalization has allegedly undermined the social project by marginalizing the political one. In some renderings, globalization must therefore be fought, while in others, it has already triumphed and there is little to do except lament the passing of the nation-state, of national trade union movements, of empowered citizenries.[3]

Finally comes the Dance of the Flows and the Fragments. This argument accepts much of the other two—the reality of globalization in the present and its destabilizing effect on national societies—but makes another move. Rather than homogenize the world, globalization reconfigures the local—but not in a spatially confined way. People's exposures to media—to dress, to music, to fantasies of the good life—are highly fragmented; bits of imagery are detached from their context, all the more attractive because of the distant associations they evoke. Hollywood imagery influences people in the African bush; tropical exoticism sells on rue du Faubourg St. Honoré. This detachment of cultural symbolism from spatial locatedness paradoxically makes people realize the value of their cultural particularity. Hence, a sentimental attachment to "home" by migrants who don't live there but who contribute money and energy to identity politics. As flows of capital, people, ideas, and symbols move separately from one another, the dance of fragments takes place within a globalized, unbounded space.[4]

There is something in each of these conceptions. What is wrong with them is their totalizing pretensions and their presentist periodization. The relationship of territory and connectivity has been reconfigured many times; each deserves particular attention.[5] Changes in capital markets, transnational corporations, and communications in the last decades deserve careful attention, but one shouldn't forget the vast scale in which investment and production decisions were made by the Dutch East Indies Company—linking the Netherlands, Indonesia, and South Africa and connecting to ongoing trading networks throughout Southeast Asia—in the seventeenth century. Some scholars argue that the "really big leap to more globally integrated commodity and factor markets" was in the second half of the nineteenth century, that "world capital markets were almost certainly as well integrated in the 1890s as they were in the 1990s." Such arguments work better for OECD countries than elsewhere and do not adequately express qualitative change, but economic historians still stress that the great period of expansion of international trade, investment, and interdependence was the decades before 1913, followed by a dramatic loss of economic integration after 1913. For all the growth in international trade in recent decades, as a percentage of world GDP it has only barely regained levels found before World War I. Paul Bairoch finds a historical record of "fast internationalization alternating with drawback" rather than evidence of "globalization as an irreversible movement." The extensive work now being done on specific patterns of production, trade, and consumption, on national and international institutions, and on existing and possible forms of regulation is salutary; however, fitting it all into an "-ization" framework puts the emphasis where it does not belong.[6]

The movement of people, as well as capital, reveals the lumpiness of cross-border connections, not a pattern of steadily increasing integration. The high point of intercontinental labor migration was the century after 1815. Now, far from seeing a world of lowering barriers, labor migrants have to take seriously what states can do. France, for example, raised its barriers very high in 1974, whereas in the supposedly less globalized 1950s Africans from French colonies, as citizens, could enter France and were much in demand in the labor market. Aside from family reconstitution, labor migrations to France have become "residual."[7] Clandestine migration is rampant, but the clandestine migrant cannot afford the illusion that states and institutions matter less than flows. Illegal (and legal) migration depends on networks that take people some places but not others. Other sorts of movements of people follow equally specific paths. Movements of diasporic Chinese within and beyond Southeast Asia is based on social and cultural strategies that enable mobile businessmen and migrating workers to adjust to different sovereignties while maintaining linkages among themselves. As Aihwa Ong argues, such movements do not reflect diminishing power of the states whose frontiers they cross or undermine those states; rather, such states have found new ways of exercising power over people and commodities.[8] We need to understand these institutional mechanisms, and the metaphor of global is a bad way to start.

The deaths of the nation-state and the welfare state are greatly exaggerated. The resources controlled by governments have never been higher. In OECD countries in 1965, governments collected and spent a little over 25 percent of GDP; this has increased steadily, reaching close to 37 percent in the supposedly global mid 1990s.[9] Welfare expenditures remain at all-time highs in France and Germany, where even marginal reductions are hotly contested by labor unions and social democratic parties and where even conservatives treat the basic edifice as a given. The reason for this is contrary to both the Bankers' Boast and the Social Democrat's Lament: politics. This point has been emphasized in regard to Latin America: both France and Brazil face tough international competition, but in France the welfare state can be defended within the political system, whereas in Brazil globalization becomes the rationale for dismantling state services and refraining from the obvious alternative—taxing the wealthy. In the more developed Latin

American countries, taxes as a percentage of GNP are less than half the levels of western Europe.[10] There are alternatives to acting in the name of globalization, which the Brazilian state has chosen not to pursue.

But one should not make the opposite mistake and assume that in the past the nation-state enjoyed a period of unchallenged salience and was the unquestioned reference point for political mobilization. Going back to the antislavery movements of the eighteenth and early nineteenth centuries, political movements have been transnational, sometimes focused on the empire as a unit, sometimes on civilization, sometimes on a universalized humanity. Diasporic imaginations go far back too—the importance of deterritorialized conceptions of Africa to African Americans from the 1830s is a case in point.

What stands against globalization arguments should not be an attempt to stuff history back into national or continental containers. It will not fit. The question is whether the changing meaning over time of spatial linkages can be better understood in a some other way than globalization.

Globalization is itself a term whose meaning is not clear and over which substantial disagreements exist among those who use it. It can be used so broadly that it embraces everything and therefore means nothing, but for most writers, it carries a powerful set of images, if not a precise definition. Globalization talk takes its inspiration from the fall of the Berlin Wall, which offered the possibility or maybe the illusion that barriers to cross-national economic relations were falling. For friend and foe alike, the ideological framework of globalization is liberalism—arguments for free trade and free movement of capital. The imagery of globalization derives from the World Wide Web, the idea that a weblike connectivity of every site to every other site is a model for all forms of global communications. Political actors and scholars differ on "its" effects: diffusion of the benefits of growth versus increasing concentration of wealth, homogenization of culture versus diversification. But if the word means anything, it means expanding integration, and integration on a planetary scale. Even differentiation, the globalizers argue, must be seen in a new light, for the new emphasis on cultural specificity and ethnic identification differs from the old in that its basis now is juxtaposition, not isolation.

For all its emphasis on the newness of the last quarter century, the current interest in the concept of globalization recalls a similar infatuation in the 1950s and 1960s: modernization.[11] Both are "-ization" words, emphasizing a process, not necessarily fully realized but ongoing and probably inevitable. Both name the process by its supposed endpoint. Both were inspired by a clearly valid and compelling observation: that change is rapid and pervasive. And both depend for their evocative power on a sense that change is not a series of disparate elements but their movement in a common direction. Modernization theory failed to do the job that theory is supposed to do, and its failure should be an illuminating one for scholars working in the globalization framework. Modernization theory's central argument was that key elements of society varied together and this clustering produced the movement from traditional to modern societies: from subsistence to industrial economies, from predominantly rural to predominantly urban societies, from extended to nuclear families, from ascriptive to achieved status, from sacred to secular ideologies, from the politics of the subject to the politics of the participant, from diffuse and multifaceted to contractual relationships (see chapter 5).

The flaws of modernization theory parallel those of globalization. The key variables of transition did not vary together, as much research has shown. Most important, modernization, like globalization, appears in this theory as a process that just happens, something self-propelled. Modernization talk masked crucial questions of the day: were its criteria Eurocentric, or even based on an idealized vision of what American society was supposed to be like? Was change along such lines just happening or was it being driven—by American military might or the economic power of capitalist corporations?

The contents of the two approaches are obviously different, and I do not wish to push the parallel beyond the observation that modernization and globalization represent similar stances in relation to broad processes. Both define themselves by naming a future as an apparent projection of a present, which is sharply distinguished from the past. For the social scientist, the issue is whether such theories encourage the posing of better, more precise questions or slip over the most interesting and problematic issues of our time.

CAPITALISM IN AN ATLANTIC SPATIAL SYSTEM—AND BEYOND

So let me start somewhere else, with C. L. R. James and Eric Williams.[12] These books are both solidly researched analyses, and they are political texts. I intend to talk about them in both senses, to emphasize how reading them allows us to juxtapose space and time in a creative way. James was born in the British colony of Trinidad in 1901. He was a Pan-Africanist and a Trotskyite, an activist in anti-imperialist movements in the 1930s that linked Africa, Europe, and the Caribbean. *Black Jacobins* (1938) was a history of the Haitian revolution, from 1791 to 1804, and it showed that in the eighteenth century as much as the twentieth economic processes and political mobilization both crossed oceans.

To James, slavery in the Caribbean was not an archaic system. The organizational forms that became characteristic of modern industrial capitalism—massed laborers working under supervision, time-discipline in cultivation and processing, year-round planning of tasks, control over residential as well as productive space—were pioneered on Caribbean sugar estates as much as in English factories. The slaves were African; the capital came from France; the land was in the Caribbean. Eric Williams, historian and later prime minister of Trinidad, elaborated the process by which the transatlantic connections were forged, arguing that the slave trade helped bring about capitalist development in England, eventually the industrial revolution.

Slavery was not new in Africa or in Europe. What was new was the interrelationship of Africa, Europe, and the Americas, which changed the way actors in all places acted, forced a change in scale, and gave a relentless logic to the expansion of the system into the nineteenth century.

When the Declaration of the Rights of Man and of the Citizen was being discussed in Paris, it did not occur to most participants that the categories might embrace people in the colonies. But colonials thought they did, first planters who saw themselves as property-owning Frenchmen, entitled to voice the interests of their colony vis-à-vis the French state, then the *gens de couleur*, property-owning people of mixed origin, who saw themselves as citizens too, irrespective of race. Then slaves became aware both of universalistic discourse about rights and citizenship coming from Paris and the weakening of the state as republicans, royalists, and different planters fought with each other. James stresses the "Jacobin" side of the rebellion: the serious debate in Paris over whether the field of application of the universal declaration was bounded or not, the seizure by slaves of this discourse of rights, the mixture of ideals and strategy that led a French governor to abolish slavery in 1793 and try to rally slaves to the cause of Republican France, and the multisided and shifting struggle of slave-led armies, full of alliances and betrayals, which ended in the independence of Haiti. He mentioned that two-thirds of the slaves at the time of the revolution were born in Africa, but he was not particularly interested in that fact or its implications.

The year of *Black Jacobins'* publication, 1938, was the centenary of Great Britain's decision to end the intermediary status ("apprenticeship") through which slaves passed as they were emancipated. The British government, which had for years emphasized its emancipatory history, now banned all celebrations of the centenary. A series of strikes and riots had taken place in the West Indies and central Africa between 1935 and 1938; celebrating emancipation might have called attention to the meagerness of its fruits. James brings this out in his text. His intervention tied a history of the liberation accomplished in 1804 to the liberation he hoped to see— in the British as well as in the French empires—in his own time.

His text had another significance. Haiti did not go down in history as the vanguard of emancipation and decolonization; it was for colonial elites the symbol of backwardness and for nineteenth-century abolitionists an embarrassment. James wanted to change that record, to make the Haitian revolution a modern uprising against a modern form of exploitation, the vanguard of a universal process. Michel-Rolph Trouillot has called attention to what James left out in order to do this, what he calls the "war within the war," another layer of rebellion by slaves of African origin who rejected the compromises the leadership was making—for it was seeking to preserve plantation production, some kind of state structure, and some kind of relationship with the French—all of which these slaves rejected. Trouillot notes that the upper class of Haiti likes to claim direct descent from the nationalists of 1791; to do so takes a willful act of silencing.[13]

In spite of all James left out for his 1938 purposes, he disrupts present-day notions of historical time and space in a fruitful way. The revolution happened too early. It began only two years after the storming of the Bastille. The nation-state was being transcended as it was being born; the universe to which the rights of man applied was extended even as those rights were being specified; slaves were claiming a place in the polity before political philosophers had decided whether they belonged; and transoceanic movements of ideas were having an effect while territorially defined social movements were still coming into their own. Many of the questions being debated in James's time were already posed, with great forcefulness, between 1791 and 1804. So too some of the questions James didn't want to pose, as Trouillot has reminded us.

Looking at 1791 and 1938 together allows us to see politics in cross-continental spatial perspective, not as a binary opposition of local authenticity against global domination, and to emphasize struggle over the meaning of ideas as much as their transmission across space. The French Revolution installed liberty and citizenship in the lexicon of politics, but it did not fix their meanings, the spatial limits of the concepts, or the cultural criteria necessary for their application. If some political currents (in 1791 or 2000) sought a narrow, territorially or culturally bounded definition of the rights-bearing citizen, others (in 1791 or 2000) developed deterritorialized political discourses. This dialectic of territorialization and deterritorialization has undergone many shifts since then.

James's argument is an "Atlantic" one, Williams's as well. Both emphasize a specific set of connections, with worldwide implications to be sure, but whose historical actuality is more precisely rooted. The development of capitalism is at the core of their argument: capital formation via the African-European-American slave trade, the interconnectedness of labor supply, production, and consumption, and the invention of forms of work discipline in both field and factory. The struggle *against* this transoceanic capitalism was equally transoceanic.

Atlantic perspectives have been considerably extended via Sidney Mintz's analysis of the effects of Caribbean sugar on European culture, class relations, and economy, and Richard Price's studies about the cultural connections of the Caribbean world. Such studies do not point to the mere transmission of culture across space (as in other scholars' search for "African elements" in Caribbean cultures), but look instead at an intercontinental zone in which cultural inventiveness, synthesis, and adaptation take place, both reflecting and altering power relations.[14]

The Atlantic perspective does not necessarily have this ocean at its core. There were many shorelines and islands that were all but bypassed by the colonizing-enslaving-trading-producing-consuming system, even at its eighteenth-century peak. And there were places in other oceans (such as Indian Ocean sugar-producing islands) that were Atlantic in structure even if they were in another ocean. Powerful as the forces James and Williams wrote about, they had their histories, their limitations, their weaknesses. One can, as these authors show, write about large-scale, long-term processes without overlooking specificity, contingency, and contestation.

OCEANS, CONTINENTS, AND INTERTWINED HISTORIES

But the history of long-distance connections goes back farther than the history of capitalism centered in northwestern Europe and the Atlantic Ocean. Take the following sentence from an historian's article: "There have been few times in history when the world has been so closely interconnected— not only economically, but also in culture and tradition."[15] Is she writing about the globalization era of the late twentieth century? Actually, she is describing the Mongol empires of the fourteenth century: an imperial system stretching from China to central Europe, laced with trade routes and featuring linked belief systems (a marriage of kinship and warrior ideology from East Asia and Islamic learning and law from western Asia), a balance of nomadic, agricultural, and urban economies, and a communications system based in relays of horsemen that kept the imperial center informed.

Analyzing regional connections and culture—in large empires or networks of trade and religious linkages—means coming to grips with the lumpiness of power and economic relations and the way such asymmetries shifted over time.[16] Attempts to posit a transition from multiple worlds to a single world system with a core and a periphery have been mechanistic and inadequate to understand the unevenness and the dynamics of such a spatial system. Rather than arguing for a sixteenth- or seventeenth-century world system—and then assigning causal weight to the logic of the system itself—one can argue that structures of power and exchange were not so global and not so systematic and that what was new was in the domain of political imagination.[17] With the widespread Portuguese and Dutch voyages and conquests, it became possible to think of the world as the ultimate unit of ambition and political and economic strategy. But it still required considerable scientific progress, in cartography for example, to give content to such imaginings, let alone to act on such a basis. The relationship among different regional trading systems, religious networks, projections of power, and geographical understandings presents a complex and highly uneven historical pattern.

Empires are a particular kind of spatial system, boundary-crossing and also bounded. There is now abundant scholarship on their ambiguity: their structure emphasizes difference and hierarchy, yet they also constituted a single political unit, and hence a potential unit of moral discourse. Jurists in Spain from the sixteenth to the eighteenth century debated the moral authority of an imperial ruler to subordinate certain subjects but not others, to take the land of some but not others. Imperial forces often recognized and profited from preexisting circuits of commerce, but they could also be threatened by networks they did not control and by the unpredictable effects of interaction between agents of empire and indigenous commercial and political actors. Empires generated creole societies that might distance themselves from the metropole even as they claimed "civilizational" authority by association with it.[18]

A seminal intervention into these issues—in some ways breathing new life into the James-Williams argument—comes from a historian of China, Kenneth Pomeranz. He notes that the economies of Europe and China before 1800 operated in quite different ways but that it makes little sense to say that one was better, more powerful, or more capable of investment and innovation than the other. Instead of a single center of a world economy, he finds several centers with their own peripheries. The central regions in China and those in northwestern Europe were not notably unequal in their access to resources needed for industrialization. But after 1800, they diverged. He argues that different kinds of relations with regional peripheries shape this divergence. China's trading and political connections with Southeast Asia brought it into relationship with a periphery that was in many ways too similar: rice-growing, trade-oriented communities. European expansion, however, both built upon and built differentiation, in terms of ecology and in terms of labor. The slave plantation in European colonies developed resource complementarities with key regions in Europe that the Chinese empire could not emulate. China could not overcome resource blockages in food and fuel that the industrializing regions of Western Europe were able to surmount. The different forms of imperial projection—the specific blockages overcome or not overcome—shaped the divergence.[19]

Africa's place within such a picture is crucial: the possibility of moving—by force—labor from Africa to parts of the Americas (where indigenous populations had been marginalized or killed off) allowed European empires to develop labor complementarities and to turn land complementarities into something useable. African slaves grew sugar on Caribbean islands that supplied English workers with calories and stimulants. But how could such a frightful complementarity come about? Only with powerful commercial and navigational systems to connect parts of this Atlantic system. Only with an institutional apparatus—the colonial state—capable of backing up the coercive capability of individual Caribbean slave owners, of defining an increasingly racialized system of law that marked enslaved Africans and their descendants in a particular way, and of enforcing property rights across different parts of an imperial system, but whose power was vulnerable in ways James pointed out. Only by developing connections to African states, mostly unconquered, and African trading systems, and then by influencing those relationships in a powerful—and horrendous—manner.[20]

But to understand the contrast—and the interrelation—of coastal West Africa and the heartlands of capitalist agriculture and early industrialization in England, one must look at the ways in which production was organized, not just the way it fit into a wide spatial system. Marx stressed the importance in the seventeenth and eighteenth centuries of "primitive accumulation," the separation of producers from the means of production. It was this process that forced the possessors of land and the possessors of labor power to face each day the necessity to combine their assets with some degree of efficiency. Feudal landlords, slave owners, and peasants all could respond—or not respond—to market incentives, but capitalists and workers were trapped.

One can argue that in most of Africa one is at the other extreme, and therefore Africa should play a crucial role in the study of capitalism, however paradoxical this might now appear. For a combination of social and geographic reasons, what Albert Hirschman calls the "exit option" was particularly open in Africa.[21] There were a few places with the resources for prosperity, but many places with adequate resources for survival, and corporate kinship structures made mobility into a collective process. Africa's islands of exploitation were linked by trading diasporas and other sociocultural linkages, so that movement and the juggling of alternative political and economic possibilities remained key strategies. This does not mean that Africa was a continent of tranquil villages, for efforts were being made to overcome precisely the challenges of kinship groups and physical dispersal. The would-be king tried to get hold of detached people—those who fell afoul of kinship group elders or those whose own groups had fallen apart—to build a patrimonial following. But anyone who built up land resources had to face the problem that laborers could flee or use their corporate strength to resist subordination. Expanding production often meant bringing in outsiders, often through enslavement. Power depended on controlling the external.

And here we have an intertwining of histories that cannot simply be compared. The British economy in the seventeenth and eighteenth centuries was prepared to use its overseas connections in a more dynamic way than had the Iberian imperialists of an earlier epoch. African kings were vulnerable at home and found strength in their external connections. The slave trade meant different things to different partners: for the African king it meant gaining resources (guns, metals, cloth and other goods with redistributive potential) by seizing someone else's human assets, rather than facing the difficulties of subordinating one's own population. Raiding slaves from another polity and selling them to an outside buyer externalized the supervision problem as well as the recruitment problem. Over time, the external market had increasing effects on the politics and economics of parts of West and Central Africa, effects that were unpredictable to the first rulers who became enmeshed in this transatlantic system. It fostered militarized states and more efficient slave-trading mechanisms. This militarization was, from the point of view of African participants in the process, an unintended consequence of the fatal intertwining: outlets for war captives created a new and insidious logic that began to drive the entire system of slave catching and slave marketing.

So while one set of structures were enhanced in Africa by the slave trade, another set—the "modern" institutions of production, commercialization, and capital movement described by James and Williams—developed between the Caribbean and Europe. The Atlantic system depended on the connection of vastly different systems of production and power and had different consequences for each point in the system.

When Europeans finally decided in the early nineteenth century that the slave trade was immoral, the odium of it was attached to Africans who continued to engage in such practices, and Africans moved from being the Enslavable Other to the Enslaving Other, an object for humanitarian denunciation and intervention.[22] What was most "global" in the nineteenth century was not the actual structure of economic and political interaction, but the language in which slavery was discussed by its opponents: a language of shared humanity and the rights of man, evoked by a transatlantic social movement that was both Euro-American and Afro-American. This language was used first to expunge an evil from European empires and the Atlantic system and, from the 1870s onward, to save Africans from their alleged tyranny toward each other. The actual impetus and mechanisms of European conquest were of course more particular than that. Colonial invasions entailed the concentration of military power in small spaces, the movement of colonial armies onward, and a strikingly unimpressive colonial capacity to exercise power systematically and routinely over the territories under European rule. A globalizing language stood alongside a structure of domination and exploitation that was lumpy to an extreme.

This is little more than a sketch of a complex history. From the sixteenth-century slave trade through the nineteenth-century period of imperialism in the name of emancipation, the interrelation of different parts of the world was essential to the histories of each part of it. But the mechanisms of interrelation were contingent and limited in their transformative capacity—as they still are. In that sense, the Atlantic system was not entirely systematic, nor was it an eighteenth-century "globalization."

DOING HISTORY BACKWARDS: COLONIZATION
AND THE ANTECEDENTS OF GLOBALIZATION

Scholars working within globalization paradigms differ over whether the present should be considered the latest of a series of globalizations, each more inclusive than the last, or else a global age distinct from a past in which economic and social relations were contained within nation-states or empires and in which interaction took place among such internally coherent units. Both conceptions share the same problem: writing history backwards, taking an idealized version of the "globalized present" and working backwards to show how everything either led up to it ("proto-globalization") or how everything, until the arrival of the global age itself, deviated from it. In neither version does one watch history unfold over time, producing dead ends as well as pathways leading somewhere, creating conditions and contingencies in which actors made decisions, mobilized other people, and took actions that both opened and constrained future possibilities.[23]

Let us take an example from where I left off in the last section: colonization by European powers in Africa in the late nineteenth century. At first glance, this fits a metahistory of integration—however ugly some of its forms may have been—of apparently isolated regions into what was becoming a singular, European-dominated globality.[24] Colonial ideologists themselves claimed that they were "opening" the African continent. But colonization does not fit the integrative imagery associated with globalization. Colonial conquests imposed territorial borders on long-distance trading networks within Africa and imposed monopolies on the growing external trade of this time, damaging or destroying more articulated trading systems crossing the Indian Ocean and the Sahara Desert and lining the West African coast. Africans were forced into imperial economic systems focused on a single European metropole. More profoundly, colonial territories were highly disarticulated politically, socially, and economically: colonizers made their money by focusing investment and infrastructure on extremely narrow, largely extractive forms of production and exchange.[25] They taught some indigenous peoples some of what they needed to interact with Europeans, and then tried to isolate them from others whose division into allegedly distinct cultural and political units ("tribes") was emphasized and institutionalized. There might be a better case for calling colonization deglobalization rather than globalization, except that the prior systems were constituted out of specific networks, with their own mechanisms and limits, and except that colonial economies were in reality crosscut by numerous networks of exchange and socio-cultural interaction (also dependent on specific mechanisms and bounded in particular ways). To study colonization *is* to study the reorganization of space, the forging and unforging of linkages; to call it globalization, distorted globalization, or deglobalization is to hold colonization against an abstract standard with little relation to historical processes.

Was decolonization a step toward globalization? It was literally a step toward *internationalization*—that is, a new relationship of nation-states, which is what globalizers, with reason, try to distinguish from globalization. Newly independent states were at pains to emphasize their national quality, and economic policy often relied on import-substitution industrialization and other distinctly national strategies to shape such an economic unit.

Does the era of Structural Adjustment Plans, imposed on now-hapless African states by international financial institutions such as the IMF, at last represent the triumph of globalization on a resistant continent? That certainly was the goal: IMF policy is consistent with the Banker's Boast, an imposed lowering of barriers to capital flows, reduction of tariff barriers, and aligning of currency on world markets.

But was that the effect? It takes a big leap to go from the Banker's Boast to a picture of actual integration. In fact, Africa's contribution to world trade and its intake of investment funds was *larger* in the days of national economic policy than in the days of economic openness.[26] Shall we call this the age of globalizing deglobalization in Africa or of distorted globalization? Is Africa the exception that proves the rule, the unglobalized continent, and is it paying a heavy price for its obstinacy in the face of the all-powerful world trend? The problem with making integration the standard—and measuring everything else as lack, failure, or distortion—is that one fails to ask what is actually happening in Africa.

The downsizing of governments and the loosening of investment and trade regulations are important trends, but they reflect the force of pro-globalization *arguments* within institutions like the IMF more than an ongoing *process*. Rule-making is not production, exchange, or consumption. All of those depend on specific structures, and these need to be analyzed in all their complexity and particularity. Africa is filled with areas where international investors do not go—even when there are minerals that would repay investors' efforts. To get to such places requires not deregulation, but institutions and networks capable of getting there.

One could make related arguments about China—where the state's economic role and importance in mediating relations to the outside world are far too strong for the globalization paradigm–or Russia, where oligarchs and mafias imply a model focused on networks more than integrative world markets. Africa now appears to belong to the half of the globe that is not globalized. Better, however, to emphasize not a globalizing (or deglobalizing) Africa (or China, or Russia), but rather changing *relationships* of externally based firms and financial organizations, indigenous regional networks, transcontinental networks, states, and international organizations.[27] Some linkages, such as the relationships of transnational oil companies to the state in Nigeria or Angola, are narrowly extractive in one direction and provide rewards to gatekeeping elites in the other. There is nothing weblike about this. At another extreme are the illicit networks that sent out diamonds from the rebel-controlled areas of Sierra Leone and Angola and brought in arms and luxury goods for warlords and their followers. Such networks were built out of youth detached from their villages of origin (or kidnapped from them), and flourished in contexts where young men had few routes to a future other than joining the forces assembled by a regional warlord. These systems were linked to diamond buyers and arms sellers in Europe (sometimes via South Africa, Russian, or Serbian pilots), but they depended on quite specific mechanisms of connection. Rather than integrating the regions in which they operated, they reinforced fragmentation and reduced the range of activities in which most people in a violence-torn region could engage.[28] The diamond-arms nexus recalls the slave trade of the eighteenth and early nineteenth centuries, for there too, as James and Williams understood very well, were historical processes unfolding in Africa that made no sense except in their relationship to the Atlantic system. The modern version provides a product to be enjoyed by people in distant lands—who do not necessarily ask where the diamond came from, any more than the consumers of sugar in nineteenth-century England wanted to know about the blood in which their sugar was soaked. And now, there are "international issue networks" developing to tell the diamond users in Europe and North America about this blood, using a universalistic language similar to that of the antislavery movement of the early nineteenth century.

MORE THAN LOCAL AND LESS THAN GLOBAL: NETWORKS, SOCIAL FIELDS, DIASPORAS

How does one think about African history in ways that emphasize spatial connection but do not assume the global? The vision of the colonial official or the 1930s anthropologist, of Africa divided neatly into culturally distinct, self-conscious units, did not work, despite the tendency of official myths to create their own reality. By the 1950s and 1960s, anthropologists were using other concepts: the "social situation," the "social field," and the "network." The first two emphasized that in different circumstances Africans constructed distinct patterns of affinity and moral sanction and moved back and forth between them; class affiliation might be operative in a mine town, deference to elders in a village. Conquest itself created a "colonial situation," as Georges Balandier described it in his pathbreaking article of 1951, defined by external coercion and racialized ideology within a space marked by conquest boundaries; Africans, far from living within their bounded tribes, had to maneuver within—or try to transform—the colonial situation. The network concept stressed the webs of connection that people developed as they crossed space, countering the somewhat artificial notion of situations as being spatially distinct.[29]

These terms did not provide a template for analyzing a structure, but they directed the researcher toward empirical analysis of how connections were formed, toward defining units of analysis by observation of the boundaries of interaction. They encouraged studying the channels through which power was exercised. These concepts thus had their limits, and they did not address the kinds of macro-processes to be found in the historical analysis of James or Williams. Nevertheless, one can use such a framework to study the merchant diasporas of West Africa—in which Islamic brotherhoods as well as kinship and ethnic ties maintained trust and information flows across long distances and during transactions with culturally distinct populations—or the long-distance migrant labor networks of southern Africa.[30] The network concept puts as much emphasis on nodes and blockages as on movement, and thus calls attention to institutions—including police controls over migration, licensing, and welfare systems. It thus avoids the amorphous quality of an anthropology of flows and fragments.

These concepts open the door to examination of the wide variety of units of affinity and mobilization, the kinds of subjective attachments people form and the collectivities that are capable of action. One is not limited by supposedly primordial identifications, to the tribe or race for instance, or to a specific space. One can start with identification with Africa itself and study the diasporic imagination, for Africa as a space to which people attached meaning was defined less by processes within the continental boundaries than by its diaspora. If slave traders defined Africa as a place where they could legitimately enslave people, their victims discovered in their ordeal a commonality that defined them as people with a past, a place, a collective imagination.

When African American activists in the early nineteenth century began to evoke images of Africa or "Ethiopia," they were making a point within a Christian conception of universal history more than a reference to particular cultural affinities. The meanings of Africa-consciousness have been varied, and their relationship to the particulars of Africa even more so. J. Lorand Matory argues that certain African "ethnic groups" defined themselves in the course of an African-American dialogue under the influence of former slaves who returned to the region of their fathers and advocated forms of collective identification that transcended local divisions and were based as much on an imagined future as a claimed past.[31]

The spatial imagination of intellectuals, missionaries, and political activists, from the early nineteenth to the mid twentieth century was thus varied. It was neither global nor local, but was built out of specific lines of connection and posited regional, continental, and transcontinental affinities. These spatial affinities could narrow, expand, and narrow again. Pan-Africanism was more salient in the 1930s and early 1940s than in the 1950s, when territorial units became more accessible foci of claims and when political imagination became (for a time at least) more national. French officials in the postwar decade tried to get Africans to imagine themselves in a different way, as citizens of a Union Française, and African politicians tried to use this imperial version of citizenship to make claims on the metropole. But imperial citizenship was riddled with too many contradictions and hypocrisies to constitute to most Africans a plausible case for supranational identification. French officials, aware of the cost of making imperial citizenship meaningful, backed away from it, using the word *territorialization* in the mid 1950s to emphasize that in conceding power to Africans the government was devolving on them the responsibility of meeting the demands of citizens with the resources of individual territories.[32] Among the various possibilities—pan-African visions, large-scale federations, and imperial citizenship—the territorially bounded citizenship that Africans received was the product of a specific history of claims and counterclaims.

One needs to look at other circuits: religious pilgrimages to Mecca and networks of training that Muslim clerics followed all over the Sahara Desert, from the eighth century, and intensely from the eighteenth; regional systems of shrines in Central Africa; religious connections between Africans and African American missionaries. The linkage between intra-African and extra-African networks is an old one: the Brazil-Angola-Portugal slave-trading nexus; trans-Saharan commercial, religious, and scholarly networks connecting to Hausa and Mandingo systems within West Africa; a trading system extending from Mozambique Island through the Red Sea, southern Arabia, and the Persian Gulf to Gujarat; a Dutch-pioneered system that connected Indonesia, South Africa, and Europe, with tentacles reaching into the interior of southern Africa; the network of merchants and professionals across coastal West Africa, with links to Brazil, Europe, the Caribbean, and the West African interior, shaping racially and culturally mixed coastal communities; and, more recently, the horrifically effective networks of diamond and arms smugglers connecting Sierra

Leone and Angola to Europe. One cannot argue that networks are soft and cozy whereas structures are hard and domineering.[33]

And one can look at the border-crossing "issue networks," of which the antislavery movement of the early nineteenth century was the great pioneer.[34] Anticolonial movements from the 1930s onward were able to make the once-ordinary category of "colony" into something unacceptable in international discourse largely because they linked activists in African towns and cities with principled groups in metropoles, who in turn tied those issues to the self-conception of democracies. In South Africa in the early twentieth century, scholars have found in a single rural district linkages to church groups emphasizing Christian brotherhood, to liberal constitutionalist reforms in cities, to African American movements, and to regional organizations of labor tenants.[35] The shifting articulations of local, regional, and international movements shaped a political repertoire that kept a variety of possibilities alive and suggested ways of finding help in the African diaspora and in Euro-American issue networks. In the end, South African whites, who prided themselves on their connections to the "Christian" and "civilized" west, lost the battle of linkages.

Perhaps social democrats have better things to do than lament. The current efforts of trade unions and NGOs to challenge "global" capitalism via "global" social movements—such as those against sweat shops and child labor in the international clothing and shoe industries or the movement to ban "conflict diamonds"—have precedents going back to the late eighteenth century, and they have won a few victories along the way. Arguments based on the rights of man have as good a claim to global relevance as arguments based on the market. And in both cases, discourse has been far more global than practice.

RETHINKING THE PRESENT

The point of these short narratives is not to say that nothing changes under the sun. Obviously, the commodity exchange system, forms of production, the modalities of state interventions into societies, capital exchange systems, let alone technologies of communication, have changed enormously. The slave-sugar-manufactured goods commodity circuits of the eighteenth century had a vastly different significance for capitalist development in that era than the diamond-arms circuit does today. My argument is for precision in specifying how such commodity circuits are constituted, how connections across space are extended and bounded, and how large-scale, long-term processes, such as capitalist development, can be analyzed with due attention to their power, their limitations, and the mechanisms that shape them. One can, of course, call all of this globalization, but that is to say little more than that history happens within the boundaries of the planet and therefore all history is global history. However, if one wants to use globalization as the progressive integration of different parts of the world into a singular whole, then the argument falls victim to linearity and teleology. The globalizers are right to tell us to look at long-distance connections. The difficulty is to come up with concepts that are discerning enough to say something significant about them. Like modernization theory, globalization draws its power from uniting diverse phenomena into a singular conceptual framework and a singular notion of change. And that is where both approaches occlude rather than clarify historical processes.

But what about reversing the argument—admitting that there is little point in refining globalization by adding a historical dimension, and turning instead to the other position that some globalizers take: that the global age is now, and it is clearly distinguished from the past? Here, my argument has not been against the specificity of the present, but whether characterizing it as global distinguishes it from the past. Communications revolutions, capital movements, and regulatory apparatuses all need to be studied and their relationships, mutually reinforcing or contradictory, explored. But we need more refined theoretical apparatus and a less misleading rhetoric than that provided by globalization—whether Banker's Boast, Social Democrat's Lament, or the Dance of the Flows and Fragments. I have argued this both by looking at the variety and specificity of cross-territorial connecting mechanisms in past and present, and the misleading connotations of the "global" and the "-ization."

The point goes beyond the academic's quest for refinement: a lot is at stake in the kinds of questions brought to the fore by the conceptual apparatus. International financial institutions that tell African leaders that development will follow if they open their economies will not get to the bottom of that continent's problems unless they address how specific structures within African societies, within or across borders, provide opportunities and constraints for production and exchange and how specific mechanisms in external commodity markets provide opportunities and blockages for African products. State institutions, oligarchies, warlords, regional mafias, commercial diasporas, oligopolistic foreign corporations, and varied networks shape the nature of capitalism and its highly uneven effects. Capitalism remains lumpy.[36]

It is no surprise that journalists and academics alike react with a sense of wonder to the multiplicity of forms of communication that have opened up (but are available only to some) and to the border-crossing strategies of many firms (but not others). The globalization fad is an understandable response to this sense of connectivity and opportunity, just as modernization theory was to the collapsing rigidities of European societies in the 1950s and the escape from the constraints of colonial empires. Globalization can be invoked to make a variety of claims, but it can also constrict the political imagination, occlude the power and importance of the long history of transnational mobilizations, and discourage focus on institutions and networks that can offer opportunities as well as constraints.

Of course, all the changing forms of transcontinental connections, all the forms of integration and differentiation, of flows and blockages, of the past and present can be seen as aspects of a singular but complex process, which we can label globalization. But that is to defend the concept by emphasizing how little it signifies. Words matter. The incessant talk about globalization—the word, the images associated with it, and arguments for and against "it"—both reflect and reinforce fascination with boundless connectivity. Yet scholars do not need to choose between a rhetoric of containers and a rhetoric of flows. They do not need to decide whether Africa is part of a necessary and universal trend or a peculiar and frustrating exception; instead they can analyze how it and other regions are linked and bounded. Not least of the questions we should be asking concerns the present: what is actually new? What are the limits and mechanisms of ongoing changes? And above all, can we develop a differentiated vocabulary that encourages thinking about connections and their limits?

5 Modernity

The word *modernity* is now used to make so many different points that continued deployment of it may contribute more to confusion than to clarity. Scholars who use the term are trying to address issues of great importance for debates over past, present, and future. Modernity is evoked in public debate, and such uses demand attention. But modernity is not just a "native's category"; it is employed as an analytic category as well—defining a subject for scholarly inquiry—and that is where its value is in doubt. Four perspectives on modernity run through much of the academic literature:

1. Modernity represents a powerful claim to singularity: it is a long and continuing project, central to the history of Western Europe, and in turn defining a goal to which the rest of the world aspires. This singularity is applauded by those who see new opportunities for personal, social, and political advancement as liberation from the weight of backwardness and the oppressiveness of past forms of Western imperialism.

2. Modernity, again, is a bundle of social, ideological, and political phenomena whose historical origins lie in the West, but this time it is condemned as itself an imperial construct, a global imposition of specifically Western social, economic, and political forms that tames and sterilizes the rich diversity of human experience and the sustaining power of diverse forms of community.

3. Modernity is still singular; it is indeed a European project and a European accomplishment, to be defended against others who may knock at the gate but whose cultural baggage renders the mastery of modernity unattainable.

4. Modernity is plural. We have "multiple modernities" and "alternative modernities." These arguments either bring out the way in which non-Western peoples develop cultural forms that are not mere repetitions of tradition but bring their own perspectives to progress. Or else such interpretations focus on colonized intellectuals or leaders who explicitly engage the claims of Western agents to represent all that was modern and seek to put forward alternatives that are forward-looking but self-consciously distinct.

The first three usages of modernity are centered on Europe, whether in a positive or negative sense. The fourth version is more pluralistic, but is open to a double critique. On the one hand, it is not clear why an alternative modernity should be called a modernity at all. If any form of innovation produces a modernity, then the term has little analytic purchase. On the other hand, if alternative modernities all represent alternatives to a European modernity, then one package of cultural traits is being awarded a European pedigree while other packages are being linked across time to a people, however defined, as in Chinese modernity or Islamic modernity. Both the idea of package-making and its time-transcending, essentializing association with a particular people demand scrutiny.

The vast literature keeps multiplying a further confusion: is modernity a *condition*—something written into the exercise of economic and political power at a global level? Or is it a *representation*, a way of talking about the world in which one uses a language of temporal transformation while bringing out the simultaneity of global unevenness, in which "tradition" is produced by telling a story of how some people became "modern"? If we are talking about a condition, then the question is whether modernity, as an analytic category, encourages us to ask good questions about what that condition is. If we are talking about representations, then the question is whose? Might a scholar's conviction of the importance of the modernity problematic lead to the imposition of one modernity, or any modernity, on other people's conceptual schemas? Some insist that modernity is both a condition and a representation of that condition, indeed that it is *the* condition, *the* predicament of the present: "Modernity is a global condition that now affects all our actions, interpretations, and habits, across nations and irrespective of which civilizational roots we may have or lay claim to."[1] But if modernity is everything and everything is modernity, is the concept helping us distinguish anything from anything else?

A few brave souls have come to question the usefulness of the concept: John Kelly wishes "not for alternative modernities but alternatives to 'modernity' as a chronotope necessary for social theory."[2] But most soldier on, in their own ways, quite inconsistent with each other. Whether modernity appears as a bright but distant star—the aspirations of diverse people for a world with less poverty and less tyranny—or as the hubris of those who would remake the world by the dictates of their own notions of rationality, these are powerful concerns, and the question is not whether they are worth pondering, but whether the concept of modernity has enough clarity to advance thinking about them.

The usual response of a scholar faced with the conceptual confusion that bedevils modernity is to plunge more deeply into the subject: let the users of the term fight it out; may the best modernity win. My argument is the reverse: scholars should not try for a slightly better definition so that they can talk about modernity more clearly. They should instead listen to what is being said in the world. If modernity is what they hear, they should ask how it is being used and why; otherwise, shoehorning a political discourse into modern, antimodern, or postmodern discourses, or into "their" modernity or "ours," is more distorting than revealing.

In colonial studies, modernity has had an especially powerful valence, producing both a useful critique and a constricting abstraction. The power of the concept comes from the assertion that modernity has been the model held up before colonized people: a marker of Europe's right to rule, something to which the colonized should aspire but could never quite deserve. The critique of modernity seethes with resentment and longing. In weaving together modernity and colonialism, critics have tried to force a rethinking not only of colonialism but of an entire vision of change that continues to condemn Africans and Asians to the role of "catching up." This is an important, in some ways essential, critique to think with and through. But it is also a confining one, both as a way of studying history and as a political project. In both senses, the critique itself keeps modernity on an intellectual pedestal, and the insistence that modernity be the reference point in a quest for alternatives makes it more difficult to talk about salient issues in altogether different terms.

Modernity has been a claim-making concept—in certain moments of history, not all moments, and not all places at the same time. Imperial ideologues, at various points in the nineteenth and twentieth centuries, put forth either transformative or static versions of a modernity argument: that bringing the backward into the modern world justified colonization, or that Europe's essential modernizing capacity compared to Africa's inherent backwardness justified long-term rule over Africa. But to argue, as does Partha Chatterjee, that "the question that frames the debate over social transformation in the colonial period is that of modernity" is to mistake arguments *within* colonial history—set against other arguments and other tendencies—for an essence of colonialism.[3]

For the political activist, modernity is only one of the terms in which claims can be made. The act of abstracting a claim from its specific referents and reframing it in terms of modernity has the virtue of linking it to other claims but the weakness of diminishing the stakes that women and men might have in the specific issue at hand. An argument phrased in terms of modernity may be convincing to someone for whom the self-image of being on the side of progress is important, and it may be repulsive to someone who fears the loss of familiar solidarities. It is good historical practice to recognize the discursive and material constraints within which colonized people asserted themselves and to see how in the course of struggle certain options were precluded, but if we start out with an assumption of an "incommensurable" difference between a package of Western modernity and alternatives packages rooted in African or Asian communities, the possible trajectories of political action, past and future, are narrowed from the start.[4] The trade unionists of French West Africa in the 1950s whom I have studied (see chapter 7) did very well for their members by translating colonial officials' desire to see their policies as progressive into concrete claims for wages, family allowances, and other benefits. That trade unionists found a useful lever within imperial ideology does not mean that they—let alone the rank and file—bought the package French officials had in mind or used resources to build the kinds of families French officials wanted for them. Their strategy had political, social, and cultural costs too, and understanding them is part of the story of decolonization and its aftermath.

The colonial question is not the modernity question, even if issues of modernity arise within colonial history. And if we recognize that about the colonial past, perhaps we can pose issues about the future with more precision and without reproducing the polarities that we want to dismantle. In the following pages, I point both to the proliferation of meanings of modernity—and hence its confusion when used in the singular—and to the proliferation of modernities, and the vanishing analytical utility of the term in the plural. The most incisive tenet of modernization theory, its insistence that modernity constituted a package, has been modified in more recent scholarship by a willingness to consider that packages might differ from each other, without focusing on the issue of packaging itself. But, I will argue, posing the issue at that level of abstraction gives an artificial coherence to the concept of modernity and separates it from the debate and struggle that have attended the use of such constructs in historical situations. The use by historians and others of the concept of colonial modernity flattens history, elevating messy histories into a consistent project and underplaying the efforts of colonized people to deflect and appropriate elements of colonizing policies, taking apart the packaging that the critics of modernity leave intact. Even less helpful is language in which the abstract category "modernity" becomes a causal agent. Although colonization was *of* the era in which it occurred, to identify the villain as modernity is to avoid rather than foster debate over the political and ethical issues that matter most.

OF "-ITY"S AND "-IZATION"S

For someone of my generation, coming of intellectual age in the 1970s, there is an irony to the modernity fad of the 1990s and 2000s. We cut our eye teeth—the ones that chew up concepts—on modernization. This concept was the most sweeping of all the "-ization"s that were then in vogue: urbanization, commercialization, industrialization, proletarianization. These words seemed to take the life out of politics and history, for they posited self-propelled movements of large-scale change that could be analyzed scientifically, leaving little room for the actions of human agents or for the importance of struggle. Of all such concepts, modernization was the one we loved to hate. Its best-known texts, W. W. Rostow's for instance, seemed unreflexively to assume that American society—as understood in the 1950s—represented the telos toward which all the world would converge.[5] Modernization theory was both analytic and normative, its insistence on the historical inevitability of modernization its most powerful argument for jumping on the bandwagon.[6]

There were many critiques of modernization theory.[7] Some were empirical: the theory implied an observable trend toward global homogenization around critical social indicators, while research indicated divergent pathways toward ends that were not so clear. Others thought American modernization theorists were looking toward the wrong modernity; they reversed Rostow's anticommunist manifesto to argue that Marxism defined a preferable form of modernization. By the mid 1970s, world-systems theory turned modernization into a global dualism: modernization really happened in the "core" because the "periphery" was blocked in its backwardness. But adding peripheralization to the self-propelling "-izations" did not solve the problem of understanding the causes and limits of integrating tendencies.[8]

Someone my age is thus struck by the irony of opening virtually any scholarly journal, from *International Organization* to *Social Text,* and finding that the most teleological of the teleologies are still alive and well, espoused not only by apologists for the World Bank's economic policies, but by people who regard themselves as critics. Some of the apologists have revived modernization in the form of globalization—just as self-propelled and homogenizing, but now with the discipline of all-pervasive, near-instantaneous market transactions and continent-hopping media substituted for the broader social logic of modernization theory. Some of their critics lament globalization without questioning that "it" defines our era (see chapter 4).

Meanwhile, the scholarly reader has in the last few years been inundated with book after book sporting titles like *Habitations of Modernity, Modernity at Large, Other Modernities, Modernity: An Ethnographic Approach, Consuming Modernity, Overcome by Modernity, Critically Modern,* and *African Modernities,* or with such subtitles as *Village Modernity in West Africa* or *The Dialectics of Modernity on a South African Frontier.*[9]

Do the "-ity"s imply that the "-ization"s have done their work and produced the condition toward which the labeled process was leading? Has all the work that has gone into critical theory merely reproduced American sociology of the 1950s, reversing modernity's valence from positive to negative, while leaving it intact?

In its time, the idea of modernization could be attractive and inspiring, evoking an aspiration for a life that could be understood and changed for the better. A younger generation in the two decades after World War II—in Africa, India, or Europe itself—could distinguish itself from the stodgy traditionalism of its ancestors. Modernity could also provoke anxiety over the loss of intimacy and community, the increasing power of impersonal institutions over social and cultural life, and the dangers of projects of social transformation destroying individual freedom—an anxiety that appeared all the more acute in Europe after World War II. But the possibilities of attaining modernity were most attractive to those who did not have it, and by the 1950s much of the world's colonized population was insisting their aspirations be taken into account. Claims to be for or against modernity have not gone away, nor have the aspirations that inspired such claims been fulfilled.

Both the anxieties and the aspirations deserve to be pondered; it is no wonder that discussions of modernity are often fraught. For both scholar and activist, the question is whether considering modernity as a coherent construct enables one to express the range of aspirations for a better life and whether such a construct points to the realities of an imperious, totalizing imposition. To emphasize the irony that self-proclaimed efforts to free slaves, emancipate women, and improve economies led to the arrogance and destructiveness of colonialism might capture important moments within a broader history yet miss others, not least of them the poignancy of claims coming from people once excluded from the material and cultural resources Europe claimed as its own.

THE MULTIPLYING MODERNITIES

The Now and the New

The most ordinary meaning of *modern* is that which is new, that which is distinguishable from the past.[10] In this sense, modernity is, was, and always will be with us, a point nicely illustrated in a recent debate over the types of art that belong in the Museum of Modern Art. A major donor of important art work claimed that *modern* indeed means "new" and that after fifty years a painting should be transferred out of the Modern to a museum whose task was to preserve the old. Against this claim, critics argued that modern art "has a recognizable style very different from what preceded it in the West." Hence "great works of modernism will always be modern, much as the masterpieces of the Renaissance will always be Renaissance masterpieces." If one holds to the former notion of modern art, then it is a moving category: something that is modern today will no longer be modern tomorrow. If one holds to the second, then one has to take up the challenge of defining what makes a style distinct. On this point, the 1950s modernizers had no doubts: they knew modernity when they saw it and didn't hesitate to specify the criteria.[11]

The modern as "now" conception produces another kind of difficulty: is everything and everyone modern? In Peter Geschiere's ethnography of witchcraft in contemporary Cameroon, *The Modernity of Witchcraft*, his deep research and careful argumentation show that witchcraft accusations are part and parcel of struggles over material and political resources as they actually exist, not some sign of ongoing tradition. The argument is persuasive, the link to the state and regional economies compelling, but it is not clear whether anything in contemporary Cameroon could be other than modern. Such arguments have been useful antidotes to the typical representation of African cultural and religious practice as backward, but once tradition is peeled off the spectrum, modernity occupies the entire space. Twenty years from now everything will still be modern, but it could possibly be quite different. Trying to escape from the false dichotomy of modern and traditional, we find ourselves with a concept whose main value is to correct past misuses of the same word.[12]

A Set of Attributes (Good Ones)

Hence the importance of thinking carefully about the opposite approach, which defines modernity by its attributes. Classic modernization theory derived its notion of a transition from tradition to modernity from Talcott Parsons's concept of "pattern variables." The interrelation of these attributes over time gave the theory its force. Daniel Lerner's 1968 formulation included self-sustaining growth in the economy, public participation in the polity, "diffusion of secular-rational norms in the culture," increased mobility—including personal freedom of physical, social, and psychic movement—and transformation of "the modal personality that equips individuals to function effectively in a social order that operates according to the foregoing characteristics." The modern personality is "striving."[13] Wilbert Moore put industrialism at the center, and saw it as shaping an entire way of life: a rational perspective on decision-making, adapting to labor markets, working in a hierarchical structure, and adapting to new social situations in places of residence.[14] Some modernization theorists thought that movement in one variable—economic growth was often seen as the instigator—would bring about change in predictable directions in the others. Others, such as Rostow, thought a minimum threshold of change was necessary to trigger the others. Still others set out modernization as a clearly delineated path that some people might choose not to follow—at a tremendous cost.[15] Then came the pessimistic and authoritarian modernizers, convinced that some if not most non-Western peoples would not follow the—still singular—path, leading to political and social pathologies that would have to be kept in check by those who had made the transition.[16]

If the early modernizers saw their focus as society, economics, and politics, their critical concepts were also cultural, and in later considerations of the project of modernity, as in the writing of Daniel Bell, this element came to the fore: modernity entailed a "sea change of consciousness. . . . What defines the modern is a sense of openness to change, of detachment from place and time, of social and geographical mobility, and a readiness, if not eagerness, to welcome the new, even at the expense of tradition and the past." Modernity implied a market economy, but an antibourgeois spirit, a rejection of the stuffiness of the past, of the taken-for-grantedness of social arrangements and forms of expression as well as of the received Word of religion; it entailed "rejection of classicism; of order, symmetry, proportion; of realism"; it questioned the "exact relation of sign to object"; it proposed a "pragmatic theory in which usage and experiment dictate interpretation and meaning."[17]

The empirical critique of modernization theory took apart such associations: the linkage of market economies to secularization worked neither for the classic case of capitalist development in the Britain—where religion was a potent force—nor for the trading diasporas of Islamic communal groups in West Africa; elites claiming sacred authority, from northern Nigeria in the 1960s to Iran today, used up-to-date media technologies to underscore their status; nineteenth-century Europeans reacted to the loosening of certain social constraints by fascination with the occult, spiritualism, and new forms of religious expression as much as by individualistic rationalism; agricultural innovators in late-nineteenth-century Africa used extended kinship networks to mobilize capital and labor, and far from development turning extended families into nuclear ones, it brought new resources into larger kinship groups. The covariance of commercialization, secularization, achievement orientation, rationalism, and individuation fit poorly in the history of "modern" Europe or "modernizing" Africa or Asia.[18]

A Set of Attributes (But Not So Good)

The package in some of the most recent work is not radically different. Take Charles Taylor: "By *modernity* I mean that historically unprecedented amalgam of new practices and institutional forms (science, technology, industrial production, urbanization), of new ways of living (individualism, secularization, instrumental rationality), and of new forms of malaise (alienation, meaninglessness, a sense of impending social dissolution)." Modernity lay at the end of a "long march," which "is perhaps ending only today."[19]

For the critics of modernity, the package is the problem: the creation of a certain kind of politics and a certain kind of subject. For Dipesh Chakrabarty,

> The phenomenon of "political modernity"—namely, the rule by modern institutions of the state, bureaucracy, and capitalist enterprise—is impossible to *think* of anywhere in the world without invoking certain categories and concepts, the genealogies of which go deep into the intellectual and even theological traditions of Europe. Concepts such as citizenship, the state, civil society, public sphere, human rights, equality before the law, the individual, distinctions between public and private, the idea of the subject, democracy, popular sovereignty, social justice, scientific rationality, and so on all bear the burden of European thought and history.[20]

Thus if someone like Bell sees modernity as expanding the possibilities of thought, Chakrabarty sees it as constricting. For the human to be thought of as an abstract figure and for reason to be the mode in which the question of a better life was broached entailed a loss of other ways of thinking and other ways of putting together community life. Not only did the concepts that constituted modernity fit together, but their emergence can be located in European history, hence the claim by Chakrabarty and others to be producing a critique of "post-Enlightenment rationality."

An Epoch

The critique of modernity slips from a conception of modernity as a package of concepts and institutions to modernity as an epoch: a "distinct and discontinuous period of human history."[21] The modern era stretches from the Enlightenment to a time when the categories and institutions in question lost their grip on people's imaginations, sometimes identified as postmodernity. If postmodernity hasn't yet come about, it is what the critics of modernity would like to encourage, by destabilizing our supposedly universalistic, self-confident assumptions about the use of reason to understand the world and change it.

The critique of modernity is influenced by Foucault, the object of whose critical analysis is the modern governmentality that emerged from the Enlightenment era. Some scholars refer to a "colonial modernity" or a "colonial governmentality" that is the manifestation of the Foucauldian process of creating a certain kind of subject (see below). To the extent that modernity can be defined by notions like governmentality, there are at least some contents that define the era.[22] But this move comes at a high cost, for it projects these concepts onto a two-century-long history of Europe that is much messier than that. Secularism remained embattled to different degrees and in different ways throughout Western Europe, the relationship of reason to subjectivities of different sorts was shifting and deeply preoccupying for centuries, and—most important—the very critiques of disciplining processes, of positivist reason, of rule-bound expression that some herald as the "post-" of postmodernism were in fact fundamental to debates among self-conscious modernists. When Chakrabarty asserts that European thought, especially that of "leftist intellectuals," was so sodden with the notions of secularism and reason that it "ceded to the fascists all moments of poetry, mysticism, and the religious and mysterious" and that "Romanticism now reminds them only of the Nazis," he reveals how far the Europe he wants to "provincialize" is from any Europe that existed. Instead of looking at the conflicting ways in which inhabitants of this province actually thought, he has been content to let the most simplistic version of the Enlightenment stand in for the European Province's much more convoluted history.[23]

The strange fate of the word *modernism* is indicative of a more general problem. Modernism is now used to denote the ideology that strives for modernity. Yet this view of modernism is largely an invention of postmodernism, which needed (contradicting its own claims to avoid metanarrative) a clearly bounded modernism that it could critique, transcend, and succeed. But the people who called themselves modernists in the late nineteenth and early twentieth centuries defined themselves—"bitterly," as one scholar puts it—*against* "the modernity of our industrial civilization and its major ideologies."[24] Many saw themselves as an avant-garde situated in opposition to the stuffiness of bourgeois culture, against formalism in art, and in favor of subjectivist, self-critical understanding of human experience. They were part of a longer, multisided debate beginning in the Enlightenment itself over the uncertainties of ways of knowing.[25] If the postmodernists write as if modernist social theorists were all incarnations of Talcott Parsons and modernist architects were all versions of Le Corbusier, the modernism of social theory at the juncture of the nineteenth and twentieth centuries was antipositivist, and its art gave rise to dada, constructivism, and surrealism.[26] In short, modernism entailed a critique of what is today identified as . . . modernism.

The issue here is more profound than a misreading of European intellectual and cultural history. The effort to provincialize Europe would be more meaningful if the all-dominating post-Enlightenment rationality were seen in relation to the questioning, contestation, and critique that were and are part of history.

If much of the discussion of modernity flattens time during the last two hundred years, it ignores much of what went before, not just in Europe but elsewhere. The benchmark technologies of nineteenth-century European governmentality—censuses and cadastral surveys, a professional bureaucracy watching and classifying a population, mechanisms to monitor and correct misallocations of the food supply—were already centuries old in the Chinese empire. A leading student of comparative politics pushes China's "modern structure" back to the seventh century.[27] Modernity must have begun a long time ago.

Bernard Yack addresses the underlying issue, arguing against the conflation of modernity as substance—a set of distinct attributes—and modernity as an epoch. For modernity to constitute an era, he points out, whatever makes it distinct must not only be present but also be its defining feature. To think of a modern epoch brings us back, yet again, to identifying features that define it, hence to something like the bundle of traits signaled by 1960s modernization theorists.[28] The idea of a modern period—usually post-1789—has an obvious appeal, not least to history departments, who routinely classify their courses as premodern and modern, a distinction dubious enough when applied to Europe but often exported elsewhere. There is an "of course" dimension to this distinction when one thinks about a twelfth-century French peasant juxtaposed with a twenty-first-century Parisian, just as there is when one compares the Parisian to a stereotypical African pastoralist. Perhaps looking at Europe from the vantage point of its former colonies—and noting the confusions of temporality and simultaneity to which "modernity" gives rise—will point to the misleading coherence implied by the notion of a modern era, and the need for more precise ways of thinking about change, in all parts of the world.

A Process (Singular), or "Capitalism-Plus"

While the marking of a modern era—with an artificial coherence and minus its conflicts and contradictions—is misleading, a more supple move has been to narrate modernity, to see it as an unfolding of related processes over time. Modernity is the consequence of the rise of capitalism, of states, and of bureaucracy. Anthropologist Charles Piot calls modernity "those everyday forms of culture, politics, and economy associated with the rise of industrial capitalism in Europe of the sixteenth, seventeenth, and eighteenth centuries and disseminated globally by European imperial expansion—forms, however, which have no essence and whose content is unstable and shifting."[29] Or take this definition from sociologists Roger Friedland and Deirdre Boden: "We treat modernity simply as the intertwined emergence of capitalism, the bureaucratic nation-states, and industrialism, which, initiating in the West but now operating on a global scale, has also entailed extraordinary transformations of space and time."[30] And finally this from political scientist Timothy Mitchell: "We should acknowledge the singularity and universalism of the project of modernity, a universalism of which imperialism is the most powerful expression and effective means; and, at the same time, attend to a necessary feature of this universalism that repeatedly makes its realization incomplete. . . . If the logic and movement of history—or of capitalism, to use an equivalent term—can be produced only by displacing and discounting what remains heterogeneous to it, then the latter plays the paradoxical but unavoidable role of the 'constitutive outside.'"[31]

These authors define modernity by its cause: capitalism did it, or some combination of capitalism, imperialism, and state-building. But they are much less clear about what it is whose causation they delineate. This conception only *appears* historical: the history they evoke is canned, a three-hundred- or four-hundred-year story that we need only name. There is a significant divergence here from classic modernization theory: these approaches refuse the notion of a certain pathway that others, in their separate ways, will follow. Modernity exists and can exist only on a global scale, and the task of the scholar is not to compare discrete instances of it but to analyze the relationship of particular cases to the totality.[32] The long story of modernity is still about the making of a package, but we have only an evocation of the process of making and no specification of its contents.

Let us call this way of narrating movement toward modernity "capitalism-plus." The development of capitalism in Europe and its extension via imperialism and world markets to the rest of the world (never mind that empires linking distant territories predate capitalism by centuries) are seen as the motor of history, but seeking to avoid the economistic version of Marxist theory, such arguments bring in state-building and bureaucratization. Going beyond the Parsonian notion of covariance of social, cultural, and economic pattern variables, these arguments insist on a causative priority for capitalism, with the other variables going along with it.

Anthony Giddens also hinges his view of modernity on the capitalism-plus argument, but, like 1950s modernization theorists, he specifies its results. Modernity is the homogenization of space and time, from the rich and varied ways in which people situated themselves in their contexts to an impersonal interchangeability. The argument derives from Marx's analysis of commoditization—the way in which the development of capitalism makes human labor, like material objects, into goods exchangeable for any other goods from any place. The workers' time becomes sellable by the hour, regardless of social context. These arguments can be extended, via an analysis of bureaucracy or the participation of individual citizens in electoral processes, into a notion of disenchantment (Weber's term), the depersonalization of social interaction, and the transformation of different forms of personal affinity and emotionally laden connections into transactions among individuals and between individual citizens and the state.[33]

The best historical scholarship on capitalism has emphasized that the story needs to be pulled apart rather than mushed together: it brings out different trajectories of capitalist development; the extent to which different forms of production are articulated with each other; the importance of state protection, regulation of markets, and support to particular capitalist classes; the varied trajectories of capitalist economies; the unevenness and segmentation of labor markets; the varied roles of gender in the organization of production; and the importance of territorially bounded institutions for containing the contradictions and dangers of capitalism and deterritorialized exchange.[34] If, on the contrary, one moves beyond the *specific* effects of capitalist development (or state-building, for that matter), one recreates modernization theory's problem of treating modernity as fully integrated and coherent. One misses the reappropriations of the tangibleness of space or the particularity of conceptions of time, from Manchester to Madras. The new modernity, like the old modernization, puts such emphasis on secularization that it misses the acute importance of religion to the most dynamic periods of British and American history in the nineteenth century (or in the United States today), let alone the great variety of relationships between religion and social change elsewhere in the world.[35] In slipping all too easily from identifying the importance of capitalism as a mode of production to making broad assertions about cultural and political life, the capitalism-plus school leaves us with a generic picture of the very processes whose importance it has emphasized.

Responses to modernity, in these arguments, are sometimes varied, and some analyses (see below) give more weight than others to the variations. But modernity can only be singular and universal.[36] "It" has concrete manifestations—visible in the landscape, describable in government institutions, tangible in our taken-for-granted social relations, in our conceptions of space and time, in the place of religion in our lives, in our notions of private zones and public life, in our aesthetic notions, and in our sense of who we are.

But what if we think of modernity as a representation, as the end point of a certain narrative of progress, which creates its own starting point (tradition) as it defines itself by its end point? To see modernity as the story of the "it"—without necessarily accepting the tangibility of the it—is a useful way of seeing things, but it is a demanding one, for it is convincing only as an empirical argument: Do people tell a story of progress? Which people? Is it a story about the West, about the United States, about England, about China, about the world as a whole? Is tradition modernity's invention of its negation in some or all such representations? If the narrative is our concern, how do we write about the fact that in a single place some intellectuals might believe that modernity can be defined scientifically and that their society fulfills those criteria, while others may disagree on either or both points? Some believe modernity is a good (and identifiable) thing, some a bad thing, and some that it is a good story or a bad story. It might be a story told by intellectuals or by ordinary people, by the person writing the account in question or the people about whom the account is written.

A Process (Multiple)

But if some emphasize the global, unitary process of capitalist development and European imperialism, others emphasize that its effects were multiple: Donald M. Nonini and Aihwa Ong use the plural to define their focus:

"global capitalism and its modernities."[37] The possessive pronoun makes modernities wholly derivative from capitalism but implies that one needs another term to designate capitalism's effects. Here we have the pluralizing version of the capitalism-plus argument.

Indeed, even some veteran modernization theorists, like Shmuel Eisenstadt, have joined the multiple modernities school. Conceding that the convergence theory does not work, they add theme and variations to the older modernization theory, softening but not giving up the notion of connected socio-cultural traits moving from tradition to modernities.[38] Others take off from the capitalism-plus argument and permit a wider degree of variation. Lisa Rofel writes, "Modernity enfolds and explodes by means of global capitalist forms of domination in conjunction with state techniques for normalizing its citizens." But "if one relocates modernity by viewing it from the perspective of those marginalized or excluded from the universalizing center, then it becomes a mutable project developed in unequal cross-cultural dialogues and contentions." Her book not only documents particular forms of the project in Communist and post-Communist China, but the diverse understandings one can develop of its effects and meanings through the lens of gender.[39] Another China scholar, Aihwa Ong, goes further. She emphasizes "how non-western societies themselves make modernities *after their own fashion,* in the remaking of the [sic] rationality, capitalism and the nation in ways that borrow from but also transform western universalizing forms."[40] Her argument goes against the contention that modernity must be singular and global, emphasizing that the making of modernity, not just responses to it, is plural.

Others go still farther toward autonomous modernities. For Huri Islamoglu, the goal is "bringing into focus the universality of the experience of modernity, beyond the narrow confines of western Europe." With Peter Perdue, she defines modernity as "the multiple institutional forms, or orderings of social reality, that since the sixteenth century responded to and enabled commercial expansion and competition among different political entities."[41] That leaves virtually nothing out. The concept of modernity, multiplied, therefore runs the gamut, from a singular narrative of capitalism, the nation-state, and individualism—with multiple effects and responses—to a word for everything that has happened in the last five hundred years.

The Avant-Garde, the Tradition of Modernity, or Just About Anything

At the extreme, we have truly arrived at the telos. To Arjun Appadurai and Carol Breckenridge, "Modernity is now everywhere, it is simultaneously everywhere, and it is interactively everywhere."[42] Or else modernity is conflated with all of human history in the last several centuries. Marshall Berman takes Marx's famous phrase from the *Manifesto*, "All that is solid melts into air," and moves beyond Marx's focus on the way commodity relations dissolve social ties. From the sixteenth to the eighteenth century, "people are just beginning to experience modern life"; after the 1790s, "a great modern public abruptly and dramatically comes to life"; in the twentieth century, "the process of modernization expands to take in virtually the whole world." Modernity, to Berman, was experienced as adventure, power, flux, and joy, as well as disintegration and anguish. His is a restless modernity, avant-gardist, a project as much as a realization. He links a Marxist historical conception to the famous evocation of Baudelaire: "Modernity is the transitory, the fugitive, the contingent." And he anticipates what Harry Harootunian says about interwar Japan: "For Japanese, modernity was speed, shock, and the spectacle of constant sensation."[43] These are grand themes of intellectual and cultural history, but Berman's schematization does not do the necessary historical work in regard to Europe, let alone elsewhere. The interplay of change and stability in social thought and social behavior is much more convoluted than his celebrationist/condemnatory rhetoric.

Bernard Yack is well justified in his riposte: "All that is solid is not melting." He cites the example of the supposedly most modern of the modern political systems, the United States, where an attitude prevails that is close to "ancestor worship" of the Constitution and where political institutions of 2002 as much as 1802 exhibit high degrees of inertia.[44] Some British historians claim that the special feature of British modernity is a high degree of continuity, avoidance of too much avant-gardism and too much imagination, and the care with which a tradition of Britishness is preserved amid incremental change.[45] The stability of property regimes in Western democracies is notable as well, and care needs to be taken about commonplace invocations (modern or postmodern) of flux and rootlessness.

As Jürgen Habermas points out, conservative writers on modernity like Daniel Bell juxtapose the avant-gardist, restless, all-questioning aspect of cultural modernism to a social, political, and economic modernity that they see as rationalist, orderly, and disciplined. The latter is claimed as the achievement of European history; the former is blamed for the ills of the present: hedonism, failure of social identification, a culture of transgressivity, narcissism, withdrawal from the mundane affairs of the world. This bifurcated notion of modernity, Habermas points out, obscures the complexity of the social, political, and economic processes in a capitalist world—the destructiveness of capitalism as well as its failures to fulfill promises of social betterment. Postmodernists, while celebrating (and claiming for themselves) the cultural transgressivity that alarms Bell, are also wont to overlook the gritty details of social and economic life and to hold a disdainful irony toward those (modernists!) who actually think they can do something to make life a little better.

As the modernities proliferate, the capacity to distinguish modernity from anything else is diminished. John and Jean Comaroff take this tendency to its logical conclusion, "In itself, 'modernity' has no a priori telos or content. It is colorless, odorless, and tasteless. . . . [M]odernity is not an analytic category. It is an ideological formation; an unstable, often inchoate one, to be sure, but an ideological formation nonetheless." But do they mean it to be quite as colorless as this quotation implies? Not really: "Modernity, itself always historically constructed, being understood here as an ideological formation in terms of which societies valorize their own practices by contrast to the specter of barbarism and other marks of negation." This formulation would make ancient Rome and China of two thousand years ago modern, and makes the observer, not the native, the one who decides when modernity appears. And then the Comaroffs' modernity gets even less like a native's category, whether the native be Rostow or a Tswana elder: "Modernity, as an ideological formation, may have grown out of the history of European capitalism. But, like capitalism, it has not remained there. It has seeded itself, in various and complex ways, across the globe." Here we have the " 'multiple' and 'alternative' modernities." Yet there is an "it" that is seeded and multiplied, a story of Western capitalism, now with the emphasis on its varied ideological effects, on the richness and variety of its representations. We may not know, in advance, what these representations are, but we already know, it seems, what is being represented. If people have different modernities, the reason the Comaroffs consider these representations to be modernities is that they assume that each person's narration is linked to theirs: that each person is telling a tale of progress, whose roots are in capitalism and imperialism—even if it takes an anthropologist to point that out.[46]

In the second volume of their rich and insightful study *Of Revelation and Revolution*, subtitled *The Dialectics of Modernity on a South African Frontier*, the modernity in question has become more coherent and more clearly part of a grand narrative. They are interested in "the postenlightenment self that was especially vital to its place in Protestant theology, practice theory, and the history of modernity." In studying how Protestant missionaries brought such a self to Africa, they show how the missionary message and the missionary practice insinuated a series of practices into Tswana life: they describe forms of dress, house styles, cleanliness—personal habits that mark the individual—and they analyze the undermining of collective habits, particularly notions of healing and ritual. They end up with the "struggle—endemic to colonialism in general and to the civilizing mission in particular—over the making of the modernist [sic] subject. . . . All of these things came together in the construction of the right-minded, right-bearing, propertied individual; a being untangled from 'primitive' webs of relations and free to enter both contracts and the church." What they will find in the "fissures" of this discourse will turn out to be the roots of "black resistance," but the struggle—"conversation," they sometimes term it—between missionaries and Tswana has indeed produced a modernity out of which new phases of struggle come.[47] There is much to mull over in this valuable ethnography and complex analysis, but in the end, whose modernity is it about?

A case *can* be made for a modernity that situates itself as an alternative to one laid out by missionaries or colonizers intent on remaking indigenous societies. The most explicit case for this comes in the essays of Dipesh Chakrabarty and other subalternists, notably their elucidation of a Bengali-modern position. Chakrabarty documents that a number of Bengali intellectuals in the late nineteenth century engaged British claims to represent progress and British indictments of features of Hindu culture. He shows that the goal of these thinkers was to lay out a progressive Hinduism that sought to make good use of aspects of British technology, law, and social practices, but which also saw that Hindu civilization was not static and that elements of it could be built upon to create a more prosperous and progressive India that was still true to its cultural values. The crucial question in such examinations is empirical: Did such thinkers specifically fight their battles on the turf of modernity, engaging a vision that represented itself as modernizing and proposing an alternative to it? Or can one characterize their thought more precisely using other terminology, and particularly can one avoid confusion of present-day frameworks with those of their own time?[48]

In less historically rich cases, the danger is that any notion of improvement or progress—of directed change or change welling up from social processes—becomes another modernity.[49] Whether one emphasizes the engagement of non-European thinkers with European thought or their use of frameworks that can be called "their own," the formulation of alternative modernity is empty unless one can demonstrate both the alternative and the modernity. That depends on analysis of how people formulate their conceptions, which might or might not fall into a language or a form of argument that they see as modernity.[50] Setting out to do an anthropology of modernity, in other words, is not a good research strategy. *Finding* a discourse of modernity could be a revealing demonstration.

The alternative modernity argument of Chakrabarty or Gyan Prakash has the virtue of bringing out the diversity and complexity of the ways in which South Asian thinkers came to grips with a situation in which they confronted not only the material might of a colonizing power but that power's claim to represent progress. The force of their argument depends on their juxtaposition of the multiplicity of forms of reason in South Asia with the singularity of post-Enlightenment rationality in Europe, the uniformity of European modernity throughout the entire era after the Enlightenment.[51] The pleasure of seeing Europeans become the people without history is offset by the difficulty this juxtapositional approach poses to seeing if the writings and actions of people in the colonies ever forced Europeans to rethink their own ideological constructs.

Making Claims and Making Revolutions

The intellectual cost of proliferating modernities has been powerfully spelled out by James Ferguson, for it is precisely the singularity and universality of the modern that made it so compelling in a certain historical moment. Ferguson points out that the appeal of modernization—to African mineworkers in the 1950s and 1960s as much as to political leaders or development professionals—has been its claim that economic and social standards can be made to converge *at the level of the most affluent societies.* For most Africans, he insists, modernity has quite concrete meanings—health facilities, education, decent pensions, opportunity to sell one's crops and obtain useful commodities from elsewhere—and the language of modernization gave them a basis for asserting claims: if you think we should be modern, help us find the means. In his sensitive ethnography of Zambian mine workers in an era when their hard-won wages and pensions have been eroded by inflation, when facilities that once seemed to be improving have collapsed, when childhood mortality that seemed to be declining is resurgent, Ferguson writes the story of modernization as a story of claims made, expectations that they might at least in part be realized, and bitter disappointment about the modernization that never came to be.

The issue here is not whether modernity *is* singular or plural, but how the concept is *used* in the making of claims. Modernization—as a policy as much as a theory—pointed in its heyday to the depth of global hierarchy and promised that eventually material standards would converge upward. Not only have such hopes been dashed—especially since the crises of the 1970s wiped out most of the modest but significant economic growth many

African countries had experienced previously—but influential international organizations and many academics have turned modernization from
a policy goal into a static hierarchy, as Ferguson argues. A new economic
orthodoxy in the 1980s and 1990s spurned policy initiatives to promote development, but classified countries by how well their economies did according to the criteria of the market. Meanwhile, Ferguson notes, anthropologists looking for multiple modernities miss the importance and the
tragedy of this story of possibilities opened and closed in a decolonizing
world.[52]

Donald Donham makes a different case for a singular notion of modernity being used to mobilize a population during the Ethiopian revolution.
Focusing on a rural area far from the center of the old Ethiopian monarchy,
he shows how an ideology that emphasized repudiation of the regime—and
the Ethiopian past—in favor of a radically new future gained force through
the interaction of peasants, mission converts, students, and soldiers. His
analysis is compelling because he locates a specific conjuncture in the
1970s, when Haile Selassie's own project of top-down modernization came
apart and Marxist radicals portrayed the status quo as backwardness. By
the 1980s, this forward-looking, mobilizing ideology had turned into a new
form of state coercion, and by the 1990s the modernizing impetus was
lost.[53] This historically located approach contrasts with the metahistorical
one, where the specificity of claims, representations, and ideological positioning disappears into a three-hundred-year history that is named (capitalism, bureaucratization, modernity) rather than analyzed.

The ghost of Talcott Parsons hovers over current writing about modernity as much as his personage hovered over the modernization debate.[54]
But as soon as one takes apart the fixity of his package of pattern variables
and posits multiple trajectories leading to multiple modernities, the intu-
itive salience of the label *modern* becomes more problematic. Everything is
simultaneously modern; modernity is everything that history made;
modernity is everywhere the constructed relationship of the modern to the
traditional. Such conceptions beg many historical questions, not least of
them when and why the "moderns" tried to make everyone else modern
and when and why they did not.

PACKAGING, REPACKAGING, AND UNPACKING MODERNITY

In modernization theory, the idea that changes in economic, political, de-
mographic, and cultural life all changed together added up to a compelling

vision of an entire world remade. The critics of modernization theory were most effective in taking apart the package, forcing a more careful examination of different elements of a changing social picture and their connection to each other.

The critique of modernity restores the package, now insisting that it is a bad one. The alternative modernity argument is a repackaging argument, for it leaves intact the Western notion of modernity, then proposes alternative packages.[55] As long as the package idea is retained, the alternative contains a premise that has political implications as dangerous as those of the modern in the eyes of its critics. To call, in Japan of the 1920s and 1930s, for example, for a Japanese modernity was to posit a bounded Japanese entity moving forward through time, in contrast to both the imperialist modernity of the West and the modernities—or worse still, nonmodernities—of other peoples. Harry Harootunian has shown the diverse ways in which Japanese intellectuals took apart the package of modern culture they perceived as the consequence of Western capitalism, but the effort of some of these people to put together another package created an "eternalized" order with a reified sense of what it meant to be Japanese.[56] Whether such discourses in other instances followed this direction—toward national chauvinism—is a problem for historical analysis, but my point here is that one has to be just as careful about celebrating multiple modernities as about attributing to a singular modernity more coherence than it has.

If one's focus is on how different people respond to colonization and capitalism, it is important to keep the spectrum of possibilities open: empirical analysis might well reveal a singular modernity to which people laid claim; or the package might be seen as singular but rejected in the name of "tradition"; or people might see both opportunities and constraints in the economic niches and social networks that open up, to which they will react with varying mixtures of instrumentality and enthusiasm; or they might think their thoughts and make their claims with little regard to the traditional/modern, internal/external polarities.[57] Here is where the scholars' modernity—that is, modernity as an analytic category—is likely to get in the way of understanding whatever indigenous categories need to be investigated.

What does it mean, in Europe or elsewhere, to claim to *be* modern? Bruno Latour reverses European assertions of making a breakthrough in scientific and social thought when he insists, "We have never been modern." In order to be modern, he argues, "the moderns" had to distinguish themselves from the ancients, rejecting the "entire work of mediation," yet the moderns have created the types of analysis that make possible modes of mediation and hybridity. Modern reason depends on making distinctions that determine how humans will act and how humans will understand their world—between nature and society, between ancient and modern—yet reason shows the impossibility of these distinctions, the proliferation of "hybrids." The modern who narrates European history since the eighteenth century in terms of modernity does so by willfully occluding everything that doesn't fit, violating the very canons of modern reason.[58]

If one can follow Latour in taking modernity away from the Europeans and follow many scholars of Asia and Africa who insist that "we have always been modern," one is left with a concept that has played an important role in making claims but does little analytic work.[59] Most problematic of all is giving the package of modernity causal significance. Modernity appears as an agent in this typical phrase: "Modernity changed the representation of space and time." Or again, the agency of the modern appears in a scholar's call for "a critical interrogation of the practices, modalities, and projects through which modernity inserted itself into and altered the lives of the colonized."[60] Perhaps this is abbreviated, imprecise phraseology; the author really means to say that people who operated within the representational framework of modernity did the acting. But the writing is indicative of a deeper problem: the package of modernity substitutes for analysis of debates, actions, trajectories, and processes as they took place in history.[61]

What does it mean to make modernity the agent? Colonialism is an aspect of modernity in the here-and-now sense of modernity, but then it could hardly be anything else. The people responsible for the murderous wars of colonial conquest, for the cruelties of colonial labor recruitment, for the wanton violence of repression from the 1904–7 Herero revolt to the 1947 Madagascar revolt were "moderns."

Colonialism was very much part of the twentieth century. So too was anticolonialism. So was fascism and antifascism, racism and antiracism. People made their moral and political choices. They did so within specific, often conflicting, ideological constructs and historical contexts. Some may have claimed to speak for modernity when arguing for or against racial discrimination, but neither those actors nor those frameworks can be reduced to modernity. And colonialism, like Nazism, drew vitally on notions whose history—from empires with a long continuous history to notions of command and status—extends back in time and cannot be reduced to post-Enlightenment rationality, liberalism, or science. It is no more helpful to credit the end of colonialism in the 1960s to the march of modernity than to claim that modernity conquered the Zulu in the 1870s. That the moderns' capacity for rational organization was used to organize transportation of deportees to Auschwitz and to police the migrations of Africans in apartheid South Africa is not an argument against building railroads, and the murderous consequences of such "development" projects as Stalin's or Mao's versions of forced collectivization are not convincing arguments against efforts to build national healthcare institutions.[62] A whiggish view of progress, in which evil after evil falls before the increasing power of human rationality, is more persuasively countered by efforts to locate ideological and political responsibility historically than by maintaining the argument at the level of agentless abstractions.

These concerns are all too real today. While some (but not all) Islamic mullahs attack "Western modernity" as a degenerate, antireligious totality, some (but not all) American mullahs attack Islam as being "antimodern." Difficult issues are being debated about the options open to societies in the Middle East and elsewhere, about the constraints, limits, and effects of American power in different regions, about the relevance in different contexts of "universal" notions of the rights of women and "Islamic" notions of modesty and status.[63] Historians have no privileged vantage point to intervene on such issues, but they can remind people of the range of ways in which problems can be framed and that any framing will have its consequences. Framing debates in terms of modernity, antimodernity, and alternative modernities has not provided a precise or suggestive vocabulary for analyzing the relationship of different elements of change, the alternative ways in which political issues can be framed, or conflicting dreams of the future.

THE CRITIQUE OF UNIVERSALISM— AND OF PARTICULARISM

Both the value and the limits of thinking about modernity in colonial situations may be approached by contrasting two arguments, one well disseminated and well received in the American academy, by the Indian historian Dipesh Chakrabarty, the other little known beyond francophone Africanist circles and controversial within them, by the Cameroonian journalist Axelle Kabou. The contrast will be revealing. Let us begin with Chakrabarty's contribution to the critique of modernity.[64]

Chakrabarty is in no way attempting a blanket denial of social science theory tainted by association with the West—he has himself both contributed to and used Marxist theory.[65] He does not want to allow—as many Marxists and others have done—a stylized interpretation of Western history to become a benchmark for all other histories, positing a modernity that others cannot quite attain. Instead, he insists that "modernist" conceptions of modernity miss the way imperialism constructed Europe and India in the same process, as modernity and backwardness incarnate. He argues that the most deadly manifestation of backwardness—ethnic chauvinism and intolerance—is itself part of the modernizing project, for its impetus to classify and enumerate the population turned shades of difference into rigid units around which power was organized and resources allocated. Liberal theory is incapable of understanding—and certainly incapable of fashioning the political mechanisms to deal with—communal feeling or religious values because of its insistence that the relevant unit of understanding is the universal human being, the individual.[66] A modernity of enlightenment and secularism implies a tradition of irrationality and superstition. But, he argues, it is precisely in recognizing the limits of rational analysis—the existence of worlds not amenable to classification and enumeration, of cultural practices not reducible to either irrationality or rational calculation—through a philosophy of "difference" and "noncommensurability," that one can better understand how India was produced and acquire a fuller sense of how diverse people within those boundaries understand themselves and articulate their aspirations.[67]

Chakrabarty denies that he seeks "a simple rejection of modernity, which would be, in many situations, politically suicidal." He accepts "the immense practical utility of left-liberal political philosophies," and hopes that a fuller understanding of just what these notions signify historically will "help teach the oppressed of today how to be the democratic subject of tomorrow."[68] It is not so much the thought of rejecting liberal ideals with which Chakrabarty wants to leave his readers, but his sense of the loss that attends the history of modernity.

Axelle Kabou fears the loss that attends Africa's failure to engage with modernity. Her book has a question as its title: *What If Africa Refused Development?*[69] She admits most readers would think the question absurd—African governments have made the "battle for development" into the rationale for their existence. Yet she argues that this assertion is a myth, for African elites' reaction to the idea of development is not that they should organize to promote it, but quite the contrary: elite ideology revolves around on the one hand a culture of blame—a history of slaving and colonization and of a "neocolonial plot" responsible for Africa's woes—and on the other hand a claim that cultural authenticity defines a higher value than Western-oriented development allows. Development is central to elite ideology not because it sets a goal to which people can aspire (and against which an elite's performance could therefore be measured), but precisely because its failure reinforces the elite's continued claim to power, as the guardians of African authenticity against neocolonialism. When such an elite talks about development, it is therefore to demand handouts from abroad—reparations, aid—rather than to demand efforts from within. The origins of such a way of thinking, she acknowledges, lie in the brutality and humiliation of colonization. But now, elite ideology encourages a view that "development is 'something for whites,' " while the elite gives itself over to pursuit of its own narrow interests and to extravagance and waste. It has no desire to encourage "coherence, transparence, rigor," let alone analysis of what causes poverty and how it can be countered, but claims authority as the representative of "cultural self-defense." Kabou insists that a "culture of particularism" is invoked by an elite to justify "the most retrograde behavior and the actions most prejudicial to the liberty and dignity of Africans."[70]

If her contempt is directed at a corrupt and dictatorial leader like Mobutu—whose political program went by the name of "authenticity"—she is also critical of the more intellectually serious arguments, such as those of Cheikh Anta Diop, which invoke African cultural particularism in opposition to the West. Kabou's argument is not that one should abandon the one for the other, but that those aspects of African cultures that can be used creatively and positively should be encouraged and the others discarded. She in effect argues that the cultural incommensurability between Western and non-Western cultures that Chrakrabarty asserts is what needs to be overcome. The vision of an authentic African culture opposed to a neocolonial West is for Kabou self-serving for a corrupt elite and "suicidal" for Africa as a whole.[71]

Whereas Chakrabarty seeks to undermine the power of universality, Kabou rejects the ideological power of particularity. And her conclusion goes directly against the critique of Enlightenment rationality central to Chakrabarty's arguments: "The Africa of the 21st century will be rational or it won't be."[72]

Neither of these arguments is uncontested within its own geographic reference point.[73] To some extent, African intellectuals might be reacting to a colonial discourse that compartmentalized Africa into tribes, whereas Indian intellectuals react to the colonial construction of an essentialized, singular India. In any case, these two regions have much in common: not just terrible poverty that has resisted national development programs and foreign assistance, but the failure of state institutions to provide all people with education and health facilities, and widespread discrimination against women in regard to education, marriage, and inheritance.[74] In both regions, intercommunal conflict stems not from primordial cultural particularism but from a colonial and postcolonial history that hardened differentiation into institutionalized distinction. Postcolonial states failed to enhance or fairly distribute the resources that all needed, encouraging political and cultural entrepreneurs to turn sentiments of affinity into the mobilization of a communal faction that fought others for their due.[75]

The critique of universalism and the critique of particularism refer to different longings and different anxieties that are important parts of colonial and postcolonial experience. Both of these thoughtful and important arguments help us understand that the ways in which issues are framed in political discourse are neither self-evident nor innocent of the exercise of power in colonial and postcolonial situations. But both remain at too high a level of abstraction to explain *how* any framing developed in the course of interaction or struggle or to help us reframe issues in the future and discuss responsibility for specific actions.

There are real political dilemmas here, as the long debate among scholars of India about the past and present relationship of women's rights and community values has brought out.[76] Which right trumps which: that of an individual—a woman—to choose her spouse or make another decision as she wishes, or the right of a collectivity to "its" particularistic belief, which subordinates her right to make such decisions to that of other members, say male elders? Some would argue that the "liberal" position—that the woman should be free to choose, even if she chooses her own subordination—should govern here, but the critique of modernity holds that this response is insufficient. An individual woman might exercise choice, but she can choose to abide by the values of the community only if those values are preserved. Yet liberalism or citizenship theory have little to say about preserving communities, except to treat them as voluntary organizations. The survival of a community, one can argue, depends on its ability to police its boundaries, to hold its members to the values fundamental to it, and to make community membership more than something people turn on and off at will. Because a question like marriage is not simply a private matter, but one in which state and community both have an interest, the modern, liberal notion of religion or culture as a separate domain doesn't help us out of the dilemma. But if one goes too far in such a defense of community, we are left with a view of community and culture as self-contained—a position that is historically and sociologically inaccurate and politically untenable, for it immunizes any political system from interrogation except in the terms of those who dominate it. This logic brings us back to Kabou's fears.

What gets us out of the dilemma—or at least to a better understanding of it? Veena Das asks a very simple but profound question: Who has the most at stake? Where can a woman find support against the intrusiveness of her community as well as against the intrusiveness of the state or do-gooder outsiders? In an argument over a woman's rights and duties in marriage, the woman herself should be at the center, for her entire framework of relationships and individual and familial affinities is affected. Similarly, in writing about arguments between advocates of gender equality and of patriarchal traditions in South Africa, Cathi Albertyn and Shireen Hassim emphasize the importance of activists and the invocation of constitutional norms in forcing a debate, while insisting that the debate be pragmatic and specific, and not a zero-sum confrontation between feminism and traditionalism.[77] Such confrontations are by no means certain to produce compromises and mutual understanding, but the traditional as well as the national communities in question are themselves products of centuries of interaction and confrontation. One outcome is predictable: in a cultural confrontation over gender questions between a side that keeps uttering "universal human rights" and another that keeps saying "community values," the issues and the stakes the women face are likely to be lost.

The interconnection—and commensurability—of different parts of the world is not only a historical fact but a resource, for good, for bad, and for much that lies in between. Rights talk is effective insofar as it provides a resource—for example, for women critical of patriarchy to find allies and arguments beyond the local, regional, or national system of gender relations. Its power lies less in its association with "modernity" than with links to issue networks beyond a community.[78] Community talk is a resource as well, deployed against overbearing forces that threaten to sweep people before the tide of a supposedly universal history. One can recognize, with Chakrabarty, that "universal" values come with the baggage of colonial history and, with Kabou, that appeals to cultural specificity can be self-serving and constraining, but recognize that imposition from outside and defense of autonomy are not the only two alternatives. Organizational and discursive resources can bring together people across borders—contingently and with awareness of the asymmetrical power relations involved. How such confrontations play out cannot be predetermined: the gentle and the good do not necessarily triumph over the harsh and the oppressive. But, as Sheldon Pollock observes, if we can think about the tensions of universality and particularity without making "particularity ineluctable" or "universalism compulsory," we can think more historically about the past and more constructively about the future.[79]

Critics of modernity have been accused at times of giving aid and comfort to communitarian sentiments that, in practice, entail intolerance, indirectly lending credence to a right-wing argument for a specifically Hindu conception of Indian society. This is far from the intention or the arguments of such critics as Chatterjee and Chakrabarty. The problem is rather that they do not provincialize Europe enough, allowing community to appear as the antidote to imperialistic universality, or "our modernity" to be contrasted with "theirs." That universalism was less universal and less European in practice than it was in theory, shifting in response not only to the particularities encountered in the colonies but to reconfigurations of ideologies and practices some Europeans thought were their own. Having revealed how much the modern and the traditional were constructed in the process of colonialism, critics of modernity keep constructing these categories rather than finding ways to break out of them.[80] There is little to be gained in arguing that the solutions to the world's problems lie within modernity or outside it. A historical simplification leads to a misframing of contemporary issues.

This leads me to my second major example of how the concept of modernity frames debate in a less than fruitful way: James C. Scott's much-cited *Seeing Like a State*. Scott's target is what he calls "high modernism," by which he means a "muscle-bound" version of "the rational design of social order commensurate with the scientific understanding of natural laws."[81] Scott, like many others, misuses the word *modernism*, ignoring the critique, dissent, subjectivity, indeed wild creativity that was fundamental to modernism (see above), and leaving only a one-dimensional view of scientific rationality. From there, Scott argues that high modernism combined with what he calls "state simplifications," the administrative ordering of nature and society in a way that rendered it "legible" to planners who wished to reorder nature and society, plus two more factors, an authoritarian state and a weak civil society, to produce a "pernicious combination" responsible for the cases described in his book. Scott cites many ways in which the state's urge to produce "legibility" resulted in sterile, grid-like layouts in planning of city maps and in large-scale schemes for reordering productive systems. He concentrates on extreme cases, notably high-modernist urban planning in Brasília, the capital of Brazil, Lenin's revolutionary party and Stalin's collectivization, compulsory villagization in Tanzania after 1968, and various experiments in agricultural planning. The example of the Nazis hovers around the edges, mentioned but not analyzed as a "high-modernist utopianism of the right."[82] In contrast to the high modernism that he condemns, Scott uses the Greek work *mētis,* which he glosses as practical, locally rooted knowledge, the mixture of ideals for change with acceptance of the messiness of life, a more personal sense of human relations.

The best example of high modernism that appears in Scott's text is James C. Scott himself. He has simplified each of his cases to render it "legible," taking away the patron-client relationships and mechanisms of personal rule that fingered enemies and turned plans into political infighting in the Soviet Union, the ways in which local power brokers in rural Tanzania manipulated their local and central connections to build a very unrationalized form of power, the networks that sprang up among the poor in Brasília or in Tanzania to gain access to resources outside of official channels, the way in which landowners in areas of supposedly modernist agriculture turned appeals to market rationality and scientific practice into particularistic access to resources, undermining reform in the interests of self-aggrandizement. The simplifying logic of high modernism, in each of Scott's cases, turns out to be anything but simplifying, not so much because of resistance as because the supposedly modern apparatus of rule was itself laced through with particularistic mechanisms. Scott acknowledges some of the difficulty in demonstrating that modernism was ever truly high, claiming that the difficulties of implementing high-modernist plans show their inherent impossibility. But throughout the book he slips in the opposite direction, from projects that meet his extreme criteria to denunciation of the very fact of "seeing like a state."[83]

Lacking here is a "control group"—forms of *mētis* that are distinct from high modernism and produce preferable outcomes. Let me suggest an example of "high mētis" to be set against Scott's examples of high modernism: the Zaire of Mobutu Sésé-Séko. No modernist he, no believer in making the state the instrument of a social ideal. Mobutu practiced the politics of personal fiefdom. He was known to claim supernatural as well as governmental powers; his local knowledge was acute. He operated through henchmen whose ties to him and to their own followers were highly personal. And he worked quite cooperatively and pragmatically with international banks, with architects who built modern-looking buildings, and so on. The outcome in Mobutu's Zaire is not an obvious improvement on that achieved in Nyerere's Tanzania.

That is not to defend Nyerere's villagization program, let alone Stalinism, nor is it to deny the dangers of excess zeal in the direction of too much planning or, for that matter, too much faith in nonregulated markets or in the notion that "small is beautiful." But what Scott has failed to show is that his two central concepts, the state and high modernism, are helpful in separating hubristic excess from balanced social reform. In the future, we will face, as in the past, situations where people claim that knowledge and planning will improve lives. Some problems may be confronted on a large scale only, some would best not be. The grandiose has indeed appeared in state projects, but has hardly been limited to the modern world: pyramids, road networks, aqueducts, and claims to constitute a universal empire were part of ancient empires. Scott is at pains to insist that he is not for banishing every reformist ideal from the realm of politics, but he can only add another layer of rationalist analysis—the critique of the big plan—to his denunciation of rationalist social planning, missing the spirit of critique and skepticism that has been intrinsic to modernism.[84] Scott's passing claim that he does not mean to favor unfettered market capitalism begs the question of what kinds of structures are capable of countering the power of corporate capitalism.[85] We need to make distinctions, and condemning the systematic and celebrating the messy will not help us make them.

COLONIAL MODERNITY?

I have already suggested that viewing the history of Europe through the frame of modernity obscures the ongoing, unresolved conflicts at the heart of European culture and politics. The same can be said about the history of nineteenth- and twentieth-century colonization. The notion of *colonial modernity* has attained a certain cachet in history and other disciplines. To the extent that some, most famously Schumpeter, have argued that colonialism was atavistic—that colonies gave a field of play to an aristocratic, militaristic outlook no longer tenable in Europe itself—refutation of the nonmodern character of colonialism is in order.[86]

But colonial modernity signifies something stronger than the here-and-now definition. "In the colonial world," writes David Scott, "the problem of *modern* power turned on the politico-ethical project of producing subjects and governing their conduct." The "formation of colonial modernity" represented a "discontinuity in the organization of colonial rule characterized by the emergence of a distinctive political rationality—a colonial governmentality—in which power comes to be directed at the destruction and reconstruction of colonial space so as to produce not so much extractive-effects on colonial bodies as governing-effects on colonial conduct."[87] Antoinette Burton refers to "the determination of the colonial state and its cultural agencies to produce colonial modernities through the regulation of cultural difference as read onto the bodies of men and women—through technologies of science, the law, ethnography, spirituality, motherhood, marriage, travel-writing and the postcard." Achille Mbembe asserts, "Like Islam and Christianity, colonization is a universalizing project. Its ultimate aim is to inscribe the colonized in the space of modernity."[88]

There were colonial initiatives in the nineteenth and twentieth centuries that might be described this way.[89] But does it make sense to say that the sum of such efforts produced a "colonial modernity" or that colonial policy makers in this era, or some section thereof, intended them to do so? The formulations cited above mistake arguments *within* colonial regimes for an essence of colonial rule in the "modern" era.

The most vigorous case for the imposition of modern governmentality on colonies comes from historians of India. It hinges on the importance British officials attached to institutions that defined the subject in relation to the state: the census, the cadastral survey, and more generally the collection of knowledge that defines a "population" and can be used to maintain surveillance and superintend social change. Bernard Cohn's pioneering analyses of knowledge-gathering mechanisms convincingly showed that India was as important a laboratory for working out such systems in the nineteenth century as were the British Isles.[90] But if an Indian history of censuses and classifications is supposed to reveal colonial modernity in the nineteenth century, then what is one to make of the fact that the first census in Kenya that counted indigenous people was conducted only in 1948, and that before then officials showed no interest in taking one?[91] Colonial states did not necessarily want or need to see individual subjects in relation to the state or to classify and enumerate them on various axes; they belonged in tribes and could be governed through the collectivity. Whereas European governments may have wanted to separate populations into the sane and the insane, the criminal and the orderly, and to devise institutions that marked their subjects, colonial institutions often put more stress on the maladjustment of the collectivity than of the individual, and colonial penology continued into the post–World War II era to make use of precisely those punishments that from a Foucauldian perspective should have been supplanted by modern governmentality—flogging, collective punishment of villages and kinship groups, and penal sanctions for contract violations.[92] Colonial regimes in Africa were notably unable to routinize and normalize their exercise of power, and they were equally incoherent in their efforts to harness "tradition" and "traditional rulers" to a stable pattern of governance.[93]

Certainly, several nineteenth-century colonial regimes had their versions of James Mill, who saw little possibility of progress within indigenous cultural traditions and hoped for a thoroughgoing remaking of India.[94] But then one should consider the extent to which the Indian government pulled its punches: its unwillingness to undertake the necessary risks and expenditures to foster economic development, the constraints it felt because of the delicacy of its relationship with Indian elites, its caution in individualizing land tenure or developing industry, its miserable record in education and health, and its willingness to live, to an embarrassingly large extent, from indigenous land revenue collection and commercial networks.[95] If many officials thought better knowledge of Indian society would convey more power, ignorance was just as characteristic of the regime, and "information panics and ideological frenzies . . . reflected the weakness of the new quasi-bureaucratic state in its own hinterland."[96]

In colonial Africa, modernization projects were important in certain moments and certain contexts. Meanwhile, the inability and disinterest of regimes in establishing an apparatus of routine control lay behind some of the worst instances of colonial violence; early-twentieth-century economic policy included the coercive, brutal extraction of resources in King Leopold's Congo or the "old empire" style of the concessionary company in France's Equatorial Africa, and conflicts continued between colonizers who favored the grab-what-one-can approach and those who sought to build structures favoring long-term profitability and expansion. The best success stories of colonial economies, such as cocoa production in the Gold Coast or Nigeria, reflected above all the initiatives of African farmers, and colonial authorities happily benefited from their efforts without asking too many questions about the producers' subject positions or how they adapted "traditional" kinship systems to agricultural innovation.[97]

If one is to take seriously the "civilizing mission" enunciated by the government of the French Third Republic at the end of the nineteenth century, then one should take note of the important argument of J. P. Daughton that colonial rulers devoted few resources—teachers, doctors, engineers—to the cause, but that the inveterate foes of secular republicanism, the Catholic Church, sent a vastly larger body of men into the empire, aimed not at civilizing but at converting, at fostering a social order far more hierarchical and traditionalist than that advocated at home and overseas by republican modernizers. And one should note as well that even the republican government backed off its civilizing mission after World War I in favor of a politics of retraditionalization.[98] If British missionaries sought to extract individuals from a web of social relations and integrate them as individuals into markets and institutions of governance, then what is one to make of the effort of the state to marginalize those people—labeled "detribalized natives"—who had gone the farthest in detaching themselves from custom and kinship? Religious conversion and education had proponents who wished to colonize minds, but the empires spent little money on such objectives until, after 1945, they realized in near panic that their effort to relegitimize and reinvigorate their empires demanded skilled personnel whom they had not produced and forms of political incorporation that they had heretofore blocked.

Should one consider colonial campaigns against indigenous forms of slavery, widow burning, or child marriage as part of a coherent campaign to impose a universal notion of the rights-bearing individual on backward cultures? Or is there something pathetic about these colonial initiatives, an admission that their transformative ambitions could never be realized and that the best they could do was to mark certain "primitive practices," to isolate them from their social context, to try to excise them from a "traditional society," and then to represent the colonial state's failure to do so as evidence of the irredeemable backwardness of the colonized?[99] In the first decades after conquest in both French and British Africa, some policy makers advocated vigorous programs to turn slavery into wage labor and to open new areas to commerce, but they soon learned the limits of how much they could manipulate African productive systems.[100] In the 1920s and 1930s, France and Britain considered and rejected programs of using metropolitan resources to build better infrastructure in African colonies and contented themselves with a less dynamic vision of colonial economies, colonial labor, and rule over "traditional" societies.

But by the 1940s, policy makers in France and Britain felt they needed a more systematic effort to develop productive resources, a more thorough program of socializing workers to regular employment and urban living, and a more forward-looking image for colonial policy.[101] There is therefore a good case to be made for identifying projects of modernization within specific conjunctures in colonial history, just as one can distinguish moments when the nontransformation of "traditional societies" played a key role in colonial ideology. But designating the entire experience as colonial modernity takes the force out of such arguments and discourages asking why and through what processes they emerged in a particular moment. Most importantly, one could easily pass over the way in which African mobilizations—as in the critical moments during and after the world wars—forced colonial regimes to reconfigure their policies, which in turn presented African social and political movements with new fissures to widen in the regime, new strategies of rule to counter, and new bases for large-scale mobilization.[102]

In the period after World War II, colonial modernizers, ahead of the academic modernization theorists, saw a package of covarying characteristics as markers of progress on the road from stultifying tradition to dynamic modernity. The question of whether the mission convert, newly trained teacher, or skilled worker accepted the package as a whole was now important. Colonial officials in the 1950s feared that an African who had acquired the technical skills to perform a certain job still might lack the motivation and social reinforcement to adapt to all aspects of an industrial or urban situation and might—like the partially converted Christian—backslide. Many officials were so taken with their modernizing role that they saw Africans who did not follow the script as willfully hostile to progress rather than quaintly backward, which helps to explain the bitter brutality of the repression of supposedly antimodern movements, notably Mau Mau.[103]

Extensive historical, anthropological, and sociological research on how such initiatives played out has revealed the *unpackaging* of this modernization effort. The mission station, even earlier, could become a site for continuing older patterns of kinship and peasant production protected from the predations of white settlers or rival communities. The payment of family wages intended to wean African workers from the resources of home villages could instead give men resources to promote extended families and to combine wage labor with trading networks and peasant farming. Urban migrants could reinforce rather than discard their rural connections and build within the city varied associational and personal networks. Western medicine could be incorporated into an enlarged repertoire of healing methods. Literacy could be used to record "tradition," to assert the contributions of Africa to humanity, or to forge networks of letter writers and petitioners who could challenge missionaries and government authorities. At the same time, economic expansion and modernization projects themselves exacerbated cleavages and insecurities, and people worked hard to develop old and new social networks, to straddle different kinds of economic activities, and to make use of different kinds of cultural resources to reduce insecurity and, hopefully, to build a better future.[104]

Neither the temporal patterns nor the contents of change fit the colonial modernity package—or alternative packages—but the story of this volatile moment (see chapter 7) suggests another way of looking at the language of modernity: as a claim-making device. A vivid example of the deployment of such a discourse came from unions representing African government employees during a major strike in Senegal in 1946. At the bargaining table, the union spokesmen silenced their French counterparts by saying, "Your goal is to elevate us to your level; without the means, we will never succeed."[105] Such claims were powerful because they linked well-organized social movements to colonial officials' eagerness to find a basis of legitimacy for an inclusive and unified imperial polity and their hope that Africans could, in fact, become productive and orderly participants in such a polity. Such claims would soon challenge the French government's illusions that it could direct—and pay for—a modernized imperialism.

Only by renouncing the central tenets of empire could the French government escape the implications of its modernizing ideology, notably the claim on French resources. But if France was willing at this point to move away from the logic of empire, it did not repudiate the logic of modernization. Indeed, officials were able to accept giving up colonial administration in part because they convinced themselves that Africans had acquired a vested interest in maintaining the "modern" structures that they had put in place, hence in continued cooperation with France, now between sovereign nations with unequal economic resources.[106] Such an argument made decolonization imaginable, but the very idea of the package that was modernization occluded rather than fostered officials' understanding of how postcolonial African polities would evolve.

We see here how the idea of modernization was *used* in a particular context, and we can trace the effects of its usage and its relation to politics on the ground. It is the intensity of this historically rooted process of making claims and counterclaims in the name of modernization that John Comaroff misses when he asserts that the multiple modernities he wishes to examine "have nothing to do with processes of modernization."[107]

In the postwar conjuncture, British and French governments and African and Asian social and political movements brought forth different modernization projects. So too did the United States government and its rival modernizer, the Soviet Union. Such diverse initiatives shaped for a time an international consensus that put modernization alongside sovereignty among the objectives of international organizations. For some state actors, the goal was to manage change in the era of decolonization. But for others, the point was to open new issues, to make claims on the resources of the "developed" world. For academics, the evident need for new knowledge and new theory gave them a part to play in a global drama. In this context, modernization theory both emerged and was called into question.[108]

How wide was the opening for intellectuals and activists to think about issues such as these? The critique of modernity recognizes that political contestation takes place within frameworks, and the history of colonization and decolonization has shaped the structures within which economic and social issues are debated, and the language with which they are discussed—

structures that remain unequal and languages that privilege certain modes of understanding. The question is whether treating colonial modernity as a package focuses on a set of closures without recognizing the openings that have been pried wider in the recent and more distant pasts. Literary scholar Simon Gikandi, for example, brings out the effort of Nigerian novelist Amos Tutuola to write, in his imaginative and evocative *The Palm Wine Drinkard,* outside the "symbolic economy of European modernity." But the critic won't let the novelist have his way: he insists that modernity must be for Africans an impossibility and a necessity, an impossibility because modernity "established its normativity by marking the African as one of its 'others,' subjects excluded from the informing categories of modern identity," and a necessity "because we cannot think of African pasts and futures except through the institutions and philosophies imposed on the continent through the modern (colonial) project." Yet Gikandi, like other critics, carries forth the work that he claims modernity has done, insisting that there really was a "modern project," that colonialism was part of it, and that there are no alternatives.[109] The literary imagination, as much as the political one, is being pushed back into the categories of tradition, modernity, antimodernity, and postmodernity—by scholars who claim to be revealing their conceptual tyranny. Perhaps a reading of the past giving more space to openings—to different ways of framing and reframing visions and issues—will provide a less closed outlook on the future.

CONCLUSION

We seem to be living modernization twice, the first time as earnestness, the second time as irony. But in juxtaposing the dream of using reason to make the world more prosperous, egalitarian, and responsive to the wishes of its inhabitants with the hubris of social engineering and the reinscription of hierarchy within nominally egalitarian systems, we risk missing the power and poignancy of dreams and aspirations and the range and complexity of efforts at transforming colonized societies. The critics lay bare the dangers of modernity's invention of "universal man" to be the model for the entire world, erasing the colonial origins of that man and the invention of his traditionalist, non-European "other" as his foil. But if they insist that modernity *is* a set of attributes or that modernity has a *genealogy* that can be reduced to capitalism and imperialism, critics award "modernity" to the most West-centered version of the story and look away from the importance of debate and struggle in shaping what reason, liberalism, equality, and rights can be claimed to mean.

The struggles were unequal, but they were not one-sided. Colonial voices might have to shout to be heard in European capitals, but at critical moments, the intensity of colonial conflicts, uncertainties about colonial policies, disagreements between those who wanted to save souls and those who wanted to exploit bodies, and competing visions of national missions and national interests provided fissures that colonized subjects, from Olaudah Equiano or Toussaint L'Ouverture in the 1790s to Muslim Indian activists in 1900 London to Senghor and Césaire in Paris in the 1930s and 1950s—along with known and unknown union organizers, peasant rebels, participants in millennial movements, and authors of pamphlets—were able to pry open.

There has been no unidirectional trend toward political inclusiveness, toward enhancing people's choice of modes of livelihood, or toward representing their collective or individualistic aspirations in the body politic, but political opportunities, struggles, and constraints are at times reconfigured. What is lost in opposing a European, capitalist, imperialist "modernity" to "alternative modernities" or a space of the nonmodern is the boundary-crossing struggle over the conceptual and moral bases of political and social organization. The asymmetry of conceptual power—the ability to make claims stick and to alter definitions of what is a debatable issue and what is not—is all the more reason to keep one's focus on how such concepts were used in historical situations.

My purpose has not been to purge the word *modernity* and certainly not to cast aside the issues that concern those who use the word. It is to advocate a historical practice sensitive to the different ways people frame the relationship of past, present, and future, an understanding of the situations and conjunctures that enable and disable particular representations, and a focus on process and causation in the past and on choice, political organization, responsibility, and accountability in the future.

PART III

The Possibilities of History

6 States, Empires, and Political Imagination

General Charles de Gaulle, speaking in Normandy on June 16, 1946, asserted that here "on the soil of the ancestors the State reappeared." After the nightmare of defeat, the French state would now reestablish "national unity and imperial unity." This dualism of nation and empire recurred throughout the speech: the state would "assemble all the forces of *la patrie* and the French Union"; it would unite "all the Empire and all of France." De Gaulle distinguished "the metropole" from "the overseas territories attached to the French Union by very diverse ties," while evoking the "future of 110 million men and women who live under our flag and in an organization of federal form." The majority of these French people did not live in European France.[1]

The French state, de Gaulle made clear, was not the French nation, and the nation was not the state. The state, represented by its president and its parliament, was the empire, renamed the French Union. It consisted on the one hand of what de Gaulle called the Republic, the nation, or *la patrie*, recently augmented by the "overseas departments," namely France's "old colonies" of the Caribbean promoted to the same status as the departments of mainland France, and on the other hand of La France d'Outre-Mer, that is, colonies, renamed overseas territories, and associated states (formerly protectorates, like Morocco and parts of Indochina). Algeria was territorially part of the Republic but its population was not treated equally. France, in 1946, was not a nation-state, but an empire-state.

Opposition to French rule often took such broad, imperial terms as well. Movements for national independence can only be understood in relation to other movements that made claims to rights and resources on the basis of belonging to Greater France, a singular political and moral unit. Anticolonial movements were not a stage along an inevitable pathway from empire to nation, but part of a wider pattern of struggle whose culmination in the multiplication of nation-states was conjunctural and contingent.

In this chapter, I will argue that both the way the leaders of empire-states thought about their polity and the forms in which political contestation took place reflect "thinking like an empire."[2] Where to find a balance between the poles of incorporation (the empire's claim that its subjects belonged within the empire) and differentiation (the empire's claim that different subjects should be governed differently) was a matter of dispute and shifting strategies. Balances were continually upset by the actions of people in the colonies. Far from being an anachronistic political form in the "modern era," this imperial perspective applies to France, Britain, and other important states of the nineteenth and twentieth centuries.

In this brief, schematic, and selective presentation of the importance and durability of imperial systems, I will look back to the precedents of Roman and Mongol empires, and their influence on subsequent imperial systems throughout Europe and Asia. I will contend that imperial polities—"old" and "new"—constituted a system in which any serious competitor for geopolitical influence *had* to think and act like an empire.

One can claim that modern empires were projections of nation-states, and indeed some advocates of colonization in the late nineteenth century argued this way: colonies should be expressions of national power, and their resources used for national purposes. But such arguments were made within states with long histories of competing in imperial terms, and this point of view was part of a more varied address to the tension of incorporation and differentiation. Political leaders in the metropole regularly disagreed over the extent to which empires were zones of exploitation or a moral space—in which issues like slavery, forced labor, religious conversion, and education had to be confronted. The most extreme example of the pendulum swinging toward dichotomous differentiation rather than a tension of incorporation and differentiation was Nazi Germany, and there the division between German and non-German was as much within national territory as in zones of conquest. And the Thousand-Year Reich proved short-lived, in the face of the resources of the British and Soviet imperial systems, and of the empire-in-spite-of-itself, the United States.

I draw on both older and newer scholarship that has brought out the importance and durability of imperial state-making and unmaking.[3] Nation was indeed part of the repertoire of political movements and political thinkers, at least from the eighteenth century. Some argue that the roots of the national idea in Europe go back farther than that, to when the notion of the people became separable from the notion of the king.[4] Others find the

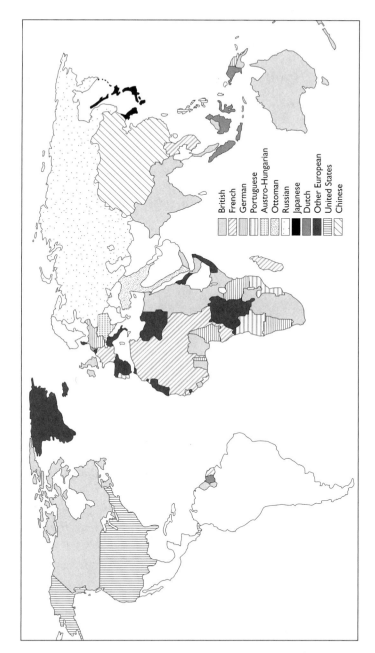

MAP 1. Empires, c. 1910.

British
French
German
Portuguese
Austro-Hungarian
Ottoman
Russian
Japanese
Dutch
Other European
United States
Chinese

origins of nationalism not in Europe, but within the wider space of European empires, as creole elites imagined their North and South American "communities" as separable from the imperial polities that had spawned them.[5] The idea of a polity built around the linguistic homogeneity of a body of people—who emphasized their "horizontal" connections with each other over "vertical" loyalty to higher authority—became a possibility that political leaders and thinkers could consider and debate, and at times it galvanized people's imaginations.

But nation was not a possibility that all political actors exercised, least of all in those states with the greatest military and political capacity at the time, Britain, Spain, and France. They did not cease to act like old empires, turn themselves into nation-states, and then conquer new territories in the interest of national power. The story of France, for example, needs to accommodate the profound ways in which the relationship of national and imperial space was thrown into question, from the Saint Domingue revolution of 1791–1804 through the differential incorporation of European spaces into the Napoleonic empire, through the debates from 1848 to 1946 over the statuses of "citizen" and "subject" in different parts of Greater France, up to the final crisis of a supranational France, challenged as much by people claiming an equal share of imperial resources as by those who wanted to exit the empire altogether. France only became a nation-state in 1962, when it gave up the last vital element of its imperial structure, Algeria.

The trajectory of empire to nation needs to be questioned for another reason. The persistence of the old empires of Eurasia—the Habsburg, Ottoman, and Romanov—until 1917–23 presents a problem for those who consider the "modern" era as the time of nation-states. The problem is usually solved by describing these empires as anachronistic holdovers from an age of aristocracy, clinging to their imperial identifications in the face of the inevitable national challenges that mounted over the course of the nineteenth century. Recent historical scholarship has made clear the power of *imperial* concepts among reformers and oppositional movements in all the empires. Nationalism was part of the repertoire of political opposition, but not necessarily the most important one.

The dismemberment of these empires after World War I should not be projected backward. And the collapse of the Russian Empire in this period gave rise to another imperial form, the Soviet Union, with its highly centralized political system intent on remaking society, yet organized around the maintenance of distinct national republics within it. Most important is the overlap of different political forms: a variety of empires and states with supranational bases of power, with dependencies, clients, and annexed territories and subordinated populations, have shared the world stage through most of history—including the recent past.[6]

Empires *did* inspire loyalty and identification from a portion of their subjects, but more often they depended on contingent accommodation.[7] They provoked opposition in the name of solidaristic identification of conquered people and opposition based on seeking contingent accommodation with a different empire. Often they were undercut by their own agents or settlers, who found ways of acquiring power and wealth by bypassing the imperial center. Imperial leaders sometimes thought they could perfectly balance incorporation and differentiation, but the greatest of empires fell victim to the hubris of thinking they could extend control indefinitely.[8]

Empires perpetrated violence because they were strong and because they were weak. Terror tactics—mass slaughter during conquests, collective punishments on villages and kinship groups thereafter—were hallmarks of colonization and lasting features of maintaining control, marrying new technology to an age-old tactic in aerial bombardments during rebellions in British-mandated Iraq and Spanish Morocco in the 1920s,[9] in British Kenya and French Algeria in the 1950s, and in Portuguese Africa in the 1970s. This terrify-and-move-on aspect of colonial control reflected the weakness of *routinized* administration and policing in colonial territories and the need to keep the costs of administration and discipline low, whatever the claims of civilizing missions or rule of law.

The old empires lasted for centuries, while the new ones, such as the African colonies of the French, British, and Belgians, lasted only decades. At first glance, the new empires had more effective technological and organizational means of exerting and maintaining power. The striking aspect of these comparisons is the extent to which "modern" European states in Africa did not exercise such power. Colonial rule was empire on the cheap, creating a patchwork of economic exploitation rather than a systematic transformation, ruling through an often ossified system of "tribal" authority rather than trying to create the docile individual subjects of supposedly modern governmentality (see chapter 5). When France and Britain at last tried to move beyond the mediocrity of their transformative efforts to forge a development-oriented empire after World War II, the entire enterprise rapidly came apart.

That strong imperial states should have found acceptable the exercise of relatively weak power in certain circumstances is so puzzling that many commentators prefer the myths of total exploitation or of modern governmentality to examining a more confusing reality. One can get partway to a better understanding of these phenomena by looking at the ambiguous relationship of imperialism and capitalism over time. Capitalists have been flexible enough to profit from and discard colonial empires; they have had a range of means—and required a range of coercive and administrative mechanisms of support—to integrate their systems of production into different parts of the world; they have encountered limits and obstacles in doing so; they will continue to need state structures to bail them out of the endless difficulties to which capitalism's unevenness leads; and they may well adapt, as in present-day Europe, to new forms of supranational politics. The course of this uneven development helps to explain why Western European powers were in a position to conquer new territory in the late nineteenth century, whereas the Ottoman and Chinese empires were on the defensive, and why European powers did not fully use their power to remake the societies they conquered, either to transform them in their own image or to maximize extraction from them. At the same time, the fact that empire was a political space helps us to understand why slavery, forced labor, and land alienation were hotly debated in nineteenth- and twentieth-century France and Britain and not just taken as acceptable means of accumulating wealth as long as they were "out there."

Despite the evocation of empire in current American political debate, we need to think about empire not because it is about to be resurrected, but because it was such an important constituent of political life for so long, until so recently, and with such important effects. We do need to think about the range of alternative political forms and of political imagination that have been available in different situations in history.

ALL ROADS LEAD TO ROME—OR TO MONGOLIA

The Arc de Triomphe, built to commemorate Napoleon's conquests, harnessed the symbolism of ancient Rome to the glorification of the emperor who followed in the footsteps of the French Revolution and the Enlightenment. The British empire, in much of its official architecture and sometimes in its rhetoric, also harked back to the Roman empire as the model of conquering glory linked to enlightened authority spread outward from a civilizational center.[10] The imperial architecture of Hitler and Mussolini deployed a stultifying classicism to symbolize the durability and authority they claimed.

Rome proclaimed itself to be a universal empire.[11] It did not see itself sharing space with other political entities, and recognized only barbarism beyond its borders. Future empires might proclaim the universality of the principles they purported to represent but had to coexist with others proclaiming similar (Western) or other (Islamic, Chinese) universalisms. The Roman Empire not only expanded at the expense of barbarians, but took slaves from outside, which gave its richest landowners alternatives to exploiting the empire's own subjects. The early empire sprang from a city-state, with authority residing not in a nationality but in a specifically Roman aristocracy and Roman citizenry, which incorporated selected members of new territories while keeping a tight hold on offices. Romans acknowledged their own mixed ancestry but asserted that they had become an "imperial people," destined to rule far and wide.[12]

As emperors extended their reach, they recruited subordinates more widely, and the Roman/non-Roman distinction was reduced in favor of a ruler/ruled distinction mediated by the recruitment of local elites. Citizenship became more attainable in the far reaches of the empire.[13] J. G. A. Pocock cites the case of St. Paul, who had "never seen Rome" but could assert the legal rights of a Roman citizen. In that way, "of the various patterns of legally defined rights and immunities available to subjects of a complex empire made up of many communities, he enjoys access to the most uniform and highly privileged there is." In 212 A.D. all nonslave subjects of the Roman Empire became citizens.[14] The imperial space of Rome was no mere authoritarian fiction. Elites from distant provinces could aspire to leadership in the empire if they obeyed authority, learned Latin, and developed the appropriate skills and connections. Roman emperors did not have to be Roman, or even Italian.

The precedent of imperial citizenship would echo in France after World War II: attempting to underscore the political and moral unity of the empire, it declared all subjects to be citizens. It then faced a barrage of claims in the name of citizenship, which in the twentieth century entailed far more burdens on the state than the notion had implied 1734 years previously.

Scholars of Roman antiquity complicate this picture of imperial radiance in ways that parallel modern-day discussion of the tensions within colonial empires. S. E. Alcock has queried the famous duo of collaboration/resistance to conquest, arguing that in the eastern Roman Empire, Greeks could make use of imperial structures and ideologies in more supple ways, playing off their own claims as a prior empire, using patronage, service, or economic niches within the Roman empire for individual and family gain, and preserving a modicum of cultural distinctiveness within the economic and cultural structures of the Roman system. Romans accepted their junior role in the genealogy of imperial culture, for as the poet Horace put it, "Greece, the captive, took her savage victor captive, and brought the arts to rustic Latium."

Nevertheless, the Roman Empire was a model for future efforts to inscribe imperial culture in time and space, in public space and the routines of daily life: through its aqueducts and roads, which constituted a level of state services not regained in Western Europe for centuries, its marking of urban space through temples, arenas, and paths, its distinctive private architecture, and its calendar and alphabet. Yet even outside Greece, as Greg Woolf has argued, the influence of the conquered upon the practices of the conquerors was considerable. While a distinctly Roman imperial culture came into being, that culture was the product of interaction across the space of empire, not a set of practices emanating from the city of Rome. Gary Miles refers to institutions and culture within the empire as "a series of regional and local hybrids, each of which combined Roman and native elements in a distinct way."[15] Hybridity—that favorite concept of postcolonial studies—seems to have begun in Rome, as did the inscription of imperialism on a colonized landscape.

The universal pretensions of the Roman Empire provide another sort of precedent: of the dangers of hubris and overextension, even in empires that have no rival of near-equivalent power and in which "national" revolts were not a factor.[16] The story of the decline and fall of the Roman Empire fascinated the British elite in the early nineteenth century and is invoked by contemporary political pundits in regard to American unipolar hegemonism. For our purposes, the story reminds us that consideration of the extension of power, whether called cultural imperialism, modern governmentality, or globalization, should always be accompanied by a consideration of limits.

A not-so-old imperial system provides another model and another ancestry for long-persisting imperial state systems—the empires of the Eurasian steppe and their offshoots of the twelfth through fifteenth centuries, including the Mongol empires of Chinggis Khan, Kublai Khan, Timur, and others. These systems are important not only for their enormous extent—at their peak from the outskirts of Vienna to the Pacific edge of Asia—which belies the notion of rapid electronic communications as the crucial variable in shrinking space, but also for their historical influence. The steppe empires spawned three of the greatest empires that persisted into the twentieth century, Qing China, Russia, and the Ottomans, just as Rome stands at the head of the putative genealogies of Byzantium, the Holy Roman Empire, Britain, France, Spain, the Netherlands, Portugal, Austro-Hungary, and Germany. The Mongols provide a contrast to Rome, for they lacked a single geographic center, yet they linked a large number of geographically dispersed, culturally diverse people into political dependence on a single authority. The polities that grew up under steppe influence were enormously varied—from the centralized bureaucratic system of Qing China to the relative autonomy of incorporated groups in the Ottoman Empire.

The Mongol empires originated in nomadic societies on the fringes of more settled areas. Their ability to change the scale of political control came from their mobility, enabling them to plunder outside their own base—particularly in regions more capable of generating an agricultural surplus—and thus to attract followers and keep the raiding and expanding going. The fundamental dynamic was not ethnic solidarity, but patrimonial affinity to a ruler and dynastic expansion. The Mongols were capable of rapidly attracting people of diverse origins, but vulnerable to breakup at times of succession, when the affinity of subordinates might be up for grabs. These empires thus existed, over time, in the plural, although the greatest of the khans established in their lifetimes singular domination over enormous territory. Khans created multiple military units, which could be played off against each other but which created high incentives for cooperation, as long as the empire kept expanding and new resources became available. Just as Mongol consolidation depended on the symbiosis of nomadic raiders and the sedentary communities that produced appropriable wealth, the ideology of their empire came to depend on the relationship of Mongol warriors to a cross-ethnic, universalistic religion, Islam. Quite distinct from the imperial systems fostered by Islam in the Arabian peninsula, Mongol polities were ruled by people from the periphery of Islamic religious incorporation. These imperial leaders became the patrons of learned Islamic scholars, largely Persian-speakers, and turned the great cities of the Mongol conquest, such as Samarkand, into centers of learning and teaching and of Islamic architecture and art.[17]

Mongol polities had to expand to survive, and they did so over extraordinary distances, with relays of horsemen keeping the moving center informed. They were vulnerable to anything that pluralized the singular direction of patrimonial loyalty.

New kinds of empire appeared at the edges of the old. The Ottomans, a Turkic-speaking group and a minor player in the region, moved into Anatolia, taking over a zone where Greeks and Romans had once ruled, and where Mediterranean traders from Venice and elsewhere had long had influence. Ottoman armies moved into the Balkans and in 1453 captured Constantinople, itself the product of imperial expansion and fission.

These conquests transformed government and administration, but not the multi-ethnic, incorporative nature of the polity. Increasingly centered on Istanbul, combining military power, tribute and land revenue, and commerce extending over the eastern Mediterranean, across Anatolia, and into central Europe, the Ottomans developed an intricate administrative apparatus, based on extensions of the sultan's household, the development of a bureaucracy, a state-sponsored hierarchy of scholars, and an "Ottoman imperial idiom in architecture, poetry, and historiography." This empire, like that of the Romans, could siphon off people of different regions into an elite that was, above all else, Ottoman, while not assimilating or destroying the distinctiveness of the people who contributed taxes, soldiers, and other resources to the imperial center. Instead, different religious and ethnic entities, termed *millets*, were recognized as collectivities within the empire.[18] Eventually, Ottoman sultans took on the mantle of defending the caliphate—the political offshoots of Mohammed's Islamic polity.

The Russian Empire also emerged from the edges of Mongol empires, from a client of a peripheral khanate. The success of the Grand Princedom of Moscow obscured its origins and eventually, thanks to influences spreading from Byzantium, produced a state attached to the Orthodox faith. The emergent Russian empire over time reoriented its claims to legitimacy against "Mongol hordes" or the "Tatar yoke." When Russia directed its expansive, Christianizing, integrating tendencies toward the Central Asian regions, it rarely acknowledged that its own political roots lay in that direction.[19]

China's Qing dynasty also sprang from Mongol-related people. The conventional wisdom has long underplayed the differentiated, imperial nature of the Chinese polity and overplayed the state's homogenizing, sinicizing tendencies. The Manchu dynasty, such arguments go, was militarily victorious over its predecessors in 1644, but Confucianism, the Mandarinate, and the Han won the culture wars, pulling the conquerors into a characteristically Chinese political system. China was an empire becoming a nation-state: large and powerful, but not reproducing the differentiation from which it sprang. Recent scholarship by historians using Manchu sources has complicated the thesis of Han Chinese cultural hegemony and with it the national character of China. Mark Elliott argues that the core of the Manchus' strategy of rule was to use the essentially Han bureaucracy, but to emphasize their own distinctiveness. Manchus dressed differently, spoke a different language, lived in separate quarters, and were organized into separate military units. In this way, the emperor was able to keep the best-trained bureaucrats at arm's length from the dynastic and military sources of power. The strategy was hard to sustain over generations, but at its height this enormous empire maintained its unity by combining systematic administration with culturally differentiated political organization. Even at the end of the nineteenth century, opponents of the imperial dynasty attacked its legitimacy because it was Manchu—foreign—thus linking their cause to struggles elsewhere against European imperialists.[20]

Just as the empire perspective suggests reconsideration of the standard wisdom of sinologists, thinking about China suggests reconsideration of the conventional association of certain forms of governmentality with post-Enlightenment Europe. The most basic aspects of Foucauldian governmentality—the development of state instruments of surveillance and intervention in regard to the individual subject—were already developed in China several centuries earlier, notably censuses and cadastral surveys, networks of state schools, and state granaries. As R. Bin Wong writes, "The Manchu state had at its disposal a repertoire of strategies for creating social cohesion developed by earlier rulers that far exceeded what European rulers of multilingual empires could even imagine."[21] If modernity has its criteria (chapter 5), imperial modernity in its Roman and Chinese variants seems to be ancient.

EMPIRE AS MORAL UNIT AND TRADING NETWORK: THEORY AND PRACTICE IN EARLY WESTERN EUROPEAN EMPIRES

The literatures on the Spanish conquest of the peoples of the Americas and the Portuguese seaborne empires are rich, so an interloper ventures into this domain with trepidation. I wish to make a simple point: such ventures defined a space of empire. They were not, indeed could not have been, an extension of national power.[22] They were vast but not global, depending on the organization of commercial, political, and military networks through key nodal points outside of which their power tailed off rapidly, and vulnerable to rival networks that might cross the lines of connection. But empires could also become a moral space, the unit in regard to which righteous political behavior was debated and which provided a framework for the propagation of religion. For all the violence of conquest, the brutality of extractive colonialism, the devastation wreaked by European diseases, the cultural violence done against small communities and large indigenous empires, and the exploitation and dependence inflicted on indigenous people and imported Africans, the Spanish empire—for one—could not escape the force of a debate among its own ideologues about the political status of the people taken into it. The famous argument of Bartolomé de Las Casas for placing limits on the subjugation of the indigenous populations of the Americas was part of an extended and passionate discussion among jurists and moral philosophers in Spain.

The Spanish Empire wasn't entirely Spanish and certainly not national; it was "a cosmopolitan conglomerate." Its rulers emerged from the confusions of European dynastic politics, and under Charles V in 1519 it extended over, but hardly integrated, much of central and eastern Europe, Burgundy, modern Holland and Belgium, Castile, Aragon, parts of Italy, and the conquered territories of the New World; it was "the most far-flung empire the world had ever known." Its emperor—a native French speaker—had to learn Castilian Spanish on the job.[23]

Its claims to moral authority were based on the defense of Christianity, on the idea of a Catholic monarchy. It saw itself operating under Catholic notions of universal law, and it expanded "Christian universalism far beyond the old boundaries."[24] The new conquests began shortly after the end of another interempire conflict: the expulsion of the Moors from Spain in 1492. Both the institutions, such as the reward of seigneurial land and privileges to warriors, and the spirit of Christian crusade affected the overseas domain. While the defeat of Muslims and the expulsion of Jews from Spain were defining events of a Christian empire, so too were the trans-European networks that made the empire possible: financial and military resources coming from places later known as Italy, Germany, and the Netherlands, and even from Jews. The navy was Genoese and scholars were trained in Italy.

Conquering the Americas depended on the ability of small bands of invaders to exploit the conflicts within American societies, especially those involving their own empires, notably the Inca. The conquistadors murdered, pillaged, and terrorized; they also made alliances and married women from indigenous nobilities, which gave them a sense of mystical association with the empires they had in fact destroyed. The Church did as much as the Crown to make settlement long-term, and missions were agricultural colonies as much as sites of conversion, and they contributed their share of exploitation.[25]

If, in the American domains, the holders of land grants (*encomienda*) originating with the Crown claimed the right to exploit Indians resident on their lands, Crown and Church asserted that the counterpart of that right was an obligation to minister to their souls—to treat them not in relation to a self-other dichotomy but as part of a hierarchical, divinely sanctioned order. Jurists and philosophers debated whether Incas and Mayas, coming from something they could recognize as civilization, could be ruled but not expropriated, whereas people lower in the hierarchy were subject to legitimate expropriation of land and other forms of wealth. Compared to territories of other empires of the era, New Spain was an elaborately administered royal domain. For the landholder, in this as in any other empire, the king was far away, and brutality and patriarchal authority ran close together. Yet settlers were still part of an imperial, hierarchical, imagined community in which juridical and moral issues were questions for the empire as a whole.[26]

What the idea of a Christian empire signified to the indigenous people of Spanish America also turns out to be complex: research highlights the interaction, for example, between Andean and European religious ideas in producing not simply a regional Christianity but a variety of religious practices. The religious possibilities would be different but equally complex in plantation zones, where African religious ideas and practices came with the slave trade.[27]

Some scholars contrast Spanish *encomienda*-based system—which incorporated land and labor—to the seaborne orientation of the Portuguese. But the most important point is that imperial systems were shaped as they developed, influenced by prior state structures and royal goals but not determined by them. To be sure, Portuguese expansion early on drew its strength from the concentration of naval power in the taking of nodal points in Indian Ocean and Southeast Asian trading networks, leading to the development of commercial/military enclaves. These empires were discontinuous, as opposed to the territorial contiguity in Spanish, British, and French mainland America.[28] But over time, notably in Brazil, Angola, Sri Lanka, and other areas, Portuguese power was drawn into deeper relations and conflict with indigenous polities, and power became more territorialized.[29] Settlers there faced the issue of obtaining or importing and controlling labor, just as in the trading enclaves they depended on interaction with indigenous trading networks and polities. Spanish colonization in the Americas was torn between brutal extraction, especially of gold and silver, and the interest of the Crown and some settlers in building a more stable, manageable, and productive New Spain, a task made no easier by the deadly effects of Old World diseases. Spain meanwhile was capable of following the Portuguese pattern of tapping into a regional trading system, as it did in the Philippines. Different modes of exercising imperial power had as much to do with the conquered as the conquering.

The so-called early modern era also witnessed the rise of the Dutch East India Company, the British East India Company, and similar entities. They were corporate actors—with national charters but primary responsibility to their shareholders—and they slid from setting up commercial outposts, trading networks, and in some cases productive enterprises into exercising administrative authority over territories and people, then more deeply into forging empire-states. They were more selective about developing territorial empires than about establishing and controlling sea routes. Particularly in their early decades, the economic force of the merchant companies derived from their ability to tap onto existing systems of trade, production, and capital formation. The very fact of administering people and territory drew the companies into an increasingly governmental, imperial mode of action. Kerry Ward describes the Dutch East India Company's transoceanic punitive strategies—exiling conquered rulers or banishing Dutch servants from Southeast Asia to South Africa, punishing South African slaves by forced labor on nearby islands—that made the Indian Ocean region into a space of imperial discipline.[30] Scholars now present a more complex picture than the earlier dichotomy between Northern European–based empires based mainly on the rational exploitation of economic linkages and Southern European empires intent on power through the extension of a monarchical, Catholic polity. All imperial ambitions were varied and changing from the start.[31]

It would be misleading to see the world after Columbus as a playing out of a singular expansionist dynamic. The success of overseas empires depended on choosing where to deepen involvement—using but not overextending increasing military disparities with non-European polities—and where to limit ambition.[32] Empires were vulnerable to the still powerful indigenous polities around them, to downturns in trading systems they did not fully control, to the vagaries of interempire warfare, and to the possibility—given that their strength was a network focused on Amsterdam or Lisbon—that their own agents or settlers might see an interest in finding a niche in a different part of the overall trading system.[33] Overseas empires provided, ever since Magellan's circumnavigation of the earth, a space of imagination that was global, but a field of power that was limited and delicate.

The different forms of colony-making, from trading enclave to plantation zone, to settlement, to various combinations of the above, posed different problems of governance, defense, and expansion. Caribbean slave plantation colonies were dependent on imperial centers to deter slave revolts and protect high-value land from other empires, but in North America community development and expectations derived from British notions of government brought to the fore questions of settler autonomy that would one day explode. Except where settlers could claim a major place in administering colonies, empires had little choice but to govern conquered indigenous communities through some form of what later was called indirect rule—they lacked the institutions and above all the revenue to do very much governing themselves—and that entailed prudence about escalating demands and reliance on authority systems whose basis in religion (local or universalistic) and other beliefs could be alien to the colonizing power.[34] Trading empires sprang into being because of the vitality of previous commercial networks, but those networks did not necessarily evolve to suit a particular imperial power.

For all the limitations to the power and transformative ambitions of the pre-1800 empires, the early colonizations had enormous influence on later expansion and consolidation. John Darwin emphasizes the importance of "bridgeheads" in the expansion of the British Empire in the Victorian era: a pragmatic government, choosing where to press different strategies for economic and diplomatic advantage, focused territorial ambitions on areas that had already been integrated into economic networks, sometimes being drawn into more aggressive action by traders, settlers, or military men on the spot.[35] Likewise, Portugal's colonization of the interiors of Angola and Mozambique was part of the late-nineteenth-century "scramble for Africa," but its being in a position to move inward reflected its earlier forms of empire in the region.

Let me skip ahead to the crisis of Spanish empire in the New World, at the beginning of the nineteenth century. Benedict Anderson has placed these revolutions at the core of his interpretation of "creole nationalism" emerging from the "imagined communities" of colonial settlers whose social "circuits" increasingly bypassed Spain, while print communications defined a national imaginary. But the pattern of the revolution qualifies this story: the *imperial* imaginary among creole elites was viable and compelling well into the revolutionary process. After Napoleon's conquest of Spain in 1808, the colonies remained a repository of sentiment in favor of the Spanish monarchy. As Spanish elites sought to restore the monarchy, the split between "Peninsulares" (the people of metropolitan Spain) and creoles was not so much a matter of people having gone separate, national ways but of a dispute over the allocation of power and the control of trade. The Spanish legislative body (the Cortes), which included representatives from both regions, declared itself part of "a single monarchy, a single nation, and a single family," then failed to make good on the premise of imperial equality, notably in regard to representation in the Cortes and protection of creoles' economic interests. Creoles also feared that metropolitan Spain would not make the moves necessary to avoid a more radical revolution: better a North American–type revolution than a Haitian one.[36] Creole nationalism was less a cause of the crisis of 1810–12 than a consequence of the breakdown of the single, imperial family, after which creoles developed a new language of nationality in the face of strong tensions within the new states of the Americas.[37] The breakup of an empire over its rulers' inability to manage an imperial polity—in which different categories of people asserted the right to rule over still others—echoed the crises of the British Empire in North America and the French in Saint Domingue and foreshadowed the end of the French and British empires 150 years later.

THE FIRST MODERN EMPIRE?
NAPOLEON BETWEEN NEW AND OLD REGIMES

The Napoleonic empire should have a prominent place in any consideration of imperialism in the era following the Enlightenment and the French Revolution. But Napoleon had the bad taste to disrupt narratives of post-Enlightenment modernity.

It would have been easier for the nation story if Napoleon's imperial adventures had been based on the French citizen's commitment to his nation and his willingness to fight for its domination over other people, and if Napoleon's openness to scientific ideas and rational, meritocratic organization had fully constructed an individual French subject in relation to the state, without mediating status groups or hierarchies. But Napoleon's history was ambiguous. The French Revolution had indeed seen the value of raising an army of volunteers motivated to fight for "la patrie en danger," but it had given up this idea well before Napoleon took power. Mass levees of soldiers began in 1793 and systematic conscription in 1798. The idea that national sentiment meant young men would willingly die for their country may be convincing to twentieth-century scholars, but it was insufficient to postrevolutionary leaders. Napoleon systematized conscription—it was indeed one of the primary mechanisms through which the state penetrated society—but the society it penetrated was not specifically French. Napoleon's conquests both demanded and fed a conscription machine in all conquered territories. Only a third of the army that attacked Russia in 1812 came from places that had been part of France before the Revolution. Within and without "France," resistance to recruitment and desertion were considerable problems. That they diminished over time reflects less the triumph of a national order than the routinization of state power throughout the empire.[38]

Michael Broers rejects the idea of the Napoleonic empire as a "pure and simple extension of France, la Grande Nation," and argues instead that some parts of what is now France, such as the Vendée, lay outside the core, while Napoleon's "inner empire" included parts of western Germany, northern Italy, and the Low Countries—reflecting a territorial conception rooted in the earlier empire of Charlemagne. The Napoleonic system was built in the core at the same time that it was built in the non-French-speaking parts of the empire.[39] The empire—which at its height encompassed 40 percent of Europe's population[40]—was differentiated space. Parts of the core were turned into departments like those of France; in other regions a dynastic principle—Napoleon's own family as local rulers—prevailed; and in others Napoleon worked through a hegemonic principle, maintaining a subordinate, allied dynasty and the fiction of still distinct states under his overrule.

The Napoleonic regime exhibited the arrogance of the revolutionary template: that France, or more accurately Paris, was the source of the formula for administering territory, and that local traditions of municipal or regional governance should be swept away in favor of administration through prefects. Napoleon's officials held Italians in contempt, considered parts of Germany backward and feudalistic, and admired parts of Germany that seemed to be like France.[41] Popular religion and church power would both be suppressed; the Napoleonic code would provide the model of civil law throughout the empire; conscription and taxation would be generalized. These measures would support an administration capable of linking the center with all localities. For a time, this project proved attractive to certain elites in the conquered territories, who saw Napoleon as liberating them from local tyrannies and feudalistic aristocracies.[42]

For all of Napoleon's interest in harnessing geography, ethnography, and other forms of scientific knowledge to the cause of rational administration, his thinking was also shaped by an older vision of empire, hence his fascination with Rome and Charlemagne. Napoleon retained important aspects of an old-regime empire. He made many of his generals and top supporters into nobles, and he did likewise with some of the elites in conquered regions. The most favored of these were awarded principates and duchies as grand fiefs, heritable under primogenitor. His armies, like those of old, were allowed to engage in undisciplined extraction, undercutting the appeal of enlightened rule to anti-aristocratic "patriots" in many conquered areas.[43] In parts of the empire where compromise with regional aristocracies was necessary, Napoleon's otherwise relentless drive against feudal and Church power was set aside and noble privileges allowed to remain.[44]

Most revealing was Napoleon's decision in 1802 to restore slavery in the Caribbean islands. The abolition of slavery in 1793–94 had followed debates, forced upon Paris by the Haitian rebellion, over whether the rights of man and the citizen applied to the empire as well as the metropole, and it reflected the calculation that France needed the military support of ex-slaves to defend itself against aristocratic counterrevolution in Saint Domingue and the invasion of rival empires (Britain and Spain). The logic of citizenship—the expectation of support in exchange for recognition of one's legitimate place in the polity—and the logic of empire combined in unpredictable ways in the post-Revolutionary empire.[45] Napoleon attempted to take all this away, failing after a long and convoluted struggle in Haiti and succeeding, despite resistance, in Martinique and Guadaloupe in 1802. This was a restorationist move in the fullest sense of the word: it reflected Napoleon's links to an ancien régime set of planters in the islands (including but hardly limited to connections through his wife Josephine, the daughter of sugar planters) and it reflected the older view of colonies as exceptional places against the Revolution's tendency to at least debate the universality of its principles and laws.

Resistance to Napoleon's rule doesn't fit the nation/empire dichotomy. Although Napoleon lost the initial support of local patriots, he gained more support by his strategies of co-optation of elites into an imperial, rather than French, nobility. There was armed opposition, most notably in Spain, Calabria, and Tyrol, but it was as much opposition to regional elites who were both collaborating with Napoleon and expropriating local resources as it was opposition to "foreign" rule.[46] An intellectual opposition—most famously from Benjamin Constant—opposed a vision of Napoleonic militarism, greed, and destruction to nations peacefully trading and interacting with each other.[47] But what stopped Napoleon were other empires, most notably the two supranational empires on the edges of Europe's central continental space, Britain and Russia, both of whom could draw resources from outside the contested region.[48]

Napoleon's only major defeat by what could be called a national liberation movement occurred at the hands of Haiti's ragtag and often divided armies of slaves, ex-slaves, and free people of color, with some help from France's imperial enemies and more from tropical microbes. Napoleon's other overseas venture, the 1798 conquest of Egypt, proved short-lived, with British intervention playing a role in leaving this territory to another imperial system, the Ottoman. His motives in Egypt were a peculiar concatenation of a desire to push his imperial genealogy back to the pharaohs and an effort to bring science and rational rule to a piece of the backward Ottoman Empire.[49] In neither case was the outcome his to determine. In 1803, Napoleon was reputed to say, "Damn sugar, damn coffee, damn colonies!" as he decided to sell off his biggest piece of New World real estate, Louisiana, to the United States for cash to finance his other imperial dreams.[50] We are left with a picture of one of the great state-building projects of the postrevolutionary era shaping a state that was neither a nation nor an empire clearly divided between a national core and a subordinate periphery, but a more finely differentiated entity, whose Frenchness was both narrower (personal, dynastic, Paris-centered) than France and wider (the claim that French values were universal).

The imperial conception of France was echoed later in a regime that called itself the Second Empire (1852–71) and whose ruler called himself Napoleon III. The first Napoleon's juridical and administrative innovations also had a wide influence in Europe, in rival empires as well as in his own. Napoleon's conquests opened up a debate about what Europe itself was, where appropriate boundaries lay, and what kinds of governments could claim legitimate authority. The 1815 Congress of Vienna, at which the victors discussed a post-Napoleonic future, was a formative event in bringing political leaders into a self-conscious discussion about how such a future could be decided. The Congress claimed to restore legitimate sovereigns, but reduced the numbers of small states and allowed France to remain a large one. It made declarations about state morality, such as an insistence that states prevent trading in slaves. With British, Germanic, Russian, and Austrian-Hungarian empires as major actors, it was far from clear that the new Europe would be a Europe of nations. It would be a Europe with a small number of serious players, interacting, competing, and at times fighting with each other, each using supranational resources in order to survive. The idea of a Europe-wide consensus among major players would be reinforced later in the century by the Conferences of Berlin (1884–85) and Brussels (1890–91), which set out the rules of the expansion of overseas empires and the definition of boundaries. Empire-making was a basic part of nineteenth-century European history.

EMPIRES AS TRANSFORMATIVE AGENTS: FRENCH AND BRITISH COLONIAL EMPIRES

The mainstreams of French and British historiography long treated colonies as something "out there," marginal to a history that remained national, or else as a projection of national culture and power. The former viewpoint has been countered by excellent studies that put metropole and colony in the same analytic field,[51] but the latter one has been given a new lease on life by the contention that the British empire offers a model for the dissemination of market economies, order, and democratic values.[52] Such arguments had a place within the histories of French and British empires. In France, the civilizing mission argument was particularly strong after 1871, during the Third Republic. France would spread liberty, equality, and fraternity. Until the worst days of the Algerian war, such arguments convinced a portion of the French Left of the possibilities of a "colonialisme du progrès," replacing both the current, exploitative version of colonialism and indigenous "feudalism." Much of the Labour Left in Great Britain, opposed as it was to the land grabbing and racism of white settlers, was likewise seduced in the mid twentieth century by the idea of British-led development and British-inspired self-government.[53]

The idea of national mission was part of a wider spectrum of colonizing ideologies. My point here is to emphasize the imperial conception of the British or French polity in the first instance. Britain was made through Scotland, Wales, Ireland, Jamaica, the Thirteen Colonies, and India. Britain grew out of a Europe-wide experience of composite monarchy—the shifting movement of sovereignties through conquest and annexation, dynastic fusion and fission. As David Armitage writes, "The rulers of composite monarchies faced problems that would be familiar to the administrators of any empire: the need to govern distant dependencies from a powerful centre; collisions between metropolitan and provincial legislatures; the necessity of imposing common norms of law and culture over diverse and often resistant populations; and the consequent reliance of the central government on the co-optation of local elites." What made an empire British was defined both by metropolitans and provincials, and the same notions of politics that gave rise to the British empire also gave rise to the American revolution.[54] France was made through Saint Domingue, French conquests and losses in North America, the Napoleonic adventure, and later Algeria, Africa, and Southeast Asia. And the power to set the boundaries of its revolutions and reactions did not just lie in Paris.

The ideas that defined a French or British sense of purpose were themselves emerging within the space of empire, where the relevance of rights, obligations, and responsibilities to different categories of people was debated. In the French case, the Haitian Revolution of 1791 laid out arguments that persisted until the end of the Algerian war in 1962, while in the British case, the abolitionist attack on "slavery under the British flag" became the basis for many arguments about abuses and responsibilities within the empire.

To say that empires were units of political and ethical debate is not to say that such debates led to a steady push to include colonized people within a universalistic, egalitarian conception of a polity. Quite the contrary. The assault on hierarchy within European polities led some political thinkers to make sharper distinctions between who was in and who was out. Such debates brought out fears of social danger—based on age, gender, race, class, status, and personal behavior—within the polity, and much anxiety about what the boundary of the polity was.[55] The uncertainties revealed in these debates, over the course of the nineteenth and twentieth centuries, gave rise to some efforts to clarify the mission of "civilized" powers and other efforts to patrol the boundary between a racially and culturally defined society and those under its control, who might serve its national interest but had no claims on it. There were many positions in between—and in practice a great deal of improvisation, contestation, and uncertainty.

The controversies over slavery occurring at a crucial period in the development of state structures in France and Britain as well as debates in Britain over the responsibility of Parliament for the actions of the British East India Company forced rulers to clarify what they meant by governing an empire. Lauren Benton argues that European empires' old practice of recognizing "legal pluralism"—different processes and different rules for people within the space of empire—was increasingly brought under the control of states. While this by no means eliminated separate justice, it did emphasize state power over differentiated judicial systems. That was part of a wider consolidation of state authority, but it had not only its limits (see below) but also its contradictory effects. Courts became another instrument through which indigenous people (bringing claims of various sorts and contesting colonial initiatives) could try to manipulate legal systems and make themselves into "legal actors." The colonial state's efforts—partial as they were—to establish the regularity of its power to lay down rules and define order also shaped possibilities for contesting how far that power could go.[56]

Any discussion of an imperial polity must be set against colonization on the ground. In the following pages, I will use the example of the French empire to illustrate the ambiguities of citizenship at the imperial level, and the case of the British empire to illustrate the ambiguity of the relationship of imperialism and capitalism.

Let us begin in Paris—and Saint Domingue. The question of the universe to which the rights of man and the citizen, as spelled out in Paris in 1788, applied was immediately thrown into question by the white planters, then the mixed-race planters, and then the slaves in Saint Domingue, and became the subject of a transatlantic pattern of argument and struggle. Black rebels and white revolutionaries at crucial points in the struggle became allies, briefly creating "a model for a different kind of imperial relationship," in which freedom and citizenship for slaves would be the return for their support of the revolution against its royalist and rival imperial enemies.[57] Only when Napoleon tried to reverse such gains did the liberation struggle take a clear turn toward independence. The creation of the state of Haiti in 1804 virtually necessitated an effort on the part of the French government—with the anxious concordance of other powers—to treat Haiti as a dangerous anomaly, a case of black mischief rather than a vanguard expanding the meaning of the French revolution. Slaves and ex-slaves, whose movements and communications in the greater Caribbean region were quite extensive, carried a more emancipatory message.[58]

How to reconcile the dimensions of inclusion and differentiation in the space of an empire-state would remain a focus of contestation until the very end of empire. To some, the ambiguities appeared resolved by the distinction between subject and citizen, the former involuntarily incorporated, with obligations but no rights and no voice, the latter a participating member of a polity (but not a homogeneous one—witness the exclusion of metropolitan French women from suffrage before 1944). Yet the relationship was always more complicated and unstable than that. The subject-citizen distinction was worked out in Algeria between 1830, when the conquest began, and 1865, when the government of the Second Empire acknowledged the citizenship of Christian settlers of Algeria (later extended to Jews), while declaring that Muslim Algerians had French *nationality* but could acquire *citizenship* only at the government's discretion and only if they gave up the right to have their civil affairs, including marriage, filiation, and inheritance, come under Islamic law. Few Muslims accepted such a constraint; fewer still were allowed to become citizens. The fiction that Algeria was not a colony but a part of France was from the start compromised by the fact that the majority of its non-Muslim settlers came from pan-Mediterranean rather than specifically French roots and that the large majority of its population were Muslims whose affinities reflected Arab and Ottoman linkages as well as a more locally defined Bedouin identification.[59] The government was following an old imperial strategy of building up a minority population strongly affiliated to the metropole in the hope of better controlling another population on a different basis—while encasing this strategy in a nineteenth-century legal framework around nationality and citizenship.

But in older colonies France followed a different strategy. After the 1848 revolution in Europe, when slaves in the empire were at last definitively emancipated, they went into the legal category of "citizen" and not into any intermediate zone, whatever prejudices French people had about ex-slaves' African origins or degraded social condition. In the small colonial trading outposts that France had maintained in Senegal, the longtime inhabitants, known as "originaires," obtained, if not the name of citizen, much of the citizen's political rights, including that of electing local assemblies. These rights expanded to electing a deputy to the French legislature, at first a mulatto but after the election of Blaise Diagne in 1914 a Black African.

In these small colonies, unlike Algeria, the exercise of citizenship was not contingent on renouncing Islamic civil status, reflecting the need of a tiny number of French officials and traders faced with a much larger surrounding African population to bring an indigenous community onto the imperial "side." But when France, beginning in the 1870s, proceeded to conquer large swaths of West and Central Africa, the conquered peoples became subjects. The citizenship ideal of the Third Republic was honored by the claim that as indigenous people became "civilized" they could apply to become citizens, provided they renounced indigenous forms of civil law and met standards of assimilation, which soon proved so high that few could meet them.[60]

In the imperial French polity, subjecthood existed alongside citizenship, a category in theory attainable but in practice withheld. The notion of *imperial* citizenship elaborated over decades in France contained within it the possibilities of both a narrow, culturally specific notion of Frenchness and a more state-centered notion focused on rights and responsibilities within a complex polity. The state might need to call on different aspects of citizenship but might also find that claims were being made upon it.[61]

Colonial regimes needed the collaboration of "local notables," educated personnel, and especially colonial soldiers. In World War I, the need for soldiers to defend France was acute. The Senegalese deputy, Blaise Diagne, was in a position to demand that in exchange for his recruitment efforts among the originaires of Senegal, their exercise of the rights of citizens would be extended by a clear declaration that they *were* citizens. The war thus entailed an expansion of citizenship within the empire, whose contributions to saving France became a standard feature of French imperial imagery.

Eugen Weber has emphasized how long it took to make "peasants" in European France into Frenchmen, into people whose provincial perspective had given way to participation in a national political culture. The army and the school, he claims, were key to the integrative process, which came to fruition around World War I. Yet the same institutions that Weber sees as so national were also operating in the French empire. They produced not a homogeneous Frenchness, but varying levels of acculturation, different forms of service to French interests, and above all a sense of simultaneous attachment, grievance, and frustrated entitlement among the segments of the population most affected—veterans and school graduates *(évolués)*.[62] The Frenchman that institutions of state produced was not quite national.

Citizenship—especially a citizenship available but not quite—proved to be too appealing a notion, especially after World War I. African, Vietnamese, and Arab ex-soldiers were not just objects of a wave of sentimentality about the "imperial community"; they demanded recognition. The expansion of claim-making in Senegal, North Africa, and Indochina, and among colonial students and workers in France—a growing presence during and after the war—was threatening. In the 1920s, the French government tried to check the citizenship process and emphasize an alternative myth: the empire as the gathering together of different cultures and nationalities, under an imperial umbrella that guaranteed peace and the ability to preserve distinct cultures and traditions.[63] In Africa, chiefs were given official blessing as the embodiments of authentic authority, while Africans who had advanced the farthest along the road to assimilation were belittled. Educational efforts languished; a proposal for a vigorous program of building economic infrastructure was rejected. Africans in many areas were subject to forced labor and to the casual cruelty of settlers and officials. If a few self-consciously progressive colonial ideologues thought *some* Africans could be treated as equivalents to metropolitan French people and others should be treated with respect as embodiments of distinct cultures, the prevailing view was that Africans lived and belonged in distinct and primitive tribes.[64]

All this changed again after World War II, as will be examined in more detail in chapter 7. Faced with the need for more effective use of imperial resources to aid France's recovery from the war yet facing an international climate where self-determination was becoming an important principle, with anticolonial movements in North Africa and Indochina already posing serious challenges, the French state took a firm position favoring inclusion over differentiation, hoping to make "France one and indivisible" the sole focus of political action. Early in 1946, the special and invidious judicial system for subjects was abolished. Forced labor was declared illegal. Ambitious programs of economic development and education were at last put in place. In May 1946, all subjects were declared to be citizens, independent of civil status regime. The 1946 Constitution posited that the French Union—the new name for the empire—was an indissoluble body that contained different sorts of entities: overseas departments fully incorporated into the polity, "associated states" under French protection, and overseas territories whose modernization was a state project. It would be a union of citizens, with representation in the Paris legislature, in territorial bodies, and in a special Assembly of the French Union.[65]

The French government soon found that the logic of imperial citizenship—the legal equivalence of all citizens regardless of their status regimes and cultural practices—became the basis for claims to equivalence of an economic and social nature: for equal wages, equal benefits, equal education, equal social services, for an equal standard of living. Some African deputies hoped that French imperialism would evolve into a kind of federalism—a multinational French polity moving beyond the tutelage of the metropole. In Algeria, the politics of citizenship was too little, too late, and was systematically undermined by the settlers. The Algerian revolution was a complex form of national mobilization mediated by a crosscutting radicalism shaped by Algerians' experience as workers in France and by transnational Islamic organization. The French government was caught between the threat that imperial citizenship would fail and that it would succeed too well: by 1956 leaders had begun to think that imperial citizenship was unaffordable and that devolving power to its overseas territories was preferable to the logic of equivalence within an indissoluble empire-state.[66]

In the case of Great Britain, let me emphasize another dimension of empire since the eighteenth century: the relationship of empire to capitalism.[67] Some political philosophers of the eighteenth and early nineteenth centuries contrasted the peaceful interaction of merchants with the warlike tendencies of empire builders—the "interests" versus the "passions." More recently, empire has been linked to capitalism, either as a good thing—the integration of people into markets—or a bad one, generalizing exploitation around the globe.[68] But the shifting and often contradictory nature of this relationship needs to be studied over time.

Slave plantations in the seventeenth and eighteenth centuries developed in colonies: labor could not have been moved on such a scale over such distances (amid violent imperial rivalries) without a well-protected place for them to go, and the coercive capacity of states was needed to ensure discipline over the vast bodies of slaves on the industrial-scale sugar plantations. The overall system mixed slave production in colonies and nonslave production/consumption in the metropole (as well as in other colonies that supplied food to the plantations), combined with nonempire sources of slaves in Africa, where the mechanisms or the consequences of enslavement and movement to the point of sale on the coasts did not concern British officials or planters.[69]

The Atlantic system had a brutal dynamic: cheap sugar became a regular ingredient in the diet of English wage workers, fostering factory production; voracious slave markets gave advantages to the most militarized of West and Central African societies.[70] But just as the slave economy depended on state power in certain—but not all—of its dimensions, the emergence in Britain itself of a class of property owners, able to defend their exclusive access to land and other property and to make the defense of property into a routine, legitimate aspect of the legal system, would not have taken place so effectively without a strong state—whose apparatus had been built up with resources from the empire in the British isles, the Caribbean, India, and North America.

Kenneth Pomeranz argues that Britain's capacity for industrialization only diverged from China's around 1800. A major factor in the British case was the complementarity that the sugar colonies allowed: a significant portion of calories to feed the growing working class could be produced without drawing on metropolitan resources in land and labor (the other biggest factor was the ready availability of fuel). The core of the Chinese empire, in contrast, extended most importantly to other regions that were agricultural and commercially active; these produced revenues but not labor/land complementarities that lowered the opportunity costs of industrial production.[71]

The mere fact of empire does not explain Britain's economic jump on other European societies, which had tropical empires too, but an interactive explanation of domestic and transoceanic changes helps to explain why Britain used empire in such a dynamic fashion. Imperial commerce and the state shaped each other: military expenses forced the state to consolidate fiscally and encourage a banking industry; military success, especially by the navy, made wider commerce safer; external sources of profit for merchants made them less dependent on paternalistic or corporatist ties at home and made property-owning elites better able to overcome resistance to land expropriation or the suppression of artisanal rights, while the ensuing capital accumulation made Britain more able to produce low-cost commodities for overseas markets; and economic success gave leaders confidence in political economists' arguments for free trade and for the universal value of labor that was both free and disciplined.[72]

The late eighteenth century, however, marked a crisis in the Empire, the loss of the Thirteen Colonies. The very strength of the imperial idea had contributed to the American Revolution through the colonists' sense of themselves as part of a British imperial polity and therefore as holders of rights that were being denied.[73] Eliga Gould argues that the loss of the Rev-

olutionary War left the British public with a "more constricted sense of nationhood," a conviction that giving up colonies was more acceptable than
changing the way things were done at home.[74] The remaining empire was
seen less as a part of British society, and hence its governance was "more
authoritarian." The sequence is important: the more Britain-centered concept of empire emerged from an imperial history, rather than an imperial
history building on a national one.

Yet the narrowing of conceptions of Britishness needs to be qualified.
Gould reports the sensation caused in the 1790s by the book and public ap-
pearances of Olaudah Equiano, whose story of enslavement and liberation
took place in the space of empire. This ex-slave contributed to what was
then becoming visible in Great Britain: an antislavery movement that
treated empire as a unit of moral discourse. A critical view of the conduct
of empire was coming not only from political economists like Adam Smith,
but from a vigorous wing of Protestantism. The shadow of Saint Domingue
loomed over the British slave islands, where continual tension and periodic
slave revolts brought home the fact that exercising power over colonized
people entailed coercion, expense, and danger as well as profits. In India,
scandals over the venality and brutality of the East India Company drew
British politics into questions of imperial governance, even as the company's deepening and widening involvement in South Asia enlarged the
space in which British claims to political hegemony and moral superiority
were in question. These debates and the continued autocratic, hierarchical
style of British imperialism were both part of empire in the age of capitalist development.[75]

Growing economic strength—alongside Britain's victory over Napoleon
and the political and military advantage that it conferred for some decades—
helps to explain why Great Britain in much of the nineteenth century was
able to benefit from what Ronald Robinson and Jack Gallagher famously
called the "imperialism of free trade."[76] They are using imperialism as
something broader than institutionalized incorporation into a polity, and
what they describe is something less than a doctrine of foreign policy. The
point is that British authorities developed a repertoire of ways in which they
could exercise power overseas, and the entire repertoire was important to a
state presiding over mobile capital and long-distance commerce. Because of
the crucial role of the City of London's financial markets, as well as the
British navy, Britain could often get its way by sending occasional gunboats
rather than administrators and police, and it could pressure Ottoman or Chinese governments to sign unequal treaties granting extraterritoriality, commercial privileges, and direct British supervision of customs receipts and

debt payments. It could champion free trade–while often practicing something more regulated than that. P. J. Cain and A. G. Hopkins see the importance of empire—as institutionalized rule—within a broader set of imperial practices, centered on finance and commercial services, that positioned Britain advantageously in coordinating asymmetrical economic relationships among economically vulnerable empires (Ottoman and Chinese), expanding economies in former colonies (Canada, Australia), primary product producers in Latin America, and industrial competitors and partners (Europe, United States, increasingly Japan).[77]

The bridgeheads of both formal and informal empire which Britain had earlier established or which its trading vanguard set up in the mid nineteenth century became a basis for territorial colonization in Africa, Asia, and the Pacific. In India, British rule became less tolerant of Indian ways of doing things, especially after the 1857 mutiny and the government's formal takeover of authority from the British East India Company. But—contrary to both Marx and advocates of market expansion—the British government still hesitated when it came to transforming the basis of production in the Indian economy, for it still needed to piggyback on indigenous authority, whose relations of dependence with landless subordinates did not dissolve into capitalist relations of production.[78]

Imperialism might have been a complex set of transnational commercial and financial linkages with different sorts of institutional arrangements, but it was more than that. Britain's initiative in abolishing the slave trade by its citizens (1807) and slavery in its colonies (1834), plus its use of diplomatic and naval power to get others to give up the slave trade cannot be explained in strictly economic terms. Abolition severely damaged the sugar economy in Britain's Caribbean islands and benefited Spain's colony of Cuba, which maintained slave production until 1886.[79] David Brion Davis has argued that the ideological, rather than the narrowly economic consequences, of capitalist development drove the antislavery movement. The moment was as much an Atlantic phenomenon as slavery itself, drawing on the growing importance of nonconformist Protestantism in middle and upper classes and gaining support from artisans, workers, and ex-slaves. Its success reflected the ideological needs of the elite: if it was to present a coherent world view that made wage labor—stripped of the protections of community and paternalism—into a naturalized part of life, it could hardly defend slavery in the same breath. It mattered to significant segments of the British public that slaves with whom it shared little cultural identification—in a British possession they had never seen—were being treated in a manner that cast a stain on the British flag.[80]

At the time of emancipation, the possibility that slaves and their de-scendants might become rational actors in a market economy or perhaps even participants in the politics of local legislatures was at least entertained by humanitarians and part of the governing elite. As Thomas Holt and Catherine Hall have shown, liberated slaves did not necessarily want to build their lives within such frameworks. That sugar production fell dras-tically in the islands was interpreted by some as the sign of a racial excep-tion to universal economic laws, while the ex-slaves' defense of another way of life was seen as a danger to political order. Some missionaries con-tinued to defend the emancipation project as a moral good, but others be-came convinced that even Christian ex-slaves would backslide unless su-pervised by whites. Increasingly harsh views of racial immutability and inferiority developed in the postemancipation encounter itself.[81]

This experiential, historically located view of growing racism should be seen alongside the approach that looks at the growth of "scientific racism" as a part of the intellectual history of Western Europe since the eighteenth century. Enlightenment categories in fact were used for building and de-bating a range of racial theories, including antiracist ones.[82] Arguments for immutable racial hierarchy increasingly resonated with and reinforced colonial experience on the ground over the course of the nineteenth cen-tury, but the extent of debate should not be forgotten. Some nineteenth-century writers pointed out that Africans along all coasts were interacting more intensively with European merchants, and took this as a sign that commerce, civilization, and Christianity might be advancing.[83] Antiracism did not imply anti-imperialism; some argued for a benevolent colonization to uplift African people. And racist arguments could be used against impe-rialism—that is, for not letting the empire get any more black.[84] The debate about race was pried open as well by African and African American intel-lectuals, and increasingly by colonial subjects who became part of intellec-tual life in London, Paris, and other European centers.[85] How racializing and univeralizing arguments played out reflected concrete issues and spe-cific struggles.

Both reluctant and eager imperialists had to engage with a shifting African reality in an age of growing but uncertain commerce along the coasts of Africa. Robinson and Gallagher's "peripheral" theory of late-nineteenth-century imperialism asserts that the conquests originated not in a set of imperatives generated within Europe, but out of the tensions within older modes of Euro-African interaction leading to a breakdown in the periphery itself, which in turn—given a highly unequal balance of mil-itary power—led to conquest.[86]

We need to step back for a moment. The "new" imperialism, especially the "scramble for Africa" from the 1870s through the 1890s, cannot be understood except in reference to "old" rivalries of empires. To the idea of a breakdown of the imperialism of free trade at the periphery, one must add both the ideological shifts that made it possible for Europeans increasingly conscious of their place in the unfolding of human progress to undertake actions that seemed to smack of old-style militarism. Whether national economic interests in colonial resources or markets could have been met by other means, capital clearly existed in relation to a wider world, was always looking for new possibilities, and had a particular need for tropical commodities. Peripheral breakdowns cannot explain why Britain was in the periphery in the first place, but it is important to see the range of options for exercising economic and political power. There were influential parties within European societies, be they the "gentlemanly capitalists" of Cain and Hopkins or the "parti colonial" of Charles-Robert Ageron, who sought vigorous state intervention and at times formal control.[87] Their influence was all the greater when they could argue from established interests, hence the importance of the bridgehead argument.[88]

Most important is the old fact of empire on the world stage: Europe in the 1870s was not a Europe of nation-states but of empires, old and would-be. It was precisely the fact that the important actors were very few in number and thought in supranational terms that turned the changing patterns of economic interaction into a scramble. Great Britain had multiple options for getting tropical resources and could put up with multiple failures. It feared, however, that other imperial powers would gain exclusive access to sources of vital supplies or lucrative trade, and the fact that a small number of European imperial powers did business with weaker and divided African polities meant that once one European power started to claim territory or exclusive access to parts of Africa, others would have to step up preemptive colonization.

The most unstable international system is one with a small number of powerful actors, neither a world of relatively equal sovereigns nor a world with a single hegemon.[89] Here the fact that Britain was losing its lead as an economic power as Germany, and to a significant extent France and Belgium, industrialized becomes important. It is not surprising that Great Britain was not the first mover in the scramble but ended up with the choicest morsels of the African cake. The paradox of imperial competition was that each power sought imperial resources and feared exclusion from other imperial spaces, but they also feared that allocating too many resources to imperial defense or imperial development could jeopardize the metropole, hence the doctrine that colonies should pay for themselves, including the costs of their own repression.

Germany's brittleness as an empire-builder reflected its catch-up position, its need to make economic advancement a specifically German project in opposition to a British empire that could defend and live off its economic lead.[90] Philipp Ther has presented a compelling argument for seeing late-nineteenth-century Germany in terms of "imperial instead of national history." The German empire, he argues, was built of pieces of neighboring imperial polities within Europe, and thus around people who "clearly did not consider themselves as Germans." The state apparatus was more German than the society. The state project of empire-building extended overseas—where the quest for resources, prestige, and outlets took on more stridency than in the British case precisely because of the consciousness of coming late to the rivalry. Racism toward Africans went along with hardening racism toward European "others," notably the Poles. The German Empire, Ter claims, "wanted to become a homogenous nation-state" but wasn't, and—if it wanted to compete with Great Britain—couldn't become one.[91]

Japan, another late industrializer and late colonizer, was caught up in the same late-nineteenth-century conjuncture: these were the two powers whose imperial projects came closest to building empire from a national core, qualified by Japan's effort to position itself as "Asian," just as Germany's effort must be qualified by the uncertainties over where in Europe Germanness was located.[92] On the ground in Africa, Germany faced the same constraints as did other powers. For all its brutality in suppressing the Herero and Maji Maji revolts, Germany, as John Iliffe shows in the case of Tanganyika, had to make compromises with indigenous elites and peasant producers in order to make empire affordable and controllable.[93]

This reality check ceased to be a factor for Germany after World War I, when it lost its colonies to the victorious empires. A self-consciously colonial power without colonies, Germany was left with not just a sense of grievance vis-à-vis its fellow European empires, but also a sense of superiority unmediated by the complexities of actually ruling over people. It was not that ruling real Africans and Asians rather than fictive ones gave British elites a fuller sense of the humanity of the people they ruled, but rather that ruling "others" gave the British a more realistic sense of the limitations of their own power.[94]

We are now faced with the central paradox of the history of colonialism: the limits faced by the colonizing powers with the seemingly greatest capacity to act and the fullest confidence in their own transformative power.

Colonial states, the British among them, were thin: they needed the legitimacy and coercive capacity of local authority to collect taxes and round up labor, and they needed local knowledge. If the category of chief under colonial administration included former kings, provincial leaders, heads of kinship groups, village elders, or sometimes people whom colonial rulers mistakenly thought influential, such people had to enforce colonial power—under threat of dismissal or worse—but they could not be pushed too far or they would become too discredited to serve the regime.[95] The structure of rule reinforced and rigidified the distinctiveness of subordinate political units within the empires. Colonialism fostered the ethnicization of Africa.[96]

Whereas colonial administrations' reliance on indigenous authorities allowed the latter to enhance and codify patriarchal dimensions of earlier social structures, missionaries tried to slot women into their own vision of domesticity, which they contrasted with the alleged cruelty toward women of pagans, Muslims, and other non-Europeans.[97] Redefining gender relations as part of an imperial, racialized order has been the focus of some of the best scholarship on nineteenth- and twentieth-century empires. Empire-building in the nineteenth century was as much (and in some ways more) a masculine operation than it had been in the sixteenth: men with guns, men on ships, men superintending mines and plantations and disciplining reluctant and dangerous native laborers, men running bureaucracies, men bringing their science, their notions of how societies and economies should work, to benighted lands. But making empire into a way of life seemed to many a quintessentially female task: women's presence would prevent white men from going native, from letting men's "old" urges for military and sexual conquest stand in the way of the civilizing mission and the establishment of bourgeois culture in colonies, for providing an example to native women of what their role should be in social reproduction. These roles entailed contradictions and conflicts, as Lora Wildenthal, for example, has brought out in the case of German colonies, where masculine notions that they could do what they want—including produce and in some cases confer legitimacy upon offspring with indigenous women—conflicted with feminine notions of restraint and domestic order, articulated in racial and gender terms.[98]

A stable gender order proved as elusive as a stable racial order: colonized women, as Luise White has shown in the case of interwar Nairobi, could find niches in colonial sites where their activities—in the provision of housing and food as much as sex—were too effective and entrepreneurial, and seemed to be reproducing the wrong kind of urban working class. The subsequent attempt of colonial regimes to "stabilize" the colonized working class—by separating workers from their rural origins and bringing up new generations near the place of work, living in families under the watchful eyes of health and education bureaucracies—had its contradictions too. The orderly relationship of male breadwinner and female homemaker was broken down not only in the "informal sector," where unsupervised labor relations gave a larger but conflict-ridden role to entrepreneurial women, but also in workers' households themselves, in which the wage packet could be used to support both an altered version of patriarchy and a more entrepreneurial role for wives than official ideology allowed.[99] The stakes that women and men acquired in the successful combination of activities within an extended household also increased the vulnerability of women to the vagaries of male fidelity, male health (even before the days of HIV), and male success in an often cruel colonial economy. Studying gender in the "modern" empire thus reveals less a terrain of successfully imposed colonial categories and rigid ordering than a terrain of conflict and contestation over roles.[100]

We should be careful not to go too far in either emphasizing the inscription of order on colonized people or celebrating cultural adaptiveness and autonomy, and we should certainly not forget that the limitations of colonial power in administering and changing its domains was often experienced as arbitrariness and brutality. Conquest had depended on the ability of invading armies to concentrate firepower, intimidate, and move on. Maintaining control, in the face of rebellions small and large, entailed exemplary punishment, reaching genocidal extremes in cases like the Herero war. Corporal punishment, collective sanctions against communities whose members had offended the colonial order, and penal sanctions for violations of private contracts remained staples of colonial discipline, even when officials recognized that modern governments were not supposed to do such things. Exemplary repression did not disappear with time, as in Sétif in French North Africa in 1945, French Madagascar in 1947, or British Central Kenya after 1952, not to mention in the Algerian war of 1954–62. Up-to-date ideas of policing and surveillance had their place too, but the thinness of colonial administrations and the insistence that colonized people pay the cost of their own oppression limited their possibilities.[101]

The crudity and humiliation that went along with colonial regimes' inability to routinize control and authority coexisted uneasily with imperialism's other pole, the notion of empire as a legitimate polity in which all members had a stake. This side emerged starkly in wars. A million Indians served Britain in World War I; around the same number came from the white dominions. Two million Africans served, mostly with little choice and mostly as carriers and laborers, around a fifth of whom died of disease. In World War II, the empire's contribution would be even greater, from both colonies and dominions.[102]

World War I, in British as in French Africa, was followed by an attempt to put the genii of imperial belonging back into tribal bottles. Even earlier, expressions of a desire to civilize or Christianize, to turn slaves into wage workers and subsistence cultivators into export farmers, were losing their appeal. Such efforts had proven too frustrating, while "detribalized" Africans were proving too demanding. In the 1920s, Britain, like France, rejected "development" programs that would have used metropolitan funds to improve infrastructure and enable a more rational exploitation of colonies, and it made a virtue of necessity, defining their mission as preserving traditional authority.

Throughout this time, islands of export productivity were carved out: mining zones surrounded by vast labor catchment areas, sites of white settlement where farmers received help from the state in recruiting and disciplining labor, and areas of cultivation by African farmers, small or medium scale, who used family labor, tenants and clients, and sometimes wage labor. Attempts to build either an indigenous or a settler capitalism ran up against the situation that most Africans had some land resources, even if they were squeezed by alienation, that colonial economies opened up new niches which were alternatives to subservience to a landowner, and that landowners themselves did not necessarily want to play by the rules of a wage-labor economy. Infrastructure focused on the narrow pathways of an import-export economy. Colonial economies fostered an urban sector, but not an urban society, with the material and social resources for workers to make a life or for officials to shape that life. Such structures permitted some firms to make large profits, but also gave every incentive to Africans to find alternatives to full involvement in a wage-labor or cash crop sector.[103]

In the mid 1930s the famous study of S. Herbert Frankel showed how small a part the "new empire" was playing in British investment patterns: most capital was going to the old, "white" colonies and to Britain's non-colonial trading partners. Neither Lenin's notion of imperialism as the highest stage of capitalism nor the apologists' notion of colonialism as the agent of development of a forward-moving market economy held up.[104]

The mediocrity of colonial economic performance made it easier for colonial powers to slough off the dislocations of the 1929 depression into a countryside they did not have to examine. By the end of the decade, however, British officials began to recognize that even weak economies in Africa and the West Indies produced social dislocation, particularly in the narrow channels of communication and islands of wage-labor production. When production haltingly increased (and with it inflation), a wave of strikes began, from Barbados to Mombasa. The Colonial Office finally got serious about a program of economic development. In India, the government's interest in development interventions only followed upon the India National Congress's effort to make economic development into a political issue.[105]

World War II was a turning point. Its profound implications included a shaking of European self-confidence and the experience of Africans and Asians—not least those who fought in armies defending some empires against others—of the contingency of imperial rule. The campaign against Hitler's racism made colonial ideologies less self-evident. The loss of Indonesia and Indochina to the Japanese Empire interrupted Dutch and French power in ways from which they could not recover, leading to two anticolonial revolutions that would remain in the minds of many as one model of decolonization.[106] In India, expectations of freedom had risen and along with them dangers of conflict, while Britain's heavy reliance on Indian troops and resources in the war had saddled it with economic and political debts from which it too could not recover.[107] The events of the 1940s shook up the apparent normality of the empire-state.

But France and Britain reacted initially to the effects of war by trying to resecure and revitalize the parts of their empires that they retained, particularly in Africa: to turn the development idea into a mechanism for proclaiming the legitimacy of rule, for building up the beleaguered imperial economy, and for raising the standard of living of colonial populations. Explaining why they failed to do so requires probing not only the changing nature of postwar capitalism—and particularly the powerful role of the United States—but also the inability of colonial powers, even given the considerable economic growth of the postwar decade, to make colonial development into a politically sustainable project within African colonies.[108]

In French and British Africa, colonial regimes fell apart as they became caught between two poles: the danger of revolutionary confrontation and an escalation of demands that threatened to turn the rhetoric of imperial legitimacy into assertions for equivalent rights, voice, and standard of living. If empire on the cheap ceased to be politically possible, governments at home would have to ask whether taxpayers were willing to pay the costs of making imperial incorporation meaningful to the poorest of imperial subjects, the costs of repressing those who wanted out, or—most likely—both.[109] Capitalist firms were weighing the advantages of operating within an imperial system against the possibilities of other relationships to state systems—and the costs of all such arrangements.[110] The escalating demands in the postwar decade for better material conditions—set alongside demands for cultural self-expression and political power—challenged European authorities, but also appealed to their hope that colonial societies would indeed become more "modern," productive, and predictable. In the postwar decade, the logic of empire and the logics of development and social democracy came to a costly confluence.

By the mid 1950s, both French and British governments were thinking more specifically than ever about the costs and benefits of particular colonies and of colonies in general. The potential gains looked uncertain, the potential costs high. Britain and France were by 1956 or 1957 looking to pass their obligations—and their power—to aspiring elites within the colonies, hoping that a positive postcolonial relationship would be more useful than a contentious and expensive colonial one.[111]

By then, India, Indonesia, and other ex-colonial nations were organizing into a bloc, turning the United Nations into a forum for anticolonial discourse, and trying with some success to use Cold War rivalries to make claims on behalf of the "third world." Important as the reconfiguration of the postwar economy was, the undoing of empire required a change in how politics was thought about—taking away the aura of normality attached to empire for millennia—and this change came about through a mix of mobilization in the colonies, international interaction, and domestic politics in metropoles, where moral qualms and financial concerns attached to both repression and reform in the colonies undermined imperial projects.

In Africa, what collapsed first was not colonialism as an obdurate, unchanging edifice, but colonialism in its interventionist moment. If the Indonesian and Indochinese revolutions demonstrated early on the dangers of failing to accommodate political movements in the colonies, the relatively nonviolent decolonizations in sub-Saharan Africa put the holdouts, including Algeria and settler colonies of southern Africa, in a vulnerable position.[112]

An imperial conception of geopolitics and an imperial sentimentality lingered afterward in policies of promoting French or British culture in ex-colonies, in preferential treatment for ex-empire commodities in European tariff regimes, and for a time in immigration rules that sought to meet labor needs from within the old empire. But the very process that created nation-states in Africa and Asia also made Britain and France national entities in a way they had not been before. The stakes in who was included and excluded in the welfare state were high. If some people within Britain and France hoped to turn the continued presence in national territory of people originally from the colonies into a culturally pluralistic sense of the nation, others—like Enoch Powell in Britain and Jean-Marie Le Pen in France—put forth a national, xenophobic view of an essential France or Britain, a form of exclusionary racism different from the imperial notion of holding subordinated peoples within the polity.[113]

The settler colonies—southern Rhodesia and Algeria, most notoriously—were the most difficult nuts to crack, for settlers had appropriated the empires' representative institutions and the ideology of development. In Algeria, the diehard elements among settlers and the military attempted a coup against the very state to which they proclaimed allegiance, while in Rhodesia, white settlers declared independence because the empire that had spawned them would no longer defend their racial privileges. In both cases—and eventually in South Africa—settlers' insistence that they were not simply their own sort of "imagined community" but the overseas vanguard of civilization, Christianity, and economic progress left them vulnerable to the repudiation of mother country and international opinion. Empire was, and remained until the 1960s, part of a global system, and when that system lost its political and moral force, its last remaining pieces could not sustain themselves.

This part of the chapter has gone over the ground best covered in the recent burst of scholarship on colonial societies: the "modern" overseas empires. What this scholarship has done best is to focus on the intertwined way in which Europe defined itself and colonized spaces in relation to each other. Scholars have shown how such colonial regimes constructed Africans as bodies to be remade to fit the modern world, as racialized, gendered selves to be molded to a particular niche in the colonial economic and social order, or as alterity incarnate. They have studied colonialism as a certain type of social order, with mental maps for placing different peoples and methods of policing boundaries among them. My emphasis here has been on how attention to the imperatives of thinking like an empire can give a fuller picture of the overseas empires of the nineteenth and twentieth centuries, both by broadening the time perspective and narrowing it. Broadening because in both new and old empires the problems of ruling over large, distant, and expanding populations in ways that institutionalized both incorporation and differentiation constrained the possibilities of implementing whatever project colonial rulers had, and because the extent and unevenness of imperial space inevitably produced tensions among colonial elites and among different colonizing ideologies and interests. Narrower because analysis of the construction of colonizer and colonized is most valuable when read not against a generalized "modernity," but against the shifting needs and constraints facing colonial regimes in specific moments, the varying ability of colonized people to deflect and reinterpret all such projects, and the actual resources devoted to mechanisms of social construction. For all the emphasis on the military, technological, bureaucratic, and cultural power of the latest round of empire-builders, the story of empires is still a story of limits.

When French and British policy most emphatically—if still inconsistently—embraced the goal of modernizing colonized societies, when they repudiated their past insistence on the immutable distinctiveness of colonized people, and when they leaned decisively toward the incorporative pole of imperial systems, then empire became definitively unsustainable. In the 1960s, a world of nation-states finally came into being, over three centuries after the peace of Westphalia, 180 years after the French and American revolutions, and 40 years after the Wilsonian assertions of national self-determination.

OLD EMPIRES IN A NEW WORLD:
OTTOMANS, HABSBURGS, AND ROMANOVS

That the embodiments of dynastic, nondemocratic, multinational polities could exist for nearly a century and a half after the apparent dawn of the modern nation-state sits uneasily with the "empire to nation" teleology.[114] Perhaps instead of preserving the grand narrative by dismissing these empires as quaintly anachronistic, we might use their histories to rethink the narrative. Recent scholarship has in fact illuminated the interplay of imperial and local elites and imperial and national ideologies within these empires, up until the moment of their imposed dissolution.

Ottoman specialists have given a picture of a dynamic empire at two levels: they demonstrate the importance of Ottoman reform efforts in the nineteenth century, to critics of the regime as well as high officials; "Ottomanism" was a compelling vision for a cosmopolitan elite. Mehmed Ali Pasha, sometimes regarded as the founder of "modern Egypt," was a thoroughly Ottomanized man of Balkan origin, at the helm of an administration from various parts of the empire whose world view was shaped by their imperial experience. There were tensions between the Turkish-speaking and Arabic-speaking parts of the Egyptian elite and between the Pasha and the Sultan—as there were between overmighty regional authorities and supreme rulers in any empire. What was at stake in Mehmed Ali's building of an army in Egypt and his efforts at restructuring Egyptian society was the nature of the empire, not a question of Egypt versus Ottoman. When British pressure on Egypt later in the century produced a rebellion, a crucial dynamic came from Egyptian perceptions that the Ottoman elite had failed to protect them against another imperialism; this rising was as much an interempire conflict as it was a specifically Egyptian one.[115]

Nineteenth-century reform from the 1839 Tanzimat onward, Selim Deringil argues, represented an attempt at a "civilizing mission" that parallels those of France and Britain: efforts to sedentarize nomads, to educate illiterate populations, to "permeate" dimensions of Ottoman society heretofore left to local elites and diverse populations. The Ottomans were in part borrowing Western European techniques better to rival these empires that were poaching on Ottoman territories in the Balkans and North Africa, and in part seeking to compromise with French and British demands for recognition of the citizenship rights of Christians and protection of Western European commercial interests. But with the sultan's wavering attitude toward constitutional reform, "Young Ottomans" and other elites articulated increasingly radical calls for political change, looking toward the French Revolution, the Russian revolution of 1905, and the Meiji revolution for precedents—still focused on revitalizing the empire as a whole.

This combination of external pressure and imperial reform had complex effects: Sultan Abdul Hamid's loss of Balkan territories led him to weaken the millet system in favor of a more specifically Islamic ideology of empire, and demands for recognition of Christian groups sometimes enhanced sectarianism. These issues were being played out in imperial space, and in conjunction with the Ottoman Empire's acute rivalry with the neighboring Habsburg and Russian Empires, and under pressure from Britain and France, but with occasional diplomatic support from Britain to keep the Russian Empire from expanding further and to ensure repayment of the empire's debts.[116]

The second trend Ottoman historiography has brought out is the relationship of Istanbul to the provinces of empire. Studies of the Arab Levant, eastern Anatolia, Yemen, and Albania complicate the picture of imposed reform by showing that elites whose power base was local developed an interest in selective accommodation with Ottoman demands. Local and regional elites were both conveyors of Ottomanist conceptions to their areas and architects of local interpretations of what being part of the empire meant, shaping what Michael Meeker calls "Ottomanist provincial society."[117]

One can make similar arguments about the Habsburg and Russian Empires: empires challenged by rival powers and social change from within responding with projects of reform at the imperial level, facing opposition that was both national and imperial. The critics of Habsburg conservatism, for instance, included many who saw the imperial unit as a possibility offering something to reform-minded intellectuals, to Jews, and to others who sought a bigger field than what became national units. The "dual monarchy," which ceded great autonomy to Hungarian elites within the empire, was both a concession to the vernacular elites' aspirations for power and a mechanism that reinforced the cooperation of German- and Hungarian-speaking rulers, for the latter feared that their own "national" domain could fragment because of the importance of non-Hungarians within it, just as they had to be concerned with the fate of Hungarians outside the boundaries of Hungary—a problem that common inclusion in a Habsburg polity helped to contain.[118]

In analyzing the Russian Empire, as Jane Burbank argues, "the use of empire and nation as distinct and antagonistic categories is problematic and obstructive." The Russian autocracy had to consolidate rule against equally imperial neighbors along some of its frontiers and elsewhere rule a spread-out, resource-poor population. Political authority was both centralized and thin, because the resources available to local elites through cooperation with the center made a decisive difference. Russian governments deployed a range of political strategies to differentially incorporate their non-Russian components, and their elites shared with intellectuals of Germany and France a geographic and ethnographic interest in acquiring knowledge about the complex cultural makeup of the empire. In its core areas as in its periphery, the Russian "autocracy could not bring itself at this critical juncture to take the giant steps toward citizenship, limited monarchy, representational politics, and inclusive programs of cultural discipline that proved so critical to the successful national projects in Europe in the nineteenth century." The "Russian" peasant, not just the Muslim Central Asian, was an "other," and the government was more autocratic than national. Interempire competition in the nineteenth century pushed the Russian, like the Ottoman, Empire in the late nineteenth century toward a more vigorous program of "civilizing" its outer reaches, but civilizing and Russifying could only go so far, given the tenuous arrangements by which administrative and judicial authority was actually exercised in distant parts of the empire. The ambiguity between empire and nation remained as much in the imagination of critical intellectuals as in that of the ruling autocracy.[119]

All three old empires had a much longer life span than the new empires in Africa, and the Russian Empire after its collapse turned into an equally imperial polity, the Soviet Union.[120] These empires did not wither away; they were destroyed as a consequence of World War I—as Britain and France brought all the force of their imperial systems to bear in a war whose conclusion was far from evident until the intervention of another sort of transoceanic power, the United States. Along the way, the Ottoman Empire, imprudently allied with the German, was still capable of teaching the British military in the Dardanelles and Iraq a few lessons about the limits of a supposedly modern empire.

These empires did have basic weaknesses—most notably that they could not equal the economic dynamism of Western Europe. What had long been a strength of the Ottoman system—the inclusion of different communities that occupied different niches in the imperial polity and economy and which benefited from their inclusion within this wider structure—turned into a weakness, for the merchants best positioned to integrate the Ottoman Empire into world trade were Christians (Greeks, Armenians, etc.) or Jews, and as the economic balance tilted increasingly toward Western Europe, they were less interested in firming up their relations with the Ottoman elite. As the sultan recognized the importance of forms of Western learning but sought to contain their effect, those who were educated in the French, English, and American schools were also tempted to move their networks and inclinations in different directions.[121] The sultan, particularly after the loss of territory in the Balkans, emphasized his role as leader of the Islamic faithful—a way of cementing his ties to the still very diverse Arabs, Turks, and others within his domains—and placed less emphasis on his role as leader of a multinational polity. Here was a fundamental vulnerability of empire: the danger of alternative networks, sources of wealth and patronage. The dangers included not simply those of secession or breakup of a multinational entity into homogeneous national blocks, but also that of networks *across* lines of religious or cultural difference that bypassed the imperial center.

The situation from the last quarter of the nineteenth century through World War I cannot be deciphered simply by comparing empires. This was a particular conjuncture. The significant actors were few in number, and each potentially drew on resources that were not limited by a particular population. Those resources were not necessarily supplied voluntarily, and the large contingents of Indians, Arabs, and Africans, as well as Canadians, New Zealanders, and Australians on the British and French sides of the world war—not to mention the material resources, obtained under forms of labor entailing varying degrees of coercion—were a part of the ultimate test of strength of these imperial systems.

Moreover, this was a time when states—empire-states, that is—were experimenting with forms of social engineering to enhance their long-term social cohesion and strength, and they were experimenting as well with ways of using populations whose distinction and subordination were clearly marked. The small number of actors and the diversity of their make-up—with the dangers that human and material resources of empire could be weakened or lost to a rival imperial formation—constituted a force for instability, all the more because it encouraged other actors to pursue imperial strategies.

World War I resulted in the coerced extinction of the Ottoman and Habsburg Empires, the transformation of the Russian Empire into a new—but still imperial—form, the parceling out of the German Empire and portions of the Ottoman to other empires, the constitution of small and vulnerable nation-states in Central Europe, and the articulation of a doctrine of national self-determination that was undercut from the start by the fact that it didn't apply to the most important empires. The basic point that Donald Quataert makes about the Ottoman Empire applies to the Habsburg and Romanov Empires as well: "Neither Turkish nor Arab nor Armenian nor Kurdish nationalism pushed a dying Ottoman state over the nationalist cliff after 1914."[122] The nation-state did not emerge triumphant from this war or from the Treaty of Versailles.[123] What did emerge were two would-be empires, Nazi Germany and a reinvigorated Japan, which wreaked havoc among weak new states in Central Europe and a mixture of states, colonies, and semicolonies in the Far East and South East Asia. They threatened the old empires and clashed with two powers that had something like the global reach of empires but insisted they were something else.

THE EMPIRE IN SPITE OF ITSELF: THE UNITED STATES

Until recently, only a few scholars—seen by some as leftwing cranks—wrote of the United States as an empire. That is no longer the case.[124] And the word *empire* has appeared in political debate, employed not only by those critical of American high-handedness in relation to its democratic pretensions, but by conservative scholars who hope to see the United States exercise the power it has. On both poles, there is a danger of confusing the word *empire* as a metaphor for extremes of power and *empire* as an analytic construct for a certain kind of polity.

I wish to make two simple points. First, the most important consideration may well be precisely the disjuncture in American history between image and reality, between a firmly "national" view of the polity and an exercise of power that was at critical times something else. The disjuncture may shape the way policy options are conceived and presented to the public. Second, the concept of empire need not be a static one: it can be a stage that a polity passes *through*. The United States may well have become a nation-state because it pretended to be one.

As Richard White shows, one should no more push back the exclusion of the Native American population after the mid nineteenth century into a founding myth of unambiguous alterity than accept a founding myth of national unity. In prerevolutionary days on the edges of European settlement, the power differentials were not so extreme, and for a time rival European empires interacted with different Indian empires—also multinational polities—via trade, military alliances, cultural connection, and sexual relations. These patterns changed "when Indians ceased to have the power to force whites onto the middle ground."[125] At a later date, Indians were referred to as "domestic dependent nations," suggesting a classic imperial concatenation of inclusion, subordination, and differentiation. Relations between the American government and Indians were governed by treaties, not dissimilar to the fiction in the late nineteenth century of African chiefs voluntarily ceding their lands and people to representatives of European states. In the Southwest's ambiguous borderlands, where the consequences of Spanish colonization, American expansion, and the shifting fortunes of different Indian polities produced a space of cultural overlap and interaction, government policy in the nineteenth century was slowly "to eviscerate the borderlands and then to push the border" southward.[126]

What was different was not only the extent of the resources that continental empire provided in North America, but also the American state's refusal of what European colonial powers took for granted: an image of itself as a colonial regime, of *keeping* conquered territories as nonequivalent parts of the polity. American institutions were at one level assimilative and incorporative: new Americans could be made and new territories could go through a series of stages until they became states, equivalent to other states.[127] The sea-to-shining-sea notion conveyed a certain naturalness to American boundaries, concealing the debates over how far the limits of continental empire would extend. That the United States had its wave of overseas conquests in the same period, the end of the 1890s, as did other powers, does not negate the fact that these were few in number and did not give rise to a doctrine of imperial rule, something all the more striking in relation to the country's military and economic capacity.[128] Within its colonies, the U.S. government shared much of its strategies and constraints with other colonial powers, but its preferred method for exercising power overseas or south of its eventual border was not conquest and incorporation, but to send in military forces, eliminate unwanted rulers, force replacement elites to agree to American terms (as in the humiliating treaty with Cuba), and then withdraw, perhaps to return again. This bash and run approach to the exercise of power overseas retains a prominent place in the American repertoire.[129]

The flip side of this process of empire as a passing stage was the harshness of exclusion for those who didn't fit. Indians were the victims of ruthless massacres and survivors ended up in reservations, bounded by fictions of a form of sovereignty and a reality of marginalization. For some, at least, there was an exit option from the reservation—but only via individual assimilation into what Americans thought of as the mainstream. Blacks, like Indians, had in the early eighteenth century not been so neatly set apart as they later were, but the effort to build a Republican movement led to an elite effort at boundary-marking. The expansion of the slave economy and the extension of a white, male franchise would rigidify the distinction.[130] After the Civil War, the 13th, 14th, and 15th constitutional amendments implied that the only place in American society for blacks was as the equivalent of everyone else, which was one reason why men of bad will worked hard to find mechanisms to enforce exclusion.

The United States has devised many mechanisms, going well beyond the military, to exercise power and influence overseas. Even as the current U.S. government is becoming more unilateralist in its foreign policy, its actions on the ground in Afghanistan and Iraq still suggest a shying away from precisely the notions of territory and long-term sovereign responsibility that empire implies. The closest echoes from an imperial past are the bash and move-on dimensions that have been part of the conduct of imperial militaries from Chinggis Khan to the British plus the "imperialism of free trade." From World War II—and abortively and with disastrous consequences after World War I—the United States portrayed itself as an advocate of a world of nation-states; it positioned itself as a mild critic of French and British empires and a virulent opponent of the Soviet one. It supported multilateral arrangements and bilateral agreements that both acknowledged the sovereignty of new and old nations and exercised influence, and at times power, over them. But it would only go so far. The United States distinguishes itself as both the most powerful actor on the world scene, and the industrial state that contributes the lowest percentage of its GNP to development assistance.

Recent patterns are thus consistent with a longer history of the American empire overseas: having made itself in the nineteenth century into one of the great continental empires of the last two centuries, on a scale comparable only with Russia and the Soviet Union (and, earlier, China), the United States stands out for its unwillingness to name what it was doing, producing a self-defined nation-state marked by fictions of equivalent inclusion and structures of stark exclusion and by conflicting visions of the role of unilateral force, rule-bound, institutionalized cooperation, and informal arrangements in an international system that is no longer a world of rival empires, no longer a world of bipolar conflict, but a world of extreme inequalities of wealth and power.

CONNECTIONS AND IMAGINATIONS WITHIN, ACROSS, AND AGAINST EMPIRE

The long arms and weak fingers of empire-states have been the focus of this chapter. But it would be misleading to juxtapose the global reach of imperialism or capitalism with the community that defends its autonomy and resists forces external to it. Aggressive empires and resistant communities are part of history, but so too are other forms of connection that cross oceans and continents, differences of religion or language, which intersect—sometimes to complement, sometimes to crosscut—the long-distance connections of empire. All I can do here is to enumerate some of the linkages that have held ambiguous relations to empire.

Trading networks are the most obvious place to start: for example, the Muslim groups that crossed the Sahara Desert, the Indian Ocean, the Arabian Peninsula, Central Asia, the Malayan Peninsula, and the islands of Southeast Asia. Such networks existed within Islamic polities and connected entrepots ruled by others. Similarly, Chinese traders developed dense networks in Southeast Asia and ventured as far as East Africa. Without Islamic and Chinese trading systems, it is far from clear that the Portuguese and Dutch empires from the sixteenth century would have been able to tap into enough wealth to pay for their administrative and maritime infrastructure. The British East India Company was in its formative years parasitic on the networks developed by Indian merchant communities. South Asian traders were installed in East Africa before European colonization, but they proved important agents of commercial development within the British possessions. In the Ottoman Empire, Armenians, Greeks, and Jews were conduits of trade and were recognized as valued but distinct collectivities within the Ottoman system. Syrio-Lebanese had a special place in both urban and rural commerce in French and British Africa in the twentieth century. Abner Cohen has argued that ethnic affinity was both a basis for and was reinforced by long-distance trading arrangements, for such traders needed relations of trust with people all along the route, and the support of a substantial community at the interface of the trade route with less mobile, local communities. But building an empire was about tying many places to one. Hence trading mechanisms were vital to empires—old and new—but could be relatively autonomous, potentially useful to imperial rivals, posing the possibility of getting around the imperial center and making it irrelevant.[131]

Religion was propagated by empire and cut across empire. The clash of rival universalisms animated the Crusades, the fifteenth-century struggles in Spain and later in the Spanish Empire, and conflict in the twenty-first century. The missionary experience was part of the history of empire, but missionaries often crossed imperial lines and could not control the religious networks that sprang up among converts. Islam's relation to empire was ambiguous ever since the fall of the early Caliphate—and if the Ottomans sometimes assumed the mantle of the caliph and guarantors of Islamic law, and sometimes the role of multiconfessional emperors, the empire was a space in which different meanings were given to Islam and different kinds of organization and mobilization developed. The Islamic pilgrimage and the training of Islamic scholars at different sites around the Islamic world shaped an enormous web of connection within and across imperial systems. The expansion of Islam during the era of European colonization in Africa and the ability of Islamic leaders to work out a modus vivendi with colonial rulers, who were sometimes as ambivalent about their own clerics as about someone else's, are other elements of the ambiguous relationship of religion and empire. African American missionaries influenced African Christianity, and African religions and African Islam influenced African Americans in Brazil, the Caribbean, and the United States. Transatlantic religious connections produced notions of African "nations" distinct from territorially or politically defined meanings.[132]

The movement of people is much more complicated than the concept of settlement conveys. The implications of the movements of colonial officials and military personnel—not to mention missionaries, technical specialists, and representatives of business firms—from colony to colony deserve examination. European settlers in colonies were part of the dynamics of empire: transforming production as well as commerce, using labor (itself subject to voluntary and involuntary migration over long and short distances) in new ways, and developing ties of kinship, religion, and trust across space—both facilitating economic interaction and fostering transcontinental communities of sentiment. Creoles at times chafed under continued rule by the governments that had spawned their settlements, sometimes turning colonies into independent states. Such a process changed but did not necessarily diminish settlers' place in imperial economic and social networks, but it reshaped international norms of sovereignty, contributing to a language of self-determination that could be used by people the settlers had exploited and tried to consign to a distinct and inferior position in imperial social formations. In places like Algeria and Rhodesia, settlers proved not so easy to get rid of when they no longer served the interests of empire: prolonged violence and chaotic "returns" of European settlers (from Dutch Indonesia, French Algeria, and Portuguese Angola and Mozambique, most notoriously) were among the consequences.[133]

The slave trade brought people into empires against their will, and indentured labor systems moved people around, making use of empires' administrative structures to enforce the semicoercive basis of labor contracts. Empires often tried to keep migrant labor within their borders, but did not necessarily succeed. The much-discussed postcolonial flows of labor from former colonies into Britain and France had their roots in earlier migratory patterns. France, after World War II, sought not just immigrants in general, but colonial immigrants—from North Africa and sub-Saharan Africa—but because they belonged to an imperial polity and after 1946 were citizens of the French Union, they had rights and claims against the polity, which made sense before decolonization and for a time thereafter, but produced increasing tension as France became more of a national polity.[134]

Such movements, as well as that of sailors and other mobile workers to imperial ports and the sojourns of students and professional people of colonial origin in European cities, gave rise to intercolonial relationships, which became the basis for political movements that linked Asians, Africans, African Americans, and others even before the Bandung conference gave rise to "third-worldism." Empire shaped notions of space in specific ways, through which certain places (London, imperial port cities) became nodes of communication and imagination.[135]

Moreover, "transnational issue networks" within, across, and against empires have a particular importance that belies the empire-conquest/community-resistance framework.[136] The antislavery movement was the model: starting among British Protestants in the late eighteenth century, largely middle-class but with important working-class elements, crossing the Atlantic to become an Anglo-American movement, invigorated by the conviction and symbolic importance of ex-slaves like Olaudah Equiano and later Frederick Douglass, linked to slave colonies by missionary stations, this complex social movement showed that empire could be a space of moral discourse.

Anticolonial and anti-apartheid movements followed in this lineage. In a territory like Algeria or South Africa, the history of political mobilization is not one of automatic unity following upon the common experience of oppression, but one of a range of activist stances and contingent affiliations, sometimes punctuated by internecine conflict. The success of anticolonial and anti-apartheid movements cannot be explained on a colony-by-colony basis, but drew on a still wider contingent affiliation of people, inside and outside metropoles and colonies, who convinced each other that the apparent normality of colonialism or white domination could not be sustained.[137] The relationship of such movements to each other shifted over time, as did the extent to which they focused on replacing empire with nation-states or developing other forms of political solidarity, such as pan-Africanism, pan-Arabism, pan-Islamism, pan-Asianism, or various forms of diasporic imagination. The emergence of a world of nations in the 1960s was the contingent outcome of a variety of other aspirations, leaving in place the possibility that new forms of long-distance affinity are still emerging and manifesting themselves in active networks and institutions.[138]

CONCLUSION

The most important point this chapter has made is the simplest: the fundamental importance of empires in world history, up to a very recent moment in the past. We need to take seriously what it meant for a polity *to think like an empire,* to conjugate incorporation and differentiation, to confront problems of long-distance extension and recognize limits of control over large and diverse populations. Thinking like an empire was not the same as thinking like a nation-state, and while territorial and cultural conceptions of "the nation" were in some situations more powerful than in others—and at times had devastating effects—the imperative of acting like an empire-state within a global system of empire-states was a compelling constraint on the range of action.

Even though we need to recognize the long-term importance of empire in modern history, we should not get carried away with the power of empires, either in the sense of a nostalgic view or of its opposite, a conception of empire as totalizing power. We should understand instead the limits of imperial power, and especially the limits that derived from the structure of empire itself. Because empires were big and had long communications routes, they depended on a range of agents, on missionaries, settlers, and fortune-seekers and on local elites who could find an interest in imperial circuits of commerce and power, and they were vulnerable not only to assertions of autonomy and resistance to central authority, but to the growth of circuits that bypassed the imperial center. And because empires reproduced rather than absorbed cultural distinction, they had to confront collectivities within their borders and networks that crossed them. Empires, old and new, had great difficulty in finding a stable balance between the incorporation and differentiation of populations they colonized, between exploiting older economic structures and building new ones, between maintaining direct, bureaucratic authority and exercising power by linking themselves to patronage structures, networks, and idioms of authority in conquered territories. Imperial strategies of rule confronted colonized populations with the terrible difficulty of preserving something of their own way of life while finding means to act within new relations of power. The confrontations that ensued had consequences that neither rulers nor ruled could anticipate, and produced lines of political connection more varied and complex than a dichotomy of superior and subaltern or the horizontal affinity characteristic of nationalism. New empires did not necessarily manage the problems of rule better than older ones, and if at times they evinced greater transformative ambitions, their interventions still had unpredictable effects as colonized people resisted, appropriated, deflected, and reconfigured such efforts.

Empires like Rome declined when they had no equivalent rivals, and they collapsed under pressure from their enemies; the role of national mobilization against empires is only part of these patterns. The colonial empires of Western European powers occupy a relatively small part of the historical horizon, and their collapse followed that of the supposedly archaic Ottoman, Habsburg, and Romanov empires by a mere three decades. The post–World War II moment was not the first interconnected, systemic crisis of empire: the North and South American revolutions, the Haitian revolution, and the Napoleonic wars, combined with crises in Islamic empires, shook up global power relations in the early nineteenth century, but not the fundamentally inter-empire structure of rivalries.[139] World War I emerged from a conflict of empires who each had the potential of harnessing resources beyond the territory in destabilizing ways. In the aftermath of war, only some empires were dismantled, and new forms of empire, with a starker distinction between a national core and internal and external "others," brought about an even greater crisis in an international system of nonequivalent states.

A generalized system of nation-states—formally equivalent but in fact riven by inequalities and asymmetrical relations of power—finally emerged in the 1950s and 1960s. That fundamental break in the organization of world power was more complicated than the emergence of national consciousness. It was more complicated than a failure of will or military and economic capacity on the part of old empires weakened by two wars or the emergence of new and rival superpowers. It was also a crisis within the empire-state form itself, always caught between poles of incorporation and difference, but now having to confront two developments with long antecedents that came together in the postwar conjuncture. The first was the crisis of racial order that the mobilization against Nazism entailed. The quest of Britain and France for a legitimate colonialism outside a framework of racial distinction rapidly proved unstable, providing no convincing answer in metropole or colony as to why rule and responsibility of some people over others still made sense.

Second was the consolidation of the welfare state and social democracy in France and Great Britain, leaving the question of whether the empire-state or the nation-state would be the unit in which "the social" was defined. The inherent uncertainty over belonging and equivalence in the empire-state not only worried rulers, but was the focus of a burst of mobilization in colonial societies. The threat to empires was not only that of secession—something the empires had faced and survived before—but that they could not afford the costs of staying whole. In the postwar context, empires faced not only movements demanding independence but movements demanding equivalence among people who now asserted themselves to be imperial citizens—without there being a clear line at which to stop such claims. Sometimes—the British in Malaya and Kenya for example—a war of liberation was successfully defeated, and independence conceded shortly thereafter. The most self-consciously progressive imperial powers cracked first, but the fact that colonial systems existed within a system of empire-states meant that the holdouts had difficulty surviving amid their independent neighbors.

The picture of national sovereignty becoming generalized in the 1950s and 1960s needs to be qualified. One reason why French elites, especially business elites, were willing to measure the costs and benefits of colonies in a critical manner in the mid 1950s was that they were already thinking about the possibilities of another sort of supranational entity, the European Economic Community, to which a part of national sovereignty would be ceded. Ex-colonies found their sovereignty compromised by less voluntary mechanisms, such as indebtedness to international financial organizations and the multidimensioned asymmetry of international relations.[140]

In 1994, after decades of struggle, majority rule came to South Africa, the last act in a long history of racialized imperialism. And in 1989 the Soviet Union gave up its hold on Eastern Europe and later on much of the Central Asian territories it had inherited from the tsarist empire. South African political movements were varied in their goals, persistent and courageous in their efforts, but their eventual success owed much to their winning the battle of connections—they, not the self-proclaimed defenders of a white, Christian civilization, placed their oppressors in an isolated, besieged situation. South Africa is now a multiracial, multicultural, democratic polity. Whether it will find a route to social and economic justice remains in question. In the Soviet Union, the communist system fell apart from its core, through elite disaffection in relation to the perceived opportunities elsewhere as much as through the long history of principled opposition and the competition of rival powers. But the peeling away of the Soviet empire in Eastern Europe and Central Asia, violent in places, surprisingly peaceful in others, was possible because it was indeed an empire, with distinct component parts. The Russian Federation itself remains multinational, and it remains to be seen if it will be pluralistic. These two instances of momentous change in the very recent past point not only to the importance of thinking precisely and historically about the vulnerability of structures of power and the possibilities of political mobilization across space, but also about possibilities of change in the future.

The most important fact about empires is that they are gone. A once ordinary part of political life became a political impossibility. Thinking about how this came about allows us to appreciate the limits of power at its most extensive, the ability of people to find niches and fissures within systems of control and constraint, the conservatism of the most progress-oriented states, and the adaptability of supposedly traditional people. Inequality of power, even extreme inequality, persists in other forms and with other names. Those forms too will become objects of mobilization across space and difference, and perhaps what is ordinary today will become politically impossible tomorrow.

7 Labor, Politics, and the End of Empire in French Africa

Having devoted most of this book to conceptual issues and historical arguments that range widely over time and space, I turn now to a specific situation. It is a small part of a bigger story, but I want to tell it with enough narrative density to establish the value of confronting original sources on the politics of decolonization and to suggest the interest in pursuing related topics.[1] But this is not just any case. The conjuncture of World War II—from a little before through the decade after—was a time of definitive change in the political forms available to state-builders. I have argued that the end of empire came not just through the titanic and violent struggle of an implacable colonialism against forces of national liberation, but also from within the system, as political fissures within imperial structures and imperial discourses were pried open by political and social movements in the empires. So this is a story of how African labor leaders in dialogue and dispute with European officials brought both sides of the colonial divide to a place where neither, in the mid 1940s, had wanted to go.

The significance of labor movements in the history of decolonization is not that they were a necessary vanguard of a national movement; the writings in Subaltern Studies have correctly warned against narratives that either privilege "Western" models of class or nationalist leadership or explain the disappointments of political history by a lack of such tendencies in colonized societies (see chapter 1). Anticolonial politics in Africa drew on anger, aspirations, and affinities expressed in a wide variety of idioms—from notions of healing the land of its ills to millennial visions of a new order to a melding of new and old visions of social roles among such "middle" people as schoolteachers and civil servants. A persuasive interpretation of the success of the political parties that challenged colonial rule in Africa is that they operated like political machines, assembling for a time diverse

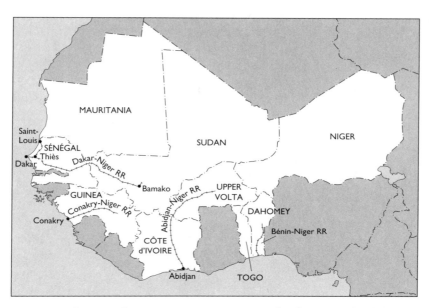

MAP 2. French West Africa. Togo was a territory mandated to France by the League of Nations and administered on a different juridical basis but in close political relation to the Federation of French West Africa.

groups of people whose grievances and aspirations focused on the state.[2] Such a process was contingent and conjunctural.

Organized labor's particular importance is twofold. First, the narrowness of colonial economies gave relatively small numbers of workers in transportation and commercial nodes and in mines the possibility of disrupting an export-import economy, threatening to drive up the costs and undermine the legitimacy of the much-touted postwar colonial effort at economic development. Second, the discourse that labor movements deployed in the postwar era—putting claims to resources in the terms in which imperial rule was now asserting its justification—made them hard to combat without calling into question the modernizing project on which France and Britain had staked so much. Labor movements revealed to colonial powers that they were endangered not only by political failure—as in the revolutions of Indochina and Algeria—but by political success, if social movements operated within the ideological and institutional structures that the postwar regimes were trying to build up and used them to demand a more progressive, more egalitarian imperial system. In the conjuncture of postwar international politics, the question of changing the standard of living of Africans—in regard to health, education, agricultural and industrial policy, as well as the conditions of workers—exposed the limits of arguments that colonization would improve the lives of the colonized but the colonizer would determine the extent and the means by which this would come about. This chapter describes an instance of colonial control coming apart on political territory the regime thought was its own.

It is precisely because this story is contingent and conjunctural that it deserves special scrutiny. In the 1950s, an acute tension arose between labor movements and nationalist politics, a tension that opened up important debates on the nature of struggle and the kind of society activists wished to build. But the advent of national rule, starting with Guinea in 1958, witnessed an attempt by new leaders to resolve that tension by insisting that the variety of mobilizations be subordinated to the task of creating a true African nation. The labor movement was prominent among the social mobilizations that had contributed to the challenge to colonial authority and which new rulers sought to tame or suppress so that they themselves would not be so challenged. This story of the opening of political space ends with the closing down of that space. It points to the limits of a certain kind of decolonization.

THE POSTWAR OPENING

As the war was coming to a close, leading figures of the French government in exile acknowledged the need to turn a new page in colonial policy. They did, but not the page they had intended to turn. The strike movement in French West Africa's capital city, Dakar, which lasted from December 1945 to February 1946, forced French officials into a confrontation with the social implications of colonial rule, cut away some of the major tenets of colonial thinking about Africans, and underscored the need for more systematic political reform at a crucial moment in the postwar constitutional debates.

Initially, the Free French vision of reform was closely bounded: "évolués," educated Africans, should be given a modest place in legislative assemblies; forced labor, excessive taxation of rural populations, extrajudicial punishments, and other of the most hated aspects of administration should be (sometimes slowly) abandoned; money should be spent to develop infrastructure for a more dynamic colonial economy; education and other services should be expanded. Very little was said about wage workers. The governor-general of French West Africa was still hoping in 1945 that the dangers of an "indigenous proletariat" could be avoided. The official sociology of Africa contained two categories, *évolué* and *paysan* (peasant). Economic development—as well as the hoped-for growth of the African population—should take place within a "customary" milieu.[3]

Dakar's workers disrupted this dualistic vision. Their challenge began from a small opening, the revival after 1944 of trade unions, dormant since 1938 or 1939, especially in Dakar and especially in the civil service.[4] Dakarois *évolué* families were relatively well integrated into urban life, and the first union leaders, such as Abbas Guèye of the metalworkers' union, Papa Jean Ka of the commercial workers' union, and Lamine Diallo, who headed the umbrella group of Dakar unions, the Union des Syndicats de Dakar, came from well-established families in the areas that had been under French control since the eighteenth century and whose inhabitants had obtained citizenship rights (see chapter 6). They were able to establish connections with the French union federation, Confédération Générale du Travail (CGT) and receive some help in establishing French-style trade union organizations.[5]

In 1944 and 1945, civil service unions were demanding more pay, while the leading Senegalese politician, Lamine Guèye, was arguing for equality for African civil servants in fulfillment of promises made by French officials. Guèye, a citizen, a socialist, former ally of the Popular Front in 1936–38, was taking up where he had left off before the war, and would soon be elected by Senegal's citizens as a deputy to the Assemblée Nationale Constituante in Paris, where he would play a major role in drafting the sections of the constitution dealing with the Union Française. So far, the demands of Senegal's civil servants fit the French framework of évolués demanding more equal treatment. While trying to hold down wage demands, the administration reorganized the civil service hierarchy, assuring Africans access to higher-paid posts while raising the standards candidates had to meet. The reform, however, led to agitation among civil servants who felt they would fall on the wrong side of the standards barrier.[6]

Workers at all levels, meanwhile, were beset by high inflation—nearly 300 percent since the beginning of the war—and shortages of imported commodities like cloth. Although there were some wage adjustments during this period, the Free French governments tried both in 1943 and 1945 to block wage increases, arguing that restraint was necessary to revive production.[7]

In December 1945, after a few episodes of "agitation" and short strikes of manual workers in various parts of French West Africa, about 2,800 dockers, metalworkers, and ordinary laborers in Dakar struck, demanding better pay and benefits. Officials tried to break the strike by using workers who had been recruited into the noncombat part of the military—a disguised form of coerced public works labor—but this proved inadequate and they had to make concessions quickly. A week later, the workers went back with a pay scale that was widened as well as raised, from a range of 3 to 7.75 francs per hour to 5.45 to 20.45 francs per hour. Officials heard the slogan "equal pay for equal work" and complained that "everyone wants to be assimilated to the European, in salary, in indemnities, in order of precedence, in access to the hospital, etc." The claims to equality were infectious: they "created a sort of psychosis of demands."[8]

In early January 1946, clerical and manual workers in the Syndicat des Employés du Commerce, d'Industrie, et des Banques (EMCIBA) in Dakar struck, paralyzing commerce and industry. Their strike stimulated the metalworkers to go out again. The administration's first instincts were authoritarian: striking workers were "requisitioned," drafted temporarily into the military. But the workers ignored the order.

By now, the various unions were acting in concert through the Union des Syndicats Confédérés under the leadership of Lamine Diallo. At a mass meeting at the racetrack, workers heard the call for a "general strike in the most absolute sense of the word" to start in three days. Diallo sent a resolution to the governor-general, telling him that "the growing development of the working class in organization and consciousness permits it to play a decisive role as the motor and guide of all the proletarian forces of French West Africa." He listed the demands of the Union des Syndicats: "Equal pay for equal work and output," union participation in classifying jobs, a minimum wage triple that of official calculations, equal rates of indemnities for family and residence for civil servants, regardless of classification, including daily and auxiliary workers. The union threatened, "This movement will eventually be extended to the whole of the Federation" (i.e., all of French West Africa).[9]

The general strike broke out as proclaimed. It embraced most sections of the working class, except for railwaymen and schoolteachers. The city was shut down, from the bureaucracy to the port to domestic service and markets catering to Europeans. Two days later, the general strike spread to Saint-Louis (seat of the territorial government of Senegal, whereas Dakar was the headquarters for the Federation of French West Africa), shutting down commerce and government operations. It spread to the port of Kaolack—from which part of Senegal's important peanut crop was exported—and to a lesser extent to other Senegalese towns. The Dakar strike lasted twelve days. Officials described the atmosphere as "calm," with restraint on both sides and relatively few incidents.

Even before the strike had become general, the governor-general admitted he had little control, telegraphing Paris: "There is hardly any more hope of seeing the conflict evolve favorably. On the contrary, some indications appear to allow predicting that the indigenous civil servants will join the current strike."[10] Not finding a solution in colonial authority, the minister in Paris sent to Dakar another type of official, Colonial Inspector Masselot, "who specializes in questions of labor conflict" and who had recently settled a dispute in Martinique.[11] Masselot pushed for the negotiation of contracts, based on French models, with each group of workers, hoping to give workers an interest in orderly collective bargaining within their own profession.

African trade unionists quickly mastered the institutions and rhetoric of industrial relations and started to shape the dialogue. Officials had begun negotiating over the *minimum vital,* the calculation of the minimal needs of a worker, which would then define the minimum wage. They kept trying to treat the process as a scientific one. But Papa Jean Ka, head of EMCIBA, politicized the debate: he protested "European methods of calculation," and argued that the lists that officials used for their calculations assumed there was an African standard of living distinct from a European one, and that this was contrary to reality and French principles. He was in effect arguing against the idea of an African way of life, an assumption heretofore unquestioned in the separate calculations of minimum wages for Africans and Europeans.[12] The protracted negotiations blew the cover off the official attempt to objectify minimum wage determination.

The rhetoric of Diallo and other strike leaders mixed an appeal to the language of patriotism for greater France with assertions of proletarian internationalism. Diallo reminded everyone that "the blacks had defended the Mother Country, now they would defend *their soil, where they do not want to be considered strangers.*" And the Union des Syndicats asserted that "the growing development of the working class in organization and consciousness permits it to play a decisive role as the motor and guide of all proletarian forces of French West Africa." It kept its focus on different measures of equality: for the private sector, it focused on the *minimum vital* for manual workers and a fair hierarchy of wages; for the public sector, the central issue was applying the same rates for calculating benefits to all workers, regardless of origin and position.[13]

Union officials in Saint-Louis displayed a capacity to manipulate French discourse similar to that of their Dakarois colleagues. At one bargaining session, a negotiator for clerical workers applied the assimilationist justification of French rule to the labor question: "The evolution of this country, the long contact of the African with whites has created needs in him. We have habits that we cannot abandon, needs which must be faced. If we have children we want to give them a secondary education, we don't want them to stay in the cadres locaux, just as we want comfort for ourselves. All this requires a costly course of life and we need the money that we are asking from you." One of his colleagues added, "Your goal is to elevate us to your level; without the means, we will never succeed." The official negotiators were left speechless by this argument, but they reported it precisely to their superiors.[14]

The strike was forcing French officials to decide if they actually believed that French models pointed the way to solutions to social problems. Under the influence of the labor expert Masselot, the bargaining turned around the formulas of French industrial relations: labor officers sought collective bargaining agreements in the major industries that included hierarchical wages, based on multiples of the minimum vital and with higher ranks receiving "salaries based on those paid to similar European employees." In the public sector, the admission of Africans into job categories largely occupied by Europeans was not the decisive question, because officials did not think many met the qualifications. The issue was whether the benefits received by the higher-ranking workers should be extended to job categories that, while formally nonracial, were largely occupied by Africans. The benefits on which union demands focused and which agonized officials the most were family allowances and the indemnity of zone: allowances, based on wages, intended to compensate for the cost of raising a family (calculated on the number of children) and for living in places with different costs of living. The public sector unions were demanding equal rates at all levels of public service, down to a lowly guard at a government office.

This was a tough demand not only because of the money involved, but because of the conceptual breakthrough: paying a government worker—not necessarily an évolué—family allowances implied that the needs of an African family were similar to those of a European one and that the state should pay the cost of reproducing its African civil service. Such notions had long been contemptuously dismissed by officials, who invoked stereotypical notions of African families—multiple wives, many children, child labor—and if Governor-General Cournarie no longer defended this panoply, he still believed that "the conditions of life of the immense majority of African civil servants are not comparable to those of their European colleagues."[15]

But the strike was dragging on. Masselot's use of the French formulas for collective bargaining agreements carried more and more weight, even among hidebound French employers. The difficulty was applying the formulas to Africans: the commercial workers' refusal to have the minimum wage set in relation to a supposedly African standard of living and civil servants' insistence that African families were not too peculiar to benefit from family allowances put pressure on officials to make a leap. They did.

In the commercial workers' negotiations, the governor-general intervened to make a classic money compromise, then worked backward to make the numbers justify the award. He proclaimed a figure of 7.40 francs per hour, a considerable increase over the 5.45 then in force and the 2.50 before the December strikes.[16] This would help to settle the strike, after another week of negotiations, while defining future battle lines: the elements of the minimum vital.

As far as family allowances for civil servants were concerned, Governor-General Cournarie knew he had to concede on the principle and could only try to contain the cost. Five days into the general strike, Cournarie offered civil servants in the lowest category (*cadres locaux*) allowances at 20 percent of the rate for the highest levels in the colonial service (*cadres généraux* and *cadres communs supérieurs*); people in the middle rank (*cadres communs secondaires*) would get 40 percent of the top rate.[17]

It was Diallo—who had helped bring the government workers into the strike—who helped take them out of it and end the general phase of the strike. The security service's secret reports on the daily meetings of strikers at the Champ de Courses reveal simultaneously a mass element—the urban population assembling as a single collectivity—and tensions within the leadership. On January 16, Diallo hinted to the daily mass meeting that a solution was near. On January 18, the crowd took the spreading of the strike to Saint-Louis as a positive sign. On January 19, Abbas Guèye, the metalworkers' leader, told the crowd, "You shouldn't give yourselves illusions: nothing has yet been done for the strikers." But Diallo appeared with a leader of the Saint-Louis strike with whom he had been in regular contact, affirmed the solidarity of all strikers, and told them of his meetings with top officials and of progress that was being made. The next day, Diallo proclaimed that the strike would end when "he, Lamine Diallo" gave the order. He criticized Abbas Guèye for his pessimism, calling him "a nothing."[18]

Finally, on January 25, Diallo told the meeting that the general issues had been resolved. "He 'gave the order' for civil servants, auxiliaries, daily workers and all other categories not having presented particular claims, among others bakers, cooks, domestics, drivers, etc . . . to go back to their posts. Despite this return, the Union [des Syndicats Confédérés] is on the side of those who remained on strike." That meant EMCIBA and the metalworkers' union.[19] The key break had been the governor-general's concessions: better minimum wages for ordinary workers—fudging the principle of what standard would be used to measure workers' needs—plus family allowances and other indemnities to all regular government workers, down to orderlies, watchmen, mailmen, and sailors, at the rate of either 25 or 50 percent of the figure used for the high-ranking civil servants, 5 and 10 percent better than the governor-general's earlier offer.[20]

In the port, clerks, office workers, and auxiliaries, following Diallo's orders, went back to work on January 25, but the port remained blocked because the foremen were members of EMCIBA and were not there to sign on and supervise the laborers. Some firms did not obey the agreement to rehire workers. Papa Jean Ka, EMCIBA's leader, asked workers to keep up the strike. Considerable tension emerged among Ka, Diallo, and Abbas Guèye, and up to five thousand people were still coming to meetings as late as January 30.[21]

EMCIBA finally agreed on February 4 to divide the workforce into seven categories, with a pay scale between 1,540 (the minimum vital) and 9,500 francs per month, plus seniority bonuses of 5 to 15 percent of the base wage. The settlement emerged as employers divided in the face of the strikers' persistence, with one association accepting the agreement and the other refusing, only to have the government, eager to restore labor peace, impose the settlement throughout the commercial sector.[22]

The metal strike dragged on, and Masselot commented, "The capacity of resistance of the strikers was maintained longer than one expected." Finally, on February 12, the employers conceded wage increases slightly higher than their earlier offer and agreed to rehire strikers, with the understanding that the final collective bargaining agreement would include a bonus for seniority and indemnities in case of layoff. The Saint-Louis strike, meanwhile, held together even when Dakar made its settlement and the civil servants in that city stayed out in support of the commercial workers, even when their own issues were settled on the basis of the Dakar accords. Finally, on February 4 the Chambre de Commerce de Saint-Louis accepted an agreement with the commercial workers based on the Dakar model. The strike movement as a whole had lasted over two months.[23]

The governor-general commented, "Thus ended in the most complete calm and without even the throwing of a punch the most important movement of workers yet recorded in A.O.F." The police conceded grudging admiration: "The mass of indigenous workers led by about a hundred leaders showed itself to be perfectly disciplined." The governor of Senegal took the strike as a serious blow to governmental authority, but one that could have been—or still could be—worse: "If the movement had had the support of the peasants, we would have witnessed the economic and financial collapse of Senegal. But if the danger is put aside for now, it continues no less to exist and we must fend it off. Because the sudden breaking out of this general strike has disclosed the existence of an organization whose ramifications extend to the most remote corners of the bush."[24]

The challenge to colonial power was a serious one. Governor-General Cournarie was more careful to note that strikers had kept the dispute strictly within the realm of labor and that the leading political figure, Lamine Guèye, had "disappointed the strikers" by avoiding any situation in which he might have had to take a stand. Masselot, the labor expert, saw the strike as "a movement for profound emancipation," even though it had focused on professional issues. For him, the challenge meant that strikes had to be anticipated, not reacted to, and the collective bargaining agreements he had helped to put in place would limit the boundaries of dispute and define issues in ways that could be handled. The wage hierarchies "will have the effect of classifying the workers of each establishment according to well-determined categories [and] will mark a very clear improvement compared to the previous situation. . . . There is a technique to organizing work, as with everything, and it cannot be improvised."[25]

The story of the strike reveals above all change during the process of conflict itself. French colonial thinking in February 1946 was not what it was in December 1945, and that reflects the persistence of a labor movement. That movement's strength was not so much an implacable opposition to everything that smacked of French colonialism, but instead an engagement with it—the molding of postwar French rhetoric into a language of claims, plunging into the details of French models of labor agreements in order to claim their benefits for colonized people. At the daily meetings in the Champ de Courses, the movement teetered between expressions of mass solidarity and a pragmatism about getting what could be won in a situation of material deprivation. Lamine Diallo was able not only to maintain balance among these tendencies but to exploit it in confronting French officials. He could threaten them with mass upheaval while negotiating with them on terms they understood.

Within the French bureaucracy, the Inspection du Travail was empowered by the events of early 1946 and by anxiety lest they repeat themselves or spread. The Inspecteurs articulated a clear rationale for their job classifications and wage differentials, as well as for using these models as a basis for collective bargaining with trade unions. They considered a differentiated workforce the key to avoiding "social trouble and a strike which would rapidly become general" as well as to "separate out an African elite and consequently maintain the attractiveness of superior positions."[26] This conception of stability, incentives, and hierarchy in wage labor was not new in the metropole, but its application to French Africa represents a dramatic reversal of policy.

Meanwhile, the labor movement built on the slogan of the strike—equal pay for equal work—to turn the language of scientific industrial relations into a language of entitlement. It campaigned for better wages, for the equalization of family allowances in the civil service and their extension to the private sector. The Administration could not counter directly the argument for equality, not only because it was an application of the assimilationist ideology through which imperial rule was now being justified, but because officials hoped that Africans might, after all, act in the manner expected of industrial men. Governor-General Cournarie wrote in March 1946—in confidential correspondence—"The Administration has always pushed for the application of the principle, 'equal pay for equal output.'" He warned against "any difference in juridical treatment" between the races and cited racially specific legislation in East and South Africa as negative examples. This was a self-serving version of labor history, but its telling shaped the terms in which other claims could be made against the state.[27] Labor unions and African politicians could use the government's egalitarian assertions to try to turn them into reality: the civil service would obtain equality of salaries and benefits—including family allowances—by legislative enactment in 1950, and unions and political leaders went from there to demand a nondiscriminatory labor code and family allowances for the private sector (see below).

The Dakar strike, like others of its era, was not exclusively the work of a highly stabilized or skilled proletariat; it cut across divisions of occupation, status, and literacy in uniting most of Dakar's 15,000 wage workers. In response, the government tried to break up the similarity of circumstances, even at the expense of conceding substantial wage increases and developing wider wage hierarchies for each occupational category. By granting low-level government workers some kind of family allowances, officials were accepting the urban labor force as a complex social entity whose conditions of production and reproduction were crucial to control, order, and productivity. The rapid shift in the rhetoric of the French government, from hoping to associate a small educated elite with its rule while assuming peasants would see their future within their own milieu, to one in which Africans and Europeans were arguing about the details of wage workers' needs and in which equality became a powerful concept across a wide social and cultural spectrum, pointed to the instability at the core of a colonial government's assertion that it could become an agent of progress within the structures and ideologies of empire.

IMPERIAL EQUALITY IN THE PARIS LEGISLATURE

The implications of contestation over equality within Greater France in the years after the 1946 strike can be seen both in debates over constitution and legislation in Paris and in continued on-the-ground struggles over labor questions in Africa. Let me briefly summarize the legislative dimension and then examine at somewhat greater length the next major episode of social struggle in French West Africa.

The year 1946 was remarkable for overturning long-established axioms of French colonial policy. Some of this was the work of about twenty Africans in the Assemblée Nationale Constituante, the body elected in November 1945 to write the constitution of the postwar French Republic and, in the meantime, to legislate. There were issues that had long remained dormant that could not survive in the open, after deputies prepared to force the issue, however small a minority, were in the seat of power. The hated *indigénat*, the body of decrees giving local administrators power to inflict arbitrary punishments on colonial subjects, was ended with little opposition in a series of legislative acts and decrees early in the year. In March the campaign led by Aimé Césaire, interwar activist, négritude poet, and deputy from Martinique, for departmental status for the West Indian colonies came to fruition. In April, what became known as the Houphouët-Boigny law, after the deputy from Côte d'Ivoire, abolished forced labor in the colonies, long practiced and either covered up or justified on the grounds that Africans' development could not be made to depend on their willingness to work for wages. In May, the Lamine Guèye law, named after the deputy from Senegal who introduced it, eliminated the distinction between citizen and subject that had for a century been a key organizing principle of French colonial society. The law was quite specific about the point that had done the most to limit the spread and the attractiveness of citizenship in the past: people were citizens regardless of their civil status, and their personal and private affairs could be regulated under Islamic or other local codes.[28] All this was enacted while constitutional debates were going on, with Lamine Guèye, Léopold Senghor, Césaire, and other colonial deputies playing particularly active roles in the hotly contested debates over institutions for governing the French Union, as the empire was renamed.

African deputies argued with only partial success for strong electoral institutions and relative autonomy *within* their colonies and more successfully for making no distinctions between the civil rights of colonial and metropolitan citizens in all the empire. White settlers wanted local governors to have wide discretion, while progressives in Paris wanted more centralized institutions that settlers couldn't control and which could promote a positive social agenda. Algerian delegates were the least successful of all, since it was all but impossible to reconcile their demands for autonomy, European settlers' insistence on dominance, and French notions of an indissoluble union. Debates over the details of the franchise and elected assemblies went on through the summer of 1946, through two constitutional referenda.

For all the ambiguity of these discussions, the message of the constitutional debate and the citizenship law—on which top officials and African political leaders agreed—was one of equality. Everyone would be under the same regime of penal law and have the same rights of speech and assembly; terms like *indigène* were banned from official publications; any citizen could enter European France and anyone could seek any job within the French civil service; all French citizens were supposed to carry equivalent identification cards.[29] Equality could be claimed without giving up difference, since the citizenship law was independent of the civil code under which personal life was administered. One could, for example, be subject to Muslim law in family matters, vote in a French election, and claim equal wages on an employment contract. As the Overseas Ministry's political bureau concluded, "The legislature wanted to mark the perfect equality of all in public life, but not the perfect identity of the French of the metropole and the overseas French."[30]

The constitution framed debates without providing a method for resolving them: some political actors would try to twist French institutions to maintain the privileges of white settlers and administrators within overseas territories; others sought to make the principle of equality meaningful in the lives of ordinary people; still others sought to break away from France altogether. But in the late 1940s, the end of the story was not known, and it would be a mistake for scholars to read the generalization of independence in the 1960s into an assumption that this was the general focus of political aspirations at an earlier date. What is striking in regard to French West Africa is how important the rhetoric of equality was *within* the imperial system, above all in reference to the French standard of wages, social benefits, and standard of living.

In the aftermath of the legislative breakthroughs and the general strike of 1946, the dialogue of officials and trade unionists continued in the campaign for a labor code, an issue I have analyzed at length elsewhere.[31] In brief, the Inspection wanted the code to bring order—a French-based order—to the workplace. They wanted a range of issues to be settled by law and others to be settled by well-defined bargaining processes. They saw unions as legitimate parts of social life, in Africa as much as in France. They were not pleased that most West African unions chose to affiliate with the Communist-linked French umbrella organization of trade unions, the Confédération Générale du Travail (CGT), but even that connection put the African unions on familiar, French territory.

The labor movement saw the labor code as guaranteeing certain entitlements regardless of their ability to bargain with often hostile employers. It wanted a code guaranteeing minimum wages based on measurable criteria for the necessities of life, limiting working hours and guaranteeing paid vacations, and making explicit the right to organize and to strike. In short, unions sought to carry the metropolitan code to the colonies, with adaptations but without any dilution of substance. African deputies in the legislature adopted this position, and defended it vigorously in the long debates.

Even employers wanted a code, for they had experienced in 1946 the dangers of chaotic mechanisms of posing demands. But they kept insisting that Africa was a special situation and the code should not replicate the metropolitan version; rather colonial officials should have heightened powers to keep demagogic unions in check and adapt regulation to colonial circumstances.

The colonial employers were able to stall the code—the debates over it took six years—but not to get their way. The pressure was maintained not just by the African deputies, who threatened to vote against the code and thus undercut its legitimacy unless provisions they cared about were enacted, but also by symbolic strikes, rallies, newspaper articles, and other actions in French West Africa throughout the period. The collective action, coordinated between Paris legislators and West African activists, culminated in a one-day strike across all of French West Africa in November 1952, just as the final, most controversial decisions were being made. It was in one of these debates that Senghor made his famous remark, "As you know, Africans now have a mystique of equality. In this domain, as in others, they want the same principles to be applied from the first in the overseas territories as in the metropole."[32]

The code came surprisingly close to meeting this aspiration in a formal sense, and its passage encouraged unions to keep up the pressure to implement its articles in favorable ways. A huge strike in Guinea in 1953 was one of the most noticed follow-up actions, and it soon gave way to West Africa–wide mobilizations to bring about s provision the code had deliberately left vague, the extension of family allowances to the private sector. This took several strikes and more strike threats and active campaigns in newspapers, but in 1956 the generalization of family allowances to regularly employed wage workers in the private sector became another labor victory.[33]

IMPERIAL EQUALITY ON THE
FRENCH WEST AFRICAN RAILWAY

Now let us turn to the most dramatic labor struggle in Africa. The strike by railway workers that began in October 1947 involved nearly 20,000 workers, their families, and their communities, and lasted, in most regions, for five and a half months. This event was made even larger by Ousmane Sembene's novel *God's Bits of Wood*, which portrays the strike as a giant step in a wider popular struggle against colonialism.[34] Yet the effectiveness of the strike lay less in the stark confrontation of subaltern and colonial power than in the ability of the strikers to widen fissures *within* the institutions and ideology of postwar colonialism. The strikers drew simultaneously on their integration into wider supportive communities in West Africa, their participation in a community of railwaymen united by a common workplace but fractured by racial tensions, and their understanding of the importance of both official rhetoric declaiming the equality of citizens in the French Union and administrators' hope that Africans could really turn out to be the productive, orderly workers that imperial modernizers wished to see. The partial success of the strike gave African workers a sense of collective empowerment—and thereby contributed to anticolonial struggle—but the nature of the demands and the strike process itself bound workers more tightly to an industrial workplace and institutions of an imperial state, in greater contrast to the conditions of life of the people whose support had helped them so much.

The strike was about the *cadre unique,* the demand of African railwaymen for a single, nonracial job hierarchy, with the same benefits package for all members, including the complicated supplements for local cost of living and family obligations. The demand followed from the victory won by civil servants in the Dakar strike of 1946—including family allowances—which had been generalized over most of the civil service in French West Africa. The cadre unique was conceded early in principle; the actual strike was over implementation, and it was really about power, whether African workers would actually have a voice in a formally nonracial work structure.

In 1946 the government had made the Régie des Chemins de Fer de l'Afrique Occidentale Française into a parastatal corporation run by a board weighted toward government officials but including representatives of railway unions and commercial interests.[35] Meanwhile, the Fédération des Travailleurs Indigènes des Chemins de Fer de l'A.O.F brought together the unions on each of the regional lines that made up the railway system: Dakar-Niger (Senegal and Sudan); Bénin-Niger (Dahomey), Conakry-Niger (Guinea), Abidjan-Niger (Ivory Coast).[36] Dakar-Niger was the most powerful branch, and the Fédération's headquarters were in Thiès, a railway junction and major maintenance center inland from Dakar. The Syndicat des Travailleurs Indigènes du Dakar-Niger dated to the 1930s. It had been the most conspicuous absentee from the 1946 general strike, largely because its leader François Gning was affiliated with the Socialists then in power in France and hence to the Government General in Dakar. His stance led to a revolt of younger trade unionists.

Gning's ouster was organized by a group from the Union des Jeunes de Thiès, who were also active members of the railway union. Here developed a conjuncture of the political ideals of a group of young, educated men and a workforce that was largely nonliterate. The Union des Jeunes was led from mid 1945 by a clerk (Abdoul Karim Sow) and a schoolteacher (Mory Tall), and included people with clerical jobs on the railway. Its goals were simultaneously political, cultural, and intellectual—to promote "our general development," one leader recalled.[37] Its meetings brought out a youthful vigor in contrast to the perceived lethargy of older Senegalese politicians, and a new combativeness toward the French, even though neither it—nor any other significant political group—was at this time calling for independence.[38] The leaders of the Union des Jeunes were Muslim, and one of them, Ibrahima Sarr, came from a family with connections to marabouts, the leaders of the Muslim brotherhoods that held great influence in rural Senegal. Sarr was a graduate of a leading trade school, "écrivain" in the *cadre local supérieure* since 1938.[39] The militants of the Union des Jeunes spearheaded a "revolution" within the railway union, attacking Gning's noncombative approach and his disinterest in nonelite workers.[40] After public meetings and demonstrations, Gning resigned and was replaced by Sarr, supported by a Comité Directeur led by other clerks but including representation of all divisions.[41]

Sarr's first speech showed he too could turn the rhetoric of imperial reform in a direction it was not necessarily intended to go. He called for "the abolition of antiquated colonial methods condemned even by THE NEW AND TRUE FRANCE which wishes that all its children, at whatever latitude they may live, be equal in duties and rights and *that the recompense of labor be a function solely of merit and capacity.*"[42]

Sarr broke out of Gning's évolué-oriented way of thinking to bring the auxiliaries into the union in a meaningful way. As of 1946, the railway employed 478 Europeans, 1,729 Africans in the various cadres, and 15,726 auxiliaries. Many auxiliaries—treated as temporary workers even after years of service—did the same work as members of the cadres, but they lacked job security, paid housing, and other indemnities.

Sarr's coup was centered on Thiès, a railway hub where workers from diverse parts of Senegal and the Sudan shared common conditions and from which the bonds formed at work traveled up and down the rail line that ran from Dakar to Bamako. Within a month of his takeover, Sarr embarked on a series of visits, beginning with the Sudan in June 1946 and culminating in a tour of the other railway lines on the eve of the 1947 strike. He appealed for cooperation across distinctions within the workforce and for support for the union and its strike fund. The union organizations on the different railway lines brought themselves together as the Fédération des Syndicats des Cheminots Africains, and ceded central direction to the Comité Directeur of the Dakar-Niger branch, headquartered in Thiès.[43]

The railway union, under Sarr, put forth a double claim in August 1946: for the *cadre unique* and for the integration of the permanently employed auxiliary into the cadre. The claim went to the Commission Paritaire, the negotiating body specified by French industrial relations law, and in April 1947 it had still not emerged. The twenty sessions of the commission were "confused, tedious, broken up by stormy discussions." The outright rejection of the *cadre unique* by the unions of white workers did not make the situation any easier. Then, the union pulled off a theatrical coup. At the moment of a visit to Senegal by the president of the Republic and of the colonial minister, Marius Moutet, it organized a three-day strike.[44]

In the presence of the important luminaries, the Government General could not publicly go against principles of equality. The Commission Paritaire accepted the *cadre unique,* while the union accepted the Régie's demand to rationalize the structure of the railway by reducing the number employed. The commission was to regulate the details.[45]

The real issue was power: much was at stake in how many auxiliaries were to be integrated and how pay scales were to be combined into a single cadre. The board of the Régie rejected the proposed settlement of the Commission Paritaire. The union felt betrayed by the rejection and mobilized for a strike, planned for October 10. The union's final list of demands—all rejected by the Régie—included making the integration of auxiliaries retroactive, revising the table of equivalences that slotted people into the wage hierarchy of the *cadre unique*, revising certain barriers to promotions within the cadre, allowing leave for family emergencies in addition to annual vacations, making company lodging available to auxiliaries rather than just to the cadres, and providing uniform, rather than hierarchical, rates for the indemnity that compensated for local variations in cost of living. The strike would take place not over the grand principles of equality, but formally over a narrower, indeed mundane, set of issues.[46]

The strike on October 10 was virtually total. Governor-General Barthes insisted that the strike was illegal while an arbitrator was considering the case. He would therefore not negotiate. Three weeks into the strike, 38 Africans were at work. The strike remained remarkably solid until January, when the Abidjan-Niger region broke away and went back to work. Even this did not lead the rest to lose heart, although there was a small drift back and considerable hiring of strikebreakers. The strike lasted over five months.

The ability of strikers to hold out so long is best explained by their integration into town-centered and family-centered networks. Through family connections, workers had access to agricultural products and fish: the strike, probably deliberately, took place after the harvests. Some railwaymen returned to their villages of origin to lessen the strain on urban resources. Women played a crucial role in pulling together such resources, although there is no evidence that the women's march that climaxes Sembene's novel ever happened. Testimonies so far collected stress the role of women within family units—their efforts to find food, their work selling at local markets and other nonwage activities to sustain family income.[47] They composed songs supporting the strike and its leaders, and taunted strikebreakers.[48] Merchants in railway towns contributed money, food, and transportation vehicles to strikers. The journal *L'A.O.F.* gave much publicity to the strike and collected donations, and the French CGT gave the union a major donation, although only enough to keep such a huge labor force supplied for about a week. The union itself had opened and stocked a cooperative, at Thiès, and for three months it gave strikers needed items on credit. One strike committee member boasted sardonically that the strikers were now like marabouts: "We do not work but we have our provisions."[49]

The strikers' discipline impressed even their opponents. Sarr had ordered his followers to "stay home and not to indulge themselves in any outside demonstration or any sabotage"—an order that was by all indications followed.[50] In Thiès, the strikers held daily open meetings, where doubts and concerns were aired and peer pressure maintained. Whenever there were signs of wavering along the Dakar-Niger line, Sarr went on tour and reaffirmed personal ties and group loyalties.[51]

This was, by any standard, a long strike, and it entailed serious hardships. The comment made by the inspecteur général du travail, Pierre Pélisson, in January is revealing: "Here the means of defense are very different—and singularly more effective—than in the case of metropolitan strikes."[52] It was, Pélisson noted, the incompleteness of workers' integration into proletarian society that gave them more diverse roots than their French comrades. Over five months, workers of various origins, working on different terms for the railway, stuck together, held to union discipline, and maintained their support networks in railway towns and surrounding villages.

The possibility of calling a general strike in support of the railwaymen came up at union meetings in Dakar, Abidjan, and Conakry in November 1947, but each time a solidarity strike was rejected, although several unions supplied money to the strikers. At Dakar, some veterans of 1946—Abbas Guèye and Lamine Diallo—argued for a general strike, but the Union des Syndicats de Dakar refused to go along. There were three reasons for the failure of working-class unity: the railway union had itself failed to join the general strike of January 1946; the railway union was unaffiliated with any union federation, while most other unions were affiliated with the CGT; and the unions of Dakar and elsewhere were at the time in the midst of renegotiating their own collective bargaining agreements. In fact, the post-1946 policy of the Inspection du Travail was paying off: each occupation had a great deal to gain by working within professional boundaries.

Political parties kept aloof. The French West Africa–wide political party, the RDA, played no role in the strike, and its newspaper, while indicating sympathy with the cause, insisted that Sarr "is not R.D.A.," and "It was the business of the railwaymen and the railwaymen alone to take up their responsibilities." Senghor is remembered by former strikers as having come privately to the strike committee on the eve of the walkout to indicate his support, but also for not speaking publicly in favor of the strike.[53] Only in December did the leading African politicians act: on the occasion of the Dakar meeting of the Grand Conseil (French West Africa's legislative body), Houphouët-Boigny and others tried to get the governor-general to intervene to effect a settlement. They were careful to make clear "their concern not to mix politics with an affair that must remain strictly professional and simply to bring their purely obliging support to settle a conflict whose importance to the country is considerable." The governor-general would not budge, and the Grand Conseil itself was so torn by partisan bickering that it could not even pass a bland appeal for a settlement.[54]

At home, Houphouët-Boigny criticized the strikers for failing to consult him, having bad timing, and acting inopportunely in not accepting a settlement and working for their demands later. When the Ivory Coast strike ended in early January 1948, over two months earlier than elsewhere, officials noted, "According to our information, this result is due to M. the Deputy Houphouet, who succeeded in persuading the African railwaymen to return to work despite the counter-propaganda of M. Sarr."[55] The importance of Ivory Coast farmers within Houphouët-Boigny's political party was undoubtedly relevant here: they stood to lose by the continuation of the strike. Senghor, meanwhile, wrote an elegant letter on the union's behalf to the minister of Overseas France appealing for a solution based "on the equality of rights and duties, without discrimination based on race or religion," but he shied away from engagement with the mundane details of a labor dispute.[56]

The Strike Committee, noting the lack of forthright support, criticized both Senghor and Lamine Guèye "for having placed themselves on the side of the Administration."[57] In January, Sudanese deputy Fily Dabo Sissoko intrigued with government officials to try to split off the crucial Sudanese workers from their Senegalese comrades on the most militant branch, the Dakar-Niger. Sarr was sufficiently shaken by the danger of a split that he thought briefly of taking up Sissoko's initiative, but his Strike Committee instructed him to reject it. When Sissoko, angered by the union's refusal, tried to get the Sudanese railwaymen to go back to work, only seven railwaymen in the Sudanese capital reported.[58] It was only after the strike, when the influence and importance of the railway union had been made clear, that the most astute of the political elite, Senghor, moved to bring Sarr and other union leaders into his orbit.

It is puzzling why the government allowed a disruptive strike to drag on so long without either resolving the less than enormous issues or using its power systematically to break it. The government did not requisition strikers into the military; it waited a month before beginning to hire replacement workers and did so diffidently and to little effect. Only in mid-November did it prosecute Sarr for ordering an illegal strike, and despite being convicted Sarr never served his sentence. Nor did the Régie play another card it had: it did not fire its workers or—despite occasional threats—expel the large number who lived in railway housing.[59]

The caution of the Régie and the administration was very much a product of the postwar conjuncture. Railway workers represented the best hope for the kind of stable, increasingly skilled workforce officials wanted to build. But the very prolongation of the strike revealed that railway workers had another foot in a different sort of social entity, and the Régie feared—probably more than was actually the case—that railwaymen could leave the labor market altogether. The issue was conceptual as well as practical. Having committed themselves to an industrial relations model of labor control, the colonial regime found it hard to go back to old-style colonialist methods.[60]

But the one point to which the administration stuck until near the end was its interpretation of the rules of the new industrial relations order. Governor-General Barthes had taken his last opportunity before the strike to lecture the union leaders on "the terms of the law and my intention of insuring that it is respected." As late as February 3, the administration insisted that the affair "end by the total execution of the arbitration ruling," refusing to let an inspector talk to the union about negotiated alternatives.[61]

The deadlock broke when a new governor-general, Paul Béchard, a Socialist politician rather than a colonial functionary, succeeded Barthes at the end of January and made a series of proposals in early March. He sustained the Régie's hierarchical scale of indemnities and its refusal to house auxiliaries, but compromised on the starting date for integrating auxiliaries, some details of reclassification, and leave policy. There would be no punishment for striking; all workers in the cadres would be rehired; and striking auxiliaries would be taken back until the staffing levels had been filled, keeping in mind that workers hired during the strike would be kept on if qualified. After a positive but still critical response from the union, Béchard agreed that the union would be involved in the process of coming up with a new staffing table—as agreed in April, the staffing structure was to be rationalized and reduced—and in deciding which workers would not be rehired. Workers also received a 20 percent wage increase, officially to compensate for the increased cost of living. Agreement was finally reached and work resumed on March 19. "It left no victors, no vanquished," Béchard concluded. "We will resume work calmly, and with discipline," were Sarr's final words, and like his previous appeals, they were systematically followed.[62]

The aftermath of the strike—even more prolonged than the main event—was the negotiations over the staff reductions. The process must have reminded the railwaymen why they had fought so hard to make clear their collective strength. The railway had initially claimed that it needed only 13,500 men, not 17,000. After discussion, it settled on a figure just under 15,000, and after further debates and attrition among the strikebreakers, relatively few auxiliaries were left at risk. In the end, Pélisson acknowledged that the union "had done its duty in defense of the railwaymen." The process of integrating auxiliaries into the *cadre unique* went on as slowly as the compressions. But the union again had something to show for its efforts: in 1950, over 30 percent of the railway workers were in the cadre, as opposed to 12 percent on the eve of the strike.[63]

The administration now knew that restructuring the colonial labor system would involve African agency as much as imperial design. When a hard-nosed inspector later complained that the cost of integrating auxiliaries into the *cadre unique* was driving up freight rates on the railway, a senior official reminded him that good labor relations in the region's largest enterprise were "necessary, as the strike of 1947 proved, for the sound functioning of the Régie itself. I believe that technical progress and social progress cannot be separated."[64]

The 1947–48 railway strike was above all a contest over power within a system of industrial relations that had only just come to French Africa. The breakthrough in accepting work, workers, and workers' organizations as part of African social reality had been made in the 1946 general strike and the April 1947 agreement. The railway job structure would look like a French job structure rather than the racial structure of backward colonialism. But the question of how power would be exercised *within* this structure had not been settled, and that was how the strike came about.

The railway workers proved that their voices would be heard. The government made its point too: African unions could fight and win, but within certain legal and institutional structures. The very battle brought both sides deeper into those structures, and the strike did not become a popular liberation struggle or an exercise in colonial repression. At the end of 1948, a government report applauded the form in which the two sides had joined their conflict: "Social peace can only profit from such a crystallization of forces around two poles, certainly opposed but knowing each other better and accepting to keep contact to discuss collective bargaining agreement and conditions of work."[65]

EPILOGUE: THE MUTUAL REPUDIATION OF THE FRENCH REFERENCE POINT

The powerful dynamic described in these pages placed both the French government and the leadership of the West African labor movement in the 1950s somewhere very different from where they began. The government started with the premise that the unity and indissolubility of Greater France was the first principle of action. The willingness to generalize citizenship and recognize the equivalence of African and European French people followed—at the cost, not fully anticipated in 1946, of facing enormous expense when poor people began to define equality in relation to the French standard of living. That situation became acute because African workers and the leaders of trade unions forced the issue, because they turned around the abstract, politically minded notion of equivalence among citizens into concrete demands, and because this rhetoric resonated between the streets of Dakar and the legislative halls in Paris. By the mid 1950s, the French state was caught between the notion of equivalence of citizens and that of the indissolubility of empire. It could not afford equivalence and had to rethink empire.

The union leadership also found itself caught in the logic of its position. Demands made in the name of equivalence kept putting African and French *wage workers* into the same category. To the extent that demands were met, the process widened the social distance between those workers and the rest of Africa, even though the support of wider communities had been essential to the success of the strikes of 1946 and 1947–48.

Moreover, a significant portion of the trade union leadership realized that, given the expanding franchise, the growing importance of legislative bodies at different levels of the French Union, and the increasing vitality of politics, they had much to gain by seeking political office and had a good platform from which to do so. But here was a problem: trade unions gave them a springboard, but the very success of trade unionism in its own terms was separating their base from the wider—and now voting—public. Sékou Touré of Guinea, one of the most effective of the radical labor leaders in the struggle to pass and then implement the labor code, was among the first to realize this as he campaigned for the territorial legislature in 1953. By 1955 and 1956, he and some of his influential colleagues were moving in a new direction: they began to separate class struggle from African unity, and make the latter the linchpin of their ideological position.

This move played out within the union movement itself, as Sékou Touré led an effort to disaffiliate African unions from French partners and sought to shift the rhetoric of the members away from class struggle and toward identification with peasants, pastoralists, and fishermen in counterposing the unity of Africa against the colonial state.[66] Sékou Touré insisted, "Although the classes of metropolitan and European populations battle and oppose each other, nothing separates the diverse African social classes." The new African trade union federation he promoted severed the ties of French West African unions with their French counterparts, and—with considerable unease and disagreement—decided that the liquidation of colonialism should "take pride of place over the class struggle."[67]

One dimension of this change is that the cards union leaders had played to make claims on the French state could also be seen as alien if not humiliating. They implied focusing on France as the reference point. That might mean something to a railway worker, whose job experience paralleled that of a French railwayman even if his home life did not, but it would not necessarily be seen as positive to a pastoralist living ten miles from a railway depot. We need to know more about the culture of politics at the local level to understand just how perceptions and rhetoric changed in the mid 1950s. There were undoubtedly major differences, depending on whether one is looking at unionized workers and army veterans (for whom a lot was at stake in the French reference point), at peasants who did not see the connection, at people immersed in Islamic or locally-defined networks whose reference points pointed elsewhere, or at intellectuals who sought to position themselves between alternative notions of affinity and to stake out new roles for themselves. We do know that expansion of the franchise and the increased tempo of electoral mobilizations produced a shift away from the rhetoric of equality so central in the late 1940s and early 1950s and toward one that put more emphasis on the unity and distinctiveness of Africa and on France as an alien, overbearing force. Within the labor movement, there is little evidence that the impetus for repudiating class struggle came from the rank and file. Rather, the evidence points to union leadership that was moving out of labor issues and into electoral politics. To say this is to note both the importance and the breadth of the feelings of humiliation that politicians sought to tap and the extent to which rank-and-file workers felt they still had something to gain from making claims within the framework of contestation laid out in the post-1946 decade.[68]

French officials had enough information about unions and trade unionists to realize that the growing nationalism of people like Sékou Touré might be an alternative to the cycle of demands being placed on them. Having opened the door to claims to equivalence in 1946—hoping to short-circuit demands for national autonomy—by 1956 they welcomed calls for national autonomy to short-circuit demands for equivalence.

The formula they found was "territorialization." It meant a devolution of power, away from the Assemblée Nationale in Paris, and toward individual colonial territories. Under the law passed by the French Assemblée Nationale in 1956, each territorial assembly would be elected under universal suffrage and would choose a cabinet to work with a French governor. The leader would be a kind of junior prime minister, and the assembly would have real budgetary authority. That meant that political leaders who depended on the vote of taxpayers would decide whether to answer demands for higher wages for government workers, for more state schools, for more health clinics, for more paved roads. The framework for the equivalence of the citizen would not be Greater France—whose resources seemed enormous viewed from Africa and limited when viewed from Paris—but the resources of the territory itself. Government leaders were quite explicit about the reasons for this reversal of the unifying, assimilating thrust of postwar colonial policy: "When you speak of assimilation to our compatriots in the overseas territories, they understand it, first and foremost, as economic and social assimilation and assimilation in regard to standard of living. And if you say to them that France wants to realize assimilation overseas, they reply: Well, give us immediately equality in wages, equality in labor legislation, in social security benefits, equality in family allowances, in brief, equality in standard of living."[69] The French government could not face the burden of an empire of citizens.

Criticism of territorialization came from civil servants' unions, who realized that the territorial treasury would be much less able to meet their pay claims than the French one, and from Senghor, who realized that territorialization would imply "balkanization"—the division of Africa into units too small to challenge European states. But it was a losing struggle, for the resources that the law devolved on the territories were real, and in each case—Senghor's Senegal included—the first generation of elected politicians quickly adapted themselves to the possibilities this sort of access gave them. After the elections of 1957, African-majority governments took power over most domestic affairs, including the budget, in their respective territories, and trade unionists were prominently placed in the ministries. Sékou Touré became head of the government in Guinea.

For once, the French political leadership guessed right. As labor conflicts inevitably emerged in Dahomey, Guinea, Senegal, and other territories, the new governments sought to contain workers' demands in the name of national development. As Sékou Touré put it, "Trade unionism for trade unionism's sake is historically unthinkable in current conditions, trade unionism of class just as much. . . . The trade union movement is obligated to reconvert itself to remain in the same line of emancipation."[70] His minister of labor, Camara Bengaly, also spelled out to the labor movement the implications of Africans coming into authority: the labor movement was expected to become "the precious collaborators of the authentic elected authorities of the people and more particularly to the young Conseil de Gouvernement in its mission to realize the happiness of all Guineans through work done in love. . . . [T]he orientation of our trade union movement must necessary correspond to the general policies desired by our populations. Any conception of trade unionism contrary to this orientation must be discarded, and courageously fought in order to be eliminated definitively."[71]

Such views did not go uncontested. David Soumah, a rival and sometime collaborator of Sékou Touré in the Guinean trade union movement, replied, "A unity which stifles the voice of free trade unionism sets back the emancipation of the laboring masses instead of facilitating it."[72] But the new governments now had the patronage mechanisms to co-opt some of the trade union leaders, the muscle to keep others under control, and for a time at least the stature to demand unity in the name of the nation. The union movement in Guinea, once a platform for launching the political career of its leaders, was harshly suppressed soon after independence. Similar stories could be told about other former colonies of French West Africa. A leader who kept the trade unionist faith during a long strike in Dahomey, defeated by a government whose labor minister was himself a former trade unionist, remarked bitterly: "It was easier to obtain satisfaction from a European Inspecteur du Travail than it is now from an African Minister."[73]

Sékou Touré meant what he said in more than one sense. Once he became vice-président du conseil in Guinea, he forced the labor movement in Guinea to tow his line of unity and African authenticity. But if such actions were consistent with French expectations, his anticolonialism and his belief in African rule were no less sincere. When President de Gaulle gave colonial territories the choice between a degree of autonomy within the French Community (as the French Union was renamed in 1958) and a total break with France, Sékou Touré alone among African leaders persuaded the people of his territory to vote for the total break. Guinea became independent in 1958, the rest of French West Africa in 1960 by a more consensual and negotiated route.

It is perfectly reasonable to argue that the relative gains of the labor movement by the mid 1950s made the assertions of leaders that peasants, pastoralists, and fishermen deserved special attention perfectly defensible. But Sékou Touré was not asking for a debate about priorities. He was not recognizing the tensions between different sorts of aspirations among a diverse population and among movements that had contributed to political mobilization. He was using the rhetoric of unity and authenticity to deny any autonomy to the labor movement, any recognition that workers might have particular claims to make. The irony of this position was that the breakup of French West Africa into distinct independent territories severed the connections among different trade unionists across French West Africa.

The new African state would not just be marked by the borders of colonial territories and not just by a kind of brittle authoritarianism that took up where colonial authority had left off. It was shaped by the rise and fall of an alternative kind of politics, in which different kinds of social and political movements, labor prominent among them, opened up space in which to make claims on imperial authority, claims that proved too much for a colonial state to accept and too threatening to their national successors to allow such movements to continue. The *process* of decolonization, not just the heritage of colonialism, shaped the patterns of postcolonial politics.

When French leaders decided in 1956 that they would save themselves from the implications of imperial citizenship, they were in effect giving up what the French Union was intended to make invincible: the notion that France was the only unit in which real power was vested and toward which aspirations could be directed. Territorialization was—although no official admitted this at the time—the decisive step toward decolonization. Either citizenship, with its premises of equivalence, or empire would have to go, and it was empire that went.

What Africans got was sovereignty. That was not the only demand that emerged from the political mobilization of the 1940s and 1950s, but that was the demand which, in the end, France was willing to concede. African labor movements had, in 1946, forced the question of achieving equality of standard of living onto the imperial agenda, and France, a decade later, had tried to remove it from that agenda. But the issues of wages, labor conditions, poverty, and opportunity never quite disappeared into the confines of national sovereignty—into questions for African and Asian governments for which outsiders had no responsibility—and they never quite disappeared into the anonymity of a world market that was supposed to allocate global resources in an optimizing manner. Those questions are still the focus of debates and of political mobilization.

8 Conclusion

Colonialism, History, Politics

How one does history shapes how one thinks about politics, and how one does politics affects how one thinks about history. I have argued throughout this book for telling a story about colonialism with full attention to the shifting trajectories of historical interaction, to the range of possibilities that people at any time could imagine for themselves and the constraints on their imaginations and on their possibilities of realizing their imaginations. The story cannot be told very well as a tale of progress toward "modernity" or as the advance of "globalization" in the face of people trying to assert their "identity" against impinging forces. It cannot be told very well as a story of the steady advance of the nation-state against the empire. Such tellings do not account for the conjuncture in which empire did in fact disappear and a world of unequal nation-states finally became the norm, at the very moment when other sorts of supranational institutions and efforts to shape norms of international development and universal human rights compromised the sovereignty that was finally being generalized.

How one writes about colonialism shapes how one thinks about the kinds of politics that challenged colonial rulers. Perhaps the fiction of a Manichean colonial state had its value, even if it simplified the ways in which colonial authority was exercised and the ways in which people living in colonies tried to make something of the situations they faced. Such a viewpoint privileged certain forms of opposition and denied legitimacy to others: a politics of unremitting struggle against an impenetrable colonial edifice rather than forms of political action and claim-making that depended on overlapping idioms and interaction between colonizer and colonized. Both kinds of politics had their place in colonial history, and it is not clear that either would have threatened the continued viability of colonial empires without the other. One kind of politics threatened colonial regimes with unending violence and the possibility of a unified opposition; the other challenged them with the possibility that political action would produce concrete gains for different categories of people within a colony, that ideologies might be reconfigured, and that notions of what is politically possible or excluded might shift. The point of historical analysis is not to commend one kind of politics or condemn another but to spell out the range of possibilities, the different consequences that could ensue from each, and the possibilities of different trajectories following upon particular combinations of actions.

The story of colonialism and the challenges to it, in my view, should reserve a large place for political struggles that crossed lines of geography and of self-identification or cultural solidarity, partly through the mobilization of political networks, partly through the coming together of different strands of political action in critical conjunctures. The antislavery movements of the late eighteenth and nineteenth centuries were pioneers; the movement of ideas and at times cooperation across the Atlantic was crucial in making an institution that was once an ordinary, acceptable part of empires into a symbol of callousness, greed, and corruption. The attack on slavery consisted of distinct, overlapping, and common struggles of slaves and abolitionists acting in different places and in different idioms. Abolitionist mobilization throughout the Atlantic world was deeply affected by the Haitian Revolution, as some tried to turn it into a warning against any challenge to authority and others tried to spread the word of its emancipatory potential. The ensuing history had deep implications for later formulations of the colonialism question.

It is correct and important to point out the dangers of writing the history of emancipation in a way that ignores how the marking of slavery (and, later, of colonialism) as evil also marked other forms of labor exploitation and social discrimination as acceptable, or which misses the way in which some abolitionists made the difficulties of ex-slaves to make their way in the "free" labor market appear to result from their failures, their lacks. Such a critique still misses the extent to which reconfigured discourses of liberation, progress, and order could be seized and turned into something else. The practice of slave emancipation, as much as slavery, put certain issues onto an international table.

Empire was an ordinary fact of political life as recently as 1935, much as slavery had been in the eighteenth century. By 1955, the legitimacy of any colonial empire was very much in question. By 1965, the colonial game was over. The two most important competitors for global power represented their power in other terms and exercised power by other means. In 1935, some political movements sought to overthrow the colonial order in the name of new nations, but others sought to expand and make meaningful imperial citizenship, while still others dreamed of nation in a diasporic, nonterritorial sense. By the 1960s, the nation-state was at last becoming the principal unit of political organization.

But the course of decolonization raised profound issues that could not be excised from the world order—about the nature of that cultural, political, and economic order as much as the accessibility of formerly colonized people to its benefits. Questions of poverty and exploitation that were once imperial have become both national and international, generating domestic opposition to governments that have failed to deliver on their promises of a better life, new transnational networks and organizations attempting to link local activists with a worldwide debate over inequality, and anxiety among leaders in wealthy countries that the existing world order is not stable or productive enough for their interests. There are, today, powerful actors who defend what they conceive of as a Western model for world order and at the same time defend the high degree of inequality of access to that model, and there are political actors who argue against both points. Coalitions around the world make claims for themselves and others in regard to the availability of medicine to treat deadly diseases, the abuses of child labor, gender inequality, environmental degradation, and the negative effects of international trade regulations on the poor. Others raise philosophically and ethically difficult questions about the ways in which peaceful interaction—within and across national borders—can be fostered while cultural difference is respected. There is no reason at this moment to be hopeful about the outcomes of these debates and struggles, but the past gives little reason to conclude that such struggles can never achieve tangible gains for those most concerned. The more one emphasizes the enormous imbalances in political power and the might of corporate capitalism today, the more important it is to remember that empires which once seemed durable and powerful eventually proved to be vulnerable and impermanent.

Not all explanations of the predicaments of the present capture the trajectories that got us here. One explanatory mode naturalizes the marginality of the poor: in Europe, the ability to innovate in science and technology, to respond effectively to markets, and to develop institutions that sustain progress and efficiency resulted in the long-term expansion of economic resources and welfare, while in other parts of the world people lacking those abilities exclude themselves (or are excluded by *their* leaders) from participation in a globalization that is both inevitable and beneficial.[1] Such a historical vision lies behind the politics of the write-off: little can be done "for" people, notably Africans, who are not making it, except to subject their governments to economic discipline, keep out their citizens who seek entry into better labor markets, and quarantine their regimes if they act like "rogue states" or "failed states." The politics of the write-off is also a politics of labeling.

A second explanation focuses on those who would self-consciously improve the world. Their project has failed: it was an effort to impose an unwanted modernity, an unwanted universality, and unwanted forms of social and economic life on diverse peoples. This is a valuable critique of arrogance and Eurocentrism within colonial and postcolonial institutions that promoted planned change, but it is far from clear that such a modernizing project ever existed. Colonial rulers, as I argued in chapters 5 and 6, were profoundly ambivalent about change, and the resulting practices were subject to selectivity, appropriation, and deflection, as well as resistance. Africans and other colonized people were able to turn the discourse of modernization into a language of claims. When development emerged as a self-avowed colonial project with metropolitan funding, it did so in the face of serious challenges from the West Indies and Africa in the 1930s and 1940s. Developmentalist colonialism was pushed farther in a postwar conjuncture when colonial states both needed to reassert their legitimacy and assure that colonial production would become more efficient and orderly—something neither "the market" nor the previous period of colonial rule had secured. The development initiatives in fact produced more conflict than they assuaged, and the escalation of claim-making from African workers, farmers, students, market women, and other groups presented colonial regimes with a potential challenge they could not meet.

Such claim-making has not gone away, as Steven Robins notes in regard to South Africa: "In fact throughout Southern Africa, calls for development have become a rallying cry in the popular struggles of the urban and rural poor demanding houses, clinics, and more state resources in a context of job losses, grinding poverty and neo-liberal fiscal austerity."[2] This ongoing effort is not sufficiently appreciated by some of today's critics, who offer, as Stuart Hall puts it, "massive, gigantic and eloquent disavowal" of Eurocentric models rather than alternative projects and alternative languages of claim-making.[3] Disavowal and critique do not provide an adequate understanding of either the struggles of the past or those of the future, in all their concreteness.

An ahistorical approach to the past reflects and encourages an apolitical approach to the present. To hold modernity responsible for the evils of colonization and the exclusions and inequities of our own time is to make such a profound observation that there is little one can do about it. To counter a linear view of progress marching ever onward with a two-century view of post-Enlightenment rationality obscures the moments and contexts in which political choices were made and provides little insight into questions of choice and responsibility today. It deflects to an abstraction the responsibility of those individuals and collectivities who chose to support brutal acts of occupation, who found reasons to condone forced labor and land seizures, and who responded to political mobilization with repression and torture. The critique of modernity or of post-Enlightenment rationality is more about *stance* than about engagement.

At the same time, the celebration of Western culture's progressive thrust—including recent arguments that assimilate empire to the promotion of global integration—use a fiction about the past as a model for the future. In this sense, and above all in their unwillingness to focus on the specificity of economic and political situations, the defenders of a putative European modernizing project and its critics converge.[4]

I began this book by noting the possibility that the valuable efforts of some scholars to emphasize the importance of the colonial question to world history might put in place a generic conception of colonialism set against European claims to be the driving force of progress, rather than bring out a contested and contingent history. I also called attention to common ways of thinking about the past that are nevertheless ahistorical: story plucking, leapfrogging legacies, doing history backward, and the epochal fallacy. All of them dissociate action and consequences. They permit the celebration of resistance, but do so by distancing it from the ongoing encounters through which the colonial rule was tested, limited, and sometimes reshaped by those who sought niches within systems of colonial power as well as those who fought it.

One can readily agree with Uday Mehta when he writes, "I do not claim that liberalism *must be* imperialistic, only that the urge is *internal* to it."[5] One could just as easily write, "I do not claim that liberalism *must be* antiimperialist, only that the urge is *internal* to it." As in the case of nineteenth-century English liberalism, the crucial questions about arguments for liberation and democratization today are not resolvable by epistemological critique, but turn on the concrete possibilities permitted by our political, economic, and social conjuncture and the political choices that people make. Which liberalism? Whose Enlightenment? What kind of development? Whose vision of progress? Which vision of an Islamic *umma*? Whose community? Which network of connections across linguistic or cultural divisions?

Critical scholars are right to point to the danger that even liberation movements can get caught up in the framing of Western conceptual categories. But the reverse is equally the case: to define modernity as the problem in today's world is to make nonmodernity the alternative, or else to promote alternative modernities that imply that each claimant to such a modernity has its own essential destiny which it pursues as others chase their own alternatives. It is salutary to warn about the dangers of assuming that such terms as *electoral democracy* and *open markets* are the only ones in which political possibilities can be discussed, obscuring the convoluted history by which those terms came to the once-colonized world and precluding a search for a wider repertoire. But we lose a great deal as well if we assume that such notions are a static package, that the powerless cannot find in the ideology of the powerful tools that are useful in confronting tyrants at home and abroad. However much we criticize Western idealists who set off to foreign lands to emancipate women or save the environment, we should not ignore the possibility that people struggling against the intolerances and inequalities that lie within most communities might find useful resonances and support from outside their boundaries.

But let us turn the question around. What is it that we can learn from a more precise historical perspective on colonization and decolonization? Can thinking historically about colonial situations help us think politically about present predicaments?

History does not offer answers, and historians do not make better prophets than anyone else. It is hard enough to do craftsmanlike work on one's own specialty, to confront but not be paralyzed by the unevenness and biases of archives and oral traditions, to imagine how people in different times and contexts thought and acted, and to recognize the assumptions within one's own conceptual apparatus. But if one can do better than story plucking, leapfrogging, doing history backward, and the epochal fallacy, at least one can engage the unfolding of historical processes. Historical analysis calls attention to two points that are worth keeping in mind as one ponders issues in the present: the range of possibility and constraint facing different political actors at any moment, and the different trajectories of possibility and constraint that follow upon acting in one's own time.

First, the most basic fact facing us today is that the world is interconnected and unequal. This fact is not new, but the ways in which connection and inequality are configured have changed again and again, through the actions of the powerful and the subordinate at the most localized of social locations and in the broadest ranges of imagination.

Capitalism provided solvents that cut into the boundedness of frameworks within which people produced and exchanged, but it did not end the fact that every product is made somewhere, services are performed somewhere, and movement of goods and ideas depends on mechanisms whose extent and power are bounded in some way. Just as the eighteenth century slave plantation—although it grew out of and shaped transoceanic connections—depended on the exercise of coercive power over people locked into a place, today's productive processes give rise to issues of labor discipline, family life, and social order in spaces that are no less specific for the fact of being interconnected. The wave of general strikes in colonial Africa in the 1940s, discussed in chapter 7, were neither replicas of European labor history nor wholly distinct from them for the fact of having occurred in Africa; understanding them still illuminates the possibilities for mobilization that occur in the reconfigured organization of capitalist production today. Questions of the social reproduction of labor (the sustenance of workers and the raising of new generations of workers), of the relationship of export production to regional ecologies, and of the relationship of networks of trade and migration to cultural affinities and divergences remain. The specificity of these issues changes over time, but they do not disappear with the proclamation that this is an "epoch" of capital mobility, of the all-determining discipline of the world market, or of a "post-Fordist" production regime. The reconfiguration of capital across space unleashes a politics of borders and border-crossings rather than a regime of borderlessness.

Second, the long history of antislavery, anticolonial, and anti-apartheid movements are important precedents for thinking about political issues today. All of these movements entailed mobilization—with vigor and courage—by victims of empire, but they succeeded not only because local mobilizations assaulted the orderly normality of colonial regimes but because mobilizations resonated and connected across space. Slavery, colonial rule, and white domination all depended on long-distance connections and on ocean-crossing ideological constructs: on the sense of normality and entitlement of colonial planters, settlers, and officials, and on publics in Europe accepting such arrangements as legitimate parts of an imperial polity, a global economy, and Western civilization. The Haitian Revolution of the 1790s and the successful colonial revolutions in Indonesia and Indochina in the 1940s and 1950s were formative parts of this reconfiguration, but so too were countless insurrections large and small that were successfully repressed, as well as mobilizations—such as those of West African labor movements—that taught colonial rulers that change within "their" ideological frameworks could be as costly as ending colonial rule.

One can rightly point to the limitations of all these movements: they did not end inequality and subordination, and their very success fed into—at least in some hands—an interpretation of an ever more enlightened West overcoming its backwardness and liberating others from their own. Yet decolonization was not a moment that suddenly produced a generalized postcolonial condition, but a process in which new possibilities for changing institutions and discourses opened up along the way—sometimes to be thwarted by new constraints or co-opted into the self-serving machinations of political elites. An ironic stance toward the language of equality and economic progress that appeared in the decolonization struggles should not obscure the appeal such concepts had, the disappointment and disillusionment that came when hopes were not fulfilled, and above all the ways in which such concepts changed when people in the colonies claimed them for themselves.

But the change in international norms regarding some of the most fundamental aspects of humanity is nonetheless part of history. These were in part the achievement of leaders who deserve heroic status and obscure people who labored and suffered and who appear anonymously in archives, newspapers, and memoirs, and in part the consequence of people who struggled for something other than national liberation—for better wages, for full citizenship within an imperial context, for a measure of social status or recognition in a changing social situation. They were not simply the achievements of the already like-minded, of the socially identical, of community triumphing over colonialism, globalization, or modernity. We have much to learn from the schoolteacher in an African colony who sought recognition for what he or she had achieved, who recorded in English the traditions of people with whom he identified and from whom he was establishing a certain distance, and who organized a trade union and campaigned for a modest increase in wages. Multiplied many times over, such people opened up the fissures in the thin, overextended apparatus of a colonial state. We could do worse than to think about how, today, analogous fissures might be opened in national regimes, transnational corporations, and international systems vulnerable precisely because of the extent of interconnection and mobility.

Third, the emphasis this book has given to the limitations of imperial power suggests reexamining the language of a very current debate in international politics. Empire and colonialism are evoked as totalizing concepts, as representing the extremes of power, cultural as well as material. On one side, one finds a reading of the history of nineteenth- and twentieth-century colonialism as the imposition of modernity, which set the rules and then belittled colonized people for being unable to play by them. On the other side is an argument that empire was a good thing, that it set a precedent for intervention in benighted, conflict-ridden societies that should be put into practice today by the one power capable of assuming the mantle of empire, the United States. Some are skeptical whether the United States is up to the high standards of the British Empire, but the point of this reading of history is important nonetheless: it is used explicitly to support new forms of the extension of American power.[6]

The historical interpretation on which this argument is based is profoundly flawed, and its flaws are the mirror image of those found within postcolonial critique. Whereas the latter uses empire to discredit modernity, the former uses modernity to give credit to empire. Empire is said to bring enlightened rule, an imposed peace, and the possibility of conducting regional and intercontinental trade under safe and predictable conditions. Never mind that the notion of enlightened and fair rule is based on a stereotype that is profoundly racial—some authors even invoke the image of the Englishman in pith helmet or the White Man's Burden of Kipling— or that the violence that colonial conquest did in fact suppress, namely that associated with slave raids and slave trading, belongs on the Euro-African side of the ledger rather than being a specifically African proclivity. Such an argument ignores the ways in which colonial rule reinforced rather than opened up distinctions among legal systems and ethnicized cultural difference. The pro-empire argument shares with the anti-modernity argument a shallow reading of the history of actual empires, which were neither the agents of the colonization of minds nor of promotion of the rule of law and market economies. Actually existing empires, British and French as much as Ottoman and Chinese, were rarely so consistent, and when, as in the post–World War II era, they tried to make themselves more forward-looking economically and more legitimate politically, they could not face the escalation of claim-making their actions encouraged, the tensions that followed from their economic interventions, and the high cost of making an empire meaningful as a unit of belonging. In the end, Britain and France abdicated responsibility for their colonial histories as they devolved power to the nation-states emerging from the decolonization process, insisting that whatever went wrong would be toted up on the African side of the historical balance sheet.

Neither the pro-empire argument nor the denunciation of an abstracted coloniality gives much weight to one of the most central features of the history of empires: their limitations. And neither wishes to see that the limits apply most strikingly to the most modern and modernizing of the empires, those of Western European powers in the late nineteenth and twentieth centuries. Capitalist empire, in India as well as Africa, turned out not to be so consistently capitalist after all, bureaucratic rule not so consistently bureaucratic, the making of colonial subjects not so consistent in their ideas of what kind of subject was to be produced.

Not just colonies, not just empires, but the very category of empire came undone in the two decades after World War II, which was a time of economic growth and systematic efforts at social engineering, in the welfare states of Europe as well as their colonies. Yet basic questions about the relationship of the world social order and the institution through which power is exercised do not go away: capital still needs protection and regulation, and hence operates in a highly uneven manner across different political units. Networks of communication and movement of people, capital, and ideas run into no-go areas, whose valuable human and material resources cannot be fully exploited and which harbor forces dangerous to wealthy states. Africa remains an area where systematic, predictable, extensive exploitation is difficult to organize, but other historic crucibles of empire—the Middle East, Central Asia, East Asia—fit poorly in images of a seamless globality extended everywhere.

The usefulness of thinking about empires is not that they represent good models for the future or a form of political power whose revival we need to fear.[7] The value of the story is in the telling, in the way in which we talk about historical trajectories, the opening and foreclosing of possibilities, the transformation of concepts as they were seized by different people, and the relationship between struggles in particular places and the reconfiguration of worldwide perspectives on what is normal and what is unimaginable. Empires may have gone, but multinational polities have not. Inequality of power is still with us. Sovereignty is still a concept that, for all its apparent indivisibility, is very much compromised and uncertain. If one tells the story as a movement from empire to nation-state—whether dated from Westphalia in the seventeenth century, France in the late eighteenth century, the Americas at the turn of the eighteenth to nineteenth century, or the Treaty of Vienna of 1815—the tale gives too much continuity, too much forward motion, too much weight to the concept of nation-state, obscuring the fact that it shared imaginative space not only with empire, in its various manifestations, but with other forms of territory-crossing political imagination. We should neither exaggerate the importance of the nation-state in the past nor exaggerate its decline in the present.

Even the generalization of the nation-state came at a time when the states that were giving up empire were contemplating participation in a very different sort of supranational institution, the European Economic

Community, and it reflected the ability of the first "new" nations to make themselves heard in international bodies and assail the apparent normality of empires. What is most important about this phase of our story is its dynamics: empires were challenged from within and without, from below and above, and their ultimate demise reflected a reconfiguration of norms of power across an entire system, not just the reversal of a particular state. The process opened space for international debates on development and economic and social rights—debates that have not ended.

Craig Calhoun has argued that solidarity should be seen not in organic so much as processual terms: as something growing out of collective action, constitution-making, and efforts to make a political system into something it was not. He raises the important question of whether such collective efforts have worked nearly as well on the international as on the national level. He worries that "the global public sphere lags dramatically," compared to other forms of international action, such as the regulation of markets or the interventions of international organizations, which are not so democratically organized.[8] The history of empires reveals important examples of efforts to make a spatially discontinuous, culturally varied, politically uneven space into a unit of political mobilization, and that is why it is worth remembering the efforts of a Toussaint L'Ouverture to bring to Haiti key claims of the French Revolution and to transform them in the process, of reformers within the Ottoman elite and the Young Ottomans who challenged them to bring constitutional reform to the Ottoman Empire while retaining its multinational configuration, and the efforts of a Léopold Sédar Senghor or an Aimé Césaire to make French citizenship meaningful to the empire, to use it as a basis for making claims to social equality and cultural recognition, and to move beyond the French Empire to make a universalistic argument for the contributions of Africa to world civilization.

In the postwar decades, the rulers of the French and British empires—and those of the United States—made clear that they could more easily tolerate the claims of nationalists to rule nation-states than they could the less bounded forms of making claims on the resources of the empire or the resources of the world economy. But the very struggle, from India to Algeria, produced a worldwide debate that could not be answered by the generalization of sovereignty and which kept returning to issues of economic exploitation, gender inequality, and access to basic resources. Transnational social movements and international organizations, ineffectual as they often have been, have kept these debates alive. Scholarship on colonialism has, in its own way, emphasized that such issues cannot be separated from the history that defined them, and it has made clear how much is at stake in the way these issues are framed. Studying colonial history reminds us that in the most oppressive of political systems, people found not just niches in which to hide and fend for themselves, but handles by which the system itself could be moved.

Notes

1. Laurent Dubois, "*La République métissée:* Citizenship, Colonialism, and the Borders of French History," *Cultural Studies* 14 (2000): 22.

2. See the considerations of the insights and blind spots in different turns in Victoria E. Bonnell and Lynn Hunt, eds., *Beyond the Cultural Turn: New Directions in the Study of Society and Culture* (Berkeley: University of California Press, 1999), especially the editors' thoughtful introduction, and William H. Sewell, Jr., "Whatever Happened to the 'Social' in Social History?" in Joan W. Scott and Debra Keates, eds., *Schools of Thought: Twenty-Five Years of Interpretive Social Science* (Princeton, N.J.: Princeton University Press, 2001), 209–26. For more turns, see Terrence J. McDonald, ed., *the Historic Turn in the Human Sciences* (Ann Arbor: University of Michigan Press, 1996); Fredric Jameson, *The Cultural Turn: Selected Writings on the Postmodern, 1983–1998* (London: Verso, 1998).

3. Antoinette Burton writes of an "imperial turn" in historical scholarship, contrasted to what she considers a "hidebound" insistence on Britain's "national" character. *After the Imperial Turn: Thinking With and Through the Nation* (Durham NC: Duke University Press, 2003), 9. I agree with much of her argument (see chapter 6), but the contrast of the hidebound and the turners does not seem to me the most effective way to make it.

4. Stephen Howe describes the mutually dismissive stances of people who call themselves postcolonial theorists and imperial historians. "The Slow Death and Strange Rebirths of Imperial History," *Journal of Imperial and Commonwealth History* 29 (2001): 131–41.

5. For the critique of modernity, one can begin with Dipesh Chakrabarty, *Provincializing Europe: Postcolonial Thought and Historical Difference* (Princeton, N.J.: Princeton University Press, 2000), while the supposed clash between those who have achieved modernity (the West) and those who are incapable of doing so (Muslims, most notably) is the theme of Samuel Hunting-

ton, *The Clash of Civilizations and the Remaking of World Order* (New York: Simon and Schuster, 1996).

6. See Eric Wolf, *Europe and the People without History* (Berkeley: University of California Press, 1982).

7. Data are from the ArticleFirst database of OCLC. Data on books from the Stanford University catalogue are similar: *modernity*, almost never used in book titles around 1980, passed *modernization* in 1991.

8. A. G. Hopkins and Niall Ferguson differ considerably in how they interpret the economic history of the British empire, but both seek to ratify their positions by associating them with globalization—a position more teleological than historical. Hopkins, ed., *Globalization in World History* (London: Pimlico, 2002); and Ferguson, *Empire: The Rise and Demise of the British World Order and the Lessons for Global Power* (London: Allen Lane, 2002).

9. Partha Chatterjee, *Our Modernity* (Amsterdam, Dakar: Sephis/Codesria, 1997), 20. Available on the web at www.sephis.org/pdf/partha1.pdf.

10. Others have attempted to define and examine differing directions within postcolonial theory, most recently Suvir Kaul and Ania Loomba, eds., *Postcolonial Studies and Beyond* (Durham, NC: Duke University Press, 2005). Subaltern Studies has been the focus of an analysis that has been both appreciative of its accomplishments and critical of some of its suppositions or tendencies. See the forum in *American Historical Review* 99 (1994): 1475–1545; and David Ludden, ed., *Reading Subaltern Studies: Critical History, Contested Meaning and the Globalization of South Asia* (London: Anthem Press, 2002).

11. Ashis Nandy, "History's Forgotten Doubles," *History and Theory* 34 (1995): 44–66.

12. Nicholas Dirks, "History as a Sign of the Modern," *Public Culture* 2, no. 2 (1990): 25. For a thoughtful discussion of critiques of history and their relation to the state, see Mamadou Diouf, "Des historiens et des histoires, pour quoi faire? L'histoire africaine entre l'état et les communautés," *Revue Canadienne des Etudes Africaines* 34 (2000): 337–74.

13. Edward Said, *Orientalism* (New York: Pantheon, 1978) and *Culture and Imperialism* (New York: Knopf, 1993). For a recent reassessment by historians of the influence of Said, see the contributions of Andrew Rotter, K. E. Fleming, and Kathleen Biddick to a forum on "Orientalism Twenty Years On," *American Historical Review* 105 (2000): 1204–49.

14. Such approaches have been strongly influenced by Michel Foucault, whom Said both used and criticized. See chapter 2. Africanists have been challenged by Valentin Mudimbe to examine how the "colonial library" shapes the ways in which the concept of Africa has been constructed, while Gaurav Desai asks us to "reimagine the colonial library as a space of contestation." V. Y. Mudimbe, *The Invention of Africa: Gnosis, Philosophy, and the Order of Knowledge* (Bloomington: Indiana University Press, 1988); Gaurav Desai, *Subject to Colonialism: African Self-Fashioning and the Colonial Library* (Durham, N.C.: Duke University Press, 2001), 4.

15. David Scott, *Refashioning Futures: Criticism after Postcoloniality* (Princeton, N.J.: Princeton University Press, 1999), 156, emphasis in original.

16. For sympathetic but critical views of the political implications of postcolonial studies, see Gayatri Chakravorty Spivak, *A Critique of Postcolonial Reason: Toward a History of the Vanishing Present* (Cambridge, Mass.: Harvard University Press, 1999); and Nicholas B. Dirks, "Postcolonialism and Its Discontents: History, Anthropology and Postcolonial Critique," in Scott and Keates, *Schools of Thought*, 244, 246; for hostile ones, see Sumit Sarkar, "The Fascism of the Sangh Parivar," *Economic and Political Weekly*, Jan. 20, 1993, 164–65; Sumit Sarkar, "The Decline of the Subaltern in Subaltern Studies," in *Writing Social History* (Delhi: Oxford University Press, 1997), 81–108; Arif Dirlik, "The Postcolonial Aura: Third World Criticism in the Age of Global Capitalism," *Critical Inquiry* 20 (1994): 328–56.

17. The interest of Chakrabarty (*Provincializing Europe*) in the "postenlightenment" does not lead him to mention the post-enlightenment of the Haitian revolutionaries; Scott doesn't mention Haiti either (*Refashioning Futures*). Robert J. C. Young, in *Postcolonialism: An Historical Introduction* (Oxford: Blackwell, 2001), cites Haiti as a slave revolt, not as a revolt that shaped debates on emancipation. It was C. L. R. James who appreciated the significance of this event. *The Black Jacobins: Toussaint L'Ouverture and the San Domingo Revolution*, 2d ed. (New York: Vintage, 1963 [1938]).

18. Stuart Hall, "When Was 'the Post-colonial'? Thinking at the Limit," in Iain Chambers and Lidia Curti, eds., *The Post-Colonial Question: Common Skies, Divided Horizons* (London: Routledge, 1996), 249. More curious is Young's statement in a book about postcolonialism: "The postcolonial does not privilege the colonial. It is concerned with colonial history only to the extent that history has determined the configurations and power structures of the present, to the extent that much of the world still lives in the violent disruptions of its wake, and to the extent that the anti-colonial liberation movements remain the source and inspiration of its politics." His postcolonialism assumes "a common political and moral consensus towards the history and legacy of western colonialism." How one would be able to judge "the extent" without studying the history is not obvious, but what counts for Young is a *stance*, taken out of the context of whatever that stance is directed against. *Postcolonialism*, 4–5.

19. Achille Mbembe's insightful and provocative *On the Postcolony* (Berkeley: University of California Press, 2001) also tends toward a generalized conception of both the postcolony and its colonial antecedent.

20. Gyan Prakash, "Subaltern Studies as Postcolonial Criticism," *American Historical Review*, 99 (1994): 1475–90.

21. Walter Mignolo sees "coloniality" as part of a singular Western history dating to the sixteenth century: "Coloniality, in other words, is the hidden face of modernity and its very condition of possibility." "The Many Faces of Cosmo-polis: Border Thinking and Critical Cosmopolitanism," *Public Culture* 12 (2000) 722. For other examples of a colonial phenomenon abstracted from time and place, see Homi Bhabha, "Of Mimicry and Man: The Ambivalence of Colonial Discourse," in Frederick Cooper and Ann Laura Stoler, *Tensions of Empire: Colonial Cultures in a Bourgeois World* (Berkeley: University of Cal-

ifornia Press, 1997),152–60; Walter Mignolo, *Local Histories/Global Designs: Coloniality, Subaltern Knowledges, and Border Thinking* (Princeton, N.J.: Princeton University Press, 2000).

22. Mamdani, *Citizen and Subject: Contemporary Africa and the Legacy of Late Colonialism* (Princeton, N.J.: Princeton University Press, 1996).

23. For another example of the leapfrogging fallacy, see Richard Price, *The Convict and the Colonel: A Story of Colonialism and Resistance in the Caribbean* (Boston: Beacon, 1998). This book is constructed around the ironic juxtaposition of a violent confrontation of police and demonstrators in the French island of Martinique in 1925 and the trivializing of the memory of colonization in the period of Price's fieldwork, when the people of Martinique were caught up in the tourist business and the French welfare state. By omitting the history in between, Price obscures the seriousness of political mobilization in the 1930s and 1940s, when a strong Caribbean movement pressed the French government to accord this colony the status of a French department, and thereby worked to lay claim to French educational and social resources equivalent to those of other French citizens. One would not know from Price's account that this movement succeeded in 1946—that the victims of the 1925 conflict did not die in vain—or that the noted writer/activist whose authority Price invokes in indicting French colonialism, Aimé Césaire, was the main leader of the departmentalization movement. The missing middle contains the politics.

24. The recent flood of books on the social construction of whiteness is an example of both the value and the problems of this approach. See Eric Arnesen, "Whiteness and the Historians' Imagination," and the debate it provoked in *International Labor and Working Class History* 60 (2001): 3–92.

25. I have discussed the relationship between nationalist politics and trade union movements in "Dialectics of Decolonization: Nationalism and Labor Movements in Postwar French Africa," in Cooper and Stoler, *Tensions of Empire,* 406–35. Michel-Rolph Trouillot makes a related point about constructivism: we can point to narratives being produced, but "the reasons why a specific story matters to a specific population are themselves historical." *Silencing the Past: Power and the Production of History* (Boston: Beacon, 1995), 13.

26. Karl Mannheim, *Ideology and Utopia: An Introduction to the Sociology of Knowledge,* trans. Louis Wirth and Edward Shils (San Diego: Harcourt Brace Jovanovich, 1985 [1936]).

27. See chapter 5 for more on the confusions of the term *modern,* in its epochal and other variants. See also Bernard Yack, *The Fetishism of Modernities: Epochal Self-Consciousness in Contemporary Social and Political Thought* (Notre Dame, IN: University of Notre Dame Press, 1997).

28. Hall, "When Was 'the Post-colonial'?" 246, also argues for a break point with decolonization. I prefer to see this as a change in the political repertoire rather than to make generalizing claims about each epoch, for example between a Manichean coloniality and a hybrid postcoloniality.

29. When Simon Gikandi states that "postcolonial theory is one way of recognizing how decolonized situations are marked by the trace of the imperial

pasts they try to disavow," he is opening the door to a valuable analysis of where those traces lie and what course they take over time. When he later states, "My assumption here is that the 'founders' of the new postcolonial nations legitimated their authority by claiming the agency of pure modernity (even as they sang praise songs for precolonial traditions) not because they were attracted to the imperial project per se but because they had no real access to modes of knowledge outside the horizon of expectations established by empire," he is preempting such an inquiry. *Maps of Englishness: Writing Identity in the Culture of Colonialism* (New York: Columbia University Press, 1996), 15, 18.

30. For a thoughtful discussion of the confusions of social type and historical era in the evocation of the modern, see James Ferguson, *Expectations of Modernity: Myths and Meanings of Urban Life on the Zambian Copperbelt* (Berkeley: University of California Press, 1999), 42–43.

31. These remarks should not detract from the illuminating work that some scholars have done using Foucauldian concepts. See especially the valuable reflections of Ann Laura Stoler, *Race and the Education of Desire: Foucault's History of Sexuality and the Colonial Order of Things* (Durham, N.C.: Duke University Press, 1995).

32. Chakrabarty, *Provincializing Europe.*

33. Chakrabarty, *Provincializing,* 237. Hegel serves the same role for Gyan Prakash, *Another Reason: Science and the Imagination of Modern India* (Princeton, N.J.: Princeton University Press, 1999), 8, 118; and Nicholas Dirks, *Castes of Mind: Colonialism and the Making of Modern India* (Princeton, N.J.: Princeton University Press, 2001), 52.

34. Arno Mayer, *The Persistence of the Old Regime: Europe to the Great War* (New York: Pantheon Books, 1981).

35. David Hollinger, "The Enlightenment and the Genealogy of Cultural Conflict in the United States," and Dena Goodman, "Difference: An Enlightenment Concept," in Keith Michael Baker and Peter Hanns Reill, eds., *What's Left of Enlightenment? A Postmodern Question* (Stanford, Calif.: Stanford University Press, 2001), 7–18 (11 quoted) and 129–47.

36. Sankar Muthu, *Enlightenment against Empire* (Princeton, N.J.: Princeton University Press, 2003); Alyssa Goldstein Sepinwall, "Eliminating Race, Eliminating Difference: Blacks, Jews, and the Abbé Grégoire," in Sue Peabody and Tyler Stovall, eds., *The Color of Liberty: Histories of Race in France* (Durham, N.C.: Duke University Press, 2003), 28–41.

37. On the role of slaves in redefining the meanings of freedom, see Robin Blackburn, *The Overthrow of Colonial Slavery, 1776–1848* (London: Verso, 1988); George Fredrickson, *Black Liberation: A Comparative History of Black Ideologies in the United States and South Africa* (New York: Oxford University Press, 1995); Thomas Holt, *The Problem of Freedom: Race, Labor, and Politics in Jamaica and Britain, 1832–1938* (Baltimore, Md.: Johns Hopkins University Press, 1992).

38. William Sewell, Jr., "Historical Events as Transformations of Structures: Inventing Revolution at the Bastille," *Theory and Society* 25 (1996):

841–81, 843 cited. I use the concept of lumpiness to make a point about space similar to the one Sewell makes about time (chapter 4).

39. One of the main achievements of African history has been to bring out not just the variety of historical trajectories found in Africa before and after colonization, but the variety of ways in which Africans have thought about them. The difficult task is to see how people worked between different modes of understanding time and process, as they came to grips with the perspectives with which colonial schools and missions confronted them. People in the middle experienced neither a smooth blending or hybridity nor a radical incommensurability of different historicities. For examples of the use of texts by people in the middle of colonial relationships in order to reconceptualize history, see Nancy Rose Hunt, *A Colonial Lexicon: Of Birth Ritual, Medicalization, and Mobility in the Congo* (Durham, N.C.: Duke University Press, 1999); Desai, *Subject to Colonialism*; and Meredith McKittrick, *To Dwell Secure: Generation, Christianity, and Colonialism in Ovamboland* (Portsmouth, NH: Heinemann, 2002).

40. The centrality of nationalism to the history of the last two hundred years is emphasized in Benedict Anderson, *Imagined Communities: Reflections on the Origin and Spread of Nationalism* (London: Verso, 1983); while the demise of the nation-state is announced in Arjun Appadurai, *Modernity at Large: Cultural Dimensions of Globalization* (Minneapolis: University of Minnesota Press, 1996), 19.

41. James, *Black Jacobins*; Laurent Dubois, *Avengers of the New World: The Story of the Haitian Revolution* (Cambridge, Mass.: Harvard University Press, 2004); idem., *Les esclaves de la République: L'histoire oubliée de la première émancipation 1789–1794* (Paris: Calmann-Lévy, 1998).

42. Eve M. Troutt Powell, *A Different Shade of Colonialism: Egypt, Great Britain, and the Mastery of the Sudan* (Berkeley: University of California Press, 2003).

43. The possibilities of putting Central Asia in an imperial perspective are illustrated in Adeeb Khalid, *The Politics of Muslim Cultural Reform: Jadidism in Central Asia* (Berkeley : University of California Press, 1998).

44. Partha Chatterjee, *The Nation and Its Fragments: Colonial and Postcolonial Histories* (Princeton, N.J.: Princeton University Press, 1993), 16.

45. Edmund S. Morgan's pioneering study of colonial Virginia brought out the increasing racial polarization that developed as elite Virginians sought to forge a republican coalition, whose class inclusiveness demanded racial exclusiveness. *American Slavery, American Freedom: The Ordeal of Colonial Virginia* (New York: Norton, 1975). For a contrast, the tsarist empire of Russia did not develop such dichotomies, for all Russians belonged to defined social categories and all were subjects of the tsar. See Jane Burbank and Mark von Hagen, eds., *Geographies of Empire* (Bloomington: Indiana University Press, forthcoming).

46. David Scott adds to his heroic view of anticolonialism and to subsequent postcolonial disillusionment a third stage, "after postcolonialism," whose hall-

mark is the revelation that everything that went before was the violence of modernity. *Refashioning Futures,* 10–14, 16–17, 45, 199. See chapter 7 for a different way of discussing openings and closures in the process of decolonization.

47. Some scholars see both possibility and danger in the fact that postcolonial theory "seems to locate itself everywhere and nowhere." Ato Quayson and David Theo Goldberg, "Introduction: Scale and Sensibility," in David Theo Goldberg and Ato Quayson, eds., *Relocating Postcolonialism* (Oxford: Blackwell, 2002), xvi.

48. The spatial dimension of colonization is both underscored and complicated by some scholars' use of the notion of internal colonialism. It is sometimes used literally—to denote the consignment of certain categories of people into specific spaces within self-governing territories, such as Indian reservations in the United States or African homelands in South Africa after its independence from Britain in 1910. Sometimes it is used metaphorically to denote extremes of categorization and discrimination of people in a polity that is formally national. The metaphoric usage requires prudence, for it risks diluting the actual experience of people in actual colonies as well as misanalyzing the specificities of categorization and differentiation in national polities.

49. Australia and the western United States in the nineteenth century provide examples of the assimilation of individuals and the destruction of cultures, of extermination, and of extreme marginalization. Scholars of Spanish America have debated since the nineteenth century the extent to which *mestisaje* is myth or reality; some China specialists see China as an empire with a strong homogenizing tendency—a movement toward becoming a very large nation-state—but others put more emphasis not just on the importance of frontier areas like Tibet or Inner Asia, but on the ethnic distinctiveness of the ruling dynasty in the long Qing period, from the seventeenth to the twentieth century. See chapter 6.

50. Michael Mann, *The Sources of Social Power: Volume II. The Rise of Classes and Nation-States, 1760–1914* (Cambridge: Cambridge University Press, 1993).

51. This is the problem with Michael Doyle's definition of empire as control of "a subordinated society by an imperial society": societies are not necessarily what does the subordinating; they may be produced in the building and evolution of empires. *Empires* (Ithaca, N.Y.: Cornell University Press, 1986), 30.

52. Robert L. Delavignette, "Action colonisatrice et paysannat indigène," *Afrique Francaise* 45 (1935): 526–30.

53. Ann Laura Stoler and Frederick Cooper, "Between Colony and Metropole: Toward a Research Agenda," in Cooper and Stoler, *Tensions of Empire,* 1–57.

54. Selim Deringil, "'They Live in a State of Nomadism and Savagery': The Late Ottoman Empire and the Post-Colonial Debate," *Comparative Studies in Society and History* 45 (2003): 311–42; Jane Burbank, "The Rights of Difference: Law and Citizenship in the Russian Empire," paper for conference "Be-

yond Europe," School of American Research, Santa Fe, New Mexico, Oct. 25–30, 2003. The civilizers, in these cases, were imposing an imperial rather than a national vision of directed change: Ottoman imperialism, not Turkish in the first instance, an imposition made on Russian peasants as much as on Central Asians in the second.

55. Dubois, *Avengers of the New World,* 3.

56. Globality is particularly amorphous—and its relationship to nation-state and colonial empires particularly murky—in Michael Hardt and Antonio Negri, *Empire* (Cambridge, Mass.: Harvard University Press, 2000). For a critique, see Frederick Cooper, "Empire Multiplied," *Comparative Studies in Society and History* 46 (2004): 247–72.

57. On the left, see Ellen Meiskins Wood, *Empire of Capital* (London: Verso, 2003); David Harvey, *The New Imperialism* (Oxford: Oxford University Press, 2003); and Michael Mann, *Incoherent Empire* (New York: Verso, 2003); and on the right, Ferguson, *Empire.*

58. Niall Ferguson, "The Empire Slinks Back: Why Americans Don't Really Have What It Takes to Rule the World," *New York Times Magazine,* April 27, 2003, pp. 52–57.

59. Revivifying empire and enforcing exclusion are at the center of Niall Ferguson's thinking. He compares the supposed dangers of Muslims immigrating to Europe to the decline and fall of the Roman empire, citing Gibbon and evoking the dangers of "a youthful Muslim society . . . poised to colonize—the term is not too strong—a senescent Europe." "Eurabia?" *New York Times Magazine,* April 4, 2004, pp. 13–14.

60. P. J. Cain and Anthony Hopkins make a good argument in the British case for examining a range of imperial strategies of which empire as a political and administrative concept is a subset, and not always the most important one. They see occasional coercion, diplomatic initiatives, and the establishment of close networks—of "kith and kin" linking Britain with colonies of settlement, of banks building ties of credit and information exchange, of merchants developing interfaces with producers in different areas—as part of an imperial project. One can argue about the strength of these networks and about the prominence of the "gentlemanly capitalists" they see at their center, but the broad view of British naval, political, economic, social, and cultural power is a useful one. It does, however, require specification of the consequences of particular strategies, including the establishment of colonial institutions over much of Asia and Africa and the selective transformation of colonial institutions into other political forms in places like Canada and Australia. *British Imperialism, 1688–2000,* 2d ed. (London: Longman, 2002).

61. International relations specialists distinguish the "hegemonic" (setting the rules of the game which others must follow) from the "imperial" (intervening in another polity without actually governing it) and the "colonial" (governing the internal affairs of a subordinated polity). The importance of such distinctions—but also the possibility of change from one category to another—are among the issues raised in Craig Calhoun, Frederick Cooper,

and Kevin Moore, eds., *Lessons of Empire* (New York: New Press, forthcoming).

62. Dipesh Chakrabarty, "Postcoloniality and the Artifice of History: Who Speaks for 'Indian' Pasts?" *Representations* 37 (1992): 2–3.

63. But not entirely, for colonial regimes trying to govern specific territories could be caught up in the historical discourses of their indigenous interlocutors. See Carolyn Hamilton, *Terrific Majesty: The Powers of Shaka Zulu and the Limits of Historical Invention* (Cambridge, Mass.: Harvard University Press, 1998).

64. Chakrabarty, "Postcoloniality," 17.

65. Seyla Benhabib, seeking to understand how people can address difficult issues across lines of cultural difference, rejects "radical incommensurability" and argues for "a pluralistically enlightened ethical universalism." There is much in her argument, but it is too abstract, for the plural units she hopes to see brought into a "conversation" with each other are left generic and equivalent. That is why—and here I agree with postcolonial theorists—the history of colonialism is so important to such debates, for it brings out the profound asymmetry in global interaction. *The Claims of Culture: Equality and Diversity in the Global Era* (Princeton, N.J.: Princeton University Press, 2002), 35–39.

66. To cite the famous phrase of Frantz Fanon, *The Wretched of the Earth,* trans. Constance Farrington (New York: Grove Press, 1963), 30.

2. THE RISE, FALL, AND RISE OF COLONIAL STUDIES

1. Among the French scholars of North Africa who contributed most to the struggle against French oppression in North Africa were Charles-André Julien, Jean Dresch, and Jacques Berque. The journal *Les Temps Modernes* was particularly important in anticolonial politics, *L'Esprit* in a more reformist direction, and *Présence Africaine* in keeping cultural questions and Pan-Africanist perspectives at the fore. Interestingly, the burst of interest in Algeria's place in French history and politics that has occurred in 2000–2001 focuses on precisely the same issue that most galvanized opinion in 1957–58: torture. See, among many other reports, *Le Monde,* 15, 20–21 May, 29 June 2001, *Le Nouvel Observateur,* 31 May–6 June 2001. Important as this issue was, the effect of the sharp focus on it turns an Algerian-French history in a "franco-français" conversation.

2. Pierre Bourdieu is both a notable exception and an exemplar of the move away from an analysis of the colonial situation. His research in Algeria in the late 1950s (following his military service there) focused on economic and social conditions in the context of a war of decolonization, and his findings shaped his approaches over many years, arguably over his entire career. The opening chapter of his study of Algerian workers invokes Balandier's "colonial situation" concept and powerfully discusses the methodological, political, and ethical dilemmas of conducting research in such a situation, notably in the midst of a colonial war. The book's empirical focus then narrows to his interpretation of

ethnographic and statistical studies of workers while the context broadens to economic dislocation and development questions. In the ensuing years, Bourdieu's trajectory of research was away from Algeria and away from phenomena that were specifically colonial. See *Sociologie de l'Algérie* (Paris: Presses Universitaires de France, 1958) and "Etude Sociologique," part 2 of *Travail et travailleurs en Algérie* (Paris: Mouton, 1963), esp. pp. 257–67.

3. Balandier later wrote about his discovery during his fieldwork in Africa after the war of "an Africa different from that which had been taught to me by the *maitres ès sociétés primitives*," first among Dakar's intellectuals, then among popular urban classes. Georges Balandier, *Histoire d'autres* (Paris: Stock, 1977), 52. The political context of this era was important as well. The war in Vietnam, the 1945 massacre at Sétif, and the repression of the 1947 revolt in Madagascar were important events in encouraging French intellectuals to question the smugly progressivist assertions of the French state. But the possibility of progress within "Greater France" also attracted considerable attention, because of the new development programs and above all the success of Africans in making demands within the institutions of the Fourth Republic.

4. Georges Balandier, "La situation coloniale: Approche théorique," *Cahiers Internationaux de Sociologie* 11 (1951): 44–79. See the only English translation, by Robert Wagoner, in Immanuel Wallerstein, ed., *Social Change: The Colonial Situation* (New York: Wiley, 1966), 34–81.

5. Georges Balandier, "La situation coloniale: Ancien concept, nouvelle réalité," *French Politics, Culture, and Society* 20 (2002): 4–10.

6. Max Gluckman, *Analysis of a Social Situation in Modern Zululand* (rpt. Manchester: Manchester University Press, 1958).

7. Michel-Rolph Trouillot, "Anthropology and the Savage Slot: The Poetics and Politics of Otherness," in Richard G. Fox, ed., *Recapturing Anthropology: Working in the Present* (Santa Fe, NM: School of American Research Press, 1991), 17–44.

8. The absence of a systematic analysis of the colonial regime in the work of the Copperbelt anthropologists is the valid point in Bernard Magubane's hatchet-job on these scholars. "A Critical Look at Indices Used in the Study of Social Change in Colonial Africa," *Current Anthropology* 12, nos. 4–5 (1971): 419–45. See also A. L. Epstein, *Politics in an Urban African Community* (Manchester: Manchester University Press, 1958).

9. Georges Balandier, *Sociologie des Brazzavilles noires* (Paris: Colin, 1955). See also the article he published in the same journal as "La situation coloniale," which sketches the research agenda for the study of modernization: "Déséquilibres socio-culturelles et modernisation des pays 'sous-développés," *Cahiers Internationaux de Sociologie* 16 (1956): 30–44. Balandier concludes by warning against "prejudging the future" by assuming that the end point of modernization is known. But his eye was firmly on the complexities of that future, no longer on the colonial situation.

10. Georges Balandier, "Urbanism in West and Central Africa: The Scope and Aims of Research," in UNESCO, *Social Implications of Industrialization*

and Urbanization in Africa South of the Sahara (Paris: UNESCO, 1956), 506, 509, 510; *Sociologie des Brazzavilles noires.*

11. Carl E. Pletsch, "The Three Worlds, or the Division of Social Scientific Labor, Circa 1950–1975," *Comparative Studies in Society and History* 23 (1981): 565–90.

12. Among of the writers who dealt most explicitly with colonial societies and colonial regimes in the 1950s was a group of self-consciously "progressive" French colonial officials, notably Henri Labouret, *Colonisation, colonialisme, décolonisation* (Paris: Larose, 1952); and Robert Delavignette, *Christianisme et colonialisme* (Paris: Arthème Fayard, 1960).

13. Among intellectuals who warned against the economic risks of independence—the dangers of victimization by new forms of imperialism or of "taudification" or "clochardisation" was Germaine Tillion, *L'Algérie en 1957* (Paris: Editions de Minuit, 1957).

14. Frederick Cooper, *Decolonization and African Society: The Labor Question in French and British Africa* (Cambridge: Cambridge University Press, 1996); Paul Clay Sorum, *Intellectuals and Decolonization in France* (Chapel Hill: University of North Carolina Press, 1977). Scholars committed to nationalist mobilization often saw the range of associations—religious, ethnic, class— as providing the social basis for political action. See for example Thomas Hodgkin, *Nationalism in Colonial Africa* (New York: New York University Press, 1957).

15. Balandier and a small number of influential African intellectuels were among the contributors to a special issue of *Présence Africaine,* published in 1952, on the problem of work. The issue combined a sense of African entitlement to the benefits of modern labor legislation with awareness that work was everywhere rooted in particular cultural practices.

16. Paul Mercier, "Aspects de la société africaine dans l'agglomération dakaroise: groupes familiaux et unités de voisinage," *Etudes Sénégalaises* 5 (1954): 11–40; idem, "La vie politique dans les centres urbaine du Sénégal: étude d'une période de transition," *Cahiers Internationaux de Sociologie* 27 (1959): 55–84.

17. Cooper, *Decolonization and African Society.*

18. Benjamin Stora, *La gangrène et l'oublie: La mémoire de la guerre d'Algérie* (Paris: Editions La Découverte, 1991)

19. A major question is the extent to which social scientists of the era of decolonization fostered the training and support of social scientists in Africa and accepted new currents of thought coming from African scholars and institutions.

20. Michael Banton, *West African City: A Study of Tribal Life in Freetown* (London: Oxford University Press, 1957) is a good example of the genre. For a review and bibliography, see Kenneth Little, *West African Urbanization: A Study of Voluntary Associations in Social Change* (Cambridge: Cambridge University Press, 1965). The Wallerstein collection that contained the translation of Balandier's "La situation coloniale" (*Social Change: The Colonial Situ-*

ation) contained numerous articles on adaptation, urban ethnicity, class, education, labor migration, and nationalism, but only two other articles with a colonial focus.

21. See the UNESCO volume, especially Daryll Forde, "Introductory Survey," 36, 38, 39, and Balandier, "Déséquilibres socio-culturels et modernisation," 44.

22. Dean C. Tipps, "Modernization Theory and the Comparative Study of Societies: A Critical Perspective," *Comparative Studies in Society and History* 15 (1973): 204.

23. W. W. Rostow's *The Stages of Economic Growth: A Non-Communist Manifesto* (Cambridge: Cambridge University Press, 1960).

24. W. Arthur Lewis, "Economic Development with Unlimited Supplies of Labour," *Manchester School* 22 (1954): 139–91; W. Arthur Lewis, *Labour in the West Indies* (London: Fabian Society, 1939); W. Arthur Lewis, *Politics in West Africa* (New York: Oxford University Press, 1965). For more on these themes, see Frederick Cooper and Randall Packard, eds., *International Development and the Social Sciences: Essays in the History and Politics of Knowledge* (Berkeley: University of California Press, 1997); and C. Choquet, O. Dollfus, E. Le Roy, and M. Vernières, eds., *Etat des savoirs sur le développement: Trois décennies de sciences sociales en langue française* (Paris: Karthala, 1993).

25. Aimé Césaire, *Discourse on Colonialism*, trans. Joan Pinkham (New York: Monthly Review Press, 1972), 11, 13, 61.

26. On the way nationalist trends in French West Africa around 1955–57 marginalized the efforts of African trade unions to obtain wages and benefits equal to those of French workers, see chapter 7.

27. Albert Memmi, *The Colonizer and the Colonized*, trans. Howard Greenfield (Boston: Beacon, 1965), 153.

28. Frantz Fanon, *The Wretched of the Earth*, trans. Constance Farrington (New York: Grove, 1965); originally published as *Les damnés de la terre* (Paris: Maspero, 1961). On Fanon in the context of colonial psychiatry, see Jock McCulloch, *Colonial Psychiatry and the "African Mind"* (Cambridge: Cambridge University Press, 1995).

29. Fanon, *The Wretched of the Earth*, 30.

30. Stora, *La gangrène et l'oublie*; Matthew Connelly, *A Diplomatic Revolution: Algeria's Fight for Independence and the Origins of the Post-Cold War Era* (New York: Oxford University Press, 2002); Sorum, *Intellectuals and Decolonization*.

31. K. O. Dike, *Trade and Politics in the Niger Delta* (Oxford: Oxford University Press, 1956). For an equivalent francophone study, thoroughly interactive in its approach, see Abdoulaye Ly, *La compagnie du Sénégal* (Paris: Présence Africaine, 1958).

32. J. F. Ade Ajayi, "The Continuity of African Institutions under Colonialism," in Terence O. Ranger, ed., *Emerging Themes in African History* (London: Heinemann, 1968), 189–200; Terence Ranger, "Connexions between 'Primary Resistance' Movements and Modern Mass Nationalism in East and Central Africa," *Journal of African History* 9 (1968): 437–53, 631–41. The domination

of precolonial and resistance histories was probably strongest in the American academy, but the French school pioneered by Yves Person had similar tendencies, and many anthropologists in France, Great Britain, and the United States also wanted to keep their Africans very African. For more thoughts on the historiography of Africa, see my "Africa's Pasts and Africa's Historians," *Canadian Journal of African Studies* 34 (2000): 298–336

33. See the monumental collection put together by editor-in-chief Wm. Roger Louis, *The Oxford History of the British Empire*, 5 vols. (Oxford: Oxford University Press, 1997–99); and several francophone equivalents, not quite as grandiose, including Jean Meyer et al., eds., *Histoire de la France coloniale* (Paris: Colin, 1990–91). Innovative work on the economics of empires was done by Jacques Marseille, *Empire colonial et capitalisme français: Histoire d'un divorce* (Paris: Albin Michel, 1984); and P. J. Cain and A. G. Hopkins, *British Imperialism*, 2d ed. (London: Longman, 2002).

34. Some of the defining work in historical anthropology, such as M. G. Smith's *Government in Zazzau, 1800–1950* (London: Oxford University Press, 1960), set out their subject in relation to the long view of African history, covering precolonial, colonial, and postcolonial. For a historically located anthropology of an African society, see Georges Balandier, *Daily Life in the Kingdom of the Kongo: From the Sixteenth to the Eighteenth Century*, trans. Helen Weaver (London: Allen & Unwin, 1968). For an overview of Africanist anthropology, see Sally Falk Moore, *Anthropology and Africa: Changing Perspectives on a Changing Scene* (Charlottesville: University Press of Virginia, 1994).

35. Walter Rodney, *How Europe Underdeveloped Africa* (London: Bogle-L'Ouverture, 1972); Immanuel Wallerstein, *The Modern World System*, 3 vols. (New York: Academic Press, 1974, 1980, 1989); Catherine Coquery Vidrovitch, *Le Congo au temps des grandes compagnies concessionnaires, 1898–1930* (Paris: Mouton, 1972); and Catherine Coquery-Vidrovitch, ed., "L'Afrique et la crise de 1930," special issue of *Revue Française d'Histoire d'Outre-Mer* 63 (1976).

36. For a broad review of this literature, see Frederick Cooper, "Africa and the World Economy," 1981, reprinted in Frederick Cooper, Steve Stern, Florencia Mallon, Allen Isaacman, and William Roseberry, eds., *Confronting Historical Paradigms: Peasants, Labor, and the Capitalist World System in Africa and Latin America* (Madison: University of Wisconsin Press, 1993). Among the most influential texts within the French Marxist tradition were Claude Meillassoux, *Femmes, greniers et capitaux* (Paris: Maspero, 1975); Maurice Godelier, *Perspectives in Marxist Anthropology*, trans. Robert Brain (Cambridge: Cambridge University Press, 1977); and Emmanuel Terray, *Marxism and "Primitive" Societies: Two Studies*, trans. Mary Klopper (New York: Monthly Review Press, 1972).

37. The neo-classical school privileged "the market" over specifically colonial economic mechanisms, but had a great deal to say about colonial institutions and policies, as well as trends in the colonial era. The most sophisticated and influential work within this genre was A. G. Hopkins, *An Economic History of West Africa* (London: Longman, 1973).

38. For examples of such approaches, see Sara Berry, *Cocoa, Custom and Socio-Economic Change in Rural Western Nigeria* (Oxford: Clarendon Press, 1975); Abner Cohen, *Custom and Politics in Urban Africa: A Study of Hausa Migrants in Yoruba Towns* (Berkeley: University of California Press, 1969); and Frederick Cooper, *From Slaves to Squatters: Plantation Labor and Agriculture in Zanzibar and Coastal Kenya, 1890–1925* (New Haven, Conn.: Yale University Press, 1980).

39. Talal Asad, *Anthropology and the Colonial Encounter* (London: Ithaca, 1973). For a francophone equivalent, see G. Leclerc, *Anthropologie et colonialisme* (Paris: Fayard, 1972).

40. Emmanuelle Sibeud, *Une science impériale pour l'Afrique? La construction des savoirs africanistes en France 1878–1930* (Paris, Editions de l'Ecole des Hautes Etudes en Sciences Sociales, 2002).

41. Godfrey Wilson, "An Essay on the Economics of Detribalization in Northern Rhodesia," *Rhodes-Livingstone Papers* 5 (Livingstone: Rhodes-Livingstone Institute, 1941).

42. Megan Vaughan, *Curing Their Ills: Colonial Power and African Illness* (Cambridge: Polity Press, 1991); Richard Grove, *Green Imperialism: Colonial Expansion, Tropical Island Edens and the Origins of Environmentalism, 1600–1860* (Cambridge: Cambridge University Press, 1995); Gwendolyn Wright, *The Politics of Design in French Colonial Urbanism* (Chicago: University of Chicago Press, 1991); Gyan Prakash, *Another Reason: Science and the Imagination of Modern India* (Princeton, N.J.: Princeton University Press, 1999); Nancy Rose Hunt, *A Colonial Lexicon: Of Birth Ritual, Medicalization, and Mobility in the Congo* (Durham, N.C.: Duke University Press, 1999); Marie-Noëlle Bourguet and Christophe Bonneuil, eds., "De l'inventaire du monde à la mise en valeur du globe: Botanique et colonisation (fin XVIIe siècle–début XXe siècle)," *Revue Française d'Histoire d'Outre-Mer* 322–23 (1999); Anne Godlewska and Neil Smith, eds., *Geography and Empire* (Oxford: Blackwell, 1994); Benoît de l'Estoile, Frederico Neiburg, and Lygia Sigaud, "Anthropologies, états et populations," *Revue de Synthèse* 4, nos. 3–4 (2000); Cooper, "Africa's Pasts and Africa's Historians," and Mamadou Diouf, "Des historiens et des histoires, pour quoi faire? L'histoire africaine entre l'état et les communautés," both in *Canadian Journal of African Studies* 34 (2000): 198–374.

43. Not surprisingly, the study of projects for social change has been particularly fraught. Some scholars see the "development" concept as nothing more than the imposition of an unwanted modernity or think that identifying its vocabulary as "modernist" is itself evidence of its denigrating and imposing nature. I have elsewhere argued that the development concept as articulated in the past fifty years is a two-edged sword, a basis for asserting the power to manage complex processes in the name of scientific knowledge but also a basis for making redistributive claims, for opening debate on the effects of inequality of wealth and power across lines of cultural and territorial distinction, for subordinate groups within particular polities to seek external allies in struggle against local or national oppressors, and for claims that "progress" be assessed

in terms of measurements of basic access to resources—such as piped water and electricity. See the different perspectives brought out in Cooper and Packard, *International Development and the Social Sciences.*

44. Edward Said, *Orientalism* (New York: Pantheon, 1978).

45. Fernando Coronil, "Beyond Occidentalism: Toward Non-Imperial Geohistorical Categories," *Cultural Anthropology* 11 (1995): 51–87; V. Y. Mudimbe, *The Invention of Africa: Gnosis, Philosophy, and the Order of Knowledge* (Bloomington: Indiana University Press, 1988).

46. Homi Bhabha, "Of Mimicry and Man: The Ambivalence of Colonial Discourse," *October* 28 (1984): 125–33, reprinted in Frederick Cooper and Ann Laura Stoler, eds., *Tensions of Empire: Colonial Cultures in a Bourgeois World* (Berkeley: University of California Press, 1997), 152–62.

47. T. O. Beidelman, *Colonial Evangelism: A Socio-historical Study of an East African Mission at the Grassroots* (Bloomington: Indiana University Press, 1982).

48. Jean Comaroff and John Comaroff, *Of Revelation and Revolution,* 2 vols. (Chicago: University of Chicago Press, 1991, 1997). See also their edited collection *Ethnography and the Historical Imagination* (Boulder, Colo.: Westview Press, 1992). For an important review, see Paul Landau, "Hegemony and History in Jean and John L. Comaroff's *Of Revelation and Revolution,*" *Africa* 70 (2000): 501–19.

49. For collections that bring out the new colonial anthropology and history, see Nicholas Dirks, ed., *Colonialism and Culture* (Ann Arbor: University of Michigan Press, 1992); and Cooper and Stoler, *Tensions of Empire*; for useful review articles, see Peter Pels, "Anthropology of Colonialism: Culture, History, and the Emergence of Western Governmentality," *Annual Review of Anthropology* 26 (1997): 163–83; and Andrew Apter, "Africa, Empire, and Anthropology: A Philological Exploration of Anthropology's Heart of Darkness," *Annual Review of Anthropology* 28 (1999): 577–98.

50. For an example of a use of the governmentality concept in a way that misses the historical specificity of different colonization regimes, see David Scott, "Colonial Governmentality," *Social Text* 43 (1995): 191–220. For more discussion and application of Foucauldian approaches, see Pels, "Anthropology of Colonialism"; Bernard Cohn, *An Anthropologist among the Historians and Other Essays* (Delhi: Oxford University Press, 1987); Vicente Rafael, *Contracting Colonialism: Translation and Christian Conversion in Tagalog Society under Early Spanish Rule* (Ithaca, N.Y.: Cornell University Press, 1988); Timothy Mitchell, *Colonizing Egypt* (Berkeley: University of California Press, 1991). Ann Stoler, *Race and the Education of Desire: Foucault's History of Sexuality and the Colonial Order of Things* (Durham, N.C.: Duke University Press, 1995) is a particularly extended and thoughtful discussion, while Vaughan, *Curing Their Ills,* is particularly critical. On the limits of colonial knowledge on social questions, see Cooper, *Decolonization and African Society.*

51. Ann Stoler, "Sexual Affronts and Racial Frontiers: European Identities and the Cultural Politics of Exclusion in Colonial Southeast Asia," in Cooper

and Stoler, *Tensions of Empire*, 198–237. For examples—among many—of studies of gender and reproduction in colonial situations, see also Lora Wildenthal, "Race, Gender, and Citizenship in the German Colonial Empire," in Cooper and Stoler, *Tensions of Empire*, 263–86; Julia Clancy-Smith and Frances Gouda, eds., *Domesticating the Empire: Race, Gender, and Family Life in French and Dutch Colonialism* (Charlottesville: University Press of Virginia, 1998).

52. Cooper, *Decolonization and African Society*. Other work in the new colonial history, specifically focusing on France, includes Isabelle Merle, *Expériences coloniales: La Nouvelle-Calédonie, 1853–1920* (Paris : Belin, 1995); Alice Conklin, *A Mission to Civilize: The Republican Idea of Empire in France and West Africa, 1895–1930* (Stanford, Calif.: Stanford University Press, 1997); and Elizabeth Thompson, *Colonial Citizens : Republican Rights, Paternal Privilege, and Gender in French Syria and Lebanon* (New York: Columbia University Press, 2000).

53. Ranajit Guha and Gayatri Chakravorty Spivak, eds., *Selected Subaltern Studies* (New York: Oxford University Press, 1988); Ranajit Guha, "Dominance without Hegemony and Its Historiography," in Ranajit Guha, ed., *Subaltern Studies VI: Writings on South Asian History and Society* (Delhi: Oxford University Press, 1989), 210–309; Dipesh Chakrabarty, *Provincializing Europe: Postcolonial Thought and Historical Difference* (Princeton, N.J.: Princeton University Press, 2000). For a critique of Subaltern Studies written from an Africanist perspective, see Frederick Cooper, "Conflict and Connection: Rethinking Colonial African History," *American Historical Review* 99 (1994): 1516–45.

54. John Lonsdale and Bruce Berman, "Coping with the Contradictions: The Development of the Colonial State in Kenya." *Journal of African History* 20 (1979): 487–506.

55. Crawford Young, *The African Colonial State in Comparative Perspective* (New Haven, Conn.: Yale University Press, 1994); Mahmood Mamdani, *Citizen and Subject: Contemporary Africa and the Legacy of Late Colonialism* (Princeton, N.J.: Princeton University Press, 1996). See the debate on Mamdani's book in *Politique Africaine* 73 (1999): 193–211.

56. Benedict Anderson, *Imagined Communities* (London: Verso, 1983).

57. The most notorious recent attempt to make otherness into a principle of international organization is Samuel P. Huntington, *The Clash of Civilizations and the Remaking of World Order* (New York: Simon and Schuster, 1996). This text is less notable as a description of a clash than as an attempt to create one.

58. Aimé Césaire, *Lettre à Maurice Thorez* (Paris: Présence Africaine, 1956), 15.

3. IDENTITY

1. George Orwell, "Politics and the English Language," in *A Collection of Essays* (New York: Harcourt Brace, 1953), 169–70.

2. For a tempered critique of identity politics, see Todd Gitlin, *The Twilight of Common Dreams: Why America Is Wracked by Culture Wars* (New York: Henry Holt, 1995); and for a sophisticated defense, Robin D. G. Kelley, *Yo' Mama's Disfunktional!: Fighting the Culture Wars in Urban America* (Boston: Beacon, 1997). For a suggestion that the high noon of identity politics may have passed, see Ross Posnock, "Before and After Identity Politics," *Raritan* 15 (Summer 1995): 95–115; and David A. Hollinger, "Nationalism, Cosmopolitanism, and the United States," in Noah Pickus, ed., *Immigration and Citizenship in the Twenty-First Century* (Lanham, MD: Rowman Littlefield, 1998).

3. Avrum Stroll, "Identity," in *Encyclopedia of Philosophy* (New York: MacMillan, 1967), 4:121–24. For a contemporary philosophical treatment, see Bartholomaeus Boehm, *Identitaet und Identifikation: Zur Persistenz physikalischer Gegenstaende* (Frankfurt: Peter Lang, 1989). On the history and vicissitudes of "identity" and cognate terms, see W. J. M. Mackenzie, *Political Identity* (New York: St. Martin's, 1978), 19–27; and John D. Ely, "Community and the Politics of Identity: Toward the Genealogy of a Nation-State Concept," *Stanford Humanities Review* 5 (1997), 76ff.

4. See Philip Gleason, "Identifying Identity: a Semantic History," *Journal of American History* 69 (1983): 910–31. The 1930s *Encyclopedia of the Social Sciences* (New York: Macmillan: 1930–1935) contains no entry on identity, but it does have one for *identification*—largely focused on fingerprinting and other modes of judicial marking of individuals (Thorstein Sellin, 7:573–75). The 1968 *International Encyclopedia of the Social Sciences* (New York: Macmillan), contains an article on *identification, political* by William Buchanan (7:57–61), which focuses on a "person's identification with a group"—including class, party, religion—and another on *identity, psychosocial*, by Erik Erikson (7:61–65), which focuses on the individual's "role integration in his group."

5. Gleason, "Identifying Identity," 914ff; for the appropriation of Erikson's work in political science, see Mackenzie, *Political Identity.*

6. Gleason, "Identifying Identity," 915–18.

7. Anselm Strauss, *Mirrors and Masks: The Search for an Identity* (Glencoe, Ill.: Free Press, 1959).

8. Erving Goffman, *Stigma: Notes on the Management of Spoiled Identity* (Englewood Cliffs, N.J.: Prentice-Hall, 1963); Peter Berger and Thomas Luckmann, *The Social Construction of Reality* (Garden City, N.Y.: Doubleday, 1966); Peter Berger, Brigitte Berger, and Hansfried Kellner, *The Homeless Mind: Modernization and Consciousness* (New York: Random House, 1973); Peter Berger, "Modern Identity: Crisis and Continuity," in *The Cultural Drama: Modern Identities and Social Ferment*, ed. Wilton S. Dillon (Washington: Smithsonian Institution Press, 1974).

9. As Philip Gleason has pointed out, the popularization of the term began well before the turbulence of the mid and late 1960s. Gleason attributes this initial popularization to the mid-century prestige and cognitive authority of the social sciences, the wartime and postwar vogue of national character studies, and the postwar critique of mass society, which newly problematized the "relationship of the individual to society" ("Identifying Identity," pp. 922ff).

10. Erikson characterized identity as "a process 'located' *in the core of the individual* and yet also *in the core of his communal culture,* a process which establishes . . . the identity of those two identities" (*Identity: Youth and Crisis* [New York: Norton, 1968], 22, italics in the original). Although this is a relatively late formulation, the link was already established in Erikson's immediately postwar writings.

11. See, for example, Craig Calhoun, "New Social Movements of the Early Nineteenth Century," *Social Science History* 17 (1993): 385–427.

12. Mackenzie, *Political Identity,* 11, reporting a seminar paper of 1974; Coles is quoted in Gleason, "Identifying Identity," 913. Gleason notes that the problem was remarked even earlier: "By the late 1960s the terminological situation had gotten completely out of hand" (ibid., 915). Erikson himself lamented the "indiscriminate" use of *identity* and *identity crisis* in *Identity: Youth and Crisis* (New York: Norton, 1968), 16.

13. Kwame Anthony Appiah and Henry Louis Gates, Jr., "Editors' Introduction: Multiplying Identities," in *Identities,* ed. Appiah and Gates (Chicago: University of Chicago Press, 1995), 1.

14. See fig. 1.

15. One might also speak of a narrower " 'identity crisis' crisis." Coined and popularized by Erikson, and applied to social and political collectivities by Lucian Pye and others, the notion of "identity crisis" took off in the 1960s. (For Erikson's own retrospective reflections on the origins and vicissitudes of the expression, see the prologue to *Identity: Youth and Crisis,* 16ff.) Crises have become (oxymoronically) chronic; and putative crises of identity have proliferated to the point of destroying whatever meaning the concept may once have had. Already in 1968, Erikson could lament that the expression was being used in a "ritualized" fashion (ibid., 16).

16. *Identities: Global Studies in Culture and Power,* which appeared in 1994, "explores the relationship of racial, ethnic and national identities and power hierarchies within national and global arenas. . . . [It] responds to the paradox of our time: the growth of a global economy and transnational movements of populations produce or perpetuate distinctive cultural practices and differentiated identities" (Statement of "aims and scope" printed on inside front cover). *Social Identities: Journal for the Study of Race, Nation and Culture,* whose first issue appeared in 1995, is concerned with "the formations of, and transformations in, socially significant identities, their attendant forms of material exclusion and power, as well as the political and cultural possibilities open[ed] up by these identifications" (statement printed on inside front cover).

17. Zygmunt Bauman, "Soil, Blood, and Identity," *Sociological Review* 40 (1992): 675–701; Pierre Bourdieu, "L'identité et la représentation: Eléments pour une réflexion critique sur l'idée de région," *Actes de la recherche en sciences sociales* 35 (1980): 63–72; Fernand Braudel, *The Identity of France,* trans. Sian Reynolds, 2 vols. (New York: Harper & Row, 1988–1990); Craig Calhoun, "Social Theory and the Politics of Identity," in Calhoun, ed., *Social Theory and the Politics of Identity* (Oxford: Blackwell, 1994); S. N. Eisenstadt and Bernhard Giesen, "The Construction of Collective Identity," *Archives européennes de*

sociologie 36, no. 1 (1995): 72–102; Anthony Giddens, *Modernity and Self-Identity: Self and Society in the Late Modern Age* (Cambridge: Polity Press, in association with Oxford: Blackwell, 1991); Jürgen Habermas, *Staatsbürgerschaft und rationale Identität: Überlegungen zur europäischen Zukunft* (St. Gallen: Erker, 1991); Claude Lévi-Strauss, ed., *L'identité* (Paris: Presses Universitaires de France, 1977); Paul Ricoeur, *Oneself as Another* (Chicago: University of Chicago Press, 1992); Amartya Sen, "Goals, Commitment, and Identity," *Journal of Law, Economics, and Organization* 2 (1985): 341–55; Margaret Somers, "The Narrative Constitution of Identity: A Relational and Network Approach," *Theory and Society* 23 (1994): 605–49; Charles Taylor, *Multiculturalism and "The Politics of Recognition"* (Princeton, N.J.: Princeton University Press, 1994); Charles Tilly, "Citizenship, Identity and Social History," in Tilly, ed., *Citizenship, Identity and Social History* (Cambridge: Cambridge University Press, 1996); Harrison White, *Identity and Control: A Structural Theory of Social Action* (Princeton, N.J.: Princeton University Press, 1992).

18. As Loïc Wacquant notes of race, the "continual barter between folk and analytical notions, the uncontrolled conflation of social and sociological understandings of 'race'" is "intrinsic to the category. From its inception, the collective fiction labeled 'race' . . . has always mixed science with common sense and traded on the complicity between them" ("For an Analytic of Racial Domination," *Political Power and Social Theory* 11 [1997]: 222–23).

19. On ethnic identity entrepreneurs, see Barbara Lal, "Ethnic Identity Entrepreneurs: Their Role in Transracial and Intercountry Adoptions," *Asian Pacific Migration Journal* 6 (1997): 385–413.

20. This argument is developed further in Rogers Brubaker, *Nationalism Reframed* (Cambridge: Cambridge University Press, 1996), chapter 1.

21. Mara Loveman, "Is 'Race' Essential? A Comment on Bonilla-Silva," *American Sociological Review* 64 (1999): 891–98. See also Wacquant, "For an Analytic of Racial Domination"; Rupert Taylor, "Racial Terminology and the Question of 'Race' in South Africa," unpublished manuscript, p. 7; and Max Weber, *Economy and Society,* ed. Guenther Roth and Claus Witlich (New York: Bedminster Press, 1968), vol. I, 385ff., for a strikingly modern argument questioning the analytical utility of the notions of race, ethnic group, and nation.

22. On nation as a political fiction, see Louis Pinto, "Une fiction politique: La nation," *Actes de la recherche en sciences sociales* 64 (Sept. 1986): 45–50, a Bourdieuian appreciation of the studies of nationalism by the eminent Hungarian historian Jeno Szucs. On race as a collective fiction, see Wacquant, "For an Analytic of Racial Domination," 222–23. The key work by Bourdieu in this domain is "L'identité et la représentation: Eléments pour une réflexion critique sur l'idée de région," *Actes de la recherche en sciences sociales* 35 (Nov. 1980), part of which is translated in Bourdieu, *Language and Symbolic Power,* trans. Matthew Adamson, ed. John B. Thompson (Cambridge, Mass.: Harvard University Press, 1991).

23. Even Durkheim's uncompromisingly objectivist sociological manifesto shies away from this extreme position; see *The Rules of Sociological Method,* chap. 2.

24. Wacquant, "For an Analytic of Racial Domination," 222. See also Wacquant's criticism of the concept of underclass in "L'*underclass* urbaine dans l'imaginaire social et scientifique americain," in Serge Paugam, ed., *L'exclusion: L'état des savoirs* (Paris: La Découverte, 1996), 248–62.

25. For a sustained and influential example, see Judith Butler, *Gender Trouble: Feminism and the Subversion of Identity* (New York: Routledge, 1990).

26. Craig Calhoun, "Social Theory and the Politics of Identity," in Calhoun, ed., *Social Theory and the Politics of Identity* (Oxford: Blackwell, 1994), 9–36.

27. Eduardo Bonilla-Silva, for example, slides from an impeccably constructivist characterization of racialized social systems as "societies . . . partially structured by the placement of actors in racial categories" to the claim that such placement "produces definite social relations between the races," where "the races" are characterized as real social groups with differing objective interests ("Rethinking Racism: Toward a Structural Interpretation," *American Sociological Review* 62 [1996]: 469–70). In their influential *Racial Formation in the United States* (2d ed., New York: Routledge, 1994), Michael Omi and Howard Winant strive to be more consistently constructivist. But they too fail to remain faithful to their constructivist definition of race as an "unstable and 'decentered' complex of social meanings constantly being transformed by political struggle . . . [and as] a concept which *signifies* and symbolizes social conflicts and interests by referring to different types of human bodies" (55). The historical experiences of "white European" immigrants, they argue, were and remain fundamentally different from those of "racial minority groups" (including Latinos and Asian Americans, as well as African Americans and Native Americans); the "ethnicity paradigm" is applicable to the former but not—because of its "neglect of race *per se*"—to the latter (14–23). This sharp distinction between ethnic and racial groups neglects the fact—now well established in the historical literature—that the whiteness of several European immigrant groups was achieved after an initial period in which they were often categorized in racial or race-like terms as nonwhite; it also neglects what might be called deracialization processes among some groups they consider fundamentally racial. On the former, see James R. Barrett and David Roediger, "Inbetween Peoples: Race, Nationality and the 'New Immigrant' Working Class," *Journal of American Ethnic History* 16 (1997): 3–44; on the latter, see Joel Perlman and Roger Waldinger, "Second Generation Decline? Children of Immigrants, Past and Present—a Reconsideration," *International Migration Review* 31 (Winter 1997): 903ff.

28. Walter Benn Michaels has argued, "There are no anti-essentialist accounts of identity. . . . [T]he essentialism inheres not in the description of the identity but in the attempt to derive the practices from the identity—we *do* this because we *are* this. Hence anti-essentialism . . . must take the form not of producing more sophisticated accounts of identity (that is, more sophisticated essentialisms) but of ceasing to explain what people do or should do by reference to who they are and/or what culture they belong to" ("Race into Culture: A Critical Genealogy of Cultural Identity," in *Identities*, ed. Appiah and Gates, 61n). Note, however, the crucial elision at the end of the quoted passage

between "do" and "should do." Essentialism inheres, pace Michaels, less in the "attempt to derive [in an explanatory mode] the practice from the identity" than in the attempt to *prescribe* the practices on the basis of an *ascribed* identity: you *ought to do* this because you *are* this.

29. See, for example, Jean L. Cohen, "Strategy or Identity: New Theoretical Paradigms and Contemporary Social Movements," *Social Research* 52 (1985): 663–716.

30. Somers, "The Narrative Constitution of Identity."

31. This opposition depends on a narrow conceptualization of the category "interest," one restricted to interests understood to be directly derivable from social structure (see, for example, ibid., 624). If interest is instead understood to be culturally or discursively constituted, to be dependent on the discursive *identification* of interests and (more fundamentally) interest-bearing units, to be "constituted and reconstituted *in* time and *over* time," like narrative identities in Somers's account, then the opposition loses much of its force.

32. Alberto Melucci, "The Process of Collective Identity," in *Social Movements and Culture*, ed. Hank Johnston and Bert Klandermans (Minneapolis: University of Minnesota Press, 1995).

33. Much recent work on gender, to be sure, has criticized as essentialist the idea that women share a fundamental sameness. Yet certain strands of recent work nonetheless predicate the sameness of some group defined by the *intersection* of gender with other categorical attributes (race, ethnicity, class, sexual orientation). See for example Patricia Hill Collins, *Black Feminist Thought: Knowledge, Consciousness, and the Politics of Empowerment* (Boston: Unwin Hyman, 1990).

34. See, for example, Harold R. Isaacs, *Idols of the Tribe: Group Identity and Political Change* (New York: Harper & Row, 1975); Walker Connor, "Beyond Reason: The Nature of the Ethnonational Bond," in *Ethnonationalism: The Quest for Understanding* (Princeton, N.J.: Princeton University Press, 1994).

35. For a sophisticated historical and philosophical account, see Charles Taylor, *Sources of the Self: The Making of the Modern Identity* (Cambridge, Mass.: Harvard University Press, 1989).

36. For a key statement by Erikson himself, see *Identity: Youth and Crisis*, 22.

37. See, for example, Calhoun, "The Problem of Identity in Collective Action"; Melucci, "The Process of Collective Identity"; Roger Gould, *Insurgent Identities: Class, Community and Protest in Paris from 1848 to the Commune* (Chicago: University of Chicago Press, 1995).

38. See, for example, Stuart Hall, "Introduction: Who Needs 'Identity'?" in *Questions of Cultural Identity*, ed. Stuart Hall and Paul du Gay (London: Sage, 1996).

39. See, for example, Richard Werbner, "Multiple Identities, Plural Arenas," in Richard Werbner and Terence Ranger, eds., *Postcolonial Identities in Africa* (London: Zed, 1996), 1–26.

40. Two important, although partial, exceptions deserve note. Walter Benn Michaels has formulated a brilliant and provocative critique of the concept of

cultural identity in "Race into Culture." But that essay focuses less on analytical uses of the notion of identity than on the difficulty of specifying what makes "our" culture or "our" past count as our own—when the reference is not to one's *actual* cultural practices or one's *actual* personal past but to some putative group culture or group past—without implicitly invoking the notion of race. He concludes that "our sense of culture is characteristically meant to displace race, but . . . culture has turned out to be a way of continuing rather than repudiating racial thought. It is only the appeal to race that . . . gives notions like losing our culture, preserving it, [or] . . . restoring people's culture to them . . . their pathos" (61–62). Richard Handler argues that "we should be as suspicious of 'identity' as we have learned to be of 'culture,' 'tradition,' 'nation,' and 'ethnic group'" (27), but then pulls his critical punches. His central argument—that the salience of identity in contemporary Western, especially American society "does not mean that the concept can be applied unthinkingly to other places and times" (27)—is certainly true, but it implies that the concept *can* be fruitfully applied in contemporary Western settings, something that other passages in the same article and his own work on Québécois nationalism tend to call into question. "Is 'Identity' a Useful Cross-Cultural Concept?" in *Commemorations: the Politics of National Identity*, ed. John Gillis (Princeton, N.J.: Princeton University Press, 1994), 27. See also Handler, *Nationalism and the Politics of Culture in Quebec* (Madison: University of Wisconsin Press, 1988).

41. Hall, "Who Needs 'Identity'?" 2. He goes on, "I use 'identity' to refer to the meeting point, the point of *suture*, between on the one hand the discourses and practices which attempt to 'interpellate,' speak to us or hail us into place as the social subjects of particular discourses, and on the other hand, the processes which produce subjectivities, which construct us as subjects which can be 'spoken.' Identities are thus points of temporary attachment to the subject positions which discursive practices construct for us" (5–6).

42. Claude Lévi-Strauss, concluding remarks to Lévi-Strauss, ed, *L'identité*, 332.

43. Lawrence Grossberg, "Identity and Cultural Studies: Is That All There Is," in Hall and du Gay, *Questions of Cultural Identity*, 87–88.

44. Melucci, "The Process of Collective Identity," 46.

45. Here the blurring between categories of analysis and categories of practice is particularly striking. As Richard Handler has argued, scholarly conceptions of nation and national identity have tended to replicate key features of nationalist ideology, notably the axiomatic understanding of boundedness and homogeneity in the putative nation (*Nationalism and the Politics of Culture in Quebec*). The same argument could be made about race or ethnicity.

46. See, for example, Isaacs, *Idols of the Tribe*; and Connor, "Beyond Reason: The Nature of the Ethnonational Bond."

47. Somers, "The Narrative Constitution of Identity," 605, 606, 614, and 618. See also Somers's "Narrativity, Narrative Identity, and Social Action: Rethinking English Working-Class Formation," *Social Science History* 16 (1992): 591–630.

48. Charles Tilly, "Citizenship, Identity and Social History," in Tilly, ed., *Citizenship, Identity and Social History* (Cambridge: Cambridge University Press, 1996), 1–17, 7 quoted.

49. Craig Calhoun, "The Problem of Identity in Collective Action," in Joan Huber, ed., *Macro Micro Linkages in Sociology* (Newbury Park, Ca: Sage, 1991), 53, 64–68.

50. Craig Calhoun, "Social Theory and the Politics of Identity," in Calhoun, ed., *Social Theory and the Politics of Identity* (Oxford: Blackwell, 1994), 9.

51. On the merits of *identification*, see Hall, "Who Needs 'Identity'?"

52. Craig Calhoun, *Nationalism* (Minneapolis: University of Minnesota Press, 1997), 36ff.

53. For an anthropological perspective, usefully extending the Barthian model, see Richard Jenkins, "Rethinking Ethnicity: Identity, Categorization and Power," *Ethnic and Racial Studies* 17 (1994): 197–223; and Jenkins, *Social Identity* (London: Routledge, 1996).

54. Peter Berger, "Modern Identity," 163–64, makes a similar point, though he phrases it in terms of a dialectic—and possible conflict—between subjective and objective identity.

55. Gérard Noiriel, *La tyrannie du national* (Paris, Calmann-Lévy, 1991), 155–80; idem, "L'identification des citoyens: Naissance de l'état civil Républicain," *Genèses* 13 (Fall 1993): 3, 28; idem, "Surveiller les déplacements ou identifier les personnes? Contribution à l'histoire du passeport en France de la Ier à la III République," *Genèses* 30 (1998): 77–100; Béatrice Fraenkel, *La signature: Genèse d'un signe* (Paris: Gallimard, 1992); Jane Caplan and John Torpey, eds., *Documenting Individual Identity: The Development of State Practices in the Modern World* (Princeton, N.J.: Princeton University Press, 2001).

56. Michel Foucault, "Governmentality," in Graham Burchell et al., eds., *The Foucault Effect: Studies in Governmentality* (Chicago: University of Chicago Press, 1991), 87–104. Similar conceptions have been applied to colonial societies, especially in regard to the way colonizers' schemes for classification and enumeration shape and indeed constitute the social phenomena (such as tribe and caste in India) being classified. See in particular Bernard Cohn, *Colonialism and Its Forms of Knowledge: The British in India* (Princeton, N.J.: Princeton University Press, 1996).

57. On the dilemmas, difficulties, and ironies involved in "administering identity," in authoritatively determining who belongs to what category in the implementation of race-conscious law, see Christopher A. Ford, "Administering Identity: The Determination of 'Race' in Race-Conscious Law," *California Law Review* 82 (1994): 1231–85.

58. Charles Tilly, *Durable Inequality* (Berkeley: University of California Press, 1998)

59. Melissa Nobles, " 'Responding with Good Sense': The Politics of Race and Censuses in Contemporary Brazil," Ph.D. diss., Yale University, 1995.

60. See, for example, Melucci, "The Process of Collective Identity"; and Martin, "The Choices of Identity."

61. Hall, "Who Needs 'Identity'?"; Somers, "The Narrative Constitution of Identity."

62. See Hall, "Who Needs Identity?" 2ff; and Alan Finlayson, "Psychology, psychoanalysis and theories of nationalism," *Nations and Nationalism* 4 (1998): 157ff.

63. Pierre Bourdieu, *The Logic of Practice*, trans. Richard Nice (Cambridge: Polity Press, 1990).

64. An extensive anthropological literature on African and other societies, for example, describes healing cults, spirit possession cults, witchcraft eradication movements, and other collective phenomena that help to constitute particular forms of self-understanding, particular ways in which individuals situate themselves socially. See studies ranging from classics by Victor Turner, *Schism and Continuity in an African Society: A Study of Ndembu Village Life* (Manchester: Manchester University Press, 1957); and I. M. Lewis, *Ecstatic Religion: An Anthropological Study of Spirit Possession and Shamanism* (Harmondsworth: Penguin, 1971); to more recent work by Paul Stoller, *Fusion of the Worlds: An Ethnography of Possession among the Songhay of Niger* (Chicago: University of Chicago Press, 1989); and Janice Boddy, *Wombs and Alien Spirits: Women, Men and the Zar Cult in Northern Sudan* (Madison: University of Wisconsin Press, 1989).

65. For a poignant example, see Slavenka Drakulic's account of being "overcome by nationhood" as a result of the war in the former Yugoslavia, in *The Balkan Express: Fragments from the Other Side of the War*, trans. Maja Soljan (New York: W. W. Norton, 1993), 50–52.

66. See, for example, Berger, "Modern Identity: Crisis and Continuity," 162.

67. See, for example, Calhoun, "The Problem of Identity in Collective Action," 68, characterizing "ordinary identity."

68. For a good example of the latter, see Mary Waters's analysis of the optional, exceptionally unconstraining ethnic "identities"—or what Herbert Gans has called the "symbolic ethnicity"—of third- and fourth-generation descendants of European Catholic immigrants to the United States in *Ethnic Options: Choosing Identities in America* (Berkeley: University of California Press, 1990).

69. Charles Tilly, *From Mobilization to Revolution* (Reading, Mass.: Addison-Wesley, 1978), 62ff.

70. On the centrality of categorical commonality to modern nationalism, see Handler, *Nationalism and the Politics of Culture in Quebec*; and Calhoun, *Nationalism*, chap. 2.

71. See, for example, the discussion of the "anti-categorical imperative" in Mustafa Emirbayer and Jeff Goodwin, "Network Analysis, Culture, and the Problem of Agency," *American Journal of Sociology* 99 (1994): 1414.

72. John Lonsdale, "When Did the Gusii or Any Other Group Become a Tribe?" *Kenya Historical Review* 5 (1977): 355–68; Abner Cohen, *Custom and Politics in Urban Africa: A Study of Migrants in Yoruba Towns* (Berkeley: University of California Press, 1969). Anthropologists were influenced by the work

of Fredrick Barth, *Ethnic Groups and Boundaries: The Social Organisation of Cultural Difference* (London: Allen & Unwin, 1969), especially Barth's "Introduction," 9–38. More recent and systematic constructivist accounts include Jean-Loup Amselle and Elikia M'Bokolo, eds., *Au coeur de l'ethnie: Ethnies, tribalisme et état en Afrique* (Paris: Editions La Découverte, 1985); Leroy Vail, ed., *The Creation of Tribalism in Southern Africa* (Berkeley: University of California Press, 1988); Terence Ranger, "The Invention of Tradition in Africa," in Eric Hobsbawm and Terence Ranger, eds., *The Invention of Tradition* (Cambridge: Cambridge University Press, 1983), 211–62.

73. Identity talk has become popular among Africanists in recent years, and the typical insistence that identity is multiple is rarely followed by explanation of why that which is multiplied should be considered identity. For a case in point, see Richard Werbner, "Multiple Identities, Plural Arenas," in Richard Werbner and Terence Ranger, eds., *Postcolonial Identities in Africa* (London: Zed, 1996), 1–26. Africanist scholars have been critical of the concepts of race and ethnicity, but often still use *identity* in an unexamined way. See, for example, the special issue of *Journal of Southern African Studies* 20, no. 3 (1994), coordinated by Edwin N. Wilmsen, Saul Dubow, and John Sharp, "Ethnicity and Identity in Southern Africa." A more reflective approach—deploying a range of terms to indicate different forms of affiliation and examining what *identical* actually means in particular contexts—may be found in Claude Fay, " 'Car nous ne faisons qu'un': Identités, équivalences, homologies au Maasina (Mali)," *Cahiers des Sciences Humaines* 31 (1995): 427–56. Identitarian positions are severely criticized by Jean-François Bayart, *L'illusion identitaire* (Paris: Fayard, 1996).

74. E. P. Evans-Pritchard, *The Nuer: A Description of the Modes of Livelihood and Political Institutions of a Nilotic People* (Oxford: Clarendon, 1937).

75. See the pioneering study of Abner Cohen, "Cultural Strategies in the Organization of Trading Diasporas," in Claude Meillassoux, ed., *The Development of Indigenous Trade and Markets* (London: Oxford University Press, 1971), 266–84.

76. Paul Richards, *Fighting for the Rain Forest: War, Youth and Resources in Sierra Leone* (Oxford: Currey, 1996), 79.

77. John Lonsdale, "States and Social Processes in Africa," *African Studies Review* 24, nos. 2/3 (1981): 139–225.

78. Jane Guyer, "Household and Community," *African Studies Review* 24, nos. 2/3 (1981): 87–137; Jean-Loup Amselle, *Logiques métisses: Anthropologie de l'identité, en Afrique et ailleurs* (Paris: Payot, 1990).

79. Sharon Hutchinson, *Nuer Dilemmas: Coping with Money, War, and the State* (Berkeley: University of California Press, 1995), 29.

80. Gerard Prunier, *The Rwandan Crisis* (New York: Columbia University Press, 1996); and Jean-Pierre Chrétien, *Le défi de l'ethnisme: Rwanda et Burundi: 1990–1996* (Paris: Karthala, 1997). Similarly, Richards's account of conflict in Sierra Leone is notable for his stress on networks over groups, on creolization over differentiation, and on overlapping moral visions over conflicts of "cultures" (Richards, *Fighting for the Rain Forest*).

81. For an elaboration of this argument, see Rogers Brubaker, "Myths and Misconceptions in the Study of Nationalism," in John Hall, ed., *The State of the Nation: Ernest Gellner and the Theory of Nationalism* (Cambridge: Cambridge University Press, 1998).

82. For a fuller version of this argument, see Brubaker, *Nationalism Reframed*, chap. 2. For a parallel argument about Yugoslavia, see Veljko Vujacic and Victor Zaslavsky, "The Causes of Disintegration in the USSR and Yugoslavia," *Telos* 88 (1991): 120–40.

83. Some peripheral Soviet regions, to be sure, had already experienced national movements in the last years of the Russian empire (and during the ensuing civil war), but even in those regions, the social basis of such movements was weak, and identification with the nation was limited to a relatively small part of the population. Elsewhere, the significance of the regime in constituting national divisions was even more prominent. On Soviet nation-making in the 1920s, see Yuri Slezkine, "The USSR as a Communal Apartment, or How a Socialist State Promoted Ethnic Particularism," *Slavic Review* 53 (1994): 414–52; Terry D. Martin, *The Affirmative Action Empire: Nations and Nationalism in the Soviet Union, 1923–39* (Ithaca, N.Y.: Cornell University Press, 2001).

84. Gitlin, *Twilight*, 134.

85. One of the best introductions to constructivist analysis in American history is Earl Lewis, "Race," in Stanley Kutler, ed., *Encyclopedia of the United States in the Twentieth Century* (New York: Scribners, 1996), 129–60. See also Barbara Fields, "Slavery, Race and Ideology in the United States of America," *New Left Review* 181 (1990): 95–118.

86. Edmund Morgan, *American Slavery, American Freedom: The Ordeal of Colonial Virginia* (New York: Norton, 1975). More recent works on this formative period include a special issue of *William and Mary Quarterly*, 3d ser., 54, no. 1 (1997), "Constructing Race: Differentiating Peoples in the Early Modern World"; and Ira Berlin, *Many Thousands Gone: The First Two Centuries of Slavery in North America* (Cambridge, Mass.: Harvard University Press, 1998).

87. The different ways in which race was configured in the Americas was one of subjects in which comparative history came into being, notably in the aftermath of Frank Tannenbaum, *Slave and Citizen: The Negro in the Americas* (New York: Knopf, 1946). An influential short statement is Charles Wagley, "On the Concept of Social Race in the Americas," in *Contemporary Cultures and Societies in Latin America*, ed. D. B. Heath and R. N. Adams (New York: Random House, 1965), 531–45. A more recent constructivist argument about the historical specificity of the idea of being white is exemplified in David Roediger, *The Wages of Whiteness: Race and the Making of the American Working Class* (London: Verso, 1991).

88. One of the foundational texts of what is sometimes considered black nationalism, Martin Delany's account of his voyage to Africa, is notable for its lack of interest in the cultural practices of the Africans he encountered. What counted for him was that a Christian of African origin would find his destiny

in ridding himself of oppression in the United States and bringing Christian civilization to Africa. See Martin R. Delany and Robert Campbell, *Search for a Place: Black Separatism and Africa, 1860,* ed. Howard H. Bell (Ann Arbor: University of Michigan Press, 1969 [1860]). For an illuminating recent book on African American–African connections—and the differing ways in which linkages were made while cultural distinctions were emphasized—see James Campbell, *Songs of Zion: The African Methodist Episcopal Church in the United States and South Africa* (New York: Oxford University Press, 1995).

89. Eric Lott, "The New Cosmopolitanism: Whose America?" *Transition* 72 (Winter 1996): 108–35.

90. For one such contribution, see Kwame Anthony Appiah, *In My Father's House: Africa in the Philosophy of Culture* (New York: Oxford University Press, 1992).

91. This is the point emphasized by Walter Benn Michaels ("Race into Culture"): the assignment of individuals to cultural identities is even more problematic than the definition of those identities.

92. Alisdair MacIntyre, *After Virtue* (Notre Dame, Ind.: University of Notre Dame Press, 1981), 22.

93. Iris Marion Young, "Polity and Group Difference: A Critique of the Ideal of Universal Citizenship," *Ethics* 99 (1989): 257, 258. See also Young's *Justice and the Politics of Difference* (Princeton, N.J.: Princeton University Press, 1990).

94. Young, "Polity and Group Difference," 267, 261.

95. Ibid., 267, 268.

96. See especially the lucid and influential books by Will Kymlicka: *Liberalism, Community, and Culture* (Oxford: Clarendon Press, 1991), and *Multicultural Citizenship: A Liberal Theory of Minority Rights* (Oxford: Clarendon, 1995).

97. Adam Przeworski, "Proletariat into a Class: The Process of Class Formation from Karl Kautsky's 'The Class Struggle' to Recent Controversies," *Politics and Society* 7 (1977): 372.

98. Pierre Bourdieu, "L'identité et la représentation: Eléments pour une réflexion critique sur l'idée de région," *Actes de la Recherche en Sciences Sociales* 35 (1980): 63–72.

99. David Laitin, "Marginality: A Microperspective," *Rationality and Society* 7 (1995): 31–57.

100. In a debate with Young, the philosopher Nancy Fraser has juxtaposed a politics of "recognition" to one of "redistribution," arguing that both are needed, since some groups are exploited as well as stigmatized or unrecognized. Strikingly, both parties to the debate treat group boundaries as clear-cut, and both therefore conceive of progressive politics as involving intergroup coalitions. Both neglect forms of political action that do not presuppose commonality or groupness. Nancy Fraser, "From Redistribution to Recognition? Dilemmas of Justice in a 'Post-Socialist' Age," *New Left Review* 212 (1995): 68–93; Iris Marion Young, " 'Unruly Categories,' A Critique of Nancy Fraser's Dual Systems Theory," *New Left Review* 222 (1997): 147–60.

101. Margaret E. Keck and Kathryn Sikkink, *Activists beyond Borders: Advocacy Networks in International Politics* (Ithaca, N.Y.: Cornell University Press, 1998); Audie Klotz, *Norms in International Relations: The Struggle against Apartheid* (Ithaca, N.Y.: Cornell University Press, 1995). See also the classic study of Jeremy Boissevain, *Friends of Friends: Networks, Manipulators and Coalitions* (Oxford: Blackwell, 1974).

4. GLOBALIZATION

1. Early on, globalization was a particularly American fad, but it has become more "global." In France, for example, *mondialisation* is much debated in politics and increasingly in academic circles. If the "pros" dominate the American debate, the "antis" are prominent in France, and they even have their public hero, José Bové, arrested for wrecking a McDonalds. The Socialist government argued that globalization could and should be regulated and controlled, but they did not question its reality. See "Procès Bové: La fête de l'antimondialisation," *Le Monde*, June 30, 2000; "Gouverner les forces qui sont à l'oevure dans la mondialisation," *Le Monde*, June 27, 2000. For different uses of the globalization concept by French academics, see GEMDEV (Groupement Economie Mondiale, Tiers-Monde, Développement), *Mondialisation: Les mots et les choses* (Paris: Karthala, 1999); Serge Cordellier, ed., *La mondialisation au delà des mythes* (Paris: La Découverte, 2000 [1997]), Jean-Pierre Faugère, Guy Caire, et Bertrand Bellon, eds., *Convergence et diversité à l'heure de la mondialisation* (Paris: Economica); and Philippe Chantpie et. al., *La nouvelle politique économique: L'état face à la mondialisation* (Paris: PUF, 1997).

2. This is the version of globalization one sees in the newspapers every day, and it can be found in vivid form in a book by *New York Times* correspondent Thomas Friedman, *The Lexus and the Olive Tree* (New York: Farrar, Straus & Giroux, 1999). However, the pro-business *Economist* has long held a more skeptical view, for it thinks the economy isn't globalized enough.

3. Susan Strange exaggerates the decline of the state but provides a valuable analysis of "non-state authorities." She finds the word *globalization* hopelessly vague. Saskia Sassen embraces globalization and treats it as a causative agent ("Globalization has transformed the meaning of . . ."). But much of her work consists of useful and insightful discussion of the intersection in cities of transnational migration and financial movements, as well as of the problems of regulation of interstate economic activities. She too emphasizes the declining relevance of states. Susan Strange, *The Retreat of the State* (Cambridge: Cambridge University Press, 1996); and Saskia Sassen, *Globalization and Its Discontents* (New York: New Press, 1998). For other versions of the decline of states, see David Held, *Democracy and the Global Order: From the Modern State to Cosmopolitan Governance* (Cambridge: Polity Press, 1995); Scott Lash and John Urry, *Economies of Signs and Space* (London: Sage, 1994); and Bertrand Badie, *Un monde sans souveraineté: Les états entre ruse et responsabilité* (Paris: Fayard, 1999). For one of many examples of the denunciatory

mode of globalization literature, see Richard Falk, *Predatory Globalization: A Critique* (Cambridge: Polity Press, 1999).

4. Arjun Appadurai, *Modernity at Large: Cultural Dimensions of Globalization* (Minneapolis: University of Minnesota Press, 1996). What is striking to a historian about this book is Appadurai's assertion of newness without the slightest effort to examine the past and his preference for inventing a new vocabulary (ethnoscapes, etc.) to characterize phenomena at a global level rather than a sustained effort to describe the mechanisms by which connections occur.

5. Some observers describe the present age as one of the "annihilation of space by time." That, of course, is a nineteenth-century idea—from Marx—and space-time compression has had many moments. David Harvey, *The Condition of Postmodernity: An Inquiry into the Origins of Cultural Change* (Oxford: Blackwell, 1989).

6. Kevin H. O'Rourke and Jeffrey G. Williamson, *Globalization and History: The Evolution of a Nineteenth-Century Atlantic Economy* (Cambridge, MA: MIT Press, 1999), 2, 4; Paul Bairoch, "Globalization Myths and Realities: One Century of External Trade and Foreign Investment," in Robert Boyer and Daniel Drache, eds., *States against Markets: The Limits of Globalization* (London: Routledge, 1996), 190; Paul Hirst and Grahame Thompson, *Globalization in Question* (Cambridge: Polity Press, 1996); and Kevin R. Cox, *Spaces of Globalization: Reasserting the Power of the Local* (New York: Guilford Press, 1997).

7. *Le Monde*, June 20, 2000.

8. Aihwa Ong, *Flexible Citizenship: The Cultural Logics of Transnationality* (Durham, N.C.: Duke University Press, 1999).

9. "A Survey of Globalisation and Tax," *The Economist*, Jan. 29, 2000, p. 6

10. Atilio Boron, "Globalization: A Latin American Perspective," unpublished paper for CODESRIA conference, Johannesburg, South Africa, 1998.

11. Dean Tipps, "Modernization Theory and the Comparative Study of Societies: A Critical Perspective," *Comparative Studies in Society and History* 15 (1973): 199–226.

12. C. L. R. James, *The Black Jacobins: Toussaint L'Ouverture and the San Domingo Revolution* (New York: Vintage, 1963 [1938]); Eric Williams, *Capitalism and Slavery* (Chapel Hill: University of North Carolina Press, 1944). See also Robin Blackburn, *The Making of New World Slavery: From the Baroque to the Modern* (London: Verso, 1997).

13. Michel-Rolph Trouillot, *Silencing the Past: The Power and the Production of History* (Boston: Beacon, 1995); Carolyn E. Fick, *The Making of Haiti: The Saint Domingue Revolution from Below* (Knoxville: University of Tennessee Press, 1990).

14. Sidney Mintz, *Sweetness and Power: The Place of Sugar in Modern History* (New York: Penguin, 1985); Richard Price, *First-Time: The Historical Vision of an Afro-American People* (Baltimore, Md.: Johns Hopkins University Press, 1983). For a more recent perspective, see Michael A. Gomez, *Exchanging Our Country Marks: The Transformation of African Identities in the Colonial and Antebellum South* (Chapel Hill: University of North Carolina Press, 1998).

15. B. A. F. Manz, "Temur and the Problem of a Conqueror's Legacy," *Journal of the Royal Asiatic Society* 8, pt.1 (1998): 22.

16. For an illuminating study of unevenness within a seaborne regional system in Southeast Asia—of the differential impact of political power and the multiple forms of connection, pilgrimage as much as trade—see Sanjay Subrahmanyam, "Notes on Circulation and Asymmetry in Two 'Mediterraneans,' 1400–1800," in Claude Guillot, Denys Lombard, and Roderich Ptak, eds., *From the Mediterranean to the China Sea* (Wiesbaden, Germany: Harrassowitz, 1999), 21–43.

17. Critiques of world-system theory in some ways parallel those of modernization and globalization. See, for example, Frederick Cooper, Allen Isaacman, Florencia Mallon, Steve Stern, and William Roseberry, *Confronting Historical Paradigms: Peasants, Labor, and the Capitalist World System in Africa and Latin America* (Madison: University of Wisconsin Press, 1993).

18. Anthony Pagden, *Spanish Imperialism and the Political Imagination: Studies in European and Spanish-American Social and Political Theory 1513–1830* (New Haven, Conn.: Yale University Press, 1990); Benedict Anderson, *Imagined Communities: Reflections on the Origin and Spread of Nationalism* (London: Verso, 1983).

19. Kenneth Pomeranz, *The Great Divergence: Europe, China, and the Making of the Modern World Economy* (Princeton, N.J.: Princeton University Press, 2000).

20. The argument is spelled out in Cooper's essay in Cooper et al., *Confronting Historical Paradigms*. For a related argument emphasizing the historical depth of contemporary patterns, see Jean-François Bayart, "Africa in the World: A History of Extraversion," *African Affairs* 99 (2000): 216–67.

21. Albert O. Hirschman, *Exit, Voice, and Loyalty: Responses to Decline in Firms, Organizations, and States* (Cambridge, MA: Harvard University Press, 1970).

22. Frederick Cooper, Thomas Holt, and Rebecca Scott, *Beyond Slavery: Explorations of Race, Labor, and Citizenship in Postemancipation Societies* (Chapel Hill: University of North Carolina Press, 2000).

23. An example of ascending globalizations can be found in the GEMDEV volume (*Mondialisation*), where Michel Beaud writes of "several globalizations," and about "archeo-globalizations" and "proto-globalizations" (11). In the same book, Gérard Kébabdjian makes the opposite argument, distinguishing between today's "globalized" structure and colonial economies, which entailed exchange within bounded regimes (54–55). A variant between the two, in the same book, comes from Jean-Lous Margolin, who looks for "preceding phases of globalization," and then writes of "the distortion into colonial imperialism of the strong globalizing wave coming from the industrial and political revolutions" (127), of "the aborted globalization surrounding Europe, 1850–1914" (130), then of the "quasi-retreat of the global economy by a third of Humanity" (under communism, 127, 130, 131). He ends up with a dazzling nonsequitur: "All this prepared the globalization, 'properly speaking,' of today" (132). All three variants reduce history to teleology with little understanding

of how human beings act in their own times and in their own contexts. More recently, A. G. Hopkins, while claiming to eschew teleology, divides history into archaic, proto-, modern, and postcolonial globalization. "Globalization: An Agenda for Historians," in Hopkins, ed., *Globalization in World History* (New York: Norton, 2002), 3–4.

24. Michael Geyer and Charles Bright present as plausible a case for a mid- or late-nineteenth-century origin for globalization as the case for the late twentieth (or for that matter the sixteenth) century, but the contention that what was created was globality is unconvincing in regard to any of these alternatives. "World History in a Global Age," *American Historical Review* 100 (1995): 1034–60.

25. On agriculture in colonial and postcolonial Africa—notably the importance of "exploitation without dispossession"—see Sara Berry, *No Condition Is Permanent: The Social Dynamics of Agrarian Change in Sub-Saharan Africa* (Madison: University of Wisconsin Press, 1993).

26. Africa's share of world trade fell from over 3 percent in the 1950s to less than 2 percent in the 1990s (1.2 percent if one excludes South Africa). Africans have the use of one telephone line per 100 people (1 per 200 outside of South Africa), compared to 1 per 50 in the world as a whole. Electricity is unavailable in many rural areas and doesn't always work in urban ones; mail services have deteriorated, and radio is often unusable because batteries are too expensive; millions of people get their information in an older way—word of mouth. World Bank, *Can Africa Claim the Twenty-First Century?* (Washington: World Bank, 2000).

27. Béatrice Hibou, "De la privatisation des économies à la privatisation des états," in Hibou, ed., *La privatisation des états* (Paris: Karthala, 1999).

28. Rather than constitute alternatives to the state, such mechanisms more likely interact with state institutions and agents. Janet Roitman, "The Garrison-Entrepôt," *Cahiers d'Etudes Africaines* 150–52 (1998): 297–329; Karine Bennafla, "La fin des territoires nationaux?" *Politique Africaine* 73 (1999): 24–49; Jean-François Bayart, Stephen Ellis, and Béatrice Hibou, *La criminalisation de l'état en Afrique* (Paris: Ed. Complexe, 1997).

29. Georges Balandier, "La situation coloniale: Approche théoretique," *Cahiers Internationaux de Sociologie* 11 (1951): 44–79; Max Gluckman, "Anthropological Problems Arising from the African Industrial Revolution," in Aidan Southall, ed., *Social Change in Modern Africa* (London: Oxford University Press, 1961), 67–82; J. Clyde Mitchell, *Social Networks in Urban Situations: Analysis of Personal Relationships in Central African Towns* (Manchester: Manchester University Press, 1969). See also chapter 2.

30. Abner Cohen, *Custom and Politics in Urban Africa: A Study of Migrants in Yoruba Towns* (Berkeley: University of California Press, 1969).

31. James T. Campbell, *Songs of Zion: The African Methodist Episcopal Church in the United States and South Africa* (New York: Oxford University Press, 1995); J. Lorand Matory, "The English Professors of Brazil: On the Diasporic Roots of the Yoruba Nation," *Comparative Studies in Society and History* 41 (1999): 72–103.

32. See chapter 7; and Frederick Cooper, *Decolonization and African Society: The Labor Question in French and British Africa* (Cambridge: Cambridge University Press, 1996).

33. The variety and time depth of diasporic phenomena, as well as the specificity of the mechanisms by which they were organized, are emphasized in Emmanuel Akyeampong, "Africans in the Diaspora; The Diaspora in Africa," *African Affairs* 99 (2000): 183–215. See also chapter 6.

34. David Brion Davis, *The Problem of Slavery in the Age of Revolution 1770–1823* (Ithaca, N.Y.: Cornell University Press, 1975); Margaret E. Keck and Kathryn Sikkink, *Activists beyond Borders: Advocacy Networks in International Politics* (Ithaca, N.Y.: Cornell University Press, 1988).

35. William Beinart and Colin Bundy, *Hidden Struggles in Rural South Africa* (Berkeley: University of California Press, 1987).

36. As Hibou ("De la privatisation") shows, the privatization of nationalized companies in Africa produced something quite different from a "private sector" of competing firms connected to world markets: officials may privatize state-owned firms to themselves, leading to private accumulation through government and narrow channels of interaction. Similarly, the Soviet Union remains vastly different from post-1989 fantasies of market integration. Markku Lonkila, "Post-Soviet Russia? A Society of Networks?" in Markku Kangaspuro, ed., *Russia: More Different Than Most?* (Helsinki: Kikimora, 1999), 98–112.

5. MODERNITY

1. Björn Wittrock, "Modernity: One, None, or Many? European Origins and Modernity as a Global Condition," *Daedalus* 129, no. 1 (2000): 59. Or what is one to make of the statement that "modernity in China, as it is globally, is a contested terrain where different experiences of the modern produce not a homogeneous modernity, but a cultural politics in which the conquest of the modern is the ultimate prize"? Or "Modernity is the illusion that defines the modern"? Arif Dirlik, "Modernity as History: Post-Revolutionary China, Globalization, and the Question of Modernity," *Social History* 27 (2002): 33.

2. John D. Kelly, "Alternative Modernities or an Alternative to 'Modernity': Getting out of the Modernist Sublime," in Bruce M. Knauft, ed., *Critically Modern: Alternatives, Alterities, Anthropologies* (Bloomington: Indiana University Press, 2002), 262. This book is notable for skepticism toward the term. Yet the editor, perhaps more than most contributors, does not want to go as far as Kelly, and for all his critical insight, contributes to the term's proliferation. See Knauft, "Critically Modern: An Introduction," esp. 32.

3. Partha Chatterjee, "Two Poets and Death: On Civil and Political Society in the Non-Christian World," in Timothy Mitchell, ed., *Questions of Modernity* (Minneapolis: University of Minnesota Press, 2000), 47. Nicholas Dirks reversed the order but to the same dehistoricizing effect: "Colonialism is what modernity was all about." "History as a Sign of the Modern," *Public Culture* 2 (1990): 29.

4. Dipesh Chakrabarty, *Provincializing Europe: Postcolonial Thought and Historical Difference* (Princeton, N.J.: Princeton University Press, 2000), 254, stresses incommensurability. Simon Gikandi refers to his own entry into cultural analysis by citing his parents, Kikuyu Christians, who "decided to break away from the traditions of their people and embrace the modern culture of colonialism, a culture that seemed to guarantee them new spaces of self-inscription in the narrative of modernity." What Gikandi has to say about the culture is revealing and insightful, but the point of departure makes his problem more difficult. He omits an important history, dating at least to the 1930s, of efforts by many Kikuyu to be both Kikuyu and Christian, to found independent churches and schools that would continue to embrace rituals and social practices of the Kikuyu people while seeking new cultural resources and building a community that avoided the dichotomy that Gikandi—like many of the missionaries—seems to say was all that was available to them. *Maps of Englishness: Writing Identity in the Culture of Colonialism* (New York: Columbia University Press, 1996), 20.

5. W. W. Rostow, *The Stages of Economic Growth: A Non-Communist Manifesto* (Cambridge: Cambridge University Press, 1961).

6. Examples of the inevitability argument come from Wilbert E. Moore, *Industrialization and Labor: Social Aspects of Economic Development* (Ithaca, N.Y.: Cornell University Press for the Institute of World Affairs, 1951); and Clark Kerr, John T. Dunlop, Frederick Harrison, and Charles A. Myers, *Industrialism and Industrial Man: The Problems of Labor and Management in Industrial Growth* (Cambridge, Mass.: Harvard University Press, 1960) .

7. The most influential summary of them is Dean Tipps, "Modernization Theory and the Comparative Study of Societies: A Critical Perspective," *Comparative Studies in Society and History* 15 (1973): 199–226. There have been some revivals of largely unreconstructed modernization, for example R. Inglehart, "Modernization, Sociological Theories of," in Neil Smelser and Paul Baltes, eds., *International Encyclopedia of the Social and Behavioral Sciences* (Amsterdam: Elsevier, 2001), 15: 9965–71. Unlike Inglehart, most of the other authors in this new edition of the *Encyclopedia* do not echo the 1968 version, which is cited below.

8. For a critical, historical approach to analyzing world systems, see Frederick Cooper, Allen Isaacman, Florencia Mallon, William Roseberry, and Steve Stern, *Confronting Historical Paradigms: Peasants, Labor, and the Capitalist World System in Africa and Latin America* (Madison: University of Wisconsin Press, 1993).

9. Dipesh Chakrabarty, *Habitations of Modernity: Essays in the Wake of Subaltern Studies* (Chicago: University of Chicago Press, 2002); Arjun Appadurai, *Modernity at Large: Cultural Dimensions of Globalization* (Minneapolis: University of Minnesota Press, 1996); Lisa Rofel, *Other Modernities: Gendered Yearnings in China after Socialism* (Berkeley: University of California Press, 1999); Daniel Miller, *Modernity, An Ethnographic Approach: Dualism and Mass Consumption in Trinidad* (Oxford: Berg, 1994); Carol Breckenridge, ed., *Consuming Modernity: Public Culture in a South Asian World*

(Minneapolis: University of Minnesota Press, 1995); Harry Harootunian, *Overcome by Modernity: History, Culture, and Community in Interwar Japan* (Princeton, N.J.: Princeton University Press, 2000); Knauft, *Critically Modern;* Jan-Georg Deutsch, Peter Probst, and Heike Schmidt, eds., *African Moderni-ties: Entangled Meanings in Current Debate* (Portsmouth, NH: Heinemann, 2002); Charles Piot, *Remotely Global: Village Modernity in West Africa* (Chicago: University of Chicago Press, 1999); Jean Comaroff and John Co-maroff, *Of Revelation and Revolution, Vol. 2: The Dialectics of Modernity on a South African Frontier* (Chicago: University of Chicago Press, 1997). Note also the existence of a journal, *Modernism/Modernity,* that began publishing in 1994. The growing popularity of *modernity* as a keyword in journal articles, compared to the stagnation of *modernization,* is illustrated in Figure 1.

10. This is how Raymond Williams uses the word *modern.* He points out that the earliest English uses of *modern* carried the sense of contemporary, in contrast to ancient, that pre-nineteenth-century uses of *modern* and its deriv-atives were generally unfavorable and nineteenth- and twentieth-century ones strongly positive. Modernism, he indicates, has a specialized meaning, "notably to the experimental art and writing of c. 1890–c.1940," while modernization's "unquestionably favourable or desirable" connotations (in his 1983 usage) "need scrutiny." *Keywords: A Vocabulary of Culture and Society,* rev. ed. (New York: Oxford University Press, 1983), 208–209. For a more detailed list of us-ages of these words, see the *Compact Edition of the Oxford English Dictionary* (Oxford: Oxford University Press, 1971), 1: 1828 (M 573–74).

11. Quotations from Arthur C. Danto, "Too Old for MOMA?" *New York Times,* Oct. 28, 1998, p. A29. On the ambiguity of modernity in relation to time, see Jacques Le Goff, *History and Memory,* trans. Steven Rendall and Elizabeth Claman (New York: Columbia University Press, 1992), 49–50.

12. Peter Geschiere, *The Modernity of Witchcraft: Politics and the Occult in Postcolonial Africa,* trans. Janet Roitman (Charlottesville: University Press of Virginia, 1997).

13. Daniel Lerner, "Modernization—Social Aspects," in David L. Sills, ed., *International Encyclopedia of the Social Sciences* (New York: Macmillan, 1968), 10: 387.

14. Moore, *Industrialization and Labor.*

15. Rostow, *Stages of Economic Growth.* The work of the Committee on Comparative Politics of the Social Science Research Council, founded in 1953, was at the center of applications of modernization theory to decolonizing situ-ations. The most famous, or notorious, example of such work is that of David Apter, including *The Gold Coast in Transition* (Princeton, N.J.: Princeton Uni-versity Press, 1955), and 1963 and 1972 editions entitled *Ghana in Transition.*

16. Samuel P. Huntington, "Political Development and Political Decay," *World Politics* 17 (1965): 386–430; idem, *The Clash of Civilizations and the Re-making of World Order* (New York: Simon and Schuster, 1996).

17. Daniel Bell, "Resolving the Contradictions of Modernity and Mod-ernism," *Society* 27, no. 3 (1990): 43, 45–46. See also Bell, *The Cultural Con-tradictions of Capitalism* (New York: Basic Books, 1976).

18. For examples of work showing how badly the tradition to modernity framework fits the case of post–World War II Nigeria, see C. S. Whitaker, *The Politics of Tradition: Continuity and Change in Northern Nigeria, 1946–1966* (Princeton, N.J.: Princeton University Press, 1970); and Sara Berry, *Fathers Work for Their Sons: Accumulation, Mobility, and Class Formation in an Extended Yoruba Community* (Berkeley: University of California Press, 1985). Or take a more recent study of a community with a strong sense of tradition and hierarchy, but quick adaptability to new commercial opportunity and the latest. technology. The author spends a lot of time trying to decide whether they are really modern, but fitting his rich data into the modernity framework becomes so awkward that he ends up saying of modernity, "you know it when you see it." Jonah Blank, *Mullahs on the Mainframe: Islam and Modernity among the Daudi Bohras* (Chicago: University of Chicago Press, 2001), 260 quoted.

19. Charles Taylor, "Modern Social Imaginaries," *Public Culture* 14 (2002): 91, 98.

20. Chakrabarty, *Provincializing Europe*, 4. Or take the description of Marilyn Ivy: "Urban energies, capitalist structures of life, and mechanical and electrical forms of reproduction . . . the problem of the nation-state and its correlation with a capitalist colonialism . . . a global geopolitical matrix from the mid-nineteenth century on. . . . the emergence of individualism and new modes of interiority . . . bureaucratic rationalisms, Taylorized modes of production, novel forms of image representation, mass media, scientific disciplines." *Discourses of the Vanishing: Modernity, Phantasm, Japan* (Chicago: University of Chicago Press, 1995), 4–5, quoted in Kelly, "Alternative Modernities or an Alternative to 'Modernity,'" 266. Parsons must be smiling in his grave at the extent to which he has shaped the conceptual apparatus of postmodern anthropology.

21. Roger Friedland and Deidre Boden, "NowHere: An Introduction to Space, Time, and Modernity," in Friedland and Boden, eds., *NowHere: Space, Time and Modernity* (Berkeley: University of California Press, 1994) , 2.

22. As Anthony Giddens notes, the problem with defining modernity as an era is often that this "leaves its major characteristics safely stowed away in a black box." *The Consequences of Modernity* (Stanford, Calif.: Stanford University Press, 1990), 1. A similar point is made by Wittrock, "Modernity: One, None, or Many?" 32.

23. *Habitations of Modernity*, 37. The important but shifting place of poetry, romanticism, subjectivism, and religiosity in European culture, on the left as well as the right, emerges clearly in H. Stuart Hughes's classic study, *Consciousness and Society: The Reorientation of European Social Thought 1890–1930* (New York: Knopf, 1958), as well as in the recent and vigorous argument of David Hollinger, "The Knower and the Artificer, with Postscript 1993," in Dorothy Ross, ed., *Modernist Impulses in the Human Sciences, 1870–1930* (Baltimore, Md.: Johns Hopkins University Press, 1994), 26–53.

24. Matei Calinescu, *Faces of Modernity: Avant-Garde, Deacadence, Kitsch* (Bloomington: Indiana University Press, 1977), 263. As J. G. A. Pocock puts it, "to be modern is to quarrel with modernity." "Modernity and Anti-modernity

in the Anglophone Political Tradition," in S. N. Eisenstadt, ed., *Patterns of Modernity, Volume I: The West* (London: Frances Pinter, 1987), 57.

25. As Hughes notes, "scoffing at the Enlightenment" was part of the intellectual fashion of the late nineteenth century—much as it is a century later. *Consciousness and Society,* 28–29.

26. David Hollinger cites the irony that "Nietzsche, after his long career as a founder of modernism, began a new career as precursor, if not a founder, of postmodernism." "The Enlightenment and the Genealogy of Cultural Conflict in the United States," in Keith Michael Baker and Peter Hanns Reill, eds., *What's Left of Enlightenment? A Postmodern Question* (Stanford, Calif.: Stanford University Press, 2001), 11.

27. Maurice Duverger, "Le concept d'empire," in Duverger, ed., *Le concept d'empire* (Paris: Presses Universitaires de France, 1980), 14. For a more thorough comparative examination by a leading historian of China, see R. Bin Wong, *China Transformed: Historical Change and the Limits of European Experience* (Ithaca, N.Y.: Cornell University Press, 1997). Within European history, one should also be careful about conflating a modern epoch with ideas of progress, for the latter have been debated for three thousand years. See Robert Nisbet, *History of the Idea of Progress* (New York: Basic Books, 1980).

28. Bernard Yack, *The Fetishism of Modernities: Epochal Self-Consciousness in Contemporary Social and Political Thought* (Notre Dame, IN: University of Notre Dame Press, 1997), esp. 4–5, 19, 29. I am more persuaded by Yack's attack on the idea of a modern epoch than by his argument that one can establish substantive criteria for what constitutes the modern that are not uniquely associated with an era. That one can establish such criteria is not in question; what purpose it would serve is.

29. Piot, *Remotely Global,* 179n1.

30. Friedland and Boden, "NowHere," 2.

31. Timothy Mitchell, "Introduction," in Mitchell, ed., *Questions of Modernity* (Minneapolis; University of Minnesota Press, 2000), xii–xiii.

32. Piot's *Remotely Global* reveals the methodological difficulties of such approaches. He breaks with the anthropological tradition of treating a village as an entity unto itself and insists that the village can be understood only in relation to the outside world and to a history going back three hundred years. But his methods are within the tradition of village ethnography—detailed, sensitive observations—and his sources do little to connect this village to the ups and downs of the history. A synchronic methodology is used to support a diachronic argument.

33. Giddens, *Consequences of Modernity.* The space-time view of modernity is emphasized by Friedland and Boden, and the flattening of time by Chakrabarty. David Harvey falls into epochal thinking in seeking to differentiate a space/time configuration of modernity from that of postmodernity. *The Condition of Postmodernity: An Inquiry into the Origins of Cultural Change* (Oxford: Blackwell, 1989).

34. A model analysis of capitalist trajectories is Geoff Eley and David Blackbourn's critique of the *sonderweg* in German history, the notion that the

story of the rise of capitalism in England constitutes the basic model and that other instances, the German one for instance, represent deviant pathways. *The Peculiarities of German History: Bourgeois Society and Politics in Nineteenth-Century Germany* (Oxford: Oxford University Press, 1984). See also Richard Biernacki, *The Fabrication of Labor: Germany and Britain, 1640–1914* (Berkeley: University of California Press, 1992).

35. The inadequacy of the secularization model is stressed by Peter van der Veer, *Imperial Encounters: Religion and Modernity in India and Britain* (Princeton, N.J.: Princeton University Press, 2001). Robert W. Hefner, in "Multiple Modernities: Christianity, Islam, and Hinduism in a Globalizing Age," *Annual Review of Anthropology* 27 (1998): 83–104, also shows that secularization doesn't fit Europe or Asia, but he stops short of examining what his argument does to the concept of modernity.

36. See, in addition to Mitchell, Rebecca E. Karl, *Staging the World: Chinese Nationalism at the Turn of the Twentieth Century* (Durham, N.C.: Duke University Press, 2002), 4. Joel Kahn ("Anthropology and Modernity," *Current Anthropology* 42 [2001]: 656) argues that the "ethnographer's insistence on the primacy of context, by relativizing and pluralizing modernity, leads us to reject any general and singular understanding of modernity and invites us to abandon the concept as caught in a hopeless contradiction." But he pulls back from this insight. His eagerness to see his area of study, Malaysia, as a "site of modernity" leads him to loosen the concept so that any place must fit it. Ibid., 655, 659, 663. A more historically rooted argument for the mutual constitution of modernity and its negation—which to my mind still does not overcome this problem—is Michel-Rolph Trouillot, "The Otherwise Modern: Caribbean Lessons from the Savage Slot," in Knauft, ed., *Critically Modern*, 220–37.

37. Donald M. Nonini and Aihwa Ong, "Chinese Transnationalism as an Alternative Modernity," in Ong and Nonini, *Ungrounded Empires: The Cultural Politics of Modern Chinese Transnationalism* (New York: Routledge, 1997), 4 (quoted), 15–16. The most important conceptual work in this article is done not by modernity but by transnationalism, particularly the authors' insistence that the significance of being Chinese be seen in relation to a circuit of movement rather than an essentialized homeland.

38. S. N. Eisenstadt, "Multiple Modernities," *Daedalus* 129, no. 1 (2000): 1–29.

39. Lisa Rofel, *Other Modernities: Gendered Yearnings in China after Socialism* (Berkeley: University of California Press, 1999), 12–13.

40. Aihwa Ong, "Anthropology, China and Modernities: The Geopolitics of Cultural Knowledge," in Henrietta Moore, ed., *The Future of Anthropological Knowledge* (London: Routledge, 1996), 64, emphasis added.

41. Huri Islamoglu and Peter C. Perdue, "Introduction," *Journal of Early Modern History* 5, no. 4 (2001): 274; and Huri Islamoglu, "Modernities Compared: State Transformations and Constitutions of Property in the Qing and Ottoman Empires," ibid., 354.

42. Arjun Appadurai and Carol Breckenridge, "Public Modernity in India," in Breckenridge, *Consuming Modernity*, 2.

43. Marshall Berman, *All That Is Solid Melts into Air: The Experience of Modernity* (New York: Penguin, 1988), 15–17; Baudelaire cited in Calinescu, *Faces of Modernity*, 4–5; Harootunian, *Overcome by Modernity*, 18.

44. Yack, *Fetishism of Modernities*, 89, 105.

45. Bernhard Rieger and Martin Daunton, "Introduction," in Daunton and Rieger, eds., *Meanings of Modernity: Britain from the Late-Victorian Era to World War II* (Oxford: Berg, 2001), 5–7. These authors take a line from the multiple modernities argument, which usually features the rich variety of processes of change outside of the West, to claim plural "modernities" for England itself. They claim that British modernity became more modern after World War II—an argument that while itself not solving terminological problems suggests that the analysis of ideologies of progress, in Europe as much as elsewhere, needs to be pinned down in time and space, not left in the metahistorical limbo of three hundred years of capitalism and state formation. Ibid, 4, 14–15.

46. The quotations are from "Interview with Jean and John Comaroff," *NAB: Newsletter of African Studies at Bayreuth University* 1, no. 1 (2002), 3–4; and Comaroff and Comaroff, *Of Revelation and Revolution*, 2: 4–6. See also the introduction to their edited volume *Modernity and Its Malcontents: Ritual and Power in Postcolonial Africa* (Chicago: University of Chicago Press, 1993). For a critique of the Comaroffs' work that also emphasizes the excessive coherence given to colonial transformations and the use of abstractions as agents, see Donald L. Donham, "Thinking Temporally or Modernizing Anthropology," *American Anthropologist* 103 (2001): 134–49. See also Paul Landau, "History and Hegemony in Jean and John L. Comaroff's *Of Revelation and Revolution*," *Africa* 70 (2000): 501–19.

47. *Of Revelation and Revolution*, 2: 33–34, 61. In responding to critics, the Comaroffs' modernity becomes even closer to the vocabulary of postwar social science. Modernity, they say, brings together "a *telos* of progress and rationalization, a positivist mode of producing knowledge and value, a stress on the primacy of the 'free' market, a liberal vision of humanity, secular society, the polity, and the citizen." Jean and John Comaroff, "Revelations upon *Revelation*: Aftershocks, Afterthoughts," *Interventions* 3 (2001): 112.

48. Chakrabarty, *Provincializing* and *Habitations of Modernity*. If Chakrabarty emphasizes the depth of critical engagement of Bengali thinkers with British modernizers, Nonini and Ong ("Transnationalism as Alternative Modernity," 15–16) emphasize the distinctiveness of Chinese "alternative modernities." Scholars of Japan emphasize the extent of engagement with the West, but also the effort to develop a distinctly Japanese version of modernity—and the dangerous political consequences of such a move. Sheldon Garon, "Rethinking Modernization and Modernity in Japanese History: A Focus on State-Society Relations," *Journal of Asian Studies* 53 (1994): 346–66; and Harootunian, *Overcome by Modernity*.

49. A different tack is taken by J. D. Y. Peel, who glosses the Yoruba word *olaju* to bring out a particular vision of progress among Yoruba, one which

stresses access to resources outside the community used to enhance the well-being of the community. " 'Olaju': A Yoruba Concept of Development," *Journal of Development Studies* 14 (1978): 139–65.

50. Ong distinguishes state modernities in Asia from subaltern ones. She makes a good case for the state versions, for they are explicit modernization projects that claim to represent a uniquely Chinese or Asian route to progress, a claim whose self-serving nature Ong criticizes. The value of applying the alternative modernity model to the diasporic Chinese she studies is less clear. Her study reveals the suppleness and flexibility of strategies of networking and self-representation by diasporic people, who engage fully with state and capitalist power in Asia and North America, while invoking Chineseness to strengthen networks. The modernity label reintroduces a traditional/modern continuum that Ong's thoughtful analysis of networks and representations seems to belie. "Chinese Modernities: Narratives of Nation and of Capitalism," in Nonini and Ong, *Ungrounded Empires*, 171–202.

51. This juxtaposition of a singular Europe and multiple colonial alternatives is particularly striking in Gyan Prakash, *Another Reason: Science and the Imagination of Modern India* (Princeton, N.J.: Princeton University Press, 1999).

52. James Ferguson, "Decomposing Modernity: History and Hierarchy after Development," in *Global Shadows: Africa in the Neoliberal World Order*, forthcoming; idem, *Expectations of Modernity: Myths and Meanings of Urban Life on the Zambian Copperbelt* (Berkeley: University of California Press, 1999). See also Steven Robins, "Whose Modernity? Indigenous Modernities and Land Claims after Apartheid," *Development and Change* 34 (2003): 265–86, who argues that the critique of modernity fails to grasp the way in which South Africans use a language of development to demand that issues of poverty be addressed.

53. Donald Donham, *Marxist Modern: An Ethnographic History of the Ethiopian Revolution* (Berkeley: University of California Press, 1999). In addition to analyzing the unambiguous modernizing ideology of the revolutionaries, Donham identifies a specifically traditionalist faction as well as others who don't fit a modernizing/traditionalizing distinction, such as missionaries who thought they were bringing old-time, fundamentalist Protestantism to Ethiopia but were seen as offering tools for progress, or the elitist modernizing ideology of Haile Selassie before his overthrow.

54. Donald Donham puts it this way: "Once the adjective has been transposed into the noun, modernity floats much more easily above the ground of ethnographic and historical specification. And floating, it has a tendency to colonize theoretical space, to gather about it all sorts of assumptions. In this context, it is perhaps too easy to appear innovative when all that is entailed is a certain inexactness." "On Being Modern in a Capitalist World: Some Conceptual and Comparative Issues," in Knauft, *Critically Modern*, 241–42.

55. Debra Spitulnik uses a different metaphor but is bothered by the same implication of the multiple modernities argument: "If there are such wide-

ranging cultural and historical particulars that fall under the umbrella of modernity, what warrants the use of the word as a single cover term in the first place?" "Accessing 'Local' Modernities: Reflections on the Place of Linguistic Evidence in Ethnography," in Knauft, *Critically Modern*, 198. She ends up with an argument similar to my call to listen to what people are saying when—and if—they talk about being modern. Ibid., 200.

56. Harootunian, *Overcome by Modernity*, esp. xxi–xxiii, 150, 303, 414. The version of "our modernity" set forth in Japan in the 1930s makes one worry about the implications of Chatterjee's call for Indians to "become the creators of our own modernity" without fully examining the dangers of the self-other dichotomy implied in the "our." *Our Modernity*, 14.

57. Sarah Whitney Womack, studying an important intellectual in colonial Vietnam, argues, "While some modernizers advocated snapping all the rotting ties of hidebound tradition, and some traditionalists condemned every perceived inroad of a vulgar and corrupting modern world, most Vietnamese held positions between the two." "Colonialism and the Collaborationist Agenda: Pham Quynh, Print Culture, and the Politics of Persuasion in Colonial Vietnam," Ph.D. diss., University of Michigan, 2003. The unpackaging by Yoruba men and women of colonial ideas of labor and family is stressed in Lisa Lindsay, *Working with Gender: Wage Labor and Social Change in Southwest Nigeria* (Portsmouth, NH: Heinemann, 2003).

58. Bruno Latour, *We Have Never Been Modern*, trans. Catherine Porter (Cambridge, Mass.: Harvard University Press, 1993 [1991]).

59. Knauft glosses Piot's *Remotely Global* (discussed above) as asserting that his village in northern Togo has "been modern for at least three hundred years" (*Critically Modern*, 19).

60. Friedland and Boden, "NowHere," 2; David Scott, *Refashioning Futures: Criticism after Postcoloniality* (Princeton, N.J.: Princeton University Press, 1999), 17.

61. These arguments are related to those about the Holocaust. Zygmunt Bauman, for example, walks a fine line between saying that the Holocaust happened within "our modern rational society" and that it was a product of that modernity and rationality. *Modernity and the Holocaust* (Ithaca, N.Y.: Cornell University Press, 2000 [1989]), x quoted.

62. The importance of making such distinctions is missing from the exchange about the relationship between the evils of colonization and the Holocaust between Vinay Lal and Omer Bartov in *American Historical Review* 103 (1998): 1187–94.

63. For discussion of the difficulties of fitting the study of Islamic politics into frameworks of modernity, see Ira Lapidus, "Islamic Revival and Modernity: The Contemporary Movements and the Historical Paradigm," *Journal of the Economic and Social History of the Orient* 40 (1997): 444–45; and Roxanne L. Euben, "Premodern, Antimodern or Postmodern? Islamic and Western Critiques of Modernity," *Review of Politics* 59 (1997): 429–59.

64. Dipesh Chakrabarty, "Modernity and Ethnicity in India: A History for the Present," *Economic and Political Weekly*, Dec. 30, 1995, 3373–80; "Radical

Histories and Question of Enlightenment Rationalism," *Economic and Political Weekly*, April 8, 1995, 751–59; and "Postcoloniality and the Artifice of History: Who Speaks for 'Indian' Pasts?" *Representations* 37 (1992): 1–26.

65. Dipesh Chakrabarty, *Rethinking Working-Class History: Bengal 1890–1940* (Princeton, N.J.: Princeton University Press, 1989).

66. "Who Speaks," 21; "Modernity," 3376, 3378, 3379, "Rationalism," 752–53. It should be noted that there is nothing particularly modern about claims to universality. Alexander the Great built a "universal empire." So did the Romans, defining what lay outside the universe as barbarism; Islamic empires aspired to universality, as the world of Islam expanded at the expense of the world of war. See chapter 7.

67. "Rationalism," 758. A contrary view of the incommensurability of distinct and hostile modes of thought is expressed by Roxanne Euben. In a study of the thought of an Islamic "fundamentalist," she argues that the framework of his thought cannot be reduced to or explained by "rationalist" perspectives. At the same time, she argues that he is "deeply engaged with and also shaped by the very categories and ideas he explicitly rejects," and that "he is also participating in a conversation that we, as Western students of politics, not only recognize, but in which we participate." *Enemy in the Mirror: Islamic Fundamentalism and the Limits of Modern Rationalism* (Princeton, N.J.: Princeton University Press, 1999), 155, 165. See also Seyla Benhabib, who rejects the notion of "radical incommensurability" not only on empirical grounds—commensurability is part of history—but on epistemological ones, namely that identifying two cultures as incommensurable implies a set of agreed-upon concepts to specify their distinction, that is on commensurability. *The Claims of Culture: Equality and Diversity in the Global Era* (Princeton, N.J.: Princeton University Press, 2002), 30.

68. "Rationalism," 756; "Postcoloniality, 22–23.

69. Axelle Kabou, *Et si l'Afrique refusait le développement?* (Paris: L'Harmattan, 1991). For a related argument, see Daniel Etounga Manguelle, *L'Afrique a-t-elle besoin d'un programme d'ajustement culturel?* (Ivry-sur-Seine: Editions Nouvelles du Sud, 1990). This genre is sometimes referred to as Afro-pessimism. Not so pessimistic, but insistent on the necessity of selective modernization is Manthia Diawara, *In Search of Africa* (Cambridge, MA: Harvard University Press, 1998).

70. Kabou, *Et si l'Afrique refusait le développement?* 19, 23, 26, 41, 118. Her critique of the self-serving uses of particularism might be compared with Aihwa Ong's criticism of the "self-orientalizing" ideology of certain ruling elites in Asia, who invoke an Asian way or a Confucian way to insist that they can have capitalist development without democracy or recognition of human rights. Ong in Nonini and Ong, *Ungrounded Empires*, 195.

71. Kabou, *Et si l'Afrique refusait le développement?* 23, 102.

72. Kabou, *Et si l'Afrique refusait le développement?* 205.

73. For arguments contrasting with Chakrabarty and other subalternists, see Rajnarayan Chandavarkar, *Imperial Power and Popular Politics: Class, Resistance and the State in India, c. 1850–1950* (Cambridge: Cambridge Univer-

sity Press, 1998); and Javeed Alam, *India: Living with Modernity* (Delhi: Oxford University Press, 1999); and for the view of a Cameroonian who shares some but not all of Kabou's view of the particularistic strategies of African elites, see Achille Mbembe, *On the Postcolony* (Berkeley: University of California Press, 2001).

74. For the comparison, see Jean Drèze ane Amartya Sen, *India: Economic Development and Social Opportunity* (Delhi: Oxford University Press, 1995).

75. See, for example, Gyanendra Pandey, *The Construction of Communalism in Colonial North India* (Delhi: Oxford University Press, 1990); and Mahmood Mamdani, *Citizen and Subject: Contemporary Africa and the Legacy of Late Colonialism* (Princeton, N.J.: Princeton University Press, 1996).

76. A historical analysis that helped open the debate is Lata Mani, "Contentious Traditions: The Debate on *Sati* in Colonial India," in Kumkum Sangari and Sudesh Vaid, eds., *Recasting Women: Essays in Indian Colonial History* (New Brunswick, NJ: Rutgers University Press, 1999), 88–126.

77. Veena Das, "Communities as Political Actors: The Question of Cultural Rights," in *Critical Events: An Anthropological Perspective on Contemporary India* (Delhi: Oxford University Press, 1995), 84–117, esp. 104–107. Cathi Albertyn and Shireen Hassim, "The Boundaries of Democracy: Gender, HIV/AIDS and Culture," in E. Everatt and V. Maphai, eds., *The Real State of the Nation*, special issue of *Development Update* (Johannesburg: Interfund, 2003). Lynn Thomas describes a telling political argument in Kenya in the late 1960s over the repeal of a law that allowed paternity suits by women in certain circumstances. Proponents of repeal insisted the law reflected a "foreign" notion of women's rights and positioned themselves as defenders of "religious and customary practices," of "African tradition." Thomas sees this as a defense of authoritarian patriarchy and an attempt to banish a debate about women's status that had begun inside Kenya. *Politics of the Womb: Women, Reproduction, and the State in Kenya* (Berkeley: University of California Press, 2003), 158–59.

78. See a new political science literature that stresses networks linking activists across continents, cultural divisions, and communities, for example Sanjeev Khagram, James V. Riker, and Kathryn Sikkink, eds., *Restructuring World Politics: Transnational Social Movements, Networks, and Norms* (Minneapolis: University of Minnesota Press, 2002). To the historical examples of transnational issue networks, such as the antislavery and anticolonial movements, one might add the Tactical Action Campaign, which linked South African and international activists on HIV/AIDS issues in a successful effort to get the South African government to reverse its refusal to make antiretroviral drugs available and to get multinational pharmaceutical companies to change their pricing policies. Here we have the state and international capitalism being forced to do things they did not want to do by border-crossing networks.

79. Sheldon Pollock, "Cosmopolitan and Vernacular in History," *Public Culture* 12 (2000): 625. Pollock is critical of arguments for the rights of collectivities that treat them as givens which "demand unequivocally to be accom-

modated just as they are." Ibid., 622. See also Martha Nussbaum, *Women and Human Development: The Capabilities Approach* (Cambridge: Cambridge University Press, 2000); and Benhabib, *The Claims of Culture.*

80. Aihwa Ong makes a similar criticism of this body of work in *Flexible Citizenship: The Cultural Logics of Transnationality* (Durham, N.C.: Duke University Press, 1999), 34.

81. James C. Scott, *Seeing Like a State: How Certain Schemes to Improve the Human Condition Have Failed* (New Haven, Conn.: Yale University Press, 1998), 4.

82. Scott, *Seeing Like a State,* 89

83. Scott (*Seeing Like a State,* 224) claims to have "stumbled across something generic about the projects of the modern developmentalist state." The sources he draws on often paint a more nuanced picture, for example James Holston's view of the "Brazilianization of Brasília" in his *The Modernist City: An Anthropological Critique of Brasília* (Chicago: University of Chicago Press, 1989), 289–318.

84. For Scott's modernist antimodernism, see his list of maxims, *Seeing Like a State,* 345.

85. Scott, *Seeing Like a State,* 8. On this point, see Fernando Coronil's critique of Scott, "Smelling like a Market," *American Historical Review* 106 (2001): 119–30.

86. Joseph Schumpeter, *Imperialism and Social Classes,* trans. Heinz Norden (New York: A. M. Kelly, 1951).

87. D. Scott, *Refashioning Futures,* 40, 52.

88. Antoinette Burton, "Introduction: The Unfinished Business of Colonial Modernities," in Burton, ed., *Gender, Sexuality and Colonial Modernities* (London: Routledge, 1999), 2; Achille Mbembe, "On the Power of the False," *Public Culture* 14 (2002): 634. For related formulations, see Dirks, "Postcolonialism and Its Discontents," 246; Chatterjee, "Two Poets and Death," 47; Saurabh Dube, "Colonialism, Modernity, Colonial Modernities," *Nepantla: Views from the South* 3, no. 2 (2002): 197–219; and Tani E. Barlow, ed., *Formations of Colonial Modernity in East Asia* (Durham, N.C.: Duke University Press, 1997).

89. The idea that modern people should develop a colonial agenda to suit their age was laid out in 1874 in a long book by Paul Leroy-Beaulieu. By 1908, it had gone through six editions. Despite the support of such leading politicians of the new French Third Republic as Jules Ferry, this position was opposed by Republicans who thought colonization too adventurous or too antidemocratic. Ferry's position got enough support to sustain colonial conquests in Africa and Southeast Asia, but hardly enough to sustain a consistent civilizing mission or even for state support for systematic exploitation of colonies. Some argue that a "colonial party" got its way not because it convinced the public or the elite of the virtues of a national project, but because the majority was indifferent and the colonial party could assemble a coalition with varying and quite particular interests in colonial territories. See Paul Leroy-Beaulieu, *De la colonisation chez les peuples modernes,* 6th ed. (Paris: Félix Alcan, 1908); James R. Lehning,

To Be a Citizen: The Political Culture of the Early French Third Republic (Ithaca, N.Y.: Cornell University Press, 2001), 128–54; and Charles-Robert Ageron, *France Coloniale ou Parti Colonial?* (Paris: Presses Universitaires de France, 1978).

90. Bernard Cohn, *Colonialism and Its Forms of Knowledge: The British in India* (Princeton, N.J.: Princeton University Press, 1996). Sumit Guha, in his study of the Indian census, rejects the idea of a "warm, fuzzy continuum of premodern collective life . . . suddenly and arbitrarily sliced up by colonial modernity," noting that precolonial polities were both divided and able to classify and enumerate their divisions. He sees a great deal of change over time, but not a break. "The Politics of Identity and Enumeration in India c. 1600–1990," *Comparative Studies in Society and History* 45 (2003): 162 quoted.

91. Thomas, *Politics of the Womb*, 110.

92. Megan Vaughan, *Curing Their Ills: Colonial Power and African Illness* (Cambridge: Polity Press, 1991); David Anderson, "Master and Servant in Colonial Kenya, 1895–1939," *Journal of African History* 41 (2000): 459–85. For a nuanced discussion from a colonial perspective of the insights and blind spots in Foucault, see Ann Laura Stoler, *Race and the Education of Desire: Foucault's History of Sexuality and the Colonial Order of Things* (Durham, N.C.: Duke University Press, 1995).

93. Thomas Spear, "Neo-Traditionalism and the Limits of Invention in British Colonial Africa," *Journal of African History* 44 (2003): 3–27.

94. See Thomas Trautmann, *Aryans and British India* (Berkeley: University of California Press, 1997) for an analysis of the shift in British thinking from an orientalizing approach that conceded to India a certain kind of civilizational attainment to a harsher view of Indian backwardness in need of systematic reform.

95. Ranajit Guha's notion of colonialism as "domination without hegemony" is relevant here; he too sees limits to colonial efforts at creating a kind of subject consistent with Europe's own nineteenth-century transformations. I would point to the limits of domination as well as of hegemony, and suggest that colonizing states at times had hegemonic projects. It is preferable to see them in their historical moment and their historical limitations than either to homogenize them into a colonial modernity or to dismiss the notion of hegemony altogether. *Dominance without Hegemony: History and Power in Colonial India* (Cambridge, Mass.: Harvard University Press, 1997). On the ambivalences of British economic and political policy, see David Washbrook, "Law, State and Agrarian Society in Colonial India," *Modern Asian Studies* 15 (1981): 649–721; and C. A. Bayly, *Rulers, Townsmen and Bazaars: Northern Indian Society in the Age of British Expansion, 1770–1870* (Cambridge: Cambridge University Press, 1983). On the state's promotion of community based on local hierarchy, kin-based connections, and the solidarity of the tribe, see David Gilmartin, *Empire and Islam: Punjab and the Making of Pakistan* (Berkeley: University of California Press, 1988).

96. C. A. Bayly, *Empire and Information: Intelligence Gathering and Social Communication in India, 1780–1870* (Cambridge: Cambridge University

Press, 1996), 171. David Cannadine inverts the argument of the colonial modernity school, and inverts its flaws as well. He interprets British imperial strategy as a deep-set tradition of hierarchy, which recognized the affinity of British and Indian notions of status and sought to build a conservative polity based on the manipulation of such affinities. The result is a one-note symphony, and although the note is not false, the result is as flat a portrayal of colonial traditionalism as the other side's portrayal of colonial modernity. *Ornamentalism: How the British Saw Their Empire* (New York: Oxford University Press, 2001).

97. On the limitations of colonial economies, see Frederick Cooper, "Africa and the World Economy," in Cooper et al, *Confronting Historical Paradigms*.

98. Alice Conklin, *A Mission to Civilize: The Republican Idea of Empire in France and West Africa, 1895–1930* (Stanford, Calif.: Stanford University Press, 1997). J. P. Daughton, "Missionaries, Colonialists, and French Identity, 1885–1914 (Indochina, Madagascar, French Polynesia)," Ph.D. diss., University of California, Berkeley, 2002.

99. David Edwards brings out the latter tendency in regard to Afghanistan, where colonial ambitions were reduced to looking for "mad mullahs." The impossibility of actually transforming Afghanistan became the rationale for colonizing it. "Mad Mullahs and Englishmen: Discourse in the Colonial Encounter," *Comparative Studies in Society and History* 31 (1989): 649–70.

100. Frederick Cooper, "Conditions Analogous to Slavery: Imperialism and Free Labor Ideology in Africa," in Cooper, Thomas Holt, and Rebecca Scott, *Beyond Slavery: Explorations of Race, Labor and Citizenship in Postemancipation Societies* (Chapel Hill: University of North Carolina Press, 2000), 107–49.

101. Frederick Cooper, *Decolonization and African Society: The Labor Question in French and British Africa* (Cambridge: Cambridge University Press, 1996).

102. One can resolve the contradiction of modernizing and traditionalizing colonies' strategies, as does John Comaroff, by pointing to the two sides of colonial states, one tending to make modern citizens available to work in modern markets, the others to reify difference. That leaves the two-faced nature of colonialism suspended in timelessness, with no way to analyze the situations in which colonial regimes leaned so sharply in one direction or another. "Governmentality, Materiality, Legality, Modernity: On the Colonial State in Africa," in Deutsch et. al., *African Modernities*, 129.

103. Cooper, *Decolonization and African Society*.

104. Even as modernization theorists in the 1950s and 1960s were spinning their unified visions of global transformation, on-the-ground research was already revealing a more complex picture, evident already in contributions to a UNESCO conference held in 1954 and published in 1956 as *Social Implications of Industrialization and Urbanization in Africa South of the Sahara* (Paris: UNESCO, 1956). The literature on the points raised in the above two paragraphs is now very large, but fine examples of how Africans reconfigured processes of social change include Meredith McKittrick, *To Dwell Secure: Generation, Christianity, and Colonialism in Ovamboland* (Portsmouth, NH:

Heinemann, 2002); J. D. Y. Peel, *Religious Encounter and the Making of the Yoruba* (Bloomington: Indiana University Press, 2000); Berry, *Fathers Work for Their Sons*; Lindsay, *Working with Gender*; and Vukile Khumalo, "Epistolary Networks and the Politics of Cultural Production in KwaZulu/Natal, 1860–1910," Ph.D. diss., University of Michigan, 2004.

105. Transcript of interview, Jan. 15, 1946, between representatives of the Union des Syndicats of Saint-Louis, and the director of personnel and the director of finance of the Government General, K 405 (132), Archives du Sénégal.

106. Related to the critique of modernity is the critique of development, an argument that also misses the importance of the development concept in claim-making. See Frederick Cooper and Randall Packard, "Introduction," in *International Development and the Social Sciences: Essays in the History and Politcs of Knowledge* (Berkeley: University of California Press, 1997).

107. Comaroff, "Governmentality, Materiality. . . . ," in Deutsch et al., *African Modernities*, 130 n.40.

108. Michael E. Latham, *Modernization as Ideology: American Social Science and "Nation Building" in the Kennedy Era* (Chapel Hill: University of North Carolina Press, 2000).

109. Simon Gikandi, "Reason, Modernity and the African Crisis," in Deutsch et al., *African Modernities*, 141, 143; Amos Tutuola, *The Palm-Wine Drinkard* (New York: Grove Press, 1953).

6. STATES, EMPIRES, AND POLITICAL IMAGINATION

1. Speech at Bayeux, June 16, 1946, reprinted in Comité National chargé de la publication des travaux préparatoires des institutions de la Ve République, *Documents pour servir à l'élaboration de la constitution du 4 octobre 1958* (Paris: Documentation Française, 1987), 1: 3–7.

2. I owe this phrase to Jane Burbank. See Jane Burbank and Mark von Hagen, eds., *Geographies of Empire* (Bloomington: Indiana University Press, forthcoming).

3. Recent studies include Anthony Pagden, *Peoples and Empires: A Short History of European Migration, Exploration, and Conquest from Greece to the Present* (New York: Modern Library, 2001); David Abernethy, *The Dynamics of Global Dominance: European Overseas Empires, 1415–1980* (New Haven, Conn.: Yale University Press, 2000); Dominic Lieven, *Empire: The Russian Empire and Its Rivals* (London: Murray, 2000); Wm. Roger Louis, ed., *The Oxford History of the British Empire* (Oxford: Oxford University Press, 1998).

4. David Bell, *The Cult of the Nation in France: Inventing Nationalism, 1680–1800* (Cambridge, Mass.: Harvard University Press, 2001).

5. Benedict Anderson, *Imagined Communities: Reflections on the Origin and Spread of Nationalism* (London: Verso, 1983). Critiques of Anderson include Partha Chatterjee, *The Nation and Its Fragments* (Princeton, N.J.: Princeton University Press, 1993); Manu Goswami, "Rethinking the Modular Nation Form: Toward a Sociohistorical Conception of Nationalism," *Comparative*

Studies in Society and History 44 (2002): 770–99; and John Kelly and Martha Kaplan, *Represented Communities: Fiji and World Decolonization* (Chicago: University of Chicago Press, 2001), ch. 1.

6. This coexistence of nonequivalent political entities, sometimes with overlapping authority over certain territories, is the problem with a large political science literature on sovereignty. Of such analyses, Stephen Krasner's is the most explicit about "alternatives to states" that have always existed (from the Holy Roman Empire to the British Commonwealth, the French Community, and the post-Soviet Commonwealth of Independent States), and to the routine acceptance of violations of norms of sovereignty. Thinking through the place of empires in history might lead one to further blur the line between normative and hypocritical behavior to examine the shifting units in which sovereignty was claimed, exercised, and contested. *Sovereignty: Organized Hypocrisy* (Princeton, N.J.: Princeton University Press, 1999), 228. See also Hendrik Spruyt, *The Sovereign State and Its Competitors* (Princeton, N.J.: Princeton University Press, 1994).

7. Michael Doyle's contention that an "imperial government is a sovereignty that lacks a community" is valid only if community requires homogeneity. Imperial communities—in the French, Ottoman, or Habsburg empires—were not coterminous with a single society but could still entail a strong sense of belonging among part of their populations. *Empires* (Ithaca, N.Y.: Cornell University Press, 1986), 36.

8. Jack Snyder, *Myths of Empire: Domestic Politics and International Ambition* (Ithaca, N.Y.: Cornell University Press, 1991).

9. For the examples of state terror in the 1920s, see David E. Omissi, *Air Power and Colonial Control: The Royal Air Force 1919–1939* (Manchester: Manchester University Press, 1990); Sebastian Balfour, *Deadly Embrace: Morocco and the Road to the Spanish Civil War* (Oxford: Oxford University Press, 2002), ch.5.

10. C. A. Bayly, *Imperial Meridian: The British Empire and the World 1780–1830* (Harrow, Eng.: Longman, 1989); Jean Tulard, "L'empire napoléonien," in Maurice Duverger, ed., *Le concept d'empire* (Paris: Presses Universitaires de France, 1980), 294.

11. Rome was not the first universal empire. Alexander the Great aspired not only to conquer the once powerful Persian empire or to use conquered people to serve the Greeks, but to be, as Plutarch later put it, the "conciliator and arbitrator of the Universe," to end the tension between Asia and Europe. See Pagden, *Peoples and Empires*, 13.

12. Greg Woolf, "Inventing Empire in Ancient Rome," in Susan E. Alcock, Terence N. D'Altroy, Kathleen D. Morrison, and Carla M. Sinopoli, eds., *Empires: Perspectives from Archeology and History* (Cambridge: Cambridge University Press, 2001), 316.

13. Gary B. Miles, "Roman and Modern Imperialism: A Reassessment," *Comparative Studies in Society and History* 32 (1990): 629–59.

14. J. G. A. Pocock, "The Ideal of Citizenship since Classical Times," in Ronald Beiner, ed., *Theorizing Citizenship* (Albany: SUNY Press, 1995), 36.

15. Miles, "Roman and Modern Imperialism," 653; S. E. Alcock, "Greece: A Landscape of Resistance?" in D. J. Mattingly, ed., *Dialogues in Roman Imperialism: Power, Discourse, and Discrepant Experience in the Roman Empire* (Portsmouth, R.I. : JRA, 1997), 103–15; Horace quoted in Susan E. Alcock, "The Reconfiguration of Memory in the Eastern Roman Empire," in Alcock, *Empires*, 329; Greg Woolf, "Beyond Romans and Natives," *World Archaeology* 28 (1997): 339–50. See also Peter Garnsey and Richard Saller, *The Roman Empire: Economy, Society and Culture* (Berkeley: University of California Press, 1987).

16. Miles, "Roman and Modern Imperialism," 630.

17. Joseph Fletcher, "The Mongols, Ecological and Social Perspectives," *Harvard Journal of Asiatic Studies* 46 (1986): 11–51; Beatrice Forbes Manz, *The Rise and Rule of Tamerlane* (Cambridge: Cambridge University Press, 1989); Thomas Allsen, *Culture and Conquest in Mongol Eurasia* (Cambridge: Cambridge University Press, 2001).

18. Cemal Kafadar, *Between Two Worlds: The Construction of the Ottoman State* (Berkeley: University of California Press, 1995), 153.

19. Donald Ostrowski, *Muscovy and the Mongols: Cross-Cultural Influences on the Steppe Frontier, 1304–1589* (Cambridge: Cambridge University Press, 1998).

20. Mark Elliott, *The Manchu Way: The Eight Banners and Ethnic Identity in Late Imperial China* (Stanford, Calif.: Stanford University Press, 2001); Peter Perdue, "Comparing Empires: Manchu Colonialism," and "Boundaries, Maps, and Movement: Chinese, Russian, and Mongolian Empires in Early Modern Central Eurasia," *International History Review* 20 (1998): 253–86; Kären Wigen, "Culture, Power and Place: The New Landscapes of East Asian Regionalism," *American Historical Review* 104 (1999): 1183–1201; Rebecca Karl, *Staging the World: Chinese Nationalism at the Turn of the Twentieth Century* (Durham, N.C.: Duke University Press, 2002).

21. R. Bin Wong, "Two Kinds of Nation, What Kind of State?" in Timothy Brook and Andre Schmid, *Nation Work: Asian Elites and National Identities* (Ann Arbor: University of Michigan Press, 2000), 112; R. Bin Wong, *China Transformed: Historical Change and the Limits of European Experience* (Ithaca, N.Y.: Cornell University Press, 1997).

22. On the non-national character of early modern empires, see J. H. Elliott, "A Europe of Composite Monarchies," *Past and Present* 137 (1992), esp. 56–59.

23. David Armitage, "Introduction," in Armitage, ed., *Theories of Empire 1450–1800* (Aldershot, Eng.: Ashgate, 1998), xviii; Henry Kamen, *Empire: How Spain Became a World Power, 1492–1763* (New York: HarperCollins, 2003), 50.

24. Pagden, *Peoples and Empires*, 43–44; Thomas A. Brady, Jr., "The Rise of Merchant Empires, 1400–1700: A European Counterpoint," in James D. Tracy, ed., *The Political Economy of Merchant Empires: State Power and World Trade 1350–1750* (Cambridge: Cambridge University Press, 1991), 130; J. H. Elliott, "Empire and State in British and Spanish America," and David Brading, "The Catholic Monarchy," in Serge Gruzinski and Nathan Wachtel, eds., *Le nouveau monde, mondes nouveaux: L'expérience américaine* (Paris: Editions Recherche

sur les Civilisations and Editions de l'Ecole des Hautes Etudes en Sciences Sociales, 1996), 365–405.

25. Kamen, *Empire*, 5, 13–22, 53–57, 63, 112, 122, 268, 351, 423; John Jay TePaske, "Integral to Empire: The Vital Peripheries of Colonial Spanish America," in Christine Daniels and Michael V. Kennedy, eds., *Negotiated Empires: Centers and Peripheries in the Americas, 1500–1820* (London: Routledge, 2002), 33–34.

26. Anthony Pagden, *Spanish Imperialism and the Political Imagination: Studies in European and Spanish-American Social and Political Theory 1513–1830* (New Haven, Conn.: Yale University Press, 1990), 1–36, 117–53; A. J. R Russell-Wood, "Introduction," in Russell-Wood, ed., *Government and Governance of European Empires, 1450–1800, Part I* (Aldershot, Eng.: Ashgate, 2000), xix–lxxxiii.

27. An interesting take on this issue comes from a historian of Rome turned specialist on the Andes, Sabine MacCormack, *Religion in the Andes: Vision and Imagination in Early Colonial Peru* (Princeton, N.J.: Princeton University Press, 1991). See also Serge Gruzinski, *La colonisation de l'imaginaire: Sociétés indigènes et occidentalisation dans le Mexique espagnol XVIᵉ-XVIIIᵉ siècle* (Paris: Gallimard, 1988); and Vicente Rafael, *Contracting Colonialism: Translation and Christian Conversion in Tagalog Society under Early Spanish Rule* (Ithaca, N.Y.: Cornell University Press, 1988).

28. Russell-Wood, *Government and Governance*, lxxiv; Sanjay Subrahmanyam, "Written on Water: Designs and Dynamics in the Portuguese *Estado da India*," in Alcock, *Empires*, 42–69.

29. Sanjay Subrahmanyam, *The Portuguese Empire in Asia, 1500–1700: A Political and Economic History* (London: Longman, 1993), 122–24, 132.

30. The indigenous origins of the colonial Indian economy are emphasized in C. A. Bayly, *Rulers, Townsmen and Bazaars: Northern Indian Society in the Age of British Expansion, 1770–1870* (Cambridge: Cambridge University Press, 1983); on exile and imperial construction, see Kerry Ward, " 'The bounds of bondage': Forced Migration from Batavia to the Cape of Good Hope during the Dutch East India Company Era, c.1652—1795 (South Africa, Indonesia)," Ph.D. diss., University of Michigan, 2002.

31. Sanjay Subrahmanyam and Luís Filipe F. R. Thomaz, "Evolution of Empire: The Portuguese in the Indian Ocean during the Sixteenth Century," in Tracy, *The Political Economy of Merchant Empires*, 298–331.

32. The military disparity is emphasized by Geoffrey Parker, who is nonetheless careful (179) not to overestimate the extent of conquering ambition. "Europe and the Wider World, 1500–1700: The Military Balance," in Tracy, *Merchant Empires*, 161–95.

33. On the last point, see Julia Adams, "Principals and Agents, Colonialists and Company Men: The Decay of Colonial Control in the Dutch East Indies," *American Sociological Review* 61, no. 1 (1996): 12–28.

34. Michael H. Fisher, "Indirect Rule in the British Empire: The Foundations of the Residency System in India (1764–1858)," *Modern Asian Studies* 18 (1984): 393–428.

35. John Darwin, "Imperialism and the Victorians: The Dynamics of Territorial Expansion," *English Historical Review* 112 (1997): 614–42.

36. Anderson emphasizes the growth of "deep, horizontal comradeship" among creoles and underestimates the vertical tensions. He notes that creole elites thought they could handle peasants and slaves more knowledgeably than metropolitan officials, but he is so convinced of the inherent power of horizontal affinity that he insists that slavery and serfdom in the Americas "*had* to go." That passes over a painful, and quite long, history. *Imagined Communities,* 16, 51, 79.

37. This argument owes much to papers presented at New York University by Jeremy Adelman based on his forthcoming book, *Struggle for Sovereignty: Empire and Revolution in the Iberian Atlantic.* See also Timothy E. Anna, "Spain and the Breakdown of the Imperial Ethos: The Problem of Equality," *Hispanic American Historical Review* 62 (1982): 254–72; Jaime E. Rodríguez, *The Independence of Spanish America* (Cambridge: Cambridge University Press, 1998); and John Lynch, ed., *Latin American Revolutions 1808–1826: Old and New World Origins* (Norman: University of Oklahoma Press, 1994); Christopher Schmidt-Nowara, *The Conquest of History: Spanish Colonialism and National Histories in the Nineteenth Century* (Pittsburgh: University of Pittsburgh Press, forthcoming).

38. Alan Forrest, *Conscripts and Deserters: The Army and French Society during the Revolution and Empire* (New York: Oxford University Press, 1989); Alan Forrest, *Napoleon's Men: The Soldiers of the Revolution and Empire* (London: Hambledon and London, 2002); Isser Woloch, *The New Regime: Transformations of the French Civic Order, 1789–1820s* (New York: Norton, 1994).

39. Michael Broers, "Napoleon, Charlemagne, and Lotharingia: Acculturation and the Boundaries of Napoleonic Europe," *Historical Journal* 44 (2001): 136; Michael Broers, "Europe under Napoleon," Conference on "Empires in Modern Times," Institut des Hautes Etudes Internationales, Geneva, March 2003.

40. Pagden, *People and Empires,* 136.

41. Michael Broers, "Cultural Imperialism in a European Context?: Political Culture and Cultural Politics in Napoleonic Italy," *Past and Present* 170 (2001): 152–80.

42. Broers, "Europe under Napoleon." On Napoleon's conception of rural France as itself an object of, in effect, ethnographic observation, see Marie-Noëlle Bourguet, *Déchiffrer la France: La statistique départementale à l'époque napoléonienne* (Paris: Editions des archives contemporaines, 1988).

43. Stuart Woolf, *Napoleon's Integration of Europe* (London: Routledge, 1991), 17, 20, 27, 43, 178–81.

44. Ibid., 129.

45. Laurent Dubois, " 'The Price of Liberty': Victor Hugues and the Administration of Freedom in Guadeloupe, 1794–1798," *William and Mary Quarterly* 56, no. 2 (April 1999): 363–92; idem, *Les esclaves de la République:*

L'histoire oubliée de la première émancipation 1789–1794 (Paris: Calmann-Lévy, 1998).

46. Woolf, *Napoleon's Integration of Europe*, 226–37.

47. Biancamaria Fontana, "The Napoleonic Empire and the Europe of Nations," in Anthony Pagden, ed., *The Idea of Europe: From Antiquity to the European Union* (Cambridge: Cambridge University Press, 2002), 124–27.

48. Dominic Lieven, "Empire's Place in International Relations," Conference on "Empires in Modern Times," Institut des Hautes Etudes Internationales, Geneva, March 2003.

49. Juan R. Cole, "Empires of Liberty? Democracy and Conquest in French Egypt, British Egypt, and American Iraq," in Craig Calhoun, Frederick Cooper, and Kevin Moore, eds., *Lessons of Empire* (New York: New Press, forthcoming). See also Henri Laurens, *L'expédition d'Egypte 1798–1801* (Paris: Colin, 1989). On Haiti, the classic account remains C. L. R. James, *The Black Jacobins* (New York: Vintage, 1963 [1938]).

50. Quoted in Jon Kukla, *A Wilderness So Immense: The Louisiana Purchase and the Destiny of America* (New York: Knopf, 2003), 249.

51. Among the best of these are Alice Conklin, *A Mission to Civilize: The Republican Idea of Empire in France and West Africa, 1895–1930* (Stanford, Calif.: Stanford University Press, 1997); and Catherine Hall, *Civilising Subjects: Metropole and Colony in the English Imagination 1830–1867* (Chicago: University of Chicago Press, 2002).

52. Niall Ferguson, *Empire: The Rise and Demise of the British World Order and the Lessons for Global Power* (London: Allan Lane, 2002).

53. Stephen Howe, *Anticolonialism in British Politics: The Left and the End of Empire, 1918–1964* (Oxford: Clarendon Press, 1993).

54. David Armitage, *The Ideological Origins of the British Empire* (Cambridge: Cambridge University Press, 2000), 8–23, 23 quoted. See also Linda Colley, *Britons: Forging the Nation, 1707–1837* (New Haven, Conn.: Yale University Press, 1992); and Bayly, *Imperial Meridian.*

55. Among the most influential works on the construction of barriers and hierarchy in terms of race and gender is that of Ann Stoler, *Carnal Knowledge and Imperial Power: Race and the Intimate in Colonial Rule* (Berkeley: University of California Press, 2002).

56. Lauren Benton, *Law and Colonial Cultures: Legal Regimes in World History, 1400–1900* (Cambridge: Cambridge University Press, 2002), esp. 257–59. See also Emmanuelle Saada, "The Empire of Law: Dignity, Prestige, and Domination in the 'Colonial Situation,' " *French Politics, Culture, and Society* 20 (2002): 47–76.

57. Laurent Dubois, *Avengers of the New World: The Story of the Haitian Revolution* (Cambridge: Harvard University Press, 2004), 4.

58. James, *Black Jacobins*; Michel-Rolph Trouillot, *Silencing the Past: Power and the Production of History* (Boston: Beacon, 1995); David Barry Gaspar and David Patrick Geggus, eds., *A Turbulent Time: The French Revolution and the Greater Caribbean* (Bloomington: Indiana University Press, 1997).

59. Benjamin Stora, "The 'Southern' World of the *Pieds-noirs*," paper for conference on "Settler Colonialism in the Twentieth Century," Harvard University, October 2002; John Ruedy, *Modern Algeria: The Origins and Development of a Nation* (Bloomington: Indiana University Press, 1992).

60. Conklin, *Mission to Civilize*; Ruth H. L. Dickens, "Defining French Citizenship Policy in West Africa, 1895–1956," Ph.D. diss., Emory University, 2001; Mamadou Diouf, "The French Colonial Policy of Assimilation and the Civility of the Originaires of the Four Communes (Senegal): A Nineteenth Century Globalization Project," *Development and Change* 29 (1998): 671–96.

61. For a stimulating discussion of how the imperial citizenship notion played out in regard to racially mixed categories in the colonies, see Emmanuelle Saada, "La 'question des métis' dans les colonies françaises: Sociohistoire d'une catégorie juridique (Indochine et autres territories de l'Empire français; années 1890–années 1950)," doctoral thesis, Ecole des Hautes Etudes en Sciences Sociales, 2001.

62. Eugen Weber, *Peasants into Frenchmen: The Modernization of Rural France, 1870–1914* (Stanford, Calif.: Stanford University Press, 1976); Conklin, *Mission to Civilize*.

63. The 1931 Colonial Exposition developed the theme of France presiding over a mixture of cultures whose integrity it guaranteed. This was highly contested by colonial students and others in Paris. See Herman Lebovics, *True France: The Wars over Cultural Identity, 1900–1945* (Ithaca, N.Y.: Cornell University Press, 1992).

64. The ups and downs may be traced in Conklin, *A Mission to Civilize*. For another example of partial openings and partial closures in citizenship discourse, see Elizabeth Thompson, *Colonial Citizens: Republican Rights, Paternal Privilege, and Gender in French Syria and Lebanon* (New York: Columbia University Press, 2000).

65. See the *Journal Officiel* of the Assemblée Nationale Constituante, April–May, August–September 1946, for exhaustive discussions on the constitution.

66. Frederick Cooper, *Decolonization and African Society: The Labor Question in French and British Africa* (Cambridge: Cambridge University Press, 1996); Matthew Connelly, *A Diplomatic Revolution: Algeria's Fight for Independence and the Origins of the Post-Cold War Era* (New York: Oxford University Press, 2002). Léopold Senghor of Senegal advocated turning empire into federalism, but French officials hijacked his idea into a process of "territorialization" that devolved real power to individual colonies but undercut possibilities of politics across the federation—or the posing of demands on metropolitan resources. See chapter 7.

67. In the British Empire, government was more decentralized and citizenship unspecified: all were subjects of the king or queen. But even that notion had a durable sentimental appeal reinforced by low barriers to entry into the British Isles for subjects. David Gorman argues that the impetus for a restrictive view came from the dominions, where sentiments of territorial solidarity

and cultural and racial exclusiveness were most acute. However, after the crucial role that Commonwealth troops played in World War II, the British government passed a nationalities act that defined broad rights of people from the colonies and dominions to enter the United Kingdom and to have privileged access to British nationality. See Daniel Gorman, "Wider and Wider Still? Racial Politics, Intra-imperial Immigration and the Absence of an Imperial Citizenship in the British Empire," *Journal of Colonialism and Colonial History* 3, no. 3 (2002), on the web at muse.jhu.edu/journals; and Kathleen Paul, *Whitewashing Britain: Race and Citizenship in the Postwar Era* (Ithaca, N.Y.: Cornell University Press, 1997).

68. Albert Hirschman, *The Passions and the Interests: Political Arguments for Capitalism before Its Triumph* (Princeton, N.J.: Princeton University Press, 1977). The classic exploitation argument is V. I. Lenin, *Imperialism: The Highest Stage of Capitalism* (London: Pluto, 1996 [1916]), while the assertion that the British empire opened global markets has most recently been propounded by Ferguson, *Empire*.

69. The pioneer study of the Atlantic origins of capitalism is Eric Williams, *Capitalism and Slavery* (Chapel Hill: University of North Carolina Press, 1944). Many of Williams's specific arguments have been effectively criticized, but his weaving together of slavery and capitalism, of the domestic economy of Great Britain and the Atlantic world, in and between empires, remains a powerful framework.

70. Sidney Mintz, *Sweetness and Power: The Place of Sugar in Modern History* (New York: Penguin, 1985).

71. Kenneth Pomeranz, *The Great Divergence: Europe, China, and the Making of the Modern World Economy* (Princeton, N.J.: Princeton University Press, 2000). On these complicated issues, see the forum "Asia and Europe in the World Economy," in the *American Historical Review* 107 (2002): 419–80, with contributions by Patrick Manning, Kenneth Pomeranz, R. Bin Wong, and David Ludden.

72. Thomas Brady makes too neat a separation in setting forth the "two faces of Europe's empire-builders: plunderers, slavers, and extortioners abroad; prudent law-abiding businessmen at home" ("The Rise of Merchant Empires, 1400–1700: A European Counterpoint," in Tracy, *Merchant Empires,* 160). Capitalist development was brutal at home too, and the rule of law was an instrument of accumulation and consolidation overseas. See Benton, *Law and Colonial Cultures.*

73. Jack Greene, "Transatlantic Colonization and the Redefinition of Empire in the Early Modern Era: The British-American Experience," in Daniels and Kennedy, *Negotiated Empires,* 267–82.

74. Eliga Gould, *The Persistence of Empire: British Political Culture in the Age of the American Revolution* (Chapel Hill: University of North Carolina Press, 2000), 199, 208.

75. Gould, *The Persistence of Empire,* 210–13; Bayly, *Imperial Meridian,* 136–63.

76. Ronald Robinson and John Gallagher, "The Imperialism of Free Trade," *Economic History Review,* n.s., 6 (1953): 1–15.

77. P. J. Cain and A. G. Hopkins, *British Imperialism, 1688–2000,* 2d ed. (Harlow, Eng.: Longman, 2002).

78. David Washbrook, "Law, State and Agrarian Society in Colonial India," *Modern Asian Studies* 15 (1981): 649–721. British imperialism was cost-conscious, fearing the effects of military burdens on the domestic taxpayer and domestic economy, and conscious as well of differing opinions within the political elite about how aggressive to be overseas, resulting in a coalition politics that restrained imperial ambition. Snyder, *Myths of Empire,* ch. 5.

79. Seymour Drescher, *Econocide: British Slavery in the Era of Abolition* (Pittsburgh: University of Pittsburgh Press, 1977).

80. David Brion Davis, *The Problem of Slavery in the Age of Revolution, 1770–1803* (Ithaca, N.Y.: Cornell University Press, 1975); Seymour Drescher, *Capitalism and Antislavery: British Mobilization in Comparative Perspective* (New York: Oxford University Press, 1987). Early critics of slavery specific drew on the notion of the slave as an imperial subject who could not simply be treated as chattel. Christopher L. Brown, "Empire without Slaves: British Concepts of Emancipation in the Age of the American Revolution," *William and Mary Quarterly* 56 (1999): 273–306.

81. Thomas Holt, *The Problem of Freedom: Race, Labor and Politics in Jamaica and Britain, 1832–1938* (Baltimore, Md.: Johns Hopkins University Press, 1992); Hall, *Civilising Subjects.*

82. Sankar Muthu, *Enlightenment against Empire* (Princeton, N.J. Princeton University Press, 2003).

83. Mary Kingsley was a leading advocate of this point of view in the late nineteenth century, and as Mary Louise Pratt writes, she was able to "locate herself within the project of empire" while opposing "domination and exploitation." *Imperial Eyes: Travel Writing and Transculturation* (London: Routledge, 1992), 215. Pratt also makes clear the importance of gender in Kingsley's argument against masculine visions of domination and possession.

84. A useful survey of varying opinions and arguments is Paul Rich, *Race and Empire in British Politics* (Cambridge: Cambridge University Press, 1986). Racist anti-imperialism is part of the story told by Christopher Schmidt-Nowara, *Empire and Antislavery: Spain, Cuba, and Puerto Rico, 1833–1874* (Pittsburgh: University of Pittsburgh Press, 1999). For two recent studies of the debates about science and race in France, see Emmanuelle Saada, "Race and Sociological Reason in the Republic: Inquiries on the Métis in the French Empire (1908–37)," *International Sociology* 17 (2002): 361–91; and Alice Conklin, "Civil Society, Science, and Empire in Late Republican France: The Foundation of Paris's Museum of Man," *Osiris* 17 (2002): 255–90.

85. West African intellectuals of the late nineteenth century, like Africanus Horton, opened an argument that Africans could be different without being inferior. Pan-African congresses beginning in 1900 shaped an antiracist agenda, while Jomo Kenyatta in London or Léopold Senghor and Aimé Césaire in Paris defended both equality and difference in the 1930s.

86. Ronald Robinson, "Non-European Foundations of European Imperialism: Sketch for a Theory of Collaboration," in Roger Owen and Bob Sutcliffe, eds, *Studies in the Theory of Imperialism* (London: Longman, 1972), 117–42; Ronald Robinson and John Gallagher, *Africa and the Victorians: The Official Mind of Imperialism* (New York: St. Martin's Press, 1961).

87. Cain and Hopkins, *British Imperialism*; Charles-Robert Ageron, *France coloniale ou parti colonial?* (Paris: Presses Universitaires de France, 1978).

88. Darwin, "Imperialism and the Victorians."

89. Some scholars are skeptical of the extent to which British power in the nineteenth century was hegemonic. See Patrick Karl O'Brien and Armand Clesse, eds., *Two Hegemonies: Britain 1846–1914 and the United States 1941–2001* (London: Ashgate, 2003).

90. The key figure at the time in arguing for a national strategy to enable Germany to catch up was Friedrich List. See Roman Szporluk, *Communism and Nationalism: Karl Marx versus Friedrich List* (New York: Oxford University Press, 1988).

91. Philipp Ther, "Imperial Instead of National History: Positioning Modern German History on the Map of European Empires," paper for the conference "History of Empires: Comparative Approaches to Research and Teaching," Open Society Institute, Moscow, June 2003. On anti-Polish racism, see Robert Nelson, " 'Unsere Frage ist der Osten': Representations of the Occupied East in German Soldier Newspapers, 1914–1918," *Zeitschrift für Ostmitteleuropa-Forschung* 51 (2002): 276–303, while George Steinmetz argues that rather than there being an essentially German form of racism, different stances emerged in different situations. See " 'The Devil's Handwriting': Precolonial Discourse, Ethnographic Acuity, and Cross-Identification in German Colonialism," *Comparative Studies in Society and History* 45 (2003): 41–95.

92. Louise Young, *Japan's Total Empire: Manchuria and the Culture of Wartime Imperialism* (Berkeley: University of California Press, 1998), stresses how the Japanese government in the 1920s and 1930s used empire-building to shape a totalizing vision of a Japanese project. Y. Tak Matsusaka, "The Japanese Hegemony in East Asia, 1895–1945," paper for conference on "Empires in Modern Times," Geneva, March 2003, brings out the on-the-ground complexities of controlling imperial space in Asia. See also Robert Eskildsen, "Of Civilization and Savages: The Mimetic Imperialism of Japan's 1874 Expedition to Taiwan," *American Historical Review* 107 (2002): 388–418.

93. John Iliffe, *Tanganyika under German Rule, 1905–1912* (Cambridge: Cambridge University Press, 1969).

94. This interruption in Germany's imperial career, its being forcibly shrunk into nation-state status, is misunderstood in arguments that lead directly from the racialized brutality of colonization to the racialized brutality of Nazi Germany. In placing such a trajectory in the context of totalitarianism, Hannah Arendt, in her pioneering and often insightful treatment of these themes, fails to appreciate the limits of colonial power, limits not faced by rulers with imaginary colonies. See *Imperialism,* in *The Origins of Totalitarianism*

(New York: Harcourt Brace, 1973 [1951]). See also Lora Wildenthal, "Notes on a History of 'Imperial Turns' in Modern Germany," in Antoinette Burton, ed., *After the Imperial Turn: Thinking With and Through the Nation* (Durham, NC: Duke University Press, 2003), 144–56.

95. John Lonsdale and Bruce Berman, "Coping with the Contradictions: The Development of the Colonial State in Kenya." *Journal of African History* 20 (1979): 487–506; Sara Berry, "Hegemony on a Shoestring: Indirect Rule and Access to Agricultural Land," *Africa* 62 (1992): 327–55; A. E. Afigbo, *the Warrant Chiefs: Indirect Rule in Southeastern Nigeria, 1891–1929* (London: Longman, 1972); Charles Ambler, *Kenyan Communities in the Age of Imperialism: The Central Region in the Late Nineteenth Century* (New Haven, Conn.: Yale University Press, 1988).

96. This position has been argued strongly by Mahmood Mamdani, too strongly perhaps. He rightly points to colonial policies aimed at creating "decentralized despotisms" through which they could rule, but underestimates the extent of crosscutting connections and misses the importance of mobilization around notions of citizenship in the final crisis of colonial rule. *Citizen and Subject: Contemporary Africa and the Legacy of Late Colonialism* (Princeton, N.J.: Princeton University Press, 1996). See also Leroy Vail, ed., *The Creation of Tribalism in Southern Africa* (Berkeley: University of California Press, 1989).

97. Martin Chanock, *Law, Custom and Social Order: The Colonial Experience in Malawi and Zambia* (Cambridge: Cambridge University Press, 1985); Jean Comaroff and John Comaroff, *From Revelation to Revolution*, 2 vols. (Chicago: University of Chicago Press, 1991, 1997); Karen Hansen, ed., *African Encounters with Domesticity* (New Brunswick, NJ: Rutgers University Press, 1992).

98. Lora Wildenthal, *German Women for Empire, 1884–1945* (Durham, N.C.: Duke University Press, 2001). Good starting points for studies of gender and empire are Stoler, *Carnal Knowledge*; Julia Clancy-Smith and Frances Gouda, eds., *Domesticating the Empire: Race, Gender, and Family Life in French and Dutch Colonialism* (Charlottesville: University Press of Virginia, 1998); special issue on "Gendered Colonialism in African History," *Gender and History* 8, no. 3 (1996); Pamela Scully, *Liberating the Family? Gender and British Slave Emancipation in the Rural Western Cape, South Africa, 1823–53* (Portsmouth, NH: Heinemann, 1997); Mrinalini Sinha, *Colonial Masculinity: The 'Manly' Englishman and the 'Effeminate Bengali' in the Late Nineteenth Century* (Manchester: Manchester University Press, 1995).

99. Luise White, *The Comforts of Home: Prostitution in Colonial Nairobi* (Chicago: University of Chicago Press, 1990); Lisa Lindsay, *Working with Gender: Wage Labor and Social Change in Southwestern Nigeria* (Portsmouth, NH: Heinemann, 2003); Aili Mari Tripp, *Changing the Rules: The Politics of Liberalization and the Urban Informal Economy in Tanzania* (Berkeley: University of California Press, 1997).

100. The most recent scholarship in African history is putting less emphasis on the imposition of roles by missionaries, teachers, and medical personnel

than on how people in the middle of colonizer/colonized relationships refashioned and contested such categories. See Nancy Hunt, *A Colonial Lexicon: Of Birth Ritual, Medicalization, and Mobility in the Congo* (Durham, N.C.: Duke University Press, 1999); Meredith McKittrick, *To Dwell Secure: Generation, Christianity, and Colonialism in Ovamboland* (Portsmouth, NH: Heinemann, 2002); Carol Summers, *Colonial Lessons: Africans' Education in Southern Rhodesia, 1918–1940* (Portsmouth, NH: Heinemann, 2002).

101. For the beginnings of a history of late colonial policing, see David M. Anderson and David Killingray, eds., *Policing and Decolonisation: Politics, Nationalism and the Police, 1917–65* (Manchester: Manchester University Press, 1992); and on the continued use of penal sanctions, Cooper, *Decolonization and African Society*, 367–68.

102. Ferguson, *Empire*, 301–303.

103. A large literature now brings out the overriding themes and important variations in different parts of Africa, but the overall argument is spelled out in Frederick Cooper, "Africa and the World Economy," in Cooper et al., *Confronting Historical Paradigms: Peasants, Labor, and the Capitalist World System in Africa and Latin America* (Madison: University of Wisconsin Press, 1993). On agrarian property relations, see Sara Berry, *No Condition Is Permanent: The Social Dynamics of Agrarian Change in Sub-Saharan Africa* (Madison: University of Wisconsin Press, 1993).

104. S. Herbert Frankel, *Capital Investment in Africa: Its Course and Effects* (London: Oxford University Press, 1938). On French and British investors' ambivalence about colonial investments, see Cain and Hopkins, *British Imperialism*; and Jacques Marseille, *Empire colonial et capitalisme français: Histoire d'un divorce* (Paris: Albin Michel, 1984).

105. Moses Ochonu, "A Colony in Crisis: Northern Nigeria, British Colonialism, and the Great Depression," Ph.D. diss., University of Michigan, 2004; Sugata Bose, "Instruments and Idioms of Colonial and National Development: India's Historical Experience in Comparative Perspective," and Frederick Cooper, "Modernizing Bureaucrats, Backward Africans, and the Development Concept," in Frederick Cooper and Randall Packard, eds., *International Development and the Social Sciences: Essays on the History and Politics of Knowledge* (Berkeley: University of California Press, 1997), 45–92.

106. The anxieties raised by this model of the late 1940s may help explain the predominance of negotiated decolonizations of the 1950s and 1960s. Of one hundred countries that became independent after World War II, sustained military uprisings were a factor in fewer than a dozen. David Abernethy, *The Dynamics of Global Dominance: European Overseas Empires 1415–1980* (New Haven, Conn.: Yale University Press, 2000), 147.

107. Clive Christie, *A Modern History of Southeast Asia: Decolonization, Nationalism and Separatism* (London: Tauris, 1996); Marc Frey, Ronald Preussen, and Tan Tai Yong, eds., *The Transformation of Southeast Asia: International Perspectives on Decolonization* (London: M. E. Sharpe, 2003); Pierre Brocheux and Daniel Hémery, *Indochine: La colonisation ambiguë, 1858–1954* (Paris: Editions La Découverte, 1995); David Marr, *Vietnam 1945: The Quest*

for Power (Berkeley: University of California Press, 1995); Sugata Bose and Ayesha Jalal, *Modern South Asia: History, Culture, Political Economy* (London: Routledge, 1998), 107–200.

108. The first type of explanation is the more typical (as in works of Cain and Hopkins, Ferguson, and Marseille cited above), but for the beginning of an explanation focused on the tensions of actually transforming Africa, see Cooper, *Decolonization and African Society*.

109. Wm. Roger Louis and Ronald Robinson call "empire on the cheap" the "terms of the metropolitan contract" with the voter. "The Imperialism of Decolonization," *Journal of Imperial and Commonwealth History* 22 (1994): 464.

110. Cain and Hopkins (*British Imperialism*) look at the importance of finance in the changing calculations about empire and its alternatives, both in regard to India in 1947 and Africa in the 1950s. See also Marseille, *Empire colonial et capitalisme français*.

111. Cooper, *Decolonization*, ch. 10.

112. As Connelly (*A Diplomatic Revolution*) shows, the brutal French campaign against the Algerian revolution largely succeeded in military terms, but failed politically by 1962. Decolonization in Africa—largely a fait accompli by the end of the 1960s—made Algeria into an anomaly, meanwhile providing havens for Algerian guerillas (as occurred later in the white settler states of sub-Saharan Africa). The anticolonial efforts of the new bloc of independent states, the interest of the United States in keeping decolonizing states out of the communist camp, and the scandals in France over torture helped to make French Algeria unsustainable.

113. Simon Gikandi expresses this well: "In the imperial period . . . the essence of a British identity was derived from the totality of all the people brought together by empire; in the postimperial period, in contrast, we find a calculated attempt to configure Englishness as exclusionary of its colonial wards." *Maps of Englishness: Writing Identity in the Culture of Colonialism* (New York: Columbia University Press, 1996), 71.

114. Empires that "failed to become nation-states" were "doomed," write Geoff Eley and Ronald Suny. "Introduction," in *Becoming National: A Reader* (New York: Oxford University Press, 1996), 19. Eric Hobsbawm, however, notes that the period 1875–1914 was "probably the period of modern world history in which the number of rulers officially calling themselves, or regarded by western diplomats as deserving the title of, 'emperors' was at its maximum." *The Age of Empire 1875–1914* (New York: Vintage, 1989), 56–57.

115. Khaled Fahmy, *All the Pasha's Men: Mehmed Ali, His Army and the Making of Modern Egypt* (Cairo: American University in Cairo Press, 1997); Juan Cole, *Colonialism and Revolution in the Middle East: Social and Cultural Origins of Egypt's 'Urabi Movement* (Princeton, N.J.: Princeton University Press, 1993).

116. Selim Deringil, " 'They Live in a State of Nomadism and Savagery': The Late Ottoman Empire and the Post-Colonial Debate," *Comparative Studies in Society and History* 45 (2003): 311–42; Nader Sohrabi, "Global Waves,

Local Actors: What the Young Turks Knew about Other Revolutions and Why It Mattered," *Comparative Studies in Society and History* 44 (2002): 45–79; Ussama Makdisi, *The Culture of Sectarianism: Community, History, and Violence in Nineteenth-Century Ottoman Lebanon* (Berkeley: University of California Press, 2000); Selim Deringil, *The Well Protected Domains: Ideology and the Legitimation of Power in the Ottoman Empire, 1876–1909* (London: Tauris, 1998). On debt, see Cain and Hopkins, *British Imperialism*, 343–47.

117. Hasan Kayali, *Arabs and Young Turks: Ottomanism, Arabism, and Islamism in the Ottoman Empire, 1908–1918* (Berkeley: University of California Press, 1997); Michael Meeker, *A Nation of Empire: The Ottoman Legacy of Turkish Modernity* (Berkeley: University of California Press, 2002), xxii; Isa Blumi, *Rethinking the Late Ottoman Empire: A Comparative Social and Political History of Albania and Yemen 1878–1918* (Istanbul: ISIS Press, 2003).

118. Robin Okey points out that had the Habsburg Empire in the nineteenth century broken into component national units, "separate states would inevitably have fallen at each other's throats over the allegiance of disputed areas." "The Habsburg Empire," paper for conference on "Empires in Modern Times," Geneva, March 2003. See also Pieter Judson, *Exclusive Revolutionaries: Liberal Politics, Social Experience, and National Identity in the Austrian Empire, 1848–1914* (Ann Arbor: University of Michigan Press, 1996); Karen Barkey and Mark von Hagen, eds., *After Empire: Multiethnic Societies and Nation-Building: The Soviet Union and the Russian, Ottoman, and Habsburg Empires* (Boulder, Colo.: Westview, 1997).

119. Jane Burbank, "The Imperial Construction of Russian and Soviet Citizens," presented at the Annual Meeting of the Social Science History Association, Chicago, November 20, 1998, published in Russian as "Imperiia i grazhdanskoe obshchestvo: Imperskaia konstruktsiia Rossii i Sovetskogo Soiuza," in *Imperskii stroi Rossii v regional'nom izmerenii (XIX-nachalo XX veka)*, ed. P. I. Savel'ev (Moscow: Moscow Public Science Foundation, 1997), pp. 19–35. Jane Burbank and David L. Ransel, eds., *Imperial Russia: New Histories for the Empire* (Bloomington: Indiana University Press, 1998); Mark Bassin, "Inventing Siberia: Visions of the Russian East in the Early Nineteenth Century," *American Historical Review* 96 (1991): 763–94; Daniel Brower and Edward Lazzerini, eds., *Russia's Orient: Imperial Borderlands and Peoples, 1700–1917* (Bloomington: University of Indiana Press, 1997); Dietrich Geyer, *Russian Imperialism: The Interaction of Domestic and Foreign Policy, 1860–1914*, trans. Bruce Little (New Haven, Conn.: Yale University Press, 1987); Yuri Slezkine, *Arctic Mirrors: Russia and the Small Peoples of the North* (Ithaca, N.Y.: Cornell University Press, 1994).

120. Ronald Grigor Suny, "The Dialectic of Empire: Russia and the Soviet Union," paper for conference on "Empires in Modern Times," Geneva, March 2003.

121. Fatma Müge Göçek, *Rise of the Bourgeoisie, Demise of Empire: Ottoman Westernization and Social Change* (New York: Oxford University Press, 1996).

122. Donald Quataert, *The Ottoman Empire, 1700–1922* (Cambridge: Cambridge University Press, 2000), 189. See also Von Hagen and Barkey, *After Empire*; and Erik-Jan Zürcher, "The Ottoman Empire 1850–1922—Reasons for Failure," paper for the conference "Empires in Modern Times," Geneva, March 2003.

123. Rogers Brubaker refers to the "unmixing of people" in Central Europe after World War I, for the new national political units that replaced the empires fit poorly with the distribution of people, resulting in violent attempts to make people fit the states and persistent tensions. *Nationalism Reframed: Nationhood and the National Question in the New Europe* (Cambridge: Cambridge University Press, 1996), 148–69.

124. The most valiant advocate of this position was William A. Williams, *The Tragedy of American Diplomacy* (Cleveland: World Publishing, 1959); and *Empire as a Way of Life: An Essay on the Causes and Character of America's Present Predicament* (New York: Oxford University Press, 1980). The new wave of empire studies can be glimpsed in two collections: Amy Kaplan and Donald E. Pease, eds., *Cultures of United States Imperialism* (Durham, N.C.: Duke University Press, 1993); and Gilbert Joseph, Catherine C. LeGrand, and Ricardo D. Salvatore, eds., *Close Encounters of Empire: Writing the Cultural History of U.S.-Latin American Relations* (Durham, N.C.: Duke University Press, 1998). See also Ann Laura Stoler, "Tense and Tender Ties: The Politics of Comparison in North American History and (Post) Colonial Studies," with responses from Ramón Gutiérrez, Lori Ginzberg, Dirk Hoerder, Mary Renda, and Robert McMahon, in *Journal of American History* 88 (2001): 829–97; and Neil Smith, *American Empire: Roosevelt's Geographer and the Prelude to Globalization* (Berkeley: University of California Press, 2003).

125. Richard White, *The Middle Ground: Indians, Empires, and Republics in the Great Lakes Region, 1650–1815* (Cambridge: Cambridge University Press, 1991), xv. See also Gregory Dowd, *War under Heaven: Pontiac, the Indian Nations, and the British Empire* (Baltimore, Md.: Johns Hopkins University Press, 2002).

126. D. W. Meinig, *The Shaping of America: A Geographical Perspective on 500 Years of History* (New Haven, Conn.: Yale University Press, 1986); Jeremy Adelman and Stephen Aron, "From Borderlands to Borders: Empires, Nation-States, and the Peoples in Between in North American History," *American Historical Review* 104 (1999): 814–41, 829 quoted.

127. In the Southwest, the switch of empires led to a conflict in property regimes, the Spanish notion being a social one, where a landowner was an authority figure with responsibilities, whereas the North American notion was one of freehold, not recognizing subsidiary rights. This made for long and bitter struggles over subordinate peoples' access to land. See Maria Montoya, *Translating Property: The Maxwell Land Grant and the Conflict over Land in the American West, 1840–1900* (Berkeley: University of California Press, 2002).

128. Meinig, *The Shaping of America*; Julian Go, "Chains of Empire, Projects of State: Political Education and U.S. Colonial Rule in Puerto Rico and the

Philippines," *Comparative Studies in Society and History* 42 (2000): 333–62; Julian Go, "Imperial Power and Its Limits: America's Colonial Empire in the Early Twentieth Century," in Calhoun, Cooper, and Moore, *Lessons of Empire*. Go concludes in regard to the Philippines, Puerto Rico, and American Pacific Islands, that "what began as an ambitious attempt to fashion a distinctly benevolent tutelary empire wound up as an empire like any other. . . . What they found there . . . was the limits of power's reach." Ibid., 14.

129. As it did, of course, in the British. This is not the comparison that those, like Ferguson, who wish the United States to assume Britain's former imperial mantle would like to emphasize, but Ferguson himself admits the importance of what he calls a "butcher and bolt" approach in British colonialism. *Empire*, 179.

130. Edmund Morgan, *American Slavery, American Freedom: The Ordeal of Colonial Virginia* (New York: Norton, 1975).

131. Abner Cohen, "Cultural Strategies in the Organization of Trading Diasporas," in Claude Meillassoux, ed., *The Development of Indigenous Trade and Markets in West Africa* (London: Oxford University Press, 1971), 266–84; Philip Curtin, *Cross-Cultural Trade in World History* (Cambridge: Cambridge University Press, 1984); Denys Lombard and Jean Aubin, eds., *Asian Merchants and Businessmen in the Indian Ocean and the China Sea* (New Delhi: Oxford University Press, 2000). Oceanic perspectives, focusing on networks, have begun to complement land-centered perspectives, which focus on rule. See Sanjay Subrahmanyam, "Notes on Circulation and Asymmetry in Two 'Mediterraneans,' 1400–1800," in Claude Guillot, Denys Lombard, and Roderich Ptak, eds., *From the Mediterranean to the China Sea* (Wiesbaden, Ger: Harrassowitz, 1999), 21–43.

132. Engseng Ho, "Empire through Diasporic Eyes: A View from the Other Boat," *Comparative Studies in Society and History* 46 (2004): 210–46; J. Lorand Matory, *Black Atlantic Religion: Tradition, Transnationalism and Matriarchy in the Afro-Brazilian Candomblé,* forthcoming; J. D. Y. Peel, *Religious Encounter and the Making of the Yoruba* (Bloomington: Indiana University Press, 2000); David Robinson, *Paths of Accomodation: Muslim Societies and French Colonial Authorities in Senegal and Mauritania, 1880–1920* (Oxford: Currey, 2000); James Campbell, *Songs of Zion: The African Methodist Episcopal Church in the United States and South Africa* (New York: Oxford University Press, 1995).

133. Andrea L. Smith, ed., *Europe's Invisible Migrants* (Amsterdam: Amsterdam University Press, 2003).

134. François Manchuelle, *Willing Migrants: Soninke Labor Diasporas, 1848–1960* (Athens: Ohio University Press, 1997); Laura Tabili, *"We Ask for British Justice": Workers and Racial Difference in Late Imperial Britain* (Ithaca, N.Y.: Cornell University Press, 1994); Paul Gilroy, *The Black Atlantic: Modernity and Double Consciousness* (Cambridge: Harvard University Press, 1993); Patrick Weil, *Qu'est-ce qu'un français? Histoire de la nationalité française depuis la Révolution* (Paris: Grasset, 2002).

135. On "intercolonial" mobilization, notably among people from diverse parts of the French Empire converging in Paris, see Brent Hayes Edwards, "The Shadow of Shadows," *Positions* 11 (2003): 11–49.

136. Margaret Keck and Kathryn Sikkink, *Activists beyond Borders: Advocacy Networks in International Politics* (Ithaca, N.Y.: Cornell University Press, 1998).

137. Connelly, *A Diplomatic Revolution.* Karl (*Staging the World*) points to the way Chinese opponents of the Manchu dynasty associated their cause with that of opponents of imperialist expansion elsewhere in the world. On South Africa, see William Beinart and Colin Bundy, *Hidden Struggles in Rural South Africa: Politics and Popular Movements in the Transkei and Eastern Cape, 1890–1930* (Berkeley: University of California Press, 1987); and Audie Klotz, *Norms in International Relations: The Struggle against Apartheid* (Ithaca, N.Y.: Cornell University Press, 1995).

138. Hence the importance of explaining *national* forms of political mobilization in a historically specific way, as is done for example in Manu Goswami, *Producing India: From Colonial Economy to National Space* (Chicago: University of Chicago Press, 2004).

139. The crisis in this period is emphasized by Bayly, *Imperial Meridian,* 164–92.

140. Marseille, *Empire colonial et capitalisme français*; Krasner, *Sovereignty.*

7. LABOR, POLITICS, AND THE END OF EMPIRE IN FRENCH AFRICA

1. For even more density, see Frederick Cooper, *Decolonization and African Society: The Labor Question in French and British Africa* (Cambridge: Cambridge University Press, 1996); "The Senegalese General Strike of 1946 and the Labor Question in Post-War French Africa," *Canadian Journal of African Studies* 24 (1990): 165–215; " 'Our Strike': Equality, Anticolonial Politics and the 1947–48 Railway Strike in French West Africa," *Journal of African History* 37 (1996): 81–118. The following abbreviations for archival sources are used in notes: AP (Affaires Politiques), AE (Affaires Economiques), and IGT (Inspection Générale du Travail), Archives d'Outre-Mer (AOM), Aix-en-Provence, France, and K (Travail) and 17G (Politiques), and D (Territorial Government of Senegal) Archives du Sénégal, and CAC (Centre d'Archives Contemporaines, Fontainebleau, France).

2. Aristide Zolberg, *Creating Political Order: The Party States of West Africa* (Chicago: Rand-McNally, 1966)

3. Extracts of letter of July 26, 1945 from the governor-general, AP 960. On postwar colonial policy, especially in regard to the 1944 planning meeting of officials at Brazzaville, see Cooper, *Decolonization,* ch. 5.

4. In the brief period of Popular Front rule (1936–38) in France, labor unions had been recognized and became active; they conducted several strikes.

The fall of the Popular Front led to the suppression of African trade unionism, especially under Vichy.

5. Cooper, "Senegalese General Strike"; Omar Guèye, "La grève de 1946 au Sénégal," mémoire de maîtrise, Université Cheikh Anta Diop de Dakar, 1990.

6. Lamine Guèye to Governor-General, Feb. 23, 1944, AP 872/3; Exposé sommaire de la situation politique de l'A.O.F. et du Togo pendant le mois d'août 1944, Nov. 15, 1944, AP 872/18. Governor, Senegal, to Governor General, Apr. 29, 1945, 17G 126; Governor General to Minister, July 16, 1945, 17G 132; Rapports politiques mensuels, Guinée, June 1945, Soudan, June 1945, K 405 (132).

7. Dakar, Inspection du Travail, Annual Report, 1944, 1945; Soldes de Personnel du Gouvernment Général, decision of Sept. 12, 1943, and Conclusions de la Commission d'Evaluation des Salaires Normaux, June 23, 1943, K 273 (26).

8. Administrator, Dakar, to Governor General, Dec. 8, 1945, and Exposé chronologique sur la crise, Jan. 12, 1946, K 327 (26); Governor General to Minister, Jan. 16, 1946, IGT, 9; AOF, Direction Générale des Affaires Politiques, Administratives et Sociales, Note sur l'évolution des salaires en vigueur à Dakar avant et après les grèves de Décembre 1945 et Janvier 1946, September 1946, K 325 (26); wages from A.O.F., *Journal Officiel,* Jan. 8, 1946, copy in AFOM 381/63/9, AOM; Renseignements, Senegal, December 1945, 17G 138. At the same time, postal workers went on strike in much of French West Africa, but curiously not in Dakar. Governor, Senegal, to Governor General, Mar. 2, 1946, K 327 (26); Governor General to Minister, Jan. 16, 1946, IGT, 9.

9. Resolution, Jan. 11, 1946, enclosed in Governor General to Minister, Jan. 16, 1946, IGT 13/3, AOM, and Renseignements, Jan. 11, 1946, K 328 (26).

10. Governor General to Minister, telegram, Jan. 10, 1946, IGT 13/3. The Governor General felt he could not resort to "measures of brutal constraint" because of international awareness, particularly through the new United Nations Organization.

11. Minister to Governor General, Jan. 12, 16, 1946, Télégrammes 903, AOM.

12. Summary report on work of Commission chargée d'évaluer le coût minimum de la vie pour un manoeuvre à Dakar, A. Becq, Président, Jan. 19, 1946, K 327 (26).

13. Renseignements, Jan. 11, 1946, K 328 (26).

14. Transcript of interview, Jan. 15, 1946, between representatives of the Union des Syndicats of Saint-Louis, and the Director of Personnel and the Director of Finance of the Government General, K 405 (132), AS.

15. Governor General to Minister, Jan. 16, 1946, IGT 13/3

16. Summary report on work of Commission chargée d'évaluer le coût minimum de la vie pour un manoeuvre à Dakar, A. Becq, Président, Jan. 19, 1946, K 327 (26); Governor General to Minister, Jan. 16, 1946, IGT 13/3.

17. Governor General to Minister, Jan. 16, 1946, IGT 13/3.

18. Renseignements, Jan. 16–20, 1946, K 328 (26).

19. Ibid., Jan. 25, 1946.

20. Secretary General, A.O.F., to Lamine Diallo, Jan. 20, 1946, K 325 (26), confirming agreement on meetings of Jan. 18–19.

21. Commissariat spécial du Port et de l'Aéroport, Renseignments, Jan. 26, 1946, K 328 (26); Renseignements, Jan. 26, 31, 1946, K 328 (26).

22. Renseignements, Jan. 29, Feb. 4, 1946, K 328 (26); Inspecteur des Colonies Masselot to Minister, Feb. 23, 1946, AP 960/syndicalisme; Governor General to Minister, Feb. 23, 1946, K 325 (26).

23. Masselot to Minister, Feb. 23, 1946, AP 960

24. Governor General to Minister, Feb. 13, 1946, K 28 (10); Renseignements, Feb. 12, 1946, K 328 (26); Commissaire de Police to Commandant du Cercle, Bas-Sénégal, February 1946, K 327 (26); Governor, Senegal, to Governor General, Feb. 9, 1946, incl. Governor General to Minister, Mar. 23, 1946, AP 960/syndicalisme.

25. Governor General to Minister, Feb. 21, 1946, Mar. 16, 1946, 17G 132; same to same, Jan. 16, 1946, IGT 13/3; same to same, Mar. 23, 1946, AP 960/syndicalisme; Masselot to Minister, Feb. 23, 1946, AP 960/syndicalisme.

26. Pierre Pélisson, "Rapport sur l'organisation de l'Inspection du Travail en A.O.F. et au Togo," Feb. 4, 1946, IGT (AOF), "Rapport Semestriel," premier semestre 1947, IGT (AOF), circular to territorial inspectors Sept. 30, 1948, IGT 75/1; Inspecteur du Travail, Senegal, to Secretary General, AOF, May 13, 1947, and "notes d'études sur l'appel de la sentence surarbitrale du 24 avril 1947," Apr. 29, 1947, IGT 13/4.

27. Governor General to Minister, Mar. 30, 1946, K 327 (26).

28. See François Borella, *L'évolution politique et juridique de l'Union Française depuis 1946* (Paris: Librarie Générale de Droit et de Jurisprudence, 1958) for a summary of the debates and the legislation.

29. Minister of Interior circular letter to Commissaires de la République and Préfets, Feb. 20, 1946, CAC 770623/83 on identify cards; Decrees of Dec. 23, 1945, Feb. 20, 1946, and Apr. 30, 1946 on suppression of restrictions on personal liberty and of the separate judicial regime. On the administrative difficulties of organizing a unitary penal system and multiple civil systems, see "Situation de la Justice en Afrique: Rapport de M. le Président Sedille, Membre du Conseil Supérieure de la Magistrature," 1952, CAC 940167/7.

30. AOF, Directeur Général des Affaires Politiques, Administratives et Sociales (Berlan), note, July 1946, 17G 152. The preamble to the constitution stated, "France forms, with the overseas peoples, a Union founded on equality of rights and duties, without distinction of race or religion. The French Union is composed of nations and people who make common and coordinate their resources and their efforts to develop their respective civilizations, to improve their well being and assure their security." Yet as juridical commentators soon pointed out, the institutions of the union were differentiated, not homogeneous. The preamble could be read as a "view of the future," not a description. Louis Rolland and Pierre Lampué, *Précis de droit des pays d'outre-mer (territoires, departements, états associés)* (Paris: Dalloz, 1952), 76–77.

31. Cooper, *Decolonization*, ch. 7.

32. Assemblée Nationale, *Débats*, Nov. 22, 1952, 5502–505. Senghor used the phrase in print (*Marchés Coloniaux* 375 [Jan. 17, 1953]: 124) and the Governor General of French West Africa used it as well to tell officials of the central passion to which they had to accommodate themselves; so too did a leading French jurist, who saw this as basic to Africans' attraction to the rule of law. "Allocution prononcée par Bernard Cornut-Gentille, Haut-Commissaire, à la séance d'ouverture de la deuxième session 1954 du Grand Conseil de l'Afrique Occidentale Française, 13 Octobre 1954, p. 20; P. F. Gonidec, "Une mystique de l'égalité: Le code du travail des territoires d'Outre-Mer," *Révue Juridique et Politique de l'Union Française* 2 (1953): 176–96.

33. Cooper, *Decolonization*, ch. 7.

34. Trans. Francis Price (Garden City, N.Y.: Doubleday, 1962). The original French edition was published in 1960. This section is based on my article, "Our Strike." See also Mor Sene, "La grève des cheminots du Dakar Niger, 1947–48," memoire de maîtrise, Ecole Normale Supérieure, Université Cheikh Anta Diop, 1986–87; Jean Suret-Canale, "The French West African Railway Workers' Strike, 1947–48," in Robin Cohen, Jean Copans, and Peter C. W. Gutkind, eds., *African Labor History* (Beverly Hills, CA: Sage, 1978), 129–54; and James A. Jones, *Colonial Labor in the Industrial World: The African Workers of the Chemin de Fer Dakar-Niger* (Portsmouth, N.H.: Heinemann, 2002).

35. Monique Lakroum, "Chemin de fer et réseaux d'affaires en Afrique occidentale: Le Dakar-Niger (1883–1960)," thesis for doctorat d'état, Université de Paris VII, 1987, 1: 300–301.

36. This union was autonomous of any of the *centrales*, in part because the largest of them, the CGT, was tainted by the racism of white railwaymen who belonged to it. The suggestion, made at the time and more recently, that the railway strike was begun at the behest of the French Communist Party—involved in a railway strike in France in late 1947—is wrong, as has been shown by C. H. Allen, "Union-Party Relationships in Francophone West Africa: A Critique of the 'Téléguidage' Interpretations," in Richard Sandbrook and Robin Cohen, eds., *The Development of an African Working Class* (London: Longman, 1975), 104–109.

37. Mory Tall, interview, Thiès, Aug. 9, 1994, conducted by Aminata Diena, Biram NDour, Alioune Ba, and Frederick Cooper.

38. Tall told an early meeting of the Jeunes of the need to "bring about in a short time a complete assimilation in all domains with Europeans and a larger participation of the indigenous element in the administration of the country." Renseignements, June 26, 1945, 11 D 1/1396; Chef du 2e Secteur du Sûreté to Commandant de Cercle, Oct. 13, 1945, 11 D 1/1396.

39. On Sarr's background, see Sene, "Grève des cheminots." His prestrike activism in the Union des Jeunes was noted by police informants. See Chef de 2e Secteur de Sûreté de Thiès to Commandant de Cercle, July 9, 1945, Note by Chef de la Police Spéciale du Réseau Dakar-Niger, Aug. 7, 1945 11 D 1/1396. Sarr was listed in the latter document as one of the editors of *Jeunesse et Democratie*. His connection to a leading Mouride marabout was described by a

well-informed strike veteran. Mansour Niang, interview, Dakar, Aug. 4, 1994, by Makhali NDiaye, Aminata Diena, Alioune Ba, and Frederick Cooper.

40. *Revolution* was the word used by a strike veteran Abdoulaye Souleye Sarr, interview, Thiès, July 22, 1990, by Mor Sene, Babacar Fall, and Frederick Cooper.

41. Renseignements, May 22, 23, 24, 25, 1946, 11 D 1/1392. This narrative and explanation is quite close to that given by informants, notably Oumar NDiaye, Amadou Bouta Guèye (Thiès, Aug. 9, 1994), Mansour Niang (Dakar, Aug. 4, 1994), and Abdoulaye Souleye Sarr (Thiès, July 22, 1990).

42. Renseignements, May 29, 1946, K 352 (26).

43. Syndicat des Travailleurs Africains de la Région Dakar-Niger, Transcript of Assemblée Générale of Feb. 9, 1947, in K459 (179); Sene, "Grève des cheminots," 47–50; Renseignements, June 20, July 2, 1946, 11 D 1/1392. A.O.F., Inspection Générale du Travail, Annual Reports, 1947, 1948. The politics of the unions in each line remain to be elucidated, as does the question of why they were willing to cede so much control to Thiès.

44. Inspecteur Général du Travail, "La Grève des Cheminots de l'A.O.F. (1/10/47–16/3/48)," IGT 13/2; A.O.F. Inspection Général du Travail, Annual Report, 1947, p. 60; Renseignements, Aug. 19, 1946, 11 D1/1392; Suret-Canale, "Railway Workers' Strike," 134–35.

45. Protocole de fin de grève, Apr. 19, 1947, K 377 (26).

46. Official positions may have hardened after the end of Communist participation in the metropolitan government in May 1947. France itself was enveloped by October in a series of major strikes. In late April and May, the Colonial Ministry also renewed its efforts to hold wages and prices down. All the official members of the Régie's board, including those on the Commission Paritaire, voted to reject the commission's proposals. Sene, "Grève des cheminots," 55–57.

47. Interview with Khady Dia, who sold peanuts by the Thiès train station, Thiès, Aug. 9, 1994, by Aminata Diena, Alioune Ba, Omar Guèye, and Frederick Cooper, plus interviews with Abdoulaye Souleye Sarr (July 22, 1990), Oumar Ndiaye and Amadou Bouta Guèye (Aug. 9, 1994).

48. Gendarmarie Nationale, Thiès, Report, Dec. 23, 1947, K 379 (26); Sene, "Grève des cheminots," 91.

49. N'Diaye Sidya, quoted in Renseignements, Oct. 29, 1947, K 457 (179). There is also evidence of support networks developing along railway branches in the Sudan, Dahomey, and other West African territories. Inspection du Travail, Dahomey, to Inspection Général du Travail, Nov. 4, 1947, K 457 (179); Renseignements, Oct. 31, Nov. 7, 1947, K 379 (26); Jones, *Colonial Labor in the Industrial World.*

50. Renseignements, Oct. 25, 1947, K 43 (1); *Réveil,* Nov. 20, 1947; Renseignements, Bamako, Oct. 11, 1947, K 43 (1).

51. Renseignements, Nov. 13, 1947, K 457 (179), in regard to Sarr's trip to the Sudan. There are extensive reports from police spies of meetings at Thiès and elsewhere. See, for example, Renseignements, Oct. 29, Dec. 25, 1947, ibid., and Renseignements, Oct. 16, 1947, K 43 (1).

52. IGT to Deputy Dumas, Jan. 6, 1948, in IGT, Report, Jan. 24, 1948, IGT 13/2.

53. *Voix de la R.D.A.*, special section of *Réveil*, Feb. 5, 1948. RDA involvement is also discounted by Allen, "Union-Party Relationships." On Senghor, evidence comes from Amadou Bouta Guèye and Oumar Ndiaye, interviews, Thiès, Aug. 9, 1994.

54. IGT to Governor General, Dec. 12, 1947, K 457 (179); Grand Conseil, *Procès Verbal*, Dec. 23, 1947, 80–81, and Jan. 31, 1948, 320–21.

55. *Réveil* 268 (Dec. 15, 1947), 269 (Dec. 18, 1947); Renseignements, Ivory Coast, Nov. 5, 18, 1947, K 379 (26), AS; IGT to M. le Deputé Dumas, Jan. 6, 1948, IGT 13/2.

56. Léopold Senghor to Minister, Nov. 26, 1947, K 457 (179).

57. Renseignements, Dec. 17, 1947, K 457 (179).

58. Sissoko planned his move with officials. Note by Pillot for the Director of the Régie, sent by latter to the President of the Conseil d'Administration, Jan. 19, 1948, K 457 (179), and Secretary General of the Government General to Sissoko, Jan. 29, 1948, copy in Inspection du Travail, Bamako, to IGT, Feb. 7, 1948, ibid. For the union response, see Moussa Dhirra, on behalf of Comité Directeur, telegram to Sarr, Jan. 29, 1948, Renseignements, Feb. 4, 1948, and Inspection du Travail, Bamako, to IGT, Feb. 7, 1948, K 457 (179).

59. Cooper, "'Our Strike'"; Sene, "Grève des cheminots"; Suret-Canale, "Railway Workers' Strike."

60. Robert Delavignette, a leading progressive in the ministry, argued this specifically: "The strong style directed at the strikers will not itself resolve the problem . . . if the government gives the impression of going back, after a detour, on trade union freedom and on the abolition of forced labor." "Grève des chemins de fer et des wharfs en A.O.F.," Dec. 13, 1947, IGT, 13/2.

61. Governor General to Minister, Oct. 11, 1947, IGT 13/2; Affaires Courantes, Dakar, telegram to Governor General Béchard, Feb. 3, 1948, IGT 13/2.

62. High Commissioner's narrative of the strike, Apr. 1, 1948, K 458 (179), AS; Renseignements, Mar. 16, 1948, K 458 (179); Sene, 104, 112.

63. IGT, "Règlement de la grève des chemins de fer africain de l'A.O.F.," Sept. 24, 1948, IGT 13/2; IGT to Inspecteur Général des Colonies, Sept. 6, 1948, K 458 (179), Directeur Fédéral de la Régie to IGT, June 30, 1950, K 43 (1).

64. Directeur Général des Finances to Inspecteur Monguillot, May 5, 1952, and High Commissioner to Monguillot, July 17, 1952, AP 2306/7.

65. "La vie syndicale en A.O.F. au cour de l'année 1948," Jan. 31, 1949, AP 3406/1.

66. This part of the story is told in detail in Cooper, *Decolonization*, ch. 11. See also Philippe Dewitte, "La CGT et les syndicats d'Afrique occidentale française (1945–1957)," *Le Mouvement Social* 117 (1981): 3–32.

67. Senegal, Sûreté, Renseignements, Feb. 21, 1956, 21G 215, Governor, Dahomey, to High Commissioner, Jan. 22, 1957, K 421 (165), AS, reporting on the UGTAN conference of the Union Générale des Travaileurs de l'Afrique Noire.

68. See Cooper, *Decolonization*, especially 413–24, for a fuller analysis and evidence on these points.

69. Pierre-Henry Teitgen, Assemblée Nationale, *Débats*, Mar. 20, 1956, 1072–73. This logic was echoed a few years later, in regard to Algeria, by President de Gaulle: "Since the first world war and especially the second, the cost of administration have gone up. The exigencies of the indigenous people for social progress have risen; and this is natural. Benefits no longer cover costs. The civilizing mission, which was at first only a pretext, has become the only justification for the continuation of colonization. But when it is so costly, why keep it up, if the majority of the population don't want any more of it?" From notes of a conversation in 1959 in Alain Peyrefitte, *C'était de Gaulle* (Paris: Fayard, 1994), 1: 57.

70. "Exposé de M. le Vice-Président Sékou Touré à l'occasion de la conférence du 2 février 1958 avec les résponsables syndicaux et délégués du personnel RDA," "Le RDA et l'action syndicale dans la nouvelle situationpolitiques des T.O.M.," PDG (9)/dossier 7, Centre de Recherche et de Documentation Africaine, Paris.

71. Speech of Camara Bengaly to Congrès Constutatif de l'UGTAN, Conakry, May 23–25, 1958, sous-dossier UGTAN, K 421 (165), AS.

72. Report of David Soumah, Secretary General, to Congress de la CATC, Abidjan, Mar. 10–12, 1958, 17G 610, AS.

73. Dahomey, Renseignements, Oct. 1957–April 1958, 17G 588. On the suppression of trade unionism in Guinea, see Claude Rivière, "Lutte ouvrière et phénomène syndical en Guinée," *Cultures et Développement* 7 (1975): 53–83. On the more nuanced situation in Senegal, see Geoffrey Hansen Bergen, "Unions in Senegal: A Perspective on National Development in Africa," Ph.D. diss., University of California Los Angeles, 1994.

8. CONCLUSION

1. Arguments for the economic and political virtues of European societies are old, but new variants keep cropping up in sophisticated circles. See David Landes, *The Wealth and Poverty of Nations* (New York: Norton, 1998); and Niall Ferguson, *Empire: The Rise and Demise of the British World Order and the Lessons for Global Power* (New York: Basic Books, 2003).

2. Steven Robins, "Whose Modernity? Indigenous Modernities and Land Claims after Apartheid," *Development and Change* 34 (2003): 281. Robins' article is framed as a critique of antidevelopment writers like Arturo Escobar and Wolfgang Sachs for missing the concrete issues at stake and the high degree of politicization of development issues.

3. Stuart Hall, "When Was 'the Post-colonial'? Thinking at the Limit" in Iain Chambers and Lidia Curti, eds., *The Post-Colonial Question: Common Skies, Divided Horizons* (London: Routledge, 1996), 258.

4. For more detailed arguments on development along these lines, see Frederick Cooper and Randall Packard, "Introduction," in *International Develop-*

ment and the Social Sciences: Essays on the History and Politics of Knowledge (Berkeley: University of California Press, 1997).

5. Uday Singh Mehta, *Liberalism and Empire: A Study in Nineteenth Century British Liberal Thought* (Chicago: University of Chicago Press, 1999), 20. The emphasis is his.

6. Niall Ferguson, "The Empire Slinks Back: Why Americans Don't Really Have What It Takes to Rule the World," *New York Times Magazine*, April 27, 2003, pp. 52–57; Deepak Lal, "In Defense of Empires," speech to American Enterprise Institute, Oct. 30, 2002, text available on www.aei.org; Max Boot, *The Savage Wars of Peace: Small Wars and the Rise of American Power* (New York: Basic Books, 2002). For a skeptical view of both sides of the current empire debate, see G. John Ikenberry, "Illusions of Empire: Defining the New American Order," *Foreign Affairs*, 83, no. 2 (2004): 144–54.

7. One should shy away from any implication of past empires as models, lest someone take such a claim seriously; according to the *New York Times,* the Bush administration commissioned a study of the ruling practices of past empires, going back to Rome and Chinggis Khan. Maureen Dowd, "What Would Genghis Do?" *New York Times*, March 5, 2003, A23.

8. Craig Calhoun, "Imagining Solidarity: Cosmopolitanism, Constitutional Patriotism, and the Public Sphere," *Public Culture* 14 (2002): 147–71, 171 quoted.

Index

Text:	10/13 Aldus
Display:	Aldus
Cartographer:	Bill Nelson
Compositor, printer, and binder:	Sheridan Books, Inc.